eat this,
san francisco

eat this,
san francisco

A Narrated
Roadmap
to Dives,
Joints, All-
Night Cafes,
Noodle
Houses,
Buffets, and
Other Cheap
Places to
Eat in the
Bay Area

dan leone

SASQUATCH BOOKS
SEATTLE

In memory of the Pit, Youngstown, Ohio, which haunts my hungry dreams all these years later and so many states away. Double wing-ding, please, sauce on the fries, one of those fried rolls, and a grape pop, thanks . . .

Printed in the United States of America.
Distributed in Canada by Raincoast Books Ltd.
03 02 01 00 99   5 4 3 2 1

The restaurant reviews in this book appeared in slightly different form in the *San Francisco Bay Guardian* from 1994 to 1999.

Cover design: Karen Schober
Cover photograph: David Wakely
Interior design and composition: Dan McComb
Copy editor: Lisa Zuniga

Library of Congress Cataloging in Publication Data
Leone, Dan.
    Eat This, San Francisco : a narrated roadmap to dives, joints, all-night cafes, noodle houses, buffets, and other cheap places to eat in the Bay area / by Dan Leone.
        p.   cm.
    Includes index.
    ISBN 1-57061-184-X
    1. Restaurants—California—San Francisco Bay Area Guidebooks.
    I. Title.
TX907.3.C22S3628   1999
647.95794'6 dc21   99-15348

Sasquatch Books
615 Second Avenue
Seattle, Washington 98104
(206) 467-4300
books@SasquatchBooks.com
www.SasquatchBooks.com

CONTENTS

"The wise therefore rule by emptying hearts and stuffing bellies, by
weakening ambitions and strengthening bones."
—Lao-tzu, from the *Tao Te Ching*

"Don't say anything bad about those restaurants. You'll get in trouble."
—Grandma Rubino

INTRODUCTION

A guy walks into a restaurant, takes a seat at the counter, and orders a napkin. (This is not a joke.) The waitressperson just looks at him. I don't understand either, and I speak excellent English. I'm sitting a few stools away, right where I like to be: facedown in a big good meal.

It's the middle of a Wednesday afternoon, which is the middle of nowhere, if you think about it. Me, I'm thinking about something else. I'm trying to remember something—anything—about Missouri.

Across the counter, all is as it should be: The cook is cooking, the prep cook is prepping, and the waitressperson is waiting for some sort of an explanation.

Should I give the guy my napkin, see what happens?

No. I'm afraid he'll just put ketchup on it and walk away, and we'll all have that much more to worry about. Then it hits me, like Chuck Daff on the bus that time: the Show-Me State.

"A napkin," the guy repeats, with a little more urgency, and the waitressperson reaches below the counter, tentatively, and comes up with one. As it turns out (to everyone's relief), he just wants to clean his glasses. "I keep bumping into things," he explains on his way out, wiping them.

I consider following but don't—so we'll never know whether or not the napkin does the trick.

The waitressperson watches him leave, then shrugs. Down the counter a street-geek begins reading some sort of a computer manual—out loud. I count, and five out of ten customers are talking to themselves. Two out of ten are younger than forty. Ten out of ten are eating alone. None out of ten look like they can afford to eat anywhere else.

San Francisco is not known for its cheap eats, I know, but if you know what you're doing, you can get three squares and a midnight snack for the same amount of money that some people spend on an appetizer, or your average barfly blows getting drunk. In fact, I estimate that for every hip/upscale/overpriced/overpublicized/overpopulated Bay Area cafe, there are roughly 1.2 hipless/downscale/cheapo/not-necessarily-clean/underfrequented dives.

I didn't want to call them "dives," but I couldn't think of a better word. And the truth is, that's what you do at these places. It's not dining—it's diving. There's no extraneous bullshit, like sniffing corks or trying to decide which fork to use. It's just you and your food, and everybody else and theirs. Although generally unpublicized and unassuming, real dives are everywhere. Forget tablecloths, lines, and fresh-brewed decaf. Instead, look for Sanka up the wazoo, same-thing-every-time regulars, and Formica at best. A dirty-looking floor is a bonus, and bugs are entirely possible. These are places, in other words, that most restaurant critics wouldn't touch with a 10-foot fork.

Take Kenny's Restaurant on South Van Ness, near Mission. In the first place, it has a perfect name. Most good dives are Someone's Something, with both parts of the name being as plain as possible—e.g., "Kenny" and "Restaurant." (Other classic "someones" include Art, Ed, and Shirley. Other "somethings": Coffee House, Coffee Shop, Hamburger.)

Inside Kenny's, you'll find a comfy old counter, well oiled by years of greasy elbows holding up years of greasy heads staring into years of bad coffee and wondering if Moose was right.

At 250 Hyde in the Tenderloin, the Lafayette Coffee Shop's counter is even better than Kenny's. In addition to cushy, back-having seats, it features a great view of the grill and really lets you in on the action—all the sizzle, all the plate-piling—right there in front of your eyes. It's kind of like having a good seat at Candlestick, except the food is a lot cheaper and foul balls are out of the question.

On the other hand, last time I was there I watched the prep cook digging into a huge pile of ground meat, weighing out and stacking up future quarter-pounders. Once or twice, when he was particularly generous with the scales, I almost jumped up and cheered.

Art's Coffee Shop (138 Church Street) is kind of halfway classy, for a dive. It has tablecloths—but they're plastic and funky. And there are flowers on the tables—but they're fake. The prices aren't great—but they're good. Maybe they're great. I guess it depends on what you're used to. I'm used to five and under, but I'm also the biggest cheapskate this side of food stamps.

At any rate, you can't argue with grease, as my Uncle Roller Coaster used to say before aliens got him; and Art's smothered pork chops go down so smooth, I'll even forgive them for not having a counter. Hell, they have everything else. Hot-pepper vinegar . . . They even imported a few flies, which I never see in restaurants around here, and somehow persuaded them to buzz around the place for the sake of atmosphere.

Under the hole-in-the-wall subdivision of dives, you've got Sam's Pizza (Broadway near Columbus). Sam's is tiny—a 10-seater counter (that's estimated seatage; yours may vary) and a few small tables. It has old-time posters on the walls and stays open late—until roughly 2:30 a.m. (depending on the crowd)—so it's especially useful for midnight snacks.

A couple of lunch-only joints that might appeal to working boys and girls are Wolfe's Lunch (1220 16th Street) and the legendary Red's Java House (Pier 28, Embarcadero).

Of the two, Red's is better. Seating accommodations include booths and wall-facing counter space, but I recommend taking your burger and beer outside and sitting on the pier itself, with the seagulls. BYO french fries. And by all means, watch out for car parts and stuff falling off the Bay Bridge.

Like Red's, Wolfe's Lunch is a self-contained little shack that draws mostly warehouse workers, but also a few briefcasers. It's a great-looking place from the outside: sort of a greasy island motif, somehow managing to be completely surrounded by streets. Of all the billions and billions of restaurants in this city, Wolfe's is probably the one most likely to get run over by a car.

Both Wolfe's and Red's are geared toward the quick-lunch-getting in-and-out crowd, which is good for them, I guess, but I'm personally a fan of the swan dive. That's where you spend a little more time in the air, spread out a bit, and have another cup of coffee, thanks.

* * *

So I guess these are restaurant reviews. The restaurants aren't all dives, but they're all fairly cheap: say, $5 to $10 per person. I'll designate the under-fivers as "cheap cheap," and the few places where you're likely to drop over $10 a head as "splurge cheap." All of the restaurants included are good, in some way, even if I didn't exactly like them myself. La Taqueria, for example, routinely wins "best burrito" awards—but I hated it. Burger Joint, JoAnn's . . . a lot of people swear by these places, so what can I say? I don't know any more about food than anyone else.

Like everyone else, however, I know what I like. A lot of these restaurants I like a lot.

If you live in the Bay Area, or if you're coming here and you don't have a ton of money, feel free to use this as a guidebook. In any case and wherever you live, even if you never make it to Ann's Cafe for a five-pound omelette or sink into a bowl of chicken-coconut soup at Yamo Thai Kitchen . . . even if you never take me up on Gravy's gumbo or Can-Cun's *carne asada* burrito or Roscoe's fried chicken and waffles . . . well, I hope you have as much fun reading these writings as I had writing them.

I wrote these pieces for the *San Francisco Bay Guardian* between 1994 and last Thursday. I present them, for the most part, in the order in which they occurred (and sometimes somewhat edited), because that's the only way the book as a whole can possibly make sense. Feel free to read it like a Richard Brautigan novel (i.e., on the can). And don't worry, guide-bookers, I indexed the hell out of it.

Now I'd like to heartfeltedly thank Miriam Wolf, my editor at the *Guardian*, and the copy editors there. (Ha ha—I put all the boners back in!) I'd also like to thank my dad, Peaches, my brother Jean-Gene the Frenchman, my buddy Bikkets, Haywire, and all the people who ate with me at all these places, but especially Rube Roy Perrotta, a.k.a. Vernon "Shortribs" Mosel, who way, way back in our Ohio days gave me the whole idea.

■ SODINI'S GREEN VALLEY RESTAURANT

I recently ate the best raviolis in the history of the world, but it wasn't at Sodini's Green Valley Restaurant in North Beach. It was at Bob Casal's mom's house.

What happened was, one day Bob started bragging all over his mother's raviolis—them being, he bragged, the best raviolis in the history of the world. Wisely, I chose not to argue, but asked outright if there might not be some way for me to get in on some.

I was only half serious—three-quarters, tops.

I didn't know Bob Casal's mom from Adam's at the time, but one miracle miraculously led to another, and the next thing I knew—thanks to the divine intervention of Bob himself—I was being introduced to Clara and her husband, Henry, and the water was on.

On my undeserving behalf (be-three-quarters, tops), Clara had happily made 136 of her historic raviolis (she counts!), and these were spread out on a table in the dining room, waiting for the water to boil. Some were square and some were round, but all 136 of them, to make a long story shorter than it would have been had I decided to discuss each one individually, were melt-in-your-mouth succulent, heavenly, and in fact the 136 best raviolis in the history of the world.

Hovering right around 141, if you'll forgive me for getting to the point, is Sodini's Green Valley Restaurant.

Sodini's, unlike Bob Casal's mom's house, features green tablecloths, wine-bottle candles, and a couple of cozy window nooks. There's just the right amount of lightlessness to facilitate relaxed, romantic conversation or a short nap before dessert, yet you will probably not fork anyone's hand without meaning to.

My most recent visit to Sodini's was with one Yatee-Yatee-Bing-Eh-Eh-Eh, which was all well and good except that she hollered at me for "jiggling" my calamari. (I contend that I was merely *brandishing* it.) At any rate, tentacles are fun, and many of Europe's most distinguished eaters have been known to hold their calamari at fork's end and wave it around in the air before eating. (This is known as *brandishing*—or, in some countries, *breathing*—the calamari.)

Sodini's fried-calamari appetizer is lightly fried, every bit as tender as the night, and stacked at least four inches up off the plate—enough squidage to amuse an army. I can't speak for the rest of the military, but it was definitely the highlight of my meal. Next time I'm getting it for dessert. This time, for dessert, I got a dinner salad.

In between, I ordered Ravioli Alla Casa—some filled with cheese and some with beef. Sodini's serves up the best over-the-counter raviolis I've had around here, but the trick is to (1) stick with the cheese-filled, no matter how much you like meat, and (2) get them in pesto or cream sauce. I've had both and they're great.

The sauce Alla Casa, on the other hand, is only decent. It's a chunky-enough meat sauce, nicely spicy, but inexplicably laden with carrots, which are good for you, sure, but not for sauce—no matter what people say. The only reason I got it was because I thought Alla Casa meant "on the house."

It didn't.

■ KUBLAI KHAN'S

One of my informants called me up and said, "All you can eat Mongolian BBQ!"

"Hey, that's my four favorite words and three favorite letters," I said.

"What's 'Mongolian'?"

She didn't know, but was pretty certain that *B, B* and *Q* were only two letters. After a brief argument, we decided to meet for lunch at the restaurant in question: Kublai Khan's on Polk Street.

Kublai Khan's
1160 Polk Street,
San Francisco. (415) 885-1378.
Lunch, dinner.
Credit cards accepted. Cheap.

I knew better than to expect ribs and chickens. In fact, I wasn't expecting anything. All I was thinking, going into it, was *all, you, can,* and *eat.* Four words.

Coming out, I was thinking: *woohoo!*

Kublai Khan's lunch buffet was one of the funnest lunches I ever ate.

The room was fun, the food was fun, and the way it works . . . well, works. A sign at the street entrance reads: "Chief cook in front of your eyes." That's when you know you're in for a good time. You know it again when you get to the top of the stairs and see another sign, which inexplicably advises: "Know your monkey." But you don't really know until you enter the restaurant and realize you're in for an Interactive Eating Experience.

They'll probably give you a menu if you ask, but I think the assumption is that you're there for the buffet. Why wouldn't you be? For only $5.50 at lunchtime or $7.95 afterward (all day on weekends/holidays), you get a big empty bowl and then pile it up with ingredients—not standard precooked, crusty, lukewarm buffet fare.

There are bins of raw bok choy, bean sprouts, potatoes, cabbage, carrots, celery, broccoli, water chestnuts, pineapples, bamboo shoots, zucchini, onions, and probably some other things that I missed.

There are noodles.

There is shaved, uncooked beef, pork, and chicken.

There is garlic, ginger, and sesame oil. There are 10 different sauces: Mongolian, Cantonese, teriyaki, Hunan, Szchuan (their spelling), *kung pau*, sweet and sour, curry, lobster, and BBQ.

There are photographic step-by-step instructions on the wall, and a chalkboard with sauce-mixing advice.

You scoop the spices and sauces you want into the ingredients you want, then hand it all over to Chief, who plops your pile onto a large, black semiglobular grill-like device, which looks more like a landing pad for a UFO than cookware.

You can tell him how you want it and watch him cook in front of your eyes if you want. Or you can go grab some appetizers. (The egg flower soup and egg rolls were great; the fried rice was not.)

When your food is finished, Chief plops it back into a bowl and sets it on the counter. If you haven't named it yet, now is the time.

I called my first dish "20-Taste Pile-Up." It contained noodles, almost every conceivable vegetable, all three kinds of meat, lobster sauce, teriyaki, BBQ oil, two scoops of ginger, and garlic. Needless to say, it was excellent.

Fearing premature insanity, however, I went with less chaotic themes my second and third times around. "Hot Hot Hot Beef with Pineapples,

Broccoli, Celery, and Onions" was exactly what its name would indicate. It was heated (x3) with Hunan, Szchuan (their spelling), and *kung pau* sauces, and came out just spicy enough to inspire nose runnage without more serious side effects, like death.

My third dish, "George," was still more focused, this time on curry. I mixed chicken, napa cabbage, water chestnuts, and carrots with garlic and three scoops of curry from the sauce bar. George was kind of bland until I went back to the bar for a revisionary scoop of Mongolian, a dark, salty sauce I'd rudely neglected my first two trips. Eat and learn, as the saying goes.

If you want to drink (but I can't guarantee that you'll learn anything), Kublai Khan's has domestic and imported Asian beers, as well as three choices of wines: red, white, and "pink."

■ TI COUZ

There are only two things worth waiting in line for. I'm not sure what either one of them is, but they are probably not crepes.

Yatee-Yatee-Bing-Eh-Eh-Eh, who says waiting *on* line, has been trying to get me to eat at Ti Couz for two years (which is especially poignant since I've only known her for one). Finally she succeeded; the only problem was that it was 8 p.m. on a Friday and the joint had a line up and out of its wazoo.

Ti Couz
3108 16th Street,
San Francisco. (415) 252-7373.
Lunch, dinner. Credit cards
accepted. Splurge cheap.

We were trying to have a dinner date, but it wasn't working because she likes places with lines and I like places with bugs. As a compromise, we wound up going back to my house, where I allowed her to stand in the hall and wait while I whipped up some fettucine Alfredo con peas.

The garlic was a tad burnt, there was way too much cream, the noodles were overdone, and some of the peas were still frozen. On the other hand, the atmosphere was delightful, the portions were generous, and the prices were quite reasonable.

The next morning, before anyone else woke up and remembered who they were, Yatee-Yatee and I snuck back down to Ti Couz. We had the place all to ourselves.

I've always had a problem with crepes, mostly because they don't come nearly as high up off the plate as pancakes do. I remembered them as little yellow skinny-ass foldy rubbery things with jelly. You had to eat 540 of them to feel satisfied.

At Ti Couz, I only needed three. That's because what the Ti Couz crepe lacks in height, it more than makes up for in width. The approximate size of a large dish, but square, each crepe is 90-some square inches big.

This style of crepe (or *krampouz* according to the menu) comes from the northwestern region of France (or Brittany), where, apparently (or obviously), they know how to crepe their crepes. Both the savory crepes, which are made out of buckwheat flour, and the sweet ones, made with wheat flour, were browned to a nice level of crispness. There was nothing yellow or rubbery or skinny-ass about them.

The crepes themselves may be faithfully authentic for all I know, but I suspect the Ti Couz fillings are to some degree influenced by California tastes. For example, the special, which was my favorite, featured ham, cilantro pesto, and *queso fresco*. OK, some of those things don't sound French.

Boy was it good, though. Standard sliced ham and a milder (better) version of feta cheese—those things were inside. On top was a dribbling of pesto. Was it cilantro *and* pesto, or was it cilantro pesto? The chalkboard had no comma between the two words, but the waiterguyperson definitely paused. I always thought pesto, by definition, was made out of basil. I didn't taste basil, but I wasn't getting much cilantro action, either, which can only mean one thing, but I'm not sure what it is.

Probably "more pesto, please," whatever the hell's in it.

My other "savory" crepe, tomato and basil, was more straightforward but not as good. It was a little skimpier on the filling, and the standard fresh cream garnish didn't work for me. If they have it and if they'll do it, I'd recommend asking for the mysterious pesto (x 2) instead.

Yatee-Yatee got the ratatouille—or "ratatatatouille," as I like to call it, being immature.

Tried it. Didn't like it.

For dessert, I chose strawberry from the sweet-crepe menu. It featured fresh strawberries inside, sweet cream *and* whipped cream on top. Yatee-Yatee got a half-size green salad, which was as big as most places' triple-size green salads. She couldn't finish it, so I did. The vinaigrette was great and garlicky, enabling me to leave the table with the right taste in my mouth.

You might have to spend 10 bucks to get filled up here, but you'll probably also have a really good time, so . . .

◼ BURGER JOINT

In order to give Burger Joint a fair shake, since I hated it long before it flipped its first burger, just from witnessing its flashiness-in-progress, I went a whole week without eating meat, hoping my heroic abstinence would help the Burger Joint burger transcend the place itself.

> **Burger Joint**
> 807 Valencia Street,
> San Francisco. (415) 824-3494.
> Lunch, dinner. Cheap.

On Day Seven, I called up my friend Haywire and said, "Meat meat meat meat."

"I'll be right there," he said.

As it turned out, Haywire had just gone a week without eating anything *but* meat, so we figured it would be a perfect opportunity to conduct a scientific study. We compared weeks. He said he went crazy and decided to move to Ohio because he was scared to death of earthquakes. I said I got a lot of work done and was very productive, then went crazy because I hadn't had any meat.

We both said, "Hmmm."

Then our burgers came and we went to town.

I'll say this for the Burger Joint burger: It's good, it's juicy, it's tasty, it's meat. And I'll say this for their fries: bleck.

They *looked* fresh-cut and good, but they were miraculously terrible. I don't know how they did it, frankly. My theory is that they were fresh-cut, then frozen, then fried, then frozen again, then fried again, and maybe hung out on the line to dry before being baked in a toaster oven and served piping hot.

I tried salt, pepper, and ketchup, and still couldn't convince them to taste like anything—not even salt, pepper, or ketchup. I mean, these fries were so dry and evil they sucked the taste out of everything they touched. But, hey, the service was friendly. One of the counterguypersons was nice enough to inform us, mid-meal, that some psycho psychic was predicting great big earthquakes the very next day, which made me laugh and gave Haywire the jitters.

I also like the simplicity of the Burger Joint menu: hamburger, cheeseburger, gardenburger, of course, all-beef hot dog, and french fries. Five things.

After springing for the burgers and fries, I'd've had to go to a cash machine to get anything to drink—even water. In the interest of responsible journalism, however, I tricked Haywire into buying a root-beer float and then tasted most of it.

(Let's see—where are my notes? Oh yeah:) It was yummy.

Like I said, the burger itself was good too—but it wasn't good enough, or big enough, for that matter, to transcend the fry fiasco or the restaurant's Essential Interior Yuckiness.

It hits you as soon as you walk into the place—in my case almost literally. (The plate-glass door was so invisibly clean I came this close to walking through it, which would almost certainly have been embarrassing.) Inside, Burger Joint features black-and-white stenciled comic-book-style art. Across the length of the ceiling is an inexplicable neon "backbone" with plastic finlike "things." The booths, tables, and floor tiles are all clashing, weird, or Day-Glo colors whose names I've never bothered to learn.

In other words, don't worry, you won't fall asleep in the middle of your meal. However, you probably won't be amused by the decor, either. You might feel, um . . . let's see, what comes between "imposed upon" and "slapped in the face"?

■ VALENCIA PIZZA & PASTA

When the Check-Inn Cafe on the corner of Valencia and 19th sadly soaped up its windows and set the old counter stools out on the sidewalk, I blamed myself. Sure, a lot of other people didn't eat there often enough, if at all, but I had walked by the place almost every day. Although I never failed to admire the Check-Inn's inner perfection, I

Valencia Pizza & Pasta
801 Valencia Street,
San Francisco. (415) 642-1882.
Breakfast, lunch, dinner.
Credit cards accepted. Cheap.

almost always failed to go in and eat. What was I thinking?

The few times I did eat there, I was happy. The food was greasy and dirt cheap, the booths were cozy, and the counter was a thing of beauty. Why wasn't anyone ever in there? Apparently the people who ran the joint asked themselves the same question, and asked it one time too many.

Valencia Pizza & Pasta, which has sprung up out of the Check-Inn's grease stains, is one-half ho-hum pizza pad, one-half North Beach wannabe, and one-half excellent cheapo breakfast establishment. Where it gets off having three halves is a matter I cannot completely address without a good team of lawyers and an overhead projector, but trust me—that's exactly what it has.

They took out the old eat-at counter and replaced it with a couple of the old booths. Where the booths were, they added a few tables and chairs. Then, where nothing in particular used to be, they put this huge, ornately ugly, fancy-looking wooden counter with a green tile top. You can't eat at it, but you wouldn't want to either.

I went there on opening night with Yatee-Yatee-Bing-Eh-Eh-Eh, my favorite dining companion. (If she doesn't like something—get this—she won't eat it!)

Here's what we got: calamari vinaigrette as an appetizer, *capellini al pomodoro e basilico* for me, and a cute little one-person pesto pizza for Yatee-Yatee. Fortunately, she hated her pizza. I didn't particularly like it either, but it was the perfect supplement to my rather smallish portion of *capellini*.

Capellini is angel-hair pasta served, in this case, beneath fresh tomatoes, basil, and garlic—not enough, not enough, and not enough, respectively. It came with an iceberg-lettuce salad and diner-style garlic bread.

But the highlight of the meal, as usual, was the calamari, which was zestfully battered, deeply fried, and just rubbery enough to slow down Yatee-Yatee—who actually prefers fresh to frozen—while I went to work.

After dinner, we went back to her place and she made herself some oatmeal while I sprawled out on the floor and started fantasizing about breakfast.

Judging from its name, my guess is that Valencia Pizza & Pasta would like to think of itself more as a pizza and pasta place than as a breakfast place. In my opinion, however, having eaten both meals there, they do a much better job with breakfast.

You can get the standard two-egg, potatoes, and toast breakfast with meat for under five bucks. I got the "Chinese breakfast" special because I had a hunch it was going to be big—and boy was it.

Basically, it was an egg-scramble (almost an omelette) with ham (or sausage or bacon), sprouts, bell pepper, celery, and carrots on a mountain of plain white rice. I was afraid all that rice might bore the dish to death, but it didn't. There was just enough going on up-top to make the meal fun and flavorful to the last bite—which took me quite a while to get to.

I'd ordered a side of sausage, just in case, but it was totally unnecessary. In fact, I had to sneak one of the links into my pocket for later. It was cold, dry, and fuzzy, but otherwise great.

I doubt if I'll revisit Valencia Pizza & Pasta for dinner, but I'll definitely be back for breakfast. And I already know what I'm getting: the two-egg breakfast with chicken. Chickens are by far my favorite animals, especially to eat, but I have to admit that it never even occurred to me to eat them for breakfast!

With eggs!

All philosophical implications aside, chickens and eggs for breakfast sounds enticing enough to me to warrant renaming the name of the place. Heck on pizza and pasta. I'd call it Valencia Chickens & Eggs.

■ PRODUCE INN

One night I went to Hanno's, this bar around the corner from the striking *Exchronamicinaler,* to see this band called Paddlefoot. I was having a beer. This guy who was four times bigger than me and five times drunker—an off-duty picketman-person—mistook me for a scab.

Luckily, my pal Punk was there to talk the guy out of killing me,

Produce Inn
321 Franklin Street, Oakland.
(510) 839-4455. Breakfast,
lunch, dinner. Cheap cheap.

because, being impressionable, I was starting to think that I *was* a scab.

"You fuckin' better fuckin' be on the right fuckin' side of the fuckin' fence," the guy stated.

"We're here to see the band," said Punk.

Hell, I wouldn't write for the *Exchronamicinaler* if it were the last two newspapers in the world. For one thing, I'd have to hobnob with Miss Manners or the fuckin' Fusco Brothers instead of Ask Isadora. For another, I probably wouldn't get an F-word in edgewise.

Hooray for the F-word!

Hooray for the Produce Inn, my favorite (so far) Oakland bar-slash-restaurant-slash-pool hall-slash-soap opera convention on Jack London Square.

The Produce Inn, a.k.a. Time to Eat, specializes in cheap food, cheap pool, extra-friendly service, plastic flowers, and beer-babe-poster art. As I understand it, the bar does most of its business in the early morning hours, when the produce district's night shift lets out.

It was almost noon by the time I'd BARTed over there, sat down with my tall friend E. B. Matt in a corner booth, and ordered the red snapper lunch special. But I hadn't had breakfast yet, so I also ordered an order of French toast.

The waitressperson didn't get it, at first. "It's up to you," she said. "Which one?"

"Both," I said. "The French toast is for breakfast."

Then she got it—so much so that she even thought to bring it on first, and it was an excellent opening act for lunch, as breakfast so often is. In fact, the French toast stole the show.

Served with oodles of already melting butter and generously snow-capped in powdered sugar, this was white-bread French toast at its best, and what with E. B. Matt helping out from his side of the table, it was gone in no time.

During the split second between the setting down of the syrup-coated forks and the arrival of lunch, we tried to have a conversation, not having seen each other in quite some time, and being, after all, relatively communicative, problem-sharing types.

"So . . . ," said E. B., but he was immediately interrupted by another waitressperson asking who ordered the deep-fried prawns. I pointed.

I got the panfried red snapper, which came with french fries and coleslaw. I hate coleslaw, speaking of serious emotional disorders, so E. B. ate mine, and I forgot to ask him how it was. The french fries were french fries. The fish was fish, but it was way too panfried, and in fact seemed to contain some of the pan. At any rate, it was grizzled solid on one side, and more-or-less dark-browned on the other, but for under five bucks, who's complaining?

■ PEASANT PIES

It was one of those rainy rain-season days and I was in the thick of a goopy novel called *Fishboy*, by Mark Richard. But I'm not a book reviewer, and this therefore isn't a book review, so I'll get right to the point:

Fish *pies*. Yum yum.

That said, let me just explain that once, many years ago, when I lived in

> **Peasant Pies**
> 4108 24th Street,
> San Francisco. (415) 642-1316.
> Also at 4117 18th Street,
> San Francisco. (415) 621-3632,
> and 1039 Irving Street,
> San Francisco. (415) 731-1978.
> Lunch, dinner. Cheap.

a trailer park in New Hampshire, I stepped on a frog by accident. I was walking in the rain and I was wearing good solid boots, not exactly watching where they were going. Then there was the second most sickening sound I ever heard, and it was right between my heel and the sidewalk, split open and clawing air like the first cook in *Fishboy*, after Lonny axes him almost in half on account of culinary crimes.

The first most sickening sound I ever heard, I'm sorry to report, was me breaking Haywire's arm arm wrestling after one of our famous New England fish fests. And the third most sickening sound I ever heard was a black cat committing suicide. It jumped off a 24th Street ledge and landed on the sidewalk right behind me—which has to be bad juju. I wish I had never turned around to see it slither, spitting blood, because I might otherwise have imagined someone had simply stomped on a Ping-Pong ball.

How this all ties in is like this: I was wearing the same old boots and a rain poncho, walking on similarly wet sidewalks down the same street and past the exact spot where the suicidal cat had landed. So if anyone saw me, now you know why I was walking that way, looking down, stepping like a ballerina, and wincing.

I was on my way to Peasant Pies, Noe Valley's new "peasant pie" place, and all-in-all it was a great day to eat seafood—frog-, cat-, and arm-related memories notwithstanding.

Peasant Pies is a one-idea place, and lucky for them it's a great idea. All they make is seven different kinds of pies: calamari, shrimp, clam, ratatouille, spinach, leek, and onion and Swiss. All the pies are made fresh, on the spot, and the fish ones use the same recipes 19th-century Mediterranean fishermen used, only different fish.

There aren't any tables, but there is an elevated, out-facing wraparound counter with about 10 stools, conducive to serious, solo, on-the-spot eating. Most of their business, however, is takeout.

All pies go for $2.40 apiece, meaning I spent just over 10 bucks eating four of them, plus coffee. My favorite was the calamari. (My favorite is always the calamari—get used to it.) This particular pie was hot out of the oven, and even though it was the last of the four and I was no longer technically starving, I didn't have the necessary patience to avoid burning one whole side of my face on it, nor the intelligence to avoid burning the other side moments later. Still, it was a thoroughly enjoyable experience, especially once I finally managed to get some of it into my mouth.

Speaking of pizza, these here pies are said to be provincial French and Spanish in origin, but they made me think of Italian. Especially the fish ones, which were also stuffed with tomato sauce, garlic, parsley, and olive oil. And then the crust is not at all flaky, like a traditional pie crust, but doughy, like a pizza pie. I guess what I'm getting at is that these were basically calzones. The fish ones were even folded over like calzones.

I love calzones.

The only veggie pie I had was spinach, which was simply spinach and garlic. It was my second favorite. Shrimp, packed with baby ones, came in third, and clam—through the process of elimination—took up the rear.

I loved Peasant Pies. The dough was perfect, and the fillings, according to the menu, are 100 percent natural (and according to me,

100 percent delicious). The price is pretty damn right, and the two guys running the place didn't even yell at me for spilling water all over one of their heads. (When you go there, you'll see how this was possible. Hint: He was on the phone.)

I weighed in (at the Meat Market Coffee Shop across the street) at 162 ½ before the big event, and that was in dripping-wet rain gear and soaked-through frog-cruncher boots, holding a hardback copy of *Fishboy*. Afterward, all drip-dried but otherwise the same way attired, I was a proud and happy 165.

Two and a half pounds. Ten bucks. I'll say no more.

■ EL TACO ZAMORANO/GORDITAS TIO TOÑO

So, we were driving around Oakland in a funny little car named Don Blando. It was me, my friend Little Him (who lives on that side of the bridge), and my other friend, Biscuits, and it was high time for burritos.

I'd never eaten a burrito in the East Bay. I just assumed they didn't have them over there, I guess, or that—being that much closer to the Midwest—they wouldn't be any good.

El Taco Zamorano
E. 14th and High Streets (restaurant at 4032 Foothill Boulevard), Oakland. (510) 536-3146. Breakfast, lunch, dinner. Credit cards accepted. Cheap cheap.

Gorditas Tio Toño
4021 E. 14th Street, Oakland. (510) 535-0961. Breakfast, lunch, dinner. Credit cards accepted. Cheap cheap.

Little Him, he was driving and tour-guiding and trying to tell me otherwise, but he couldn't decide whether to take our burritoless bellies to Gorditas Tio Toño, which is a taco truck on E. 14th Street, or El Taco Zamorano, which is another taco truck on E. 14th Street.

Naturally, I'm thinking: both.

"Well," I asked Little Him, "which one's better?"

He thought about it. Zamorano, he decided. He was wrong, but in order to find out, we had to go there and eat three burritos.

The advantage to eating burritos out of these taco trucks (or "roach coaches," as they are affectionately known among those in the know) is that they are cheap cheap cheap. A couple bucks apiece for burritos, *tortas,* or quesadillas; one buck for a taco.

The Zamorano truck is in a parking lot on the corner of E. 14th and High Streets. It's just a little trailerlike thing with a couple of over-your-head windows. The folks on the other side of these windows were not particularly friendly, probably because of overexposure to exhaust fumes.

Anyway, I got a *carne asada* burrito, Biscuits got a spicy pork (which turned out to be the best of the bunch, lucky her), and Little Him, he got a vegetarian. They were out of cheese.

We ate these three burritos on the hood of Don Blando, hot-night-at-the-drive-in style, atmospherically. While a warm darkness gently descended over the bustling parking lot, Little Him (who claims to have lived on Zamorano for years) was heard to seriously ponder: "I wonder why they call these things 'roach coaches?'"

The disadvantage of eating burritos out of these, er, taco trucks is that you don't get chips, so it's an unaccompanied meal. Oh, wait—they do toss a couple of raw radishes and scallions in the bag. (If you're not into eating the scallion, by the way, it makes a really nice boutonniere, as Biscuits fragrantly demonstrated for the rest of that evening.)

They also give you little plastic things of salsa, which was lucky for me, 'cause my burrito needed help. The green one was refreshingly, invigoratingly excellent, like diving into a cool, clear mountain stream. The spicier red one was runny and painful, like hitting your head on a rock.

In addition to being mushy and not exactly fresh, the Zamorano burrito was not big enough for me, which necessitated a quick visit to Gorditas Tio Toño, just a block or two away.

My companions sat Tio Toño out, while I had another *carne asada* burrito. (How else could I be expected to make an intelligent culinary comparison?) This one was mucho better. And bigger! Googy!

Gorditas Tio Toño is basically the same thing with the same prices in a different parking lot, except that it's a block or two away, at 4021 E. 14th, and has the distinct advantage of sharing the lot with the very restaurant (also takeout only) to which it is associated. (The actual El Taco Zamorano, on the other hand, is around the corner from its satellite truck, at 4032 Foothill.)

This may account for the fact that all of Tio Toño's ingredients—the rice, the beans, the tomatoes and onions, and especially the meat—were twice as fresh as Zamorano's.

Also, in sharp contrast to Zamorano, we had the entire parking lot to ourselves. The guy in the Tio Toño truck was downright sociable, they still had cheese, and the burrito itself was not only better but a lot bigger. So why was everyone hanging out at Zamorano?

This, I'm afraid, will remain one of life's great mysteries, right up there with *The Secret of the Old Mill.*

As for Pinter's *The Lover,* which we went to see afterward, as rendered by the Shotgun Players at LaVal's in Berkeley, well, it was very well done, darkly hilarious, and thoroughly enjoyable—but it's no longer running, nor is it food, so there would be little if any sense in reviewing it further than that.

■ ANN'S CAFE

My tall friend-for-life, E. B. Matt, tried to tell me about Ann's Cafe in Oakland. He called me up out of the blue one day after he'd been there, and he seemed to be struggling for words, out of breath, maybe even lying on his kitchen floor, dying.

Ann's Cafe
3401 Fruitvale Avenue, Oakland. (510) 531-9861. Breakfast, lunch. Cheap cheap.

"Sounds like my kind of place," I said. "When can we go?"

E. B. hedged. Not only was he in no condition to even think about ever eating again, but he wasn't sure a review would be the right thing, exactly. Eating at Ann's is one of those transcendental experiences, like finding a $50 bill on the floor of a bar, which something tells you you should probably keep under your hat. Unfortunately, something else compels you to blurt the good news to Tom, Dick, and Harry, and you wind up buying a lot of beers.

Well, I don't know if Ann's is a well-kept secret or not, but it's been around since 1957, I think, so if the poor cat's not out of the bag by now, it's either dead or too disoriented to cause any trouble.

Besides, there are plenty of reasons not to go to Ann's Cafe—you're worried about your weight, you don't like to have fun, you have a day job, you're in a bit of a hurry, health, attitude problems, vegetarianism—

regardless of whether or not it is or isn't quite possibly, in my opinion, THE BEST EAT-YOURSELF-SILLY PLACE IN THE GALAXY.

You go in, you sit down at the counter, and you're immediately drawn in. Everybody's friends. You don't even have to say anything; you're just automatically part of the action—thanks to the infectious, endearing good humor of Ann's daughter, Fran.

Frannie, a whacked-out, wisecracking Italian-American woman, has been working there since Day 1. I don't know how long she's been running the show, but she's running it right. She cooks comically huge food on a small griddle behind the counter, at her own leisurely pace, stopping to chat with, make fun of, and occasionally even hug her customers.

Before you order, Fran will slide you a bowl of soup. Then she'll shove a whole plate full of potatoes in front of you, and some two-sided griddle toast, with cheese. Be careful. If you finish, you might get more.

All this, mind you, before you've even ordered.

I got an Italian omelette, because that's what the woman next to me was staring at, giggling, and it just looked like an all-around-good idea.

Did I mention that this is a five-pound omelette?

Well, it is. I don't know how many eggs went into it, but there were three discernible kinds of meat (make that four—I asked for no mushrooms and no zucchini and she gave me ham and ham instead), onions, spinach, cheese, and a few odd green beans.

I didn't have my ruler with me, unfortunately, but I estimate that this omelette was 10 to 12 inches long, six to eight inches wide, and four to five inches tall—that's before Fran ladled two scoops of spaghetti sauce on top.

It tasted like a lot of a lot of different things—pretty fun and fantastic, actually—and, yes, I finished it.

E. B. Matt, who promised to send me a Christmas card when I'm 60 if I cleaned my plate, ordered French toast and didn't clean his. Of course, there were eight slices to contend with, and we were an hour and forty minutes into the meal by the time Fran finally got around to slapping them on the griddle.

By that time, I had finished my omelette and E. B. had cleared a plate of potatoes, two rounds of cheese toast, etc. He was nowhere near hungry, and in fact tried to back out of his order, but Fran insisted on making all eight slices and sending them home with him.

In general, people leave Ann's, when they eventually leave, with a big grin on their faces, a good feeling in their guts, and enough food either in them or on their person to last well into tomorrow.

Ann's attracts all types: us, a shy pregnant woman (she called first from next door because it sounded "like a lot of men over there"), a Catholic priest, a father/son duo who somehow appeared to be right around the same age, a couple of bodybuilders, big people in general, and a stick-figure woman.

"Don't talk to strangers," Fran advised an elderly lady (with walker) on her way out.

The old woman stopped walking her walker, turned around, pulled back the sleeve of her housedress, and flexed her muscle for us.

Over two hours after beginning the surreal experience of breakfast at Ann's, me and E. B. Matt finally staggered out ourselves, holding our stomachs and grimacing in pain/pleasure.

The damage: a little over 10 bucks, total.

■ 'CUE TIPS: BAY AREA BARBECUES

Sometimes people ask me, "Dan, why does your whole life revolve around barbecued chickens?"

"I don't know," I say, if I'm feeling surly. "Why does yours revolve around bagels?"

If I'm feeling poetic, on the other hand, I say, "Lo! How the smell of it lingers upon one's fingertips, like sex."

And if I misunderstand the question, I say, "Next Tuesday, if it doesn't rain."

Either way, people generally whap me.

But the truth of the matter, as usual, is very simple: My life revolves around barbecued chickens because I can't afford the ribs. So when the Powers that Be offered me a $250 budget to go around and "write up" various barbecue places, I naturally did three frontward somersaults, two cartwheels, and a handstand.

Finally—after years of hacking away at half-assed, heartless, and thankless writing projects when I could have been outside playing—finally, I had hit pay dirt. And let me tell you, it was worth the wait.

Two hundred and fifty is a lot of smackeroos to spend on barbecue in roughly one month. My accountant informed me that, in order to use up my budget, I would practically *have* to order ribs. In fact, I would have to order three-way combo plates *and* corn muffins *and* peach cobbler, *and* I would have to bring someone with me. So I got on the phone and shocked a few meat-eating friends by inviting them out to dinner—on me.

Then I packed up the tools of my trade—a 49ers hat and some tooth-picks—and started out in search of the Bay Area's best-smelling, weirdest-dream-inspiring, cheapest, and choicest barbecue.

Here they are—five of them, anyhow—in more-or-less-descending order of greatness:

Brother-in-Laws (705 Divisadero, San Francisco; 415/931-7427). This is the best-smelling and all-around-best barbecue place I've been to in San Francisco. You can get half a chicken for about five bucks, or a whole bird for 10, which is way cheaper than any other place I've found in the city. In fact, I've been eating chickens at Brother-in-Laws for three years, so I didn't figure I needed to eat another one, and only ordered a two-way: sliced beef and ribs. It was 11 bucks, roughly, but registered four inches UFS (Up From the Styrofoam)—a much higher pile of meat than most places give you on a three-way.

My friend Haywire, he got the chicken, and we sat there with our hats on, our coats off, and our sleeves rolled up at one of B.I.L.'s two tables, discussing relationships and carnivorating ourselves silly. Beef, ribs, and chicken . . . hey, that's three of the four major food groups right there. And for all I know there was butter involved *some*where.

Let's see, there were several things of baked beans, a side of greens, corn bread, potato salad, and two peach cobblers for dessert. But when the dust finally cleared, all that was left was a bunch of bones.

Sure, some of them still had meat on them (not mine—Haywire's), and I have to admit that I didn't even touch my cobbler until a week later, when I finally took it out of my fridge and threw it away.

Everett & Jones (1955 San Pablo Avenue, Oakland; 510/548-8261, and four other East Bay locations). Here's what happened: My ex-neighbors invited me over to their new luxury pad in Oakland for dinner. These two are great dinner-givers, but it was less than a week till deadline and, frankly, I still had over $60 to spend on barbecue. So I offered to save them some trouble by bringing the food.

I wanted to hit an East Bay place, if possible, and I was having a hard time finding time to get there. So I decided to kill half of a bird and parts of a cow and a pig with one stone, as the saying goes.

The ex-neighbors were game, so I stopped by Everett & Jones on the way over. My favorite aspect of this place is that there are only four things on the menu and they all cost the same cheap price: $5.05 for a small order, $6.80 for a large (or you can get various combinations for variously reasonable prices).

The four choices are the four obvious ones: links, beef, ribs, and chicken. In the interest of responsible journalism, I got one of each. It was so simple. "Large everythings, medium sauce," I said. "Hold the potato salad."

You can eat in at Everett & Jones, but I couldn't, because I had ex-neighbors waiting on me. So I had to get it to go, and it was pure torture in Wally the Valiant, let me tell you, with the smells I was smelling. I not only drove like a maniac, but wound up getting lost, and circled some strange neighborhood like a barbecued chicken with its head cut off.

If worst came to worst, I figured I would just have to spend several days in my car, surviving on four orders of great, cheap barbecue, medium sauce, hold the potato salad.

Unfortunately, worst did not come to worst.

Wendy's Cheesecake (4942 Third Street, San Francisco; 415/822-4959). This was the weirdest-named barbecue place I went to. I noticed it one day when I was driving around looking for junkyards, but it was closed, so I made a mental note.

Then, many weeks later, I was trying to start writing this piece, but thinking about writing about barbecue was making me hungry, so I decided to take a lunch break before I did anything. I drove to Wendy's again and it was open. Hoorah!

What a cheerful place. There were donuts, cakes, ice cream, pastries, even a popcorn machine. But—of course—I was there for the 'cue.

I got a rib sandwich with baked beans and peach cobbler, because this guy sitting at one of the tables said, "Try the peach cobbler."

I looked at him and he was wearing a neck brace, so I figured he had done his share of driving around with barbecue in the car, and probably knew what he was talking about.

As it turned out, he didn't. Or maybe I'm just not a cobbler-eating kind of guy. The ribs and beans were great, though, thanks to Wendy's excellent tangy sauce. I don't know how to describe it except to say that instead of going back to work after lunch, I took a very long nap and dreamed I was in charge.

Leon's (1911 Fillmore Street; 415/922-2436, and also 2800 Sloat Boulevard, San Francisco; 415/681-3071). This was actually the first place I went to on my recent barbecue spree, and no one ever did top Leon on the UFS scale (4⅜ inches). At the time, I thought I was paying an outrageous amount of money for any amount of food, but I later found $15 to be the going rate for three-ways this side of the bay.

And, as $15 heaps o' meat go, Leon's was the heapingest. Come to think of it, it was a four-way. The menu promised one-quarter chicken, two ribs, a hot link, and beef, but I counted a whole half of a chicken and at least three ribs, along with massive linkage and tons of beef. It was an intimidating pile of 'cue, and, as good as it was (which was pretty darn good), it was the only pile I couldn't finish—between you and me.

Big Nate's (1665 Folsom Street, San Francisco; 415/861-4242). At roughly 10 bucks for a Chicken Dinner (half a chicken) or five-something for a half order (a quarter of a chicken), Big Nate's is roughly twice as expensive as Brother-in-Laws, and not quite as good. Big Nate claims to be "SF's Best Barbeque," but he's wrong. Best greens, yes, but not the best barbecue in San Francisco. Second best, maybe.

Owner Nate Thurmond did time in Cleveland, with the Cavs; he should know that guys from Ohio, like me, can't afford to pay 10 bucks for half of a second-best chicken. I'd never have done it if I wasn't being subsidized. And—even then—it took me two tries. The first time I went there, I took one look at the menu and instinctively left.

I'm glad I wound up going back, though, because I had an excellent meal—a very good three-way (3 inches UFS) and great Mean Greens. If you have money to blow, or financial backing, I recommend Big Nate's.

In summary, my overall impression of Bay Area barbecue is that it costs too much. Of course, that's my overall impression of life in general—so there's no telling what point there was to all of this. I'm just very glad that it happened.

■ KATE'S KITCHEN

In spite of the fact that Kate's has received nothing but rave reviews from my friends, I never got around to reviewing it for.myself—until now. Deep down inside (where I used to keep the capitals of all 50 states)

Kate's Kitchen
471 Haight Street,
San Francisco. (415) 626-3984.
Breakfast, lunch. Cheap

I knew that no matter how good Kate's was, it couldn't possibly live up to the greatness of its gone-under predecessor, Delta's

Depression Dough, R.I.P.

Delta's Depression Dough, the very mention of which brings a tear to my eye and a growl to my stomach, was the home of my third-favorite breakfast ever, behind Ann's Cafe's five-pound omelette, Oakland, and the legendary Lenny's Feedbag, Portsmouth, N.H. I'm talking about Delta's plate-size chunk of fried dough smothered with chili, cheese, and onions.

Good morning, folks!

And, if you'll kindly excuse me for wandering offward, Delta's also featured the sorely missed Mr. Misty, my favorite waiterguyperson, who on hot days would wander the room watering its willing customers with a spray bottle. Just one more thing: They also had paper tablecloths that you could draw on—or drool on, in my case—while waiting for your food. My own most artistic effort was a haiku about chili, but especially good visual artists got to see their crayon-and-marker drawings on the wall, impersonating art, the next time they came in.

Call me a sentimental sap. Call me a lunkhead for evaluating a current restaurant against its spot-in-the-world's previous tenant (or for any number of other reasons). But the fact remains that Kate's, as good as it is, ain't Delta's. I'd've overlooked it if I could've—trust me.

The good news is: pancakes! meat! The bad news is: home fries. Eggs.

I can talk intelligently about all four of these things because I got the Big Guy's Breakfast, which is a West Coast version of Lenny's Feedbag, sans toast. In other words: two pancakes, two eggs, two bacons, one homemade sausage patty, and one pile of potatoes.

The undisputed champions of the meal are the great and grainy, lemon and cornmeal, melt-in-your-mouth delicious pancakes. They're way bigger than Lenny's—big enough to warrant their own plate, in fact—and they come with real Vermont maple syrup, from10 big states away (whereas Lenny's didn't, from right next door).

The bacon, to boot, is thick-cut, meaty, and perfectly sizzled (neither too dry and crumbly, nor underdone enough, like some bacons, to twist and propel a model airplane). And the homemade sausage is a plump patty— slightly fennel-heavy and salt-light, but thoroughly enjoyable nonetheless.

Surprisingly, then, the home fries are just barely edible. What's the story here? Anyone capable of creating such great pancakes and home- made sausage ought to know what to do with potatoes. I'm an eater, not a cook, and I'd normally be too intimidated to offer practical suggestions to a trained professional, especially an otherwise good one; but, in this case, since my own hack home fries are way tastier than Kate's (and I'll prove it in a court of law, if necessary), here goes: Cut 'em smaller, cook 'em harder, and don't be afraid to go a little spice crazy. May I suggest: garlic, black pepper, red pepper, thyme, maybe even some chili powder, or celery salt, or something.

I don't have any friendly suggestions for the eggs, since I can't do them either. Maybe it's all in the chicken. All I know is that I didn't miss the Big Guy's missing toast, because Kate's eggs were small-yolked to begin with, and then over over-easied, so that there was hardly anything left to sop.

But back to good news: The portions are huge. Even people who haven't had the Big Guy's Breakfast seem to think so. And there are plenty of interesting-sounding specials, like bacon-cheddar pancakes. They also do lunch, but who the hell eats lunch? Not me, not after the Big Guy. For that reason alone, I'll go back to Kate's in half of a hot second. But I won't talk it up like my friends do—not until either (*a*) the home fries get well, or (*b*) they add fried dough with chili and cheese to their specials menu.

■ AXUM CAFE

I got it in my head to go to Mally's Diner in Livermore, where they've got guns on the walls and, on the grill, the biggest, cheapest burgers you probably never heard of. So I packed up my meat-eatingest buddy, Haywire, and we headed all the way out there in Wally the Valiant.

Axum Cafe
698 Haight Street,
San Francisco. (415) 252-7912.
Lunch, dinner. Credit cards
accepted. Cheap cheap.

Well, to make a happy story sad, Mally's was closed for renovations (hopefully not the same ones the Church Street Station has been closed for since kingdom come), *and* Wally's muffler started dragging. Too disappointed and too hungry to eat anywhere else in Livermore, I crawled under the car with a trusty coat hanger, and 10 minutes later we were back on the road.

All the cows in the greater Livermore area were laughing their heads off at us, strutting around like they had all the time in the world. To spite them, we shook our fists out the windows and said, "You'll get yours, you fat pigs," then came back to the Mission and had excellent beef burritos at Taqueria Can-Cun—but that's not what I'm reviewing, either. It's Axum Cafe, this great Ethiopian place in the Lower Haight.

I went there with my pitch-playing pals Four-Bid Flick, Mr. Tea, and C. "Rogue" Fortier. These three live a block away from the restaurant and claim to be the Axum's first and only regular customers so far. (Sure enough, the waitressperson knew them by name.)

Me, I had never even eaten Ethiopian food before—there or any-where. Yatee-Yatee tried to warn me beforehand that I wouldn't like it—"It's weird bread and a bunch of mushy stuff," she said. But I wanted to see for myself.

For less than five bucks apiece, we ordered vegetarian dinners for four, and it was enough food to feed five or six, as long as none of them are me. In this case, of course, one was, so it was just the right amount, served on two round trays—one the size of an extra-large pizza, the other, say, a medium.

The meal consisted of weird bread and a bunch of mushy stuff, basically, but—unlike Yatee-Yatee, who lucky for her wasn't with us—I loved it.

Served cold and folded on separate plates, the bread also forms a foundation for everything else. It looks and feels like a cross between pancakes and some sort of pillow stuffing. But don't make fun of it; it is destined to serve as your fork.

In addition to being pretty damn tasty of its own accord, this spongy steamed bread is the perfect consistency for sopping or scooping up mush, of which there were three distinct piles, plus salad.

The biggest pile—and my favorite (at first)—was a spicy lentil mixture, which occupied the center of the circle like a big, brown, gloppy sun. Then there were smaller satellite servings of spinach ("the green stuff"), which was great, and a potato-cabbage-carrot mixture ("the yellow stuff"), which eventually became my favorite.

There was also a huge amount of salad—green lettuce, red onions, and tomato, with a light, refreshing dressing that I never did figure out, although I enjoyed it plenty. The salad was the only part of the meal that didn't go well with the bread, in my opinion, so I used my hands.

As if all this weren't enough (it were), the waitressperson showed up with a bowl of "the white stuff" right around the time we were getting ready to throw in the napkins, and she piled on four big scoops of it. This was a very spicy tabbouleh-like thing, with hot peppers and lemon, and it was served with another round of spinach (Rogue had made the mistake of saying he really liked it) and a few more sheets of bread.

A long time later, when we had finally cleared all that, the waitressperson showed up again and said, "Do you want a chicken?"

That sealed it for me: Axum is a million-star cafe, where you can eat as much as you can possibly eat (they'll see to it!) for cheap. Then, if you want, you can hang out for hours, like we did, digesting and playing pitch. Or chess, like the guys across the way. Or floor hockey, probably, if you want.

∎ PHÓ ANH DAO

Some time ago my colleague and good buddy (I wish!) Ask Isadora raised the philosophical question: "Isn't life grand?" Well, I've been thinking about it ever since, and I've finally come up with what I believe to be the correct answer: "It depends."

Phó Anh Dao
280 E. 18th Street, Oakland.
(510) 836-1566. Lunch, dinner.
Cheap cheap.

Speaking of life being grand, Bob Casal's mom, who lives in Ohio and makes the best raviolis anywhere, period, has promised to make me another 136 of them the next time I'm in town. And, as if that alone weren't reason enough to be back "in town" as soon as humanly possible, I'm also buying a 10-year-young minivan off my little brother. Yep—you heard me rightly. I'm coughing up the ultracool Wallymobile, a 1969 Plymouth Valiant that I got, literally, for a song and a dance, in order to become a shameful owner of perhaps the most soulless type of transportation imaginable. On the other hand, I'll be able to go places and carry around lots of people, or else big huge boards—so it all evens out in the end. Right?

Before leaving, I drove Wally over the bridge one last time in order to eat an East Bay dinner with married people Caterin' Caroline and the Brioschi Kid. Where they took me to (in C. C.'s cooler-than-Wally Duster—sigh) was Phó Anh Dao, a *phó* place (duh) down near the lake (Merritt).

I had never before experienced *phó*. I love soup, however, as much as if not more than the next guy, so my hopes were high. It didn't hurt that the Brioschi Kid promised "bowls so big you go crazy."

And it didn't hurt, either, that these extra-large bowls of soup go for under five bucks at Phó Anh Dao.

I got an extra-large with eye of round steak and fat brisket. C. C. got what she called "the honky special": eye of round steak and well-done brisket. And the Brioschi Kid, our most adventurous eater, went all out with eye of round steak, well-done brisket, fat brisket, soft tendon, and bible tripe.

I tried the soft tendon. It was like eating pure fat.

I tried the bible tripe. It was like eating football.

Everything else, however, really hit the spot. The beef broth, seasoned with onion and star anise, and further enhanced by do-it-yourself fresh basil, green chile peppers, and lemon, went down as smooth as, say, hockey.

The bean sprouts, also from the do-it-yourself plate, are really great in the broth. But the main "stuff" of the soup is a handful of rice noodles and a good amount of thinly sliced beef, which is dropped in raw just before serving, for maximum succulence.

Well, it was succulent. In fact, I didn't think it needed any of the table-top meat-dipping substances—such as plum sauce, fish sauce, soy sauce, etc. I tried them, but found I preferred the meat the way it was: in the soup—plain, simple, and wet.

I know, I know, it's not necessary to wash soup down, generally, but, if you're up for it, Phó Anh Dao has a very interesting selection of drinks, including "Mixed Three Color Bean" and "Iced Soda Salty Plum." I got the fresh coconut juice, which took a while to grow on me, and then grew right back off. It was basically a glass of water with a very soggy chunk of coconut at the bottom—enjoyable for about one or two sips, somewhere around the philosophically crucial half-empty/half-full point. The rest of the time it just scared me.

The *phó*, however, was excellent. And, in spite of its incredible cheap-ness, it was every bit as big a bowl as the Kid had led me to believe. Still, it was soup—so a slice of pie was necessary, for which we happily crossed the street to the Merritt. But that's another story . . .

After pie, we went back to their place, where the Kid broke open a bottle of his special-occasion top-shelf Brioschi. And, like so many other thoroughly enjoyable evenings of gluttony, this one ended with a fizz.

■ VICTOR'S PIZZA

My friend Haywire has been singing the praises of Victor's Pizza on Polk Street for quite some time. It's his number two hit, in fact, right after the one about the bus driver. ("Bus driver/Oh oh oh oh/Bus driver"—surely you've heard it.)

Victor's Pizza
1411 Polk Street, San Francisco.
(415) 885-1660. Lunch, dinner.
Credit cards accepted. Cheap.

So, anyway, we went there one night, me and him, and teamed up on 16 inches of perfectly fine pizza. However, what impressed me most was the dinner salad. Maybe I've spent too much time in the Midwest, where "dinner salad" means a handful of iceberg lettuce with soggy shredded carrots and—in select, chic cafes—two cherry tomatoes, or a few strands of red cabbage. When Victor's dinner salad was placed in front of me, I initially thought there had been some mistake; but I didn't say anything 'cause it appeared to be in my favor. It was at least two handfuls of real lettuce, plus a ton of tomatoes, red onion, cheese, salami, pepperoni, and I forget what else.

As for the pizza, I liked it OK. A "large," which is 16 inches, goes for roughly 10 bucks BT (before toppings), which is pretty reasonable. Being above all else a reasonable guy, I would have stopped there. But here's where me and Haywire don't see eye to eye: He likes his pizza loaded with toppings, and I'm basically a sauce-and-crust man, tickled to death by the mere presence of cheese.

So we compromised. We got four things and I picked all four of them: sausage, fresh tomato, black olives, and spinach. Nice combo, right?

Well, it was. The sausage was great. Everything was great, in fact, except for the sauce and the crust, which, if you were paying attention . . .

Victor also makes calzones, fresh homemade pastas, and stuffed stuff, like cannelloni, ravioli, or vegetarian lasagna.

I'll go back, sure, because the pizza's decent, which is about as much as you can hope for around here, and because of the dinner salad, and because it's a really comfortable, right-feeling place with friendly service and one of those crisscross-paddywhack-grapevine ceilings I so love to gaze up into on a warm summer indoor evening, pondering one or another of life's many minor mysteries, such as Victor's completely slanted rest room, which makes peeing even more fun than usual. Hit it, Haywire . . .

Pissing in a tilted room
Better bring a mop and broom
Shut your mouth and lock the door
And if you fall don't hit the floor
I've whizzed around the country, Lord
Hotels and rest stops, room and board
Trees and bars and filling stations
But my favorite place for urination's
Victor's! Victors! Doo-wah-ditty-wally oooh . . .

■ OUTBACK CAFE

DEAR EVERYONE WHO EVER WROTE LETTERS TO ME:

Hi. How are you? I hope you are fine. Me? In addition to being a terrible person, I am a terrible letter writer. That's why I never wrote back until now, and only now in print, because at least I'm getting paid for it. (See what I mean? I suck.)

Outback Cafe
1099-C Revere Street,
San Francisco. (415) 822-8119.
Breakfast, lunch. Cheap.

But all self-deprecating aside, I still have your letters, and I still take them out and read them every so often, and I still smile or cry or throw darts at whatever you said, depending on what you said, and I still think: "I should write back. I really should." (Sometimes I even say it out loud.)

The other day I organized them into a pile. I considered this "a start."

Next, I counted them—54, not counting promotional letters from restaurants themselves, but counting six from one person—my Epistological Stalker, so to speak, who (by the way) knows of more cool places to eat, and actually writes better than I do (yikes!)—by virtue of an even higher Exclamation Mark Per Sentence Ratio, or EMPSR [one of only two truly objective tools for measuring "good writing" (no matter what those overreactionary empiricist Tweedheads are teaching in grad school these days), the other method being, of course, the tried-and-true "Pap Smear" (as it is affectionately, acronymically known [the actual initials being PAPSR (Parenthetical Asides Per Sentence Ratio)])] than mine.

So—the Outback Cafe . . .

(One of the other things I did instead of actually answering my mail was I went through it and made a list of the many restaurants recommended therein.)

The Outback, for example, was described by one Jacqueline Geertz as "an unusual cafe in an unusual place." Hey, I like unusual cafes in unusual places, especially when they serve "delectable fare" (her words, not mine), so I minivanned on over to Bayview to check it out.

Open for breakfast and lunch only, the Outback is what I'd call an unusual cafe, located in what would have to be considered an unusual place—way down in with all them warehouses at the end of Revere Street. It took me a while to find it, but it was worth the while, for I found the fare (how shall I put it?) *delectable.*

I got a double cheeseburger and a cup of soup. And coffee.

Don't let what I got fool you, though. This is gourmet stuff.

The double burger with cheese, for example (five bucks or so), comes on a French roll with a Dijon mustard/mayo mixture if you want (no, thanks!), tomato, lettuce, pickle, and red onion. They even ask you how you like it (rare).

It was an excellent burger, even though it didn't come with french fries. But that's because they don't have a fryer—not because they're mean. In fact, all sandwiches come with a side of pasta salad. I was afraid to try mine, at first, thinking: mayonnaise. But then I asked and they said, "No mayo—sun-dried-tomato oil." So I ate it. It was fine. A friendly pile of orzo with parsley and (if my suave, discerning taste buds don't deceive me) sun-dried-tomato oil—refreshing, but not quite as good-for-you, I don't think, as french fries would have been.

The best thing about the meal was the soup, and the best thing about the soup was that they offered me a refill. They make a different home-made soup every day, and this day it was creamy turkey (with no cream) and chiffonade of spinach. I asked what *chiffonade* meant, and they told me, but I forgot. All I know is: Yum!!!!!! (Take that, E. Stalker.) I mean, nose-tinglingly flavorful—both cups—with nice-size chunks of gobbler and buoyantly fresh shredded spinach.

What with all-you-can-drink do-it-yourself coffee for a buck, the whole lunch came to more than eight bucks, but it was worth it.

The Outback is a very friendly good-food cafe with a few sidewalk tables and an unabashedly fun interior: cool flying-fork art, dangling kitchenware, and other nice touches like spilled sugar with fake plastic ants. The only thing I didn't like was the artsy three-legged pseudo-nou-veau-faux-Jetsons chairs, partly because their tiny teardrop backs were less than comfortable, and partly because I kept knocking them over, like bowling pins, every time I went to get more coffee.

Espresso happy hour, by the way, is 2:30 to 3:30 p.m., daily. See you there, OK?

(I'll be the bowling ball!)

◖ SOUPS

Speaking of free refills, there's a cool, clean, and friendly little soup counter in the Tenderloin going by the cool, clean, and friendly little name of "Soups," which bowls up 16-ounce portions of homemade soup

Soups
784 O'Farrell Street,
San Francisco. (415) 775-6406.
Lunch, dinner. Cheap cheap.

and half-bowl refills *and* coffee, tea, or milk for less than some places charge for one lousy cup.

The sign out front of Soups used to say "Good Food, Dirt Cheap"; now it says "Good Food." I asked the guy what happened to "Dirt Cheap" and he said that he raised the prices on his two vegetarian soups (potato and split pea) from $2 to $2.75.

"It's still dirt cheap, you ask me," I said, and I'll say it again, in print, for the hard-of-hearing: *It's still dirt cheap*—especially considering the refill and the coffee, tea, or milk, tax included.

Flock to Soups, folks, because it's a great idea in a not-so-great neighborhood. And because the guy behind the counter *is* . . . Mr. Nice Guy.

I ordered the clam chowder, a Monday-and-Friday-only selection, which, for $3.75, is the most expensive thing on the menu. Mr. Nice Guy took a quick whiff of the chowder, made a funny face, grabbed a spoon, and had a taste.

"I forgot to spice it," he said. "It'll be a minute."

So, OK, he sets me up with a cup of coffee and I sit and watch him spice it: white pepper, thyme, something else, something else, stir-stir-stir, and he pours me a bowl.

Now here's where the Mr. Nice Guy part comes in: If it were possible for a bowl of soup to be heaping, this bowl was. But I don't think it is, so it wasn't. However, it was as close as it could get to the edge of the edge, without runneth-ing over.

A crumpling of crackers, some black pepper of my own doing, and I'm ready to go.

Did I mention that I was hungry?

Well, yes, it's a little-known fact that I haven't had much food in my house lately, and that last week, in particular, I'd been reduced to eating popcorn for dinner, buttered tortillas for breakfast, and buttered and jellied tortillas for lunch. (Don't you worry, though—there's a check supposed to be coming in any day now.) So, yeah, I was hungry.

In fact, I don't remember actually tasting the first bowl. And then it was gone. But before I could say, "Please sir, I want some more," Mr. Nice Guy had snatched up the empty bowl and was ladling away.

What the dickens?—this weren't no "half-bowl" refill any more than I'm a half-assed critic. I'm an ass, and this was a full bowl of soup—it just wasn't overflowing, like the original.

Tastewise, it was pretty decent. Easy on the milk, plenty of clams, and plenty of clamminess. Also: potatoes and celery. I don't think the spices had quite settled in, though. It was a touch on the bland side. Not that I told him so, but Mr. Nice Guy seemed to know it. "I think I'm going to start making it on Thursdays," he said, "so it gets a little thicker by Friday." I said I liked that idea, since a lot of soups taste better leftover. Right? (Some other things are better the second or third or fourth time around: Cars. Lasagna. Life . . .)

Where were we? The soup, I think I was saying, was thinnishly fine, but the whole time I was eating it, I was also eyeballing these gigantic hot dogs making their rounds in one of those orbit-cookers directly across the counter from me. What could I do, being me, but finish up real quick with breakfast and order some lunch?

"I can't help it," I said. "Can I have one of them hot dogs?"

"Are you still hungry?"

I said what I always say under such circumstances: "That was break-fast," I said. "This is lunch."

If anyone's interested, quarter-pound all-beef kosher dogs come with potato chips or tortilla chips and coffee, tea, or milk for $2.50, 50 cents extra for chili—and here, I believe, I can accurately use the word *heaping*. I mean, Mr. Nice Guy, being nice, piled about a bowl-and-a-half's worth of chili on top of that there big boy.

"Guess it's dinner, too," I said.

He poured me a glass of milk, because technically I had another coffee, tea, or milk coming to me, and—while I went to work—he told me the story of The Guy Who Ate Six Bowls of Potato Soup and Then Two Bowls of Lentil Soup on Top of That.

It was a good story. It was a good hot dog. The chili was kind of boring, but workable with do-it-yourself cheese, onions, hot sauce, relish, jalapeños, etc.

I was too busy eating myself under the table to tell Mr. Nice Guy my own true story about The Time I Ate 10 Hot Dogs. So I'll tell him now:

One time, Mr. Nice Guy, I ate 10 hot dogs. The end.

■ MINH'S GARDEN

So, OK, went out to dinner with Ask Isadora. What else?—well, earlier that day I had a huge-ass homemade lunch with some other pals o' mine, J. F. "Dustbunny" K. and Mr. Well Baby. I only mention it because betwixt the two meals there was a certain common thread (beyond good times, camaraderie, and, you know, general hobnobbery and such). Said common thread being: Good Vietnamese grub.

Minh's Garden
208 Clement Street, San Francisco. (415) 751-8211. Lunch, dinner. Credit cards accepted. Cheap.

J. F. K. dished (or I should say *serving bowled*) up the three largest amounts of Vietnamese soup I've ever seen this side of la-la-land. I don't think there's a Vietnamese bone in her body, either; but what she lacks in authenticity, she more than made up for in quantity. I'm serious: We ate out of three-gallon serving bowls.

Thus was I still sloshing around inside myself and making various weird noises that evening as I moseyed on over to the Richmond for a Vietnamese dinner with famous person Ask Isadora, who had asked *me* to maybe get together for dinner sometime so I wouldn't have to keep referring to her as my "good buddy (I wish!) Ask Isadora." You see what I'm saying?

I ate dinner with Ask Isadora!

We met at Minh's Garden, which is a small, pleasant, downscale Clement Street establishment. I was the one with the black-and-red baseball hat instead of hair. Hers (hair, not hat) was curly and red. Neither one of us ordered soup.

What else do you want to know about her? She doesn't like seafood, and she's not the slightest bit interested in toothpicks. That's about all the dirt I can dig at this point. Besides, I'm not an Isadora reviewer, so I'll try to calm down now and write about food.

As it turns out, me and my good buddy Ask Isadora have the same favorite Vietnamese dish: *bún cha giò thit nuóng*—you know, the one with grilled pork and imperial rolls over rice noodles.

So, OK, we got that, and we got *ga xao lang,* or "special coconut-curry chicken," and we got *bi cuon,* or cold Vietnamese rolls, by way of an appetizer.

These cold rolls of shredded pork and lettuce wrapped in rice paper were refreshing and delightful, I thought, but Ask Isadora said they had "too much grass." (Meaning lettuce, I suppose, but what do you expect from a sex writer?)

Actually, I *like* eating grass (meaning grass). When in the country I have, as recently as one month ago, gone down on all fours to graze—no lie. So too much lettuce never bothers me, except when it gets stuck to my face.

The coconut-curry chicken was very good. Cooked with black mushrooms, onions, and celery and served with rice, the dish was subtle on the coconut and extremely yellow.

I don't know about Ask Isadora, 'cause I forgot to ask, but I was disappointed in the imperial rolls and barbecued pork. The bed of rice noodles over which they resided was fine and flavorful, especially drenched in fish sauce, but the too-few pieces of pork were less than succulent, maybe even overcooked, and the imperial rolls tasted mysteriously similar to stale rye bread. Why?

I've eaten at Minh's Garden a couple of times before, when I used to live near there, and I never had any complaints. I don't know if I never got that dish, or if this was just a substandard version of it, but I won't let it prevent me from going back. Minh's is dirt cheap, unpretentious, friendly, and comfortable.

We were there for two hours and talked about Everything Except Sports. I even got to sneak in a few questions about certain problems that certain, um, "friends of mine" were, you know, just wondering about.

I offered to make a guest appearance in her column, since she was doomed to do so in mine—but she didn't bite. Anyway, I have a better idea. I learned, among other things, that Ask Isadora appears in several other papers besides the *Guardian,* including the *Village Voice.* So those letters everyone reads and automatically assumes they're from me . . . well, they're not. They come from all over the country! In fact, she gets so many she can only answer a fraction of them in her column.

Here's my idea: Since I often, on the contrary, have leftover space in my column, and since many people are more interested in sex than food (even I read her first, me second), I volunteer to hereby field those left-over questions about sex, so long as they at least make mention of some type of food—preferably chickens.

■ EL ZOCALO

I had hoped this would be the second installment in a three-part series called My Dinners with Famous People, but Zippy the Pinhead did not return my calls and Jerry Rice (with my apologies to Joseph, Julie, and—if I understood him correctly— "Jughead" Rice) has an unlisted phone number. So, since that one fizzled out after just one part, the next three-part series (this one) will pick up the leftover two, and will therefore

El Zocalo
3230 Mission Street, San Francisco. (415) 282-2572. (Also at 1633 El Camino Real, South San Francisco. 650/992-1482.) Lunch, dinner. Credit cards accepted. Cheap cheap.

have five parts, but should still be considered, referred to, and officially acknowledged as a three-part series, lest I lose my accreditation.

It's called: My Dinners with Complete Strangers.

Names of the five Complete Strangers will be changed, of course, for their protection. Any resemblance to persons living, dead, or in the hospital, is either purely coincidental or entirely intentional—I'll let you know as they occur.

All disclaimers having been disclaimed . . .

Installment One: Hi, it's me—Dan—and I've been dragged, kicking and screaming, to El Zocalo, a Salvadoran restaurant in the Outer Mission, by one Thump-Chuka Thump-Chuka, a fine young hip-hopster who deejays for a living.

I wanted us to meet at Irma's, which T-C T-C had recommended to me in a letter—but she wanted to go somewhere new to her, too, and some of her pals had been talking up this El Zocalo. So that was where we met and discussed her deejay-ing, my band, and food in general over *pupusas, pastelito, pollo,* plantains, and—get this—pineapple drinks. All alliteration aside, however, it was a fine, filling lunch. But the best thing about it was: Cheap.

In fact, TC x 2 paid for it. Hooray!

And to think that I don't even know what "house music" or hip-hop *is,* let alone sounds like . . . that's OK. She returned the cluelessness by saying—after I described my band (ukulele, violin, guitar, clarinet, mandolin, etc.)—"No drums? What do you do for a *beat?*"

Thump-Chuka Thump-Chuka won me over, in spite of our musical differences, with an endearing tidbit of personal information: She once ate two (2) super burritos, on a bet. And her favorite taqueria is Can-Cun! But I'm not a person reviewer, so let me tell you about what we ate . . .

Honest engine, the *p*'s were not intentional. Without even thinking twice I ordered *plato tipico,* which consisted of two *pupusas,* one *pastelito,* and one *enchilada Salvadoreña.* And I don't know how many times she thought, but (T-C)² got *pollo Salvadoreño* (served with rice and refrieds) and *platanos fritos y crema.* And we both would have had melon drinks, I swear, except that they were out of them, so we had to settle for pineapple.

The enchilada was the best thing on my plate, although it wasn't really an enchilada, you ask me. It was a crispy corn tortilla piled up with pork, cheese, lettuce, and some other things—in other words, a taco. Well, whatever it was, it was good.

The *pupusas*—one chicken and cheese and one bean and cheese—were bland and dry until I figured out that I was supposed to wet them down and spice them up with that pickled cabbage/carrot mixture, and salsa, and whatever else was lying around. Do you know what *pupusas* are? I didn't. They're these flat fried things, see, with stuff in them. As for the *pastelito,* I still don't know what that is. Well, it's a fried thing with stuff in it, sort of, only smaller than and different from *pupusas.*

Thump-Chuka Thump-Chuka, in spite of her odd name, kindly fixed me up a sampler plate of her selections. I thought the chicken was good, the refrieds and rice were medium, and the fried plantains were bad. But then, I don't generally go for plantains, fried or otherwise, so I should probably keep my mouth shut.

Overall, I wasn't impressed with El Zocalo's food, and neither was T2C2, who does like plantains. I found the restaurant atmospherically uneventful and servically so-so. However, I can think of several reasons to go back there, or to go there, if you haven't been . . .

One: The prices really are very cheap.

Two: The menu is huge. Of all the many untried Mexican and Salvadoran dishes, I'm sure there are some great ones. (I'm pretty sure, anyway.)

And three: It's open until 3 a.m. seven days a week, and until four on Fridays—which is a rare and beautiful attribute round here, don't you think?

■ ROSE VIETNAMESE RESTAURANT

I used to always write in coffee shops. Then, for a long time, I didn't. Now I don't know what I do, but I'm writing this in a coffee shop because my house is starting to smell too much like me.

Also, I needed to get away for a while from the inexplicable, admittedly idiosyncratic activities that have taken over my days these days—things like resting my chin on a tube of toothpaste for hours on end, or swinging a baseball bat in the living room.

Rose Vietnam Restaurant
791 O'Farrell Street,
San Francisco. (415) 441-5635.
Lunch, dinner. Credit cards
accepted. Cheap cheap.

Coffee shops smell like coffee, and it's very easy to get things done.

For example, last night I ate dinner at Rose Vietnamese Restaurant (which is not a coffee shop, but here I am telling you about it, right?) with Complete Stranger #2, a guy named Bagels Begler, who just got back from honeymooning in Italy. He said the food was good. I didn't press him for details because I didn't want to know. I've got my hands full here as it is.

We ordered four things and three of them were great. (Hey—I just found a quarter!) I can see why Bagels likes this place (not the coffee shop—the restaurant), but I can also see why his new wife doesn't like to go there with him, according to him. It's in the Tenderloin—right across from Soups, my favorite soup place.

Me, I like the Tenderloin. Good cheap food, toothlessness, and sex. Who can argue with that?

Well, Mrs. Bagels can, like I said, if she wants to, but she wasn't with us. I don't know what she ate for dinner last night, but we had—in descending order of expensiveness—crab sautéed with peppercorn, shrimp cakes wrapped around sugarcane, sautéed fresh asparagus, and, of course (on my insistence), imperial rolls and barbecued pork with rice noodles.

Let me just say, first off, that this imperial roll/pork/rice noodle dish is cheaper here than anywhere else I've had it so far, including Minh's Garden. And it's as good as or better-tasting than anywhere else I've had it, with the exception of Tu Lan. It's best at Tu Lan, but it's great, and a buck cheaper, at Rose. There you have it.

As for the asparagus, it was great, too—slightly undercooked, if anything (which is the way to lean, in my opinion), and nicely spiced, with mysterious goopiness and sesame seeds. Plus there was a whole heck of a lot of it—I'd say eight or nine good, solid, pungent pisses worth.

The shrimp cake and sugarcane things, predictably, were the meal's weak link. They were edible (well, except for the sugarcanes themselves), but too cotton-pickin' *processed* for my money. I'm talking about bounceable wads of rubberized shrimpness, not to be confused with shrimp. Still, we finished every single one of them, no shit.

Having now managed to mention both forms of meaningful elimination (and don't anyone say that such talk doesn't belong in a restaurant review, 'cause it does, if you think about it—ask Newton, or Galileo, or any other dead person). But let's move on to the subject of crabs. Bagels Begler originally recommended Rose to me on the strength of its crab.

I have to confess that—much as I love them—I hadn't eaten any actual crabs since I moved here. I guess I have a problem with the expensiveness of them, having always, in the past, simply lured them out of that other ocean and into my cooler with chicken necks on the end of a string.

Fourteen, 15, 16 bucks for a crab? Back East, hell, I'd catch 20 of them in a few well-spent, pleasant hours down at . . .

"Hello—Dan? This is not 'back East.'"

True. I'll grant you that, and this *was*, after all, one kick-ass peppercorned crustacean. The menu said sautéed, but these chunked-up pieces of crab (shell and all, don't worry) seemed breaded and deep-fried— that's how chin-drippingly tasty they were. I wanted to take the empty claws home just to suck on.

So maybe I'll start eating crab again, at least on special occasions. Either way, I heartily recommend Rose for generally cheap, good Vietnamese food. There are 167 items on the menu, and—although the crab is way over—most everything else is under five bucks.

■ HARD KNOX CAFE

Get this: All four of the complete strangers I've eaten with so far for this three-part series are people who don't do the regular job thing. There was the struggling nightclub deejay (two weeks ago), a struggling writer (last week), a struggling photographer (this week), and a struggling writer/editor (next week—I already ate with him).

Hard Knox Cafe
2526 Third Street,
San Francisco. (415) 648-3770.
Breakfast, lunch, dinner. Cheap.

Three cheers for the freelance strugglers! And a moment of silence, please, for those who have to struggle on someone else's terms, often while wearing pantyhose and/or neckties.

But before you quit your job and kill your boss (or vice versa), make sure you get on down to the Hard Knox Cafe on Third Street, 'cause you'll need seven hard-earned dollars to afford the fried chicken.

Is it worth it?

Is *what* worth it? The chicken? The dollars? The struggle? Life? Freedom? (Oh how I love/hate to grapple with these philosophical questions.) The chicken is worth it, sure; money never is, was, or will be; the effort, on the other hand, is always worth the effort, whereas life itself is not; and freedom is, um, a dime a dozen, or a matter of personal preference.

But where are my manners? I forgot to introduce my Comrade in Grease, Complete Stranger #3. Reader, I'd like you to meet Drippin's, so named because she showed up for lunch drippin' sweat. (She couldn't afford a Fast Pass this month, she told me, so she has to bike everywhere she goes.) Drippin's, this is the Reader.

Now that everyone knows each other, here's the scoop on Hard Knox:

Drippin's, a transplanted Southerner (hooray!) and freelance photographer of grilled-cheese sandwiches (hooray! x3), had written to me about this place a long time ago, and I'd been meaning to get there ever since. She said it was the kind of place that makes you want to fall asleep after eating. I like that kind of place.

Ergo, I like Hard Knox.

It used to be called Inez's, but it's not Inez's anymore, but Inez still does the cooking. In fact, she came out of the kitchen in person to take our order: for me, the three-piece fried-chicken plate, which comes with two vegetables and two corn muffins for seven bucks.

The corn bread is wonderful. I also loved my two vegetables: black-eyed peas—a good-size, juicy splattering of them—and a glop of white rice with great gooey gravy. Sheesh, just mentioning it makes my eyelids heavy. Nap time!

(Dream dream dream dream dream. Boner.)

I'm back. Other available vegetables are mustard greens, red beans, string beans, yams, butter carrots, cabbage, macaroni and cheese, or potato salad. Drippin's got three of these, but I don't remember which three, and I forgot to ask for a taste. Oh well, she probably sweated into them, anyhow.

I do remember Drippin's heartily recommended the mac and cheese, but neither one of us ordered it, so I don't know what to tell you, except that anyone who takes pictures of grilled-cheese sandwiches must know their stuff.

The Hard Knox Cafe is my kind of place, but professional tell-the-truthery obliges me to point out that seven bucks is about a buck too much to pay for anything less than half a bird, and this were only just three pieces: a drumstick and two thighs.

Hey—those are the right three pieces, piecewise, but they were maybe a little bit dry. Well, yes, a little too long in the deep fryer is all, or maybe a tad overprepepared. I'm sure it won't happen again.

There will certainly be an again, though, because—like I said—it's my kind of place. I just hope Inez doesn't figure out who I am and conk me over the head with a skillet for insulting her chickens. At least not before I eat; afterward, I guess, I'll be ready for a nap, anyway.

■ ANN'S SOUP KITCHEN AND RESTAURANT

Hang onto your hats, horsies, and honeybunches, folks, 'cause—like it or not—you are about to enter the Twilight Zone, inasmuch as this is Part Four of a three-part series.

The name of the series, in case you just joined us, is My Dinners with Complete Strangers, and Complete Stranger #4, as luck would have it, does an excellent Rod Serling imitation, and did one over breakfast at Ann's Soup Kitchen and Restaurant

Ann's Soup Kitchen and Restaurant
2498 Telegraph Avenue,
Berkeley. (510) 548-8885.
Breakfast, lunch, dinner.
Cheap cheap.

without even realizing we had already entered the actual Twilight Zone, by virtue of the above-mentioned virtue (this being Part Four of a three-part series, in case you just joined us).

And if that weren't all-out weird enough . . . by cracky if I ain't writing this in just my underwear. So now you know where we stand, exactly. (Let he or she who is wearing more than just undies while reading this cast the first stone. Ouch! Whoa—)

Is everyone else done masturbating? If so, let's get on with the review.

My breakfast companion—we'll call him "Dave Bolick of Oakland, CA (510) 601-9554," seeing as he's a freelance writer/editor looking for work—well, he'd written to me twice about Ann's Soup Kitchen. So I called him up and said, "Yeah, man, let's go."

Ann's Soup Kitchen, not to be confused with Ann's Cafe in Oakland, is a pretty decent Ann-related place in its own right.

Real wood and fake brick walls, high lattice ceiling, maybe slightly overcrowded with bus-your-own (i.e., crumb-filled) tables. It feels more like a coffee shop than a restaurant, which is fine with me except that the coffee's not that great. They charge 30 cents for a refill, too, but then, the original was only 50 cents, so . . .

And there's no table service. You order your food at the counter, sit down, shut up, and wait. Then you eat.

Dave Bolick of Oakland, CA (510) 601-9554, ate the #1 Breakfast, which is the standard two-egg, home fries, and toast combo. I ate the Super Rising Sun, which is three eggs, three whole-wheat pancakes, and ham (or bacon or sausage). I also ate a side of home fries because Dave had said, in one of his letters, that they were "really really really really good."

Well, they were good. One-sidedly browned with onions, scallions, and the right amount of garlic. I don't know if I'd give them four "reallys," though—maybe because I resented having to pay for the side order when they probably should have been included in the Super Rising Sun. Speaking of which, where was the toast? What are you supposed to do with three Super Rising Sunny-Side-Ups when there's no toast to dab them with?

Those two minor complaints aside, it was a fine breakfast. The ham was really good, the eggs were really eggs, and the pancakes were really really good. I don't normally go for whole-wheat pancakes, which tend to rival black holes for the density trophy, but these were perfect. Grainy and heavy, yes, but at least syrup, if not light, could pass through them.

You can also get raisin, banana, or granola whole-wheat pancakes. And Ann's claims to have "The Best Granola in Town," although I wouldn't know, and probably never will.

For lunch: standard hot and cold sandwiches and, of course, soups (all hot, I presume), including (on that particular day) a good-sounding cream of cauliflower and five-bean veggie. I'm sorry I didn't have the appetite to sample any of these lunch items for you, but that was a pretty big breakfast, you have to admit, and I did clean my plates—both of them. Ask Dave Bolick of Oakland, CA (510) 601-9554.

◼ SHANGRI-LA VEGETARIAN RESTAURANT

Hey, if it were up to me, I'd go on eating with complete strangers until the cows come home (and then, I guess, I'd have to eat with the cows). As it turns out, it *is* up to me, but I'm still closing the curtain on this five-part three-part series, because—all bovinery aside—my actual friends probably miss eating with me by now, and they definitely miss seeing their names in print. I have to say, though, I've really lucked out on the strangers. No

> **Shangri-La Vegetarian Restaurant**
> 2026 Irving Street,
> San Francisco. (415) 731-2548.
> Lunch, dinner.
> Credit cards accepted. Cheap.

sickos or psychos, and only one vegetarian. That (the vegetarian) would be this week's complete stranger, Complete Stranger #5, or "Five Alive!" as I like to call her, her actual god-given nickname being V. Live! (exclamation mark and all). I'll admit that the "V" probably stands for vegetarian, if not Veronika (her actual *name* name), but you have to admit that it works just as well as a Roman numeral. Deal?

So, Five Alive! steered me toward Shangri-La, a vegetarian Chinese restaurant in her neighborhood, which is the Sunset. There, over lunch, we discussed things in general, vegetarianism, and careers. Of all five complete strangers (not to mention myself), Five Alive! has the realest job. She works for the circus.

I had hoped she was going to be the strong lady, or a contortionist, or a half-woman-half-toaster, or a snake-charming fire-breathing sword-swallowing hammerer of 10-inch spikes into her own nose, or something like that, but she's not. She's an usher.

Oh well—it takes all types, I suppose.

Lunch special for me—that'd be soup, egg roll, rice, tea, and (in my case) mixed vegetables. A huge bowl of *da-lu* noodles soup, emphatically recommended by Five Alive!—we'll split that, thank you. And, for her, vegetarian chicken with black-bean sauce.

Now I happen to be a pretty firm believer in the Gertrudian model of existence, according to which a chicken is a chicken is a chicken, period. Therefore, the concept of vegetarian chicken, which implies a certain chickenlessness, sits somewhat less than right with me.

Still, I tried a few chunks, and I have to admit that it wasn't bad. It wasn't good, either. It simply wasn't. My problem with tofu and bean curd and gluten and such has always been that it does not actually exist, according to the Leonian axiom: "I can taste it, therefore it is" and its obvious flip side: "I can't taste it, therefore it ain't."

Vegetables exist, and the ones involved in this fake chicken dish (carrots, onions, green peppers, water chestnuts, etc.) were tasty enough, what with a great black-bean sauce. I also liked the *da-lu* noodles soup, which featured thick noodles in a dark broth, along with assorted veggies and decent doses of garlic and ginger. For right around four bucks, this could have been a hearty meal for one person.

As for the lunch special, I liked that it came with real (as opposed to white) rice. The egg roll was fine, and the soup that came along for the ride was great—even better than the *da-lu* noodles, I thought. This clear broth was defiantly flavorful, considering no meat and yes tofu. Again, the assorted vegetables. And special thanks to cilantro, my favorite green thing, for making its surface-skimming presence known in every spoonful.

The only problem with the lunch special was with my choice of headliners—the mixed vegetables (more carrots, cabbage, onions, mushrooms, sea something-or-other, and so on). These seemed slightly overcooked, and were unimproved by a tastelessly gloopy sauce. Luckily, Five Alive! didn't like her philosophically problematic vegetarian chicken dish as much as I did, so I didn't go hungry.

But just to be safe, if you go with the lunch special, you might try "sweet and sour walnuts" or "egg and tomatoes" or "hot sauce broccoli (hot)" instead. Lunch specials are served in a fun, bright red, and bafflingly compartmentalized plastic thing. What the—?

Well, Shangri-La dishes up healthy and mostly good vegetarian fare, it seems. They use "all natural earth-grown ingredients," according to the menu, "nothing artificial," and no MSG. In other words, *plbbplbbplbbplbb*.

But the price, I have to admit, is right. We coughed up 12 or 13 bucks total for three things. Not bad.

Should you go there? Sure, if you're a vegetarian.

■ GENEVA STEAKHOUSE

It was Labor Day and I didn't have nothing better to do, like barbecuing chickens, so I went to work. By "work," of course, I mean to insinuate that I went out to eat, and ate like a racehorse.

I ate barbecued chickens. (Like a racehorse.)

Before anyone accuses me of having the easiest job in the world, I just want to say, for the record, that I do. *And* the funnest, probably. That I can think of. No one can possibly have more fun working than I do. Except maybe Jerry Rice, who got to score three touchdowns and break Jim Brown's record while I, back home, watching, washed down above-

Geneva Steakhouse
5130 Mission Street,
San Francisco. (415) 586-6685.
Lunch, dinner.
Credit cards accepted. Cheap.

mentioned birdage with about a whole half of a watermelon. (Like a racehorse.)

Hold on a second. I have to pee.

What I'm getting at is this: J. R. must make, what, three, four, five hundred thousand times what I make, and rightfully so. 'Cause as fun as wide receiving must be, and as easy as he makes it look . . . well, for one thing, he entertains (neigh, *dazzles*) millions of people a week, and I figure I'm lucky to get a chuckle out of Clark Wofford.

Also to be considered are the physical hazards of professional football versus professional eating. I mean, Rice puts his entire muscular-skeletal system on the line every time he goes up for a pass, whereas I only ever risk my arteries.

But before this train of thought gets out of hand, which I fear it already has (I'm reminded of a "compare and contrast" paper from my illustrious college years in which I compared and contrasted the character of Sir Lancelot from *La Morte d'Arthur* to my cousin Vince Chianese, who worked in a gas station) . . .

Hold on a second. I have to pee again.

OK. This time I mean business. But first: Why is it so hard to find an open barbecue joint around here? Granted, it was a holiday, but the first two places I tried looked like they were down for the count. One, sadly, was Collier's BBQ on Ocean Avenue, which looks like it was once a great place, and hopefully will be again some day.

I started getting nervous, as it was less than an hour until kickoff, so I jumped into the first and meatiest-looking place I saw: Geneva Steakhouse on the corner of Mission and Geneva. Steak struck me as a fine idea, but then I noticed they had barbecued chickens on the board, too, and I popped the big question and the guy said, "Half," so I went with it.

For five or six bucks, you get the half of a chicken, and the whole of a baked tater, and a green salad, and garlic bread. And you get to sit at one of these weirdo booths with multicolorfully squared tablecloths (don't worry—there's glass on top) and fake flowers. And you get to watch *Smokey and the Bandit* on TV.

The chicken was actually pretty damn good. The sauce was not exactly distinctive, nor was there enough of it for my money. But what the sauce lacked in presence, the meat itself more than made up for in succulence. You gotta figure—at a place like this, where your only real choice is between steak and chicken (vegetarians: BYO grilled cheese), these guys know their way around a grill like Jerry Rice knows his way around a gridiron, and like I know my way around, um . . . bones? The bathroom?

Hold on a second.

Re Baked potato. What can I say . . . what can anyone say about a baked potato? (Answer: "It was baked. There was butter. I ate it.")

Re Green salad. Yeah, some of it was green, I suppose, but mostly it was white (i.e., iceberg) lettuce and shredded red cabbage, with a few actual *green* greens tossed in for good measure, or garnish. Liked the Italian dressing, though.

Re Garlic roll. The menu board says "roll," but really it was a good-size chunk of bread, with not quite enough butter or garlic. In fact, there wasn't any actual garlic on it, I don't think, just powder. Weak. Extra-credit points, however, for sheer size.

Overall: a fine pregame meal for the price and for the atmosphere. It's cafeteria-style service, with a long, narrow dining room—one and a half rows of maybe 20 or so of those meat-eating booths I was telling you about.

I'll be back for an actual steak, because it certainly seems like a good, honest, and cheap place to eat one. And because I owe them one for getting me home in time to see the opening kick of the season, which dribbled into the end zone for a touchback.

Final score: Niners 44, Raiders 14. Me: heartburn.

▌ COUNTRY STATION

You like country music?

I do. The older stuff, mostly, and the weirdest place to listen to it has got to be Country Station. Not the one on the radio—the one on Mission Street between 17th and 18th Streets: the sushi cafe.

Now, I don't normally *do* sushi—which isn't to say that I don't enjoy it when I do. It's just that, I don't know, I kind of like my food to be big. For

Country Station
2140 Mission Street,
San Francisco. (415) 861-0972.
Dinner. Credit cards
accepted.Cheap.

example, chickens. Chickens are way bigger than sushi. It only takes one half of a chicken to put me to sleep, whereas it takes 36 sushis. And that can be expensive, so I don't normally do it. In fact, this time was my third time ever, and by as many miles (three) the best.

Country Station!

I first heard about it from one D. Troit Boingo, the ex–copy editor who apparently grew weary of x-ing out my boners and defected to New York (where, I take it, restaurant reviewers review restaurants and that is that, and what goes around comes around, and one plus one equals two, and two is company, three's a crowd, what's what, and everybody's happy—I give her six to eight weeks).

Anyway, Ms. Boingo was unable to join me for dinner, being in New York and whatnot, so I called upon my sports-talking pal Yo-Yo, who agreed to meet me after work. She's Japanese, so I figured she'd come in handy (which she did).

Until she showed up, I sat there and stared at the place. It's a small, festive, low-ceilinged room with a four-seater counter (unfortunately occupied), one big table, and a handful of smaller ones. The chairs all have names painted on them, like Derrick and Andrew (but surely you know what "names" are by now). The walls, in keeping with the "transcendence of thematic unity" theme, are hung with three or four impressionistic paintings, some cowboy hats, dried flowers, and a few black-and-white band photos.

There was a list of sushi-eating pointers on my table, and the first one was my favorite, since it gave me permission to eat with my fingers. Before I could memorize any other ones, Yo-Yo showed up and ordered everything for us, and tried to tell me what all it was. And now I'll try to tell you.

From the *nigiri* section, we had *hamachi.* Two clumps of rice with two slabs of yellowtail fish, which melted on my tongue like no yellowtail fish has ever melted on my tongue before—in part because I rarely if ever allow them there.

We also got a rabbit roll, a vegetarian selection with cabbage, carrot, cucumber, and *shiso* leaf. There was so little of everything it was difficult to distinguish any one taste, although the *shiso* leaf, I'm proud to be able to say, struck me as almost minty.

Then there was a spider roll, which was my favorite: deep-fried soft-shell crab with avocado. The two middle pieces had long crab legs sticking up and out of them, like boners. (Touch that from N.Y.C.) However, if I further describe my enjoyment of this most succulent member of our meal, I'll really be in trouble. So . . . what else?

Edamame. Oh yeah, this was great, too, and just as fun to eat as the spider roll. It's a bowl of boiled soybeans, which you eat one at a time, like this: Hold the lightly salted pod to your lips and gently squeeze until it finally cleaves open, allowing the delicious bean onto the waiting tongue.

Don't look at me. I can't help it if *eating* equals *sex* (and vice versa, in many cases).

So then we shared a couple of, um, hand rolls, which are kind of like seaweed ice-cream cones. Unfortunately, the California roll (crab and avocado) also had unannounced mayonnaise in it, prompting me to consider moving to Arizona. A whole pile of ginger and a glass of water later, I tentatively tried the Dana roll (*hamachi,* cucumber, sesame seeds, and some special Japanese sprouts). It was a good one, even though Yo-Yo had already munched off all the sprouts.

In honor of Jimmie Rodgers, the granddaddy of country music, who wrote millions of great songs without ever mentioning sushi, we also sampled an order of *yakitori,* two skewers of barbecued chicken in a thickish, dark "*yakitori* sauce," of all things.

Jimmie Rodgers often sang about chickens.

I don't know how he would have liked Country Station, but I loved it. It's a really fun place, with really good sushi, for really really cheap (for sushi), according to Yo-Yo and D. Troit Boingo and lots of other people.

I wouldn't know.

■ ABC BAKERY CAFE

Let's face it: Time flies, whether you're having fun or not. To illustrate my point: Once I was just standing there. The next thing I knew, time had flown.

Now, as I've already died, in my opinion, the flying of time does not

ABC Bakery Cafe
388 Mime Street, Oakland.
(510) 836-2288.
Also at 1068 Stockton, San
Francisco. (415) 981-0803.
Breakfast, lunch, dinner.
Cheap cheap.

sadden or worry me the way it used to, or the way it might sadden or worry a living, breathing person, such as Darren Constantino. I don't mean to insinuate that I've "died and gone to heaven," or "died a mil-

lion deaths," as the sayings go; I have died exactly two of them, by my count, and gone absolutely nowhere. So . . . well, OK, I'm done with that.

My only remaining concerns have to do with missing meals. Because sometimes, while time is flying, you wind up losing one of the three best times of day: dinnertime. And, sad to say, there isn't always food in the fridge (at least not where I live), which is why we need late-night restaurants in the world. (At least I do.) In my neighborhood, if you miss last call at Can-Cun (12:45 a.m.), you may as well go to bed hungry.

Downtown Oakland, on the other hand, has recently sprouted a killer, kick-ass, almost-all-night joint called ABC. It's open every day 7 a.m. to 3 a.m., and don't let the bright, plastic, fast-foodish interior scare you off—this 20-hour Chinatown bakery/cafe rocks and rules.

I went there one night with tall person E. B. Matt, although a much shorter person had pointed the place out to me—but he had something else to do. I can't imagine anything anyone would rather be doing late at night than sinking face-first into a mountain of steamingly delicious and alphabetically adventurous food, like "shrimp fired rice," "beeef," or (my favorite misspelling ever of my least favorite soup:) "bortsch."

Hey—at least they got their name right.

They got the food right, too. I had cream of "crab meat & sweet corns" soup, which was damn good. Smooth as all get-out, with shipwrecked chunks o' crab and kernels o' corn floating around. This came with a warm white dipping roll, coated in honey and coconut.

Did I mention that there are a million things on the menu? There are.

Some are standard American favorites, like chicken salad, T-bone steak, or "fired eggs w/ham." Some are standard Chinese: chow mein, *chow fun*, fried rice. And some are standard I-don't-know-what, such as french fried rice, fried prawn toast, and fried squid meatball. Wahoo!

ABC offers four kinds of toast, aside from the fried-prawn variety. I ordered jam-and-butter toast out of curiosity. I wanted to see what about it could possibly warrant the $2.70 price tag. Was it a loaf of toast? Was it two-inch-thick homemade bread?

Nope, nope. It was regular sliced white bread, diagonally cut, buttered, jammed, just like anywhere, the only difference being that *the crust was cut off!* What the—?

Oh well. Spend and learn.

Don't worry—there's plenty of cheap stuff, too. For example, E. B. Matt ordered "eight delights combo fun" (for only $4.90, or roughly 60 cents a delight). This was a great big bowl of great, meaty noodle soup—although by the time I got to it, there were only three delights left: pork, squid, and crab. Some of the other ones, I think, were chicken, beef, shrimp, and Matt-only-knows what else.

I also ordered squid with black-bean sauce chow mein, and it was a huge amount of memorable mealage: onions, green peppers and hot little red ones, and a generous amount of fresh-enough squid heaped over a bed of chow mein noodles and smothered in the best-tasting, best-smelling black-bean sauce I've ever encountered.

As much as I'd already eaten by then, I almost cried when the smoky smell of this dish hit my brain, then again when the taste of it hit my tongue. Inspired, I easily cleaned the plate.

What else? E. B. Matt got hot Ovaltine. I tried it, sure, but found it yucky. Some other interesting drinks that I didn't try and probably should have: mint soda, hot lemon Coke, and red bean ice.

So . . . erratically priced, eclectic, and sometimes excellent late-night food. You gotta like that, even if you don't like the atmosphere. (You won't.)

■ LA MEDITERRANÉE

Yatee-Yatee-Bing-Eh-Eh-Eh moved to another neighborhood—the Castro!—so I dialed her new phone number, 555-4444, and said, "Yatee-Yatee, do you want to go eat at La Mediterranée, a popular, bustling, yet comfortably candlelit Mediterranean cafe on Noe Street, just around the corner from your new apartment?"

La Mediterranée
288 Noe Street, San Francisco.
(415) 431-7210. Also at 2210
Fillmore Street, San Francisco.
(415) 921-2956, and 2936
College Avenue, Berkeley
(510) 540-7773. Lunch, dinner.
Credit cards accepted.
Splurge cheap.

"Why are you talking like the introductory paragraph to a restaurant review?" she said.

"Because that's what I am," I said.

"You are what you eat. Follow? So, if you write about what you eat, like me, or take pictures of it, then you must be what you write, or a photograph. In other words, one *becomes* the—"

"Hey, reader, don't believe a word of it!" Yatee-Yatee said, breaking my momentum. "He's making this up as he goes along! We never really said any of this shit."

"Don't you think they know that by now?" I said.

"One," she said, "would certainly hope," she said, "so."

The bottom line, dear reader (Hi Mom!) is that we wound up eating at La Mediterranée, in spite of its popularity. Frankly, I know one of the cooks. He always comes out to hear my band, so I figured the least I could do was go taste his tabbouleh. (Hi Scott!)

We ordered the Mediterranean Meza, which is 10 different things, including tabbouleh, for roughly 10 bucks a person. Our waitressperson assured us we had made the right decision, and I assure you, dear reader, that we had. The Meza is the way to go. All the best-looking things from the menu, including both chicken dishes, served in bowls and half-shells, lined up on our table in the shape of an X, with a small pile of pita bread in the center, marking the spot. Ten—in other words, *11* things! For $10.95 a person.

Worth it? Yep.

Two of the dishes I didn't even taste. Yatee-Yatee did, and pronounced them "good." I'm sorry, but I don't quite like hummus yet. *Baba ghanoush* I probably never will like, although it happens to have my favorite name for any kind of food ever: *baba ghanoush.* (My friend Haywire wrote a poem once about being "*baba ghanoushed* into the fourth dimension.")

I tried the *levant* sandwich, at least, even though I knew I wouldn't like it, what with cream cheese. So that leaves seven remaining things, and every which one of them, I'm happy to say, was great.

My favorite was the chicken pomegranate, two drumsticks marinated in an extremely subtle pomegranate sauce and baked with wild herbs. Then there was the *lule kebab,* two big lamb meatballs smothered in tomatoes and onions. Like the chicken pomegranate, this was served over some excellent rice pilaf, with whole chickpeas, slivers of almond, and raisins. The only other meat dish was chicken Cilicia, which is chunks of chicken with almonds, chickpeas, raisins, and cinnamon, wrapped in phyllo dough and sprinkled with powdered sugar. Sounds good, don't it? (Is.) Also from the phyllo-dough specialties section: Grecian spinach and feta, which would probably have been spanakopita, except that it was rolled into rolls instead of baked in one big piece. Well, whatever—it was melt-in-your-mouth delicious.

What else? There was dolma, of course. That's the grape leaves wrapped around rice and stuff. There was Armenian potato salad, which I liked a million times better than American potato salad. And, oh yeah, tabbouleh—one of my favorite Mediterranean things.

What with all the mint and parsley (which was all over everything), I was afraid to smile, but I was having a good time. You have to understand: There was food *everywhere,* and there were carrots and pickled peppers and cauliflowers sticking out of it, and peperoncini and olives.

Then, as if we weren't having enough fun already, it occurred to us that the carrots were there to scoop stuff out of the bowls and onto the pita. Things escalated, and by the time the parsley cleared, we were both of us a little embarrassed at the mess we'd made.

◼ ANGKOR WAT

"So," she says to me, soon as I sit down, "what's under your hat?"

Like a good boy, I take off my hat and show her. You should always take your hat off when you eat, according to my grandmother—and

Angkor Wat
4217 Geary Boulevard, San
Francisco. (415) 221-7887/8.
Lunch, dinner. Credit cards
accepted. Splurge cheap.

definitely in a restaurant, according to folks down South.

This is neither my grandmother nor the South, but I take my hat off anyway and show Ask Isadora (who doesn't like short hair, I don't think) all the little tiny half-inchers on my head. She of all people should know that size is not important—unless, of course, you're talking about the size of a cheeseburger, or chicken, or a stack of pancakes. In this case, we're talking about great big piles of great Cambodian food at Angkor Wat. It's me and my buddy Ask Isadora, so we're also talking about relationships and writing. What else is there? Well, sports, but let's not get into that now. (Eagles 40, Niners 8.)

Angkor Wat is an award-winning Richmond District Cambodian restaurant whose claim to fame is having served chicken and pineapple soup to Pope John Paul II in 1987. "He liked it so much," according to the menu, "he asked for a SECOND helping!" It doesn't say whether or not they gave it to him, but if he received a fraction of the Royal Treatment me and Ask Isadora got . . .

She's a regular, see, so they really like her—maybe even more than the pope, who only came that once. Of course, Ask Isadora lives in the 'hood. She's way more classier than me (or the pope), but she reckoned I would like the place, in spite of its cloth napkins and tablecloths, and she was absolutely right.

I knew it as soon as they brought our food out on trays—not serving trays, *eating* trays—at least two feet long and at least one foot wide (or vice versa). There was a gigantic leaflike thing on top of the tray, and then the food on top of that. Plop, plop. Great presentation!

Great food, too, and plenty of it. Before the trays showed up, we had already eaten an order of *lott,* which are tiny spring rolls served with a spicy lime sauce and pickled vegetables. The rolls themselves, stuffed with ground white chicken meat, water chestnut, "beanthread," onion, and ground peanut, are miraculously greaseless, which Ask Isadora seemed to consider a plus.

I loved the soup. It wasn't the pope's famous favorite, unfortunately, but it came along for free with the lunch plates, so who's complaining?

Not me. Tender chunks of chicken, avoidable mushrooms, fresh herbs, and some other stuff in a chicken broth so flavorful that even tofu tasted like something.

Ask Isadora got *sach ko kroeung aing,* two skewers of marinated beef charbroiled with ground peanuts and five spices (*galanga,* tumeric, kaffir lime leaves, lemongrass, and garlic). It's 10 bucks for dinner, but much less for lunch, and damn juicy either way. I tried it. "Mmm, wow," I believe, were my exact words.

On our waterguyperson's recommendation, I ordered "Cambodian five spices shark," which blew everything else out of the water, you ask me. Ask Ask Isadora and she'll tell you something else. She'd never eaten any sharks before. (They're sharks!—how could anyone *not* eat them, given the choice?) Well, she doesn't like seafood, but I talked Ask into trying a piece, using the old "tastes just like chicken" ploy. Maybe I said beef. She said pork, and she said, yes, she liked it.

For 10 bucks for dinner, six-or-seven-something for lunch, you get a heap of thinly sliced, supertender shark, panfried to perfection with peppers, chile peppers, onions, those same five spices, and those same ground peanuts. Over rice. Nice and spicy.

Both lunches also came with sautéed vegetables in a smooth-ass curry sauce. So good, again, I even ate the tofu.

For dessert, we split a crazy and wonderful dish that would best be described as "flaming bananas," because that's what it is. The technical name, I believe, is banana flambé, but Ask Isadora calls it the Batman Special. In case you've never had it, it's basically bananas in this creamy, sweet, buttery sauce. Then they set some brandy on fire and pour it over the top. ("Flaming bananas, Batman!") When the fire goes out, you dig in. It tastes like smoked heaven.

What a great place. I imagine, what with the megafriendly service, fancy-pants atmosphere, relatively cheap prices, great food, and papal blessings, they do a pretty good dinner business. But we were there for lunch, on a Friday, and we were *the only ones there.*

So, OK. You know what to do. Right?

■ CRESCENT CITY CAFE

My new van is an old Toyota minivan, but I call it "The Ford" in honor of my old LTD, Mel, R.I.P. (They're the same color, see. Maroon.) I loved Mel, and now I love The Ford. But last week somebody stole it. But then I got it back.

Crescent City Cafe
1418 Haight Street, San Francisco. (415) 863-1374. Breakfast, lunch, dinner. Credit cards accepted. Cheap.

Here's how it happened: The police called me up and said, "We found your van. Come get it." I said I'd be there in five minutes, but before five minutes passed, City Tow had hooked it up and taken it away.

Then I had to go to the police station for a release form. I was picturing something like *Barney Miller,* you know, with desks and chairs and typewriters and Wojohowitz. But that ain't how it is.

You go into a small lobby, you look at a police officer through about eight inches of bulletproof Plexi-stuff, and you pick up a phone if you want to talk. I have to say, I did feel pretty safe, even though all the guns were on the other side, and I appreciated their concern for my well-being. Overall, the policepersonpeople were helpful and courteous, whereas City Tow bites the biggest fucking one ever, and deserves to die.

I know I'm not a City Tow reviewer, but I'd rather loan my van to whoever stole it in the first place than let City Tow get its grubby hooks into it again. The stealers did about $10 worth of damage to my windshield wipers, whereas City Tow cost me $140.

But enough ranting. At least I got it back, right? And even though they took my Dolly Parton tape, which was all they took, they did replace it with a rap compilation called *West Coast Bad Boys.* So I've been driving around listening to that, trying to get cool.

And then, out of the blue, I got a Dolly Parton tape and a bottle of hot sauce in the mail from an employee of the Crescent City Cafe, who invited me to eat there—whether I reviewed it or not. She liked my column and just wanted to feed me, the letter said. Well, there's nothing I like better than being fed.

So how I worked it out ethically was like this: "Fuck ethics," I said, and I headed on down to the Haight. Crescent City. I introduced myself to the heaven-bound Dolly-and-hot-sauce-sender, counterbribed her with a tape of my band, and copped a free meal. Now I'm going to give the place a glowing review!

Truth is, I already knew that I liked Crescent City. I've eaten there lots of times. This time I got Creole gumbo because it was a rainy day and because it had my three favorite animals in it: chickens, crabs, and sausage.

The gumbo was great—a substantial bowl of thick, meaty, gloppy heat, with a pile of white rice jutting out in the middle, like an iceberg. It didn't even need any of the many varieties of hot sauce available. The meal included a salad and a couple chunks of French bread. I also got a side-order crab cake to be safe. It too was great, fried to a crisp on the outside and mushy in the middle.

For dessert I got a fried-chicken dinner with more rice, more bread, and some mighty meaty split-pea soup. I was already full, so I ordered all this to go, ate part of it at the bus stop, and then the rest for supper. Since I actually paid for it, I don't mind saying that, tasty as it was, this was another one of those goddamn bonsai chickens.

Holy cow, Chicken Farmer—take your little birdie in for its shots, why don't you? At least if it's destined to spend its afterlife on my plate. Personally, I *like* my chickens pumped up with growth hormones—they build character, you know.

One thing I like about the Crescent City is that it makes no bones about cooking up animals. In spite of the neighborhood, there are few if any concessions to vegetarianism. In fact, more than once on the menu they proudly state, "This is seasoned w/ ham hocks, it is not vegetarian!" Personally, I don't mind saying flat-out that everything tastes better with meat in it (except cornflakes and one or two other things).

As for ethical considerations, I stand by my pal Rube Roy, who recently said: "Hey, if a chicken can catch me and get me in a deep fryer, he's welcome to eat me."

■ STEVE THE GREEK

(As punishment for devoting half of that Crescent City review to automotive rather than culinary issues, I impose upon myself for this one the following restriction: I will never once wander from my accounts and

Steve the Greek
431 Polk Street, San Francisco.
Lunch, dinner. Cheap.

descriptions of the actual eating experience. No digressionary information, personal problems, vendettas, *van*dettas, gratuitous bestiality, or shameless self-promotion. Here goes . . .)

Haywire's parents are in town visiting from Maine!

Let me rephrase that: I went to eat at Steve the Greek with my pal Haywire and his two parents, Pa Haywire and Ms. Sophistication, who are in town visiting from Maine.

It was Halloween!

Let me rephrase that: Steve the Greek is a great place, in large part because the guy running it (we'll call him Steve, although I don't think that's who he is) sings loudly in Greek while preparing the food, and on the night I was there, stopped cooking and singing periodically to pass out Halloween candy to all the little (and big) Polk Street trick-or-treaters.

The kitchen is right there in the window, in front. As we walked in, Steve cheerfully greeted Haywire, who is a "regular," as well as "irregular." (Oops, let me rephrase that:) "Hi!" he said. Then he said, "Hi Ma. Hi Pa."

We ordered drinks. I got a pineapple-coconut juice, which was not fresh, of course, but very good. Everyone else, who ordered Cokes or beers, was jealous.

"So, Dan," Pa Haywire said while we were waiting for our food, "What's going on with you? What's new? Haywire told us about your van."

"Can't talk about it," I said. "How about this juice, though? Isn't it refreshing and delightful?"

"Say, boys, speaking of refreshing and delightful," said Ms. Sophistication, "how is your band, Ed's Redeeming Qualities, doing?"

Beads of sweat formed on my forehead. "Boy am I hungry for some great Greek food," I said, nudging Haywire.

"Well, Ma," he said, "we're recording a double-live album, since you asked, on Saturday, November 12, at 10 p.m."

"Where?" she said.

"At Komotion," Haywire continued, while I sat there and shook (with hunger). "It's on 16th Street near Folsom, I think. And everyone's invited."

"That's swell!" said Ms. Sophistication.

"I'll say," Pa Haywire said. "*Yodel-eh-hee-hoo!* It's been many months since you guys have played out. You must be awful excited about this show."

Haywire admitted that we were and I just sort of squeaked, and then the food came, lucky for everyone.

I got a thing called King Combination, which was some of everything: some souvlaki, a skewer of shish kebab, dolma, falafel, hummus, spinach pie, cottage fries, pita bread, Greek salad, and baklava for dessert. Didn't I tell you I was hungry?

The meat and the dolma (vegetarian) came with a subtle yogurt sauce, which I actually liked for a change. The falafel, which was excellent, came coated in hummus, which I also actually liked for a change. The spinach pie, I thought, was a bit dense and bland—not flaky enough for me. Ms. Sophistication, who ordered it on its own, said she liked it, but then, she admitted, the last spinach pie she had was in Lowell, Mass. Well, the last I had was at La Méditerranée, and it was better than Steve's.

The cottage fries were a little soggy by the time I got around to them, the pita bread was pita bread, and the salad was OK. Real olives and plenty of feta, but iceberg lettuce and no vinegar. (Haywire argued that there was in fact vinegar, offering as evidence the fact that he got some in his eye.)

The baklava was great. It wasn't oozing with honey and too sweet to eat, as baklava often is, in my opinion. Still, I had a hard time finishing it, in part because I had cleaned the rest of my plate, like a good boy, and in part because the topic of conversation had shifted to boogers.

Pa Haywire'll do that to you. And worse. I'm not even allowed to mention what other taboo topic came up while I was trying to eat dessert, since it has to do with a childhood acquaintance of his in Dallas who confessed to having "made love to a chicken."

Don't look at me. My own love for chickens is entirely platonic. I only mention it to illustrate what a terrible city Dallas is.

Steve the Greek, by contrast, is a really fun and great and relatively cheap place to eat. If for no other reason, go there to read the poignantly sad, beautiful, and ungrammatical handwritten account of Steve the Greek's struggle to survive in America. It's on the wall in the back corner, under a painting of something.

◼ EUGENE'S RANCH HOUSE

Talked to Grandma Rubino on the phone yesterday. She's 85 and my only living grandparent. As far as I know, she can still beat me at arm wrestling, but every time I talk to her I have to talk a little louder than the time before. And every time I have to explain to her that I'm not a student. I think she thinks that because I don't live in Ohio and am not married I must still be in school.

Eugene's Ranch House
4081 Hollis Street, Emeryville.
(510) 658-6507. Breakfast, lunch, dinner. Cheap cheap.

"I'm 32, Grandma," I said.

"What?" she said.

I must've had too much coffee, because I tried to explain to her that I was a writer, and that one thing I wrote was restaurant reviews for the newspaper.

"What?" she said.

I said it one notch louder.

"Wow!" she said. "You're in the paper?"

"Yeah. Every week."

"Don't say anything bad about those restaurants," she said. "You'll get in trouble. It's bad for business."

"Don't worry," I said. I said what she always says of her hundreds and hundreds of grandchildren. "I love them all equally," I said.

She said, "What?"

Before hanging up she warned me again, so I promised not to say anything bad about any restaurant ever. Then I went out to review a place I knew I would like: Eugene's Ranch House in Emeryville.

Eugene's has three different dining rooms. The first one, where me and E. B. Matt ate, was brightly lit, with several long Formica-top tables, a few small ones, and some truly hideous paintings going for $800-something, in sharp contrast to the food. Food goes for two, three, four, five-hundred tops.

E. B. Matt got the roast Tom Turkey special, with stuffing and some other things, for $4.65 (the most expensive dish on the menu). I'd just rescued him from refoundationing a house, so he was dirty and, more important, hungry. All I managed to get out of his turkey dinner was a forkful of stuffing, which was pretty good.

He also ordered split-pea soup, however, and split it with me. It was a big bowl, nice and meaty, with a big plop of white rice if you want one.

Me, I ordered sirloin-tip stew, which came with a pretty heaping heap o' smashed taters and a bunch of mixed-up vegetables—corn, peas, lima beans, you know. And there was plenty of gravy and stew juice to keep my two slices of sliced wheat bread busy.

The meat was tender and the whole meal was hearty, but it was so dang cheap that I couldn't help ordering a chili cheese dog with onions for dessert. And that's the part I've been dying to tell you about.

Get this, Grandma. I said, GET THIS, GRANDMA: They take at least one and maybe even two hot dogs—thick, juicy beef ones—and at least one and maybe even two buns; then they chop everything up willy-nilly, so that you don't know for sure how many there are, one or two, and they arrange these in spokelike fashion on a plate, then smother the whole thing with homemade chili, your choice of cheese (cheddar), and onions.

Go figure. Eugene's is one of the most down-to-earth establishments going—it's practically a truck stop, for crying out loud—and here they've got the artsiest fancy-pants presentation of a chili dog I've ever seen. And I've seen more than my share of chili dogs.

This one tasted great, and it was a lot of food for under three bucks; but I have to say, I looked real hard and only found two (2) discernible pieces of meat in all that chili. Whereas there must have been hundreds (100s) of beans. Not that I mind all that terribly much. It was good, spicy, bean-heavy chili. In all honesty, though, chili should have meat in it, don't you think? Unless it's vegetarian chili, in which case what would it be doing on a hot dog?

■ IN THE SOUP: THE SOUPS OF SAN FRANCISCO

When it's cold and wet and yucky outside, people want something warm and wet and yummy to put inside of them. Soup, right? So why don't I go out and about town, get a little wet, and round up a few good soup-related recommendations for the flu-ridden Bay Area?

OK. No problem.

When I get sick, the first thing I do is make a gigantic pot of soup, about two gallons of it. Then that's all I eat until I get better. I don't care if the soup has anything to do with the getting better, medicynically speaking—I just know that it feels right to eat it, especially if there's chickens involved.

For the purposes of this article I ate a lot of different kinds of soup in a lot of different sittings, and I enjoyed every single one of them, but I think the most perfect bowl of rainy-day soup I had was on a dark and stormy night at **La Santaneca de la Mission** (2815 Mission Street, San Francisco; 415/285-2131). It's a great little place with some really nice booths, a hoppin' jukebox, and fish soup that, I was led to believe (by reliable sources), would make my eyeballs move around independently from each other.

Who could pass up such an opportunity? So I peeled off my raincoat, sat down in the corner against the jukebox, and didn't even bother to look at the menu.

"Fish soup," I said. As an afterthought, I asked, "Is it big?"

Either the waitressperson didn't understand, or she was a liar, because her answer was no.

I don't know, there's something perhaps-not-so-mysterious about rain, especially incessant rain, that makes me want to take off all my clothes, wander out into the ocean, become a fish, and spend the rest of my days swallowing smaller ones whole. As such a move would not be practical, however, my next impulse is to sink into a good-size bowl of great seafood soup.

I'm telling you: La Santaneca de la Mission.

You get a meal-size bowl full of tasty clear broth with tomato, onion, green pepper, cilantro, one big lump of an egg, do-it-yourself lemon wedges, and—count 'em—*four* corn tortillas, for dipping.

Oh yeah, the fish. I think they just lop off its head, hack it into four or five pieces, and then toss it on in, bones and skin and all—which makes for a much funner, more interactive eating experience, you ask me. I mean, anyone who shares my kind of primo-oceanic rainy-day fantasies will love reaching down in for those prize chunks and clawing every inch of edible fish from the backbone. I certainly did.

Although La Santaneca's fish soup is the perfect thing for a rainy day, and an amazingly great meal, I'm sure, in any kind of weather, it's not the absolute best bowl of soup available in the Bay Area. For that, you just have to step into almost any Thai restaurant.

You know what I'm talking about. It's that chicken and coconut milk and *galanga* and lemongrass and chile pepper and mushroom and cilantro deal, and there are always a few other things floating around that you're not sure if you're supposed to eat or not.

It's called by different names, like *dom ka gai,* or *tom ka gai,* or something something something—always three short syllables—and it's always sweet and spicy and pungent and smooth and exotic and almost mythically exquisite, like something you might expect to sip out of a mermaid's skull for special powers.

Wherever it comes from, this whatever whatever whatever soup affects much more than the eyeballs. It'll spin your whole head around like Linda Blair's, and you might wind up in a neck brace. Extremely dangerous soup, in other words; each bowl threatens to make a drooling, babbling idiot of you.

Maybe I've had too much already.

Anyway, I started asking around for the best version of chicken coconut soup, and two different people pointed me toward **Cha Am** in Berkeley (1543 Shattuck Avenue, 510/848-9664). There's one in San Francisco, too (701 Folsom Street), but in Berkeley you can sit in this slant-ceilinged porchlike room with skylight window strips. There are other rooms, too, but I recommend the porch for a rainy day, 'cause nothing makes you happier to be inside a nice, warm, cozy restaurant, eating the soup of your life, than the sound of cold hard rain beating down on the roof over your head.

Besides *dom-ka-gai* (as they call it, with hyphens), we also got *dom-yam-gung,* which was a hot-and-sour soup with prawns, mushrooms, lemongrass, and citrus leaves. It was actually pretty great in its own right, but it might as well have been a boiled shoe, next to the *dom-ka-gai.*

Was it the best *dom-ka-gai*—the best of the best?

I don't know. Maybe. The slices of chicken, simmered in coconut milk, were especially tender, and that magical reaction between the two was accentuated by the perfect blend of everything else, with a little extra push of roasted chile to bring out the sweat. If I ever die, I hope it's at Cha Am, facedown in that deadly, delicious one-two-three.

Actually, Cha Am was our last stop (wisely so, for obvious reasons) in a three-course three-stop soup hop that started at **Ann's Soup Kitchen** (2498 Telegraph Avenue, Berkeley; 510/548-8885), where I had a warm-up bowl of cream of cauliflower. I reviewed Ann's (not to be confused with Ann's Cafe) a while back, but I went there for breakfast and neglected to even try the soup in spite of the name of the place.

Everyone says Ann's Soup Kitchen used to be better than it is now, but I wouldn't know. I've got no complaints. For only about two bucks, they dish out a fairly large bowl with one slice of margarined wheat bread. (OK, one complaint: margarine.)

I chose cream of cauliflower over vegetable and five-bean vegetarian. I'm pretty sure I made the right choice, 'cause it was pretty good soup, with celery and a few chunks of cheese. Pretty filling, too, for an appetizer.

Next, my Berkeley Soup Guide and I moseyed down Telegraph to **Cafe Intermezzo** (2442 Telegraph Avenue, Berkeley; 510/849-4592), which he translated for me as "Cafe Bohemian Cool People." They seem to specialize in coffee, soup (one kind at a time), gigantic salads, and huge hunks of homemade bread.

The soup of the day that day was lentil and ham, which should have been called lentil and mushroom, because that was about all I found in it. But the bread was big and good and *buttered*, at least.

Basic coffee shop atmosphere, but who cares? It was just a quick pit stop on our way to the main course, the real thing, the finish line, the so-on-and-so-forth.

As far as regular old American soups are concerned, I think my favorite place to go is still **Soups** (784 O'Farrell Street, San Francisco; 415/775-6406). I've written about it before, so I won't spend too much time on it now.

I just wanted to go back and ask Mr. Nice Guy, Richard Gaule, propriet-guyperson, if he did better business during the cold, rainy season.

"Do you do better business during the cold, rainy season?" I asked.

"Yes," he said.

(Or was it no?—I'm a terrible journalist.)

Anyway, while I was there, I ordered a bowl of lentil and sausage soup, with way more lentils and way more meat than Intermezzo's. Plus it included a refill, a bottomless pile of crackers, and coffee, tea, or milk.

It was great, and I got to listen to Mr. Nice Guy cracking jokes and being generally wonderful with all his wacko Tenderloin customers, including one disheveled dude who poked his head in to announce (in a drunken snarl): "I'm voting for Dan Quayle. You know why?"

Uh . . . no.

"He's the only one who knows how to spell *potato.*"

Yep, check this place out for a pleasant and quick attitude adjustment, and a good, cheap, soothing meal.

If, on the other hand, more hair on your kneecaps is what you're after, I recommend **Chava's** (3248 18th Street, San Francisco, 415/552-9387), a tough, festive, authentic Mexican restaurant where, on weekends, you can get a big bowl of *birria*— "a goat dish," they call it—with hot homemade tortillas.

Birria is fairly straightforward: It's goat in a very good, spicy goat broth, served with a plate of add-your-own cilantro, onions, lemons, and limes. Go hog-wild. Live a little. Be a man. Be whatever, just dump it all in and get to work.

I love *birria.* That's all I've ever had at Chava's, but they're also known for their other soups—chicken and vegetable, beef and vegetable, or meatball and vegetable, all of which are available every day of the week.

The best bowl of Japanese soup I've had came from **Dojima An** (219 O'Farrell Street, San Francisco; 415/956-0838). It was also the prettiest and biggest bowl of soup I've come across in my studies. It's called *nabeyaki udon,* and it's not actually a bowl of soup—it's a kettle. Handle and all, in case you want to pick it up and carry it around the restaurant to show people: "Look what I got!"

What you get is a bed of those thick *udon* noodles in a clear broth with chunks of chicken, shredded carrots, green onions, some kind of cabbage, one big mushroom cloud, two weirdo red fishy stringy thingies, seaweed, and one long breaded shrimp. The main attraction, at least aesthetically, is a center-stage sunny-side-up egg, almost raw, floating on top of it all.

As is the custom with Japanese soup, everything has its own special place in the bowl—it's up to you to mix it up, if that's your style.

However you eat it, it's a meal and a half, and everything in it is great—especially the noodles themselves, which were as flavorful a *cappella* as many full-fledged ensembles of soup I've had.

While I was there, pondering it all, I overheard this stuffed-up woman ask her waitressperson, "What kind of soup is good for a cold?"

I don't think the waitressperson understood the question. If so, she might have said: "Stop asking stupid questions. All of them!"

BEEP'S BURGERS

The boys in the band next door were practicing their next-door hearts out one night last week, and no offense but after a while I started getting a little sick of the songs. My first idea was to give up on life and watch some prime-time television. But that was a very bad idea, so then I decided to go spend a little quality time with The Ford.

Beep's Burgers
1051 Ocean Avenue, San Francisco. (415) 584-2650. Lunch, dinner. Cheap cheap.

That was a good idea. We drove around aimlessly through neighborhoods neither one of us was very familiar with—Diamond Heights, the Sunset, Outer Mission—just shooting the breeze and so forth, until we accidentally wound up near City College, where I spotted a cool neon sign for a place called Beep's Burgers. What was cool about the sign was this little neon rocket that looked like it had been there since before rockets ever happened.

"Do you see what I see, The Ford?" I said.

It said, "Yep."

So we pulled into the parking lot. Beep's Burgers is not an actual sit-down restaurant. It's takeout only. In other words: just what the situation called for. Beep's is the perfect place to have a nice, quiet, romantic dinner with your car.

It's also pretty dang cheap, as in three, four bucks for a half-pound burger, depending on what all you want up top: cheese, bacon, chili . . . Cough up another Georgie-Boy for some thick-cut fries, and you're still way under what a lot of places charge for just a half-pounder. You're also gonna make a mess of your car, but that's OK. If you're worried about it, you can always eat standing up outside at the wraparound ledge, in the drizzle.

I guess this is how folks used to do fast food in the '50s and '60s, when I was nonexistent and then sitting in my high chair getting ketchup all over everything, respectively.

So, OK, went up to the window and placed my order. Neglected to get the chili, for which I am now kicking myself. But I did get the half-pounder (hold the mayo, hold the mustard) with bacon and cheese and fries and a large root-beer float, because that's the kind of place Beep's is—the kind where you get a root-beer float.

Naturally, I was nervous that the kid in the kitchen would mess up and put the *m*-words on my burger, so I was trying to sneak a peek—but my view was obstructed by rows and columns of stark photos (mug shots, really) of unhappy-looking burgers and sandwiches with m-words oozing out of them.

Almost panicked. Didn't. Got my food and everything was fine.

The root-beer float was thick and cold and good. The fries were thick and hot and good. The burger, unfortunately, was not technically a half-pounder so much as two quarter-pounders—the sad difference being that two quarter-pounders are twice as easy to overcook.

I guess the obvious reason why cheapo churn-'em-out burger joints tend to do it that way is it's more convenient to prepare and store a million quarter-pounders and quicker to cook two of them than one big half-pound lump. Next time I'll ask them to stack the two together and cook it exactly as long as they would normally cook one skinny one. Think they'd do it?

Who cares? The point is, although it lacked any semblance of succulence, it was a decent burger, with tomato, lettuce, pickles, etc.—and a perfectly fun eating experience, overall, for not all that much money. In fact, I had no problem affording dessert.

I should have tried one of the "teriyaki bowls," because they were there and un-American. I'd also been eyeballing the barbecued-beef sandwich, but somehow I wound up getting "cheese fish" instead. I guess I liked the sound of it. Plus I was already full. As I suspected, the sandwich wasn't much of anything, just a little square of deep-fried cheese fish and a single leaf of lettuce, hold the mayo.

Now, I'm no Jacques Cousteau; I don't pretend to know anything about the cheese fish as an aquatic animal, but I think I can guess where it gets its name. It tastes exactly like regular fish with a slice of American cheese on top! (Hee hee hoo.)

And if that ain't enough high chair humor for you, check this out . . . Here's what it said at the top of my receipt, no lie: "Beep's *Bugers*"! (Pppppppkkkkfff!)

■ J & A RESTAURANT

DEAR JOHN MADDEN:

Now that the football season, even the Pro Bowl, is all the way officially over, I'd like to all the way officially invite you to eat breakfast with me. I'm thinking maybe five-pound omelettes at Ann's in Oakland. It's an All-Madden Hall of Fame nine million–star kind of place. As for me, I admit to being smaller and skinnier than Dexter Carter, and sure, Ping-Pong is my best sport; but I happen to eat like an offensive lineman. (If you're not up for a five-pounder yourself, you can always get the diet plate—roughly three and a half pounds—and I promise not to tell anyone.) So . . . whaddya say? Huh?

J & A Restaurant
5712 Mission Street, San Francisco. (415) 337-6688. Breakfast, lunch, dinner. Cheap cheap.

Here's what I have to say this week: J & A Restaurant. Way the hell out on Mission Street, past Geneva. It's yet another one of those great Chinese-American–food joints that people with my appetite-to-income ratio go both goo-goo and gaga over. In other words: cheap cheap cheap.

I celebrated the Chinese New Year there, but I had also celebrated the Chinese New Year's Eve the night before, so I didn't get going until 1, 2, 2:30 in the afternoon—an awkward time of day for eating, 'cause you don't know whether to have breakfast or lunch or supper. Can anyone guess how I solved my dilemma? (Uurrrp.) Well, you're absolutely right—every last one of you.

For breakfast I had "The All American," which was two eggs and toast and hash browns and a choice of ham, bacon, sausage, or corned-beef hash, only they didn't have corned-beef hash, so I got sausage instead. They didn't have hash browns either, come to think of it, so I wound up with french fries. No problem. That's what I get for sleeping in.

For lunch, I had "fresh squid w/black bean & pepper over rice," which is #174 on the menu, to give you some idea of its range. I also had an order of egg rolls, because I always have to try the egg rolls.

Then, for supper, I went American again with a hamburger and french fries.

Let's see—*five, nine, five, carry the one, two, nine, five, two, carry the one, three, two, one, two*—we're looking at $9.99 even—if that don't beat all. In other words, 10 bucks to eat for the cycle at J & A!

And tax and tea are included!

"Yeah, but how was everything?"

What the hell do I care, for 10 bucks? But, seeing as how my J & A fortune said, "Happiness is often a result of hard work," let me get to work and break it down for you:

Eggs: over-easied a little too hard. A lot too hard, actually. *Toast:* white. Butter your own, which I like. *Sausage:* three links (that's pretty good). *French fries:* 15 of them (that ain't). Standard run-of-the-mill freezer fries.

Number 174: my favorite meal of the day. Much better than breakfast, in fact. Plenty of delectable squids, fresh*ish*, at any rate, green pepper, and onion in a mild but tasty black-bean sauce, all over a huge mound of steamed rice. (Plenty of food right here—don't be misled by my gluttony.) *Egg rolls:* two of 'em. Decent, especially the innards, what with actual chunks of discernible pork.

Burger: pretty dry, but not bad—probably a quarter-pound. Lettuce, tomato, pickle, nice yellow roll. *French fries:* same as above, only a few more this time.

Fortune cookie: served with quartered-orange garnish and a coffee candy thing I forgot to eat. Pretty stale, but possibly because it sat there through lunch and dinner before I finally got around to it.

All in all, as far as the eating goes, I would sum it up like this: cheap, half-decent American fare, and cheap, all-the-way-decent Chinese fare, with plenty of choices to choose from.

The room itself is atmospherically sound. It's very plain but homey too, in part because it's so small (two round tables and four basic four-seaters), and in part because it's family run, complete with kids coming and going, Grandpa, etc., like a sitcom waiting to happen. Except the TV was already blaring some Chinese melodrama, competing with the sound of sizzle from the kitchen and thankfully losing.

■ VIETNAM II

I know what you're thinking. You're thinking, "Hey, what ever happened to Haywire? What, did he get fed up with the local chili scene and move back to Texas? Or did he finally freak out on Swedish meatballs and

Vietnam II
701 Larkin Street, San Francisco. (415) 885-1274. Lunch, dinner. Cheap cheap.

lock himself in the closet, there to pass the days yodeling into a hanky?"

The correct answer, as usual, lies somewhere between the two. Which is to say that he's still right where he was, doing exactly what he does: writing books for children and poems for elk (and other antlered animals). No, we didn't have a falling out—although he *was* a little miffed, come to think of it, when I refused to try the borscht at his last dinner party and opted instead for a bowl of Total.

The reason we haven't reviewed a restaurant together in so long is that we've been in a serious burrito rut, which, if you're going to be in a rut . . . But the other morning we were talking on the phone and he read me a couple of sentences he'd just written for his new book:

"Then a thing happened." (That was the first sentence.) "Little Britches came crashing out of a window with the marshal close on her heels." (That was the second.)

"Sounds like an honest day's work," I said. I was about to suggest another trip to Can-Cun for some celebratory burritos, but then it occurred to me to put in an honest day's work myself, while we were at it.

So we met at this place in his neck of the woods called Vietnam II, at Larkin and Ellis, which Neighborhood Dave Kilowatt, rock 'n' roll booker, had recommended once while handing our band $436. For some reason, it stuck with me, the name of this place, and then there we were.

Don't get your hopes up; I got what I always get: *bún cha giò thit nuóng*, or deep-fried imperial rolls and grilled pork over rice noodles. It was too cheap to pass up, in addition to being my favorite Vietnamese thing. It was $4.25. Do you realize how many times one could conceivably eat *bún cha giò thit nuóng* with $436?

(Answer: 102 times, two-fifty change.)

The grilled pork was kind of thinnish and dry, but the imperial roll was pretty tasty, and all the other stuff—the noodles, the shredded lettuce and cucumbers and mint—was all excellent, as usual, drenched with fish sauce.

The advantage to being an unadventurous food reviewer (unadventurous is worst-case scenario; I encourage you to think of me as "loyal") is that you—*I*—can make relatively intelligent, empirical comparisons between restaurants. Like this:

On the basis of *bún cha giò thit nuóng*, Vietnam II is 30 cents more than Rose (and not quite as good), $1.30 cheaper than Tu Lan (but not nearly as good), and $2.25 cheaper than Minh's Garden (and better). What you want to do with that information is entirely up to you.

"Haywire ordered *com gà nuóng chao*, or *chao* barbecued chicken over rice—"black bean flavor," according to the menu, although I think it might have been a bean-curd sauce, more accurately, because it was mysteriously white.

"All Chinese men like this dish," our waitressperson informed us, serving it up. Haywire is half Swedish and half Texan. He liked it too. Me, I was a little afraid of the white black-bean sauce, so I barely even tasted it.

Anyway, Vietnam II is best known for its seafood dishes. I would have tried some for you, but most of the fishy things were at least twice as much as $4.25, and weren't *bún cha giò thit nuóng*, and anyway I had just had Sincere Cafe fish-and-chips ($2.99) the meal before. So you'll have to take Neighborhood Dave's word for it: The fresh-killed black-pepper crab is excellent.

Some reviewer from the *Chronicle* was also talking up the seafood in an old clipping under the glass tabletop, but that review also said the place had no atmosphere—which is dead wrong.

You go in, you got tanks of living fish on either side of you, with catfish and crabs and other sea things just walking around waitin' to happen. Then there's this great, gurgly, make-believe indoor goldfish pond in the middle of the restaurant, with people's good-luck pennies and—get this—a *bag of goldfish* in it.

Now, if bags of goldfish in goldfish ponds ain't atmosphere, I don't know what is.

■ LA TAQUERIA

So one day after a rockin' game of three-way baseball—rockin' because my team won 5-4-1 and I pitched my first-ever complete game, so to speak—me and Punk and Sushi stopped in at Can-Cun to refuel.

I was experiencing considerable soreness in my elbow. Not sure I could lift a burrito, I ordered a *pechuga Suiza* instead. That's like a grilled-chicken quesadilla, and googy-googy is it good.

> **La Taqueria**
> 2889 Mission Street, San Francisco. (415) 285-7117. Lunch, dinner. Cheap.

Punk, if I remember correctly, was reverentially facedowning a burrito *mojado,* which is Can-Cun's big boy, when all of a sudden Sushi (her first time there) starts bad-mouthing the *carne asada* and talking trash about some certain taqueria up the street that she says is better all-around, you gotta go there, the best tacos, the best meat, the best *aguas frescas,* you'll love it, you gotta go.

Yeah, yeah, yeah. (Urrrp.) Pass the salsa.

So then a few days later the phone rings and it's her. I must have said I would try the place, because here she was, calling me on it. La Taqueria. Mission between 24th and 25th.

"You realize you're asking for trouble," I said. I mean, trying to convince me there's a better taqueria than Can-Cun is like offering Dracula a V-8, or telling Popeye he really should try brussels sprouts for a change.

But I must have said I would, so I did. And I swear to Chief Wahoo I went into it with an open mind. In fact, I was worried. What if Sushi's place actually *was* somehow better than Can-Cun? Well, for one thing, I would have to start walking six extra blocks for my daily bread, and I'm already taking in water through the bottoms of my shoes, poor boy, already takin' in water through the bottoms of my shooooes . . .

Not to worry, folks. My soles were saved as soon as I walked in and glanced up at the menu. Not only is La Taqueria six blocks further from home than Can-Cun, but everything's more expensive and chips and salsa are not—I repeat, *not*—included.

"You're in big trouble, Sushi," I said under my breath.

"Don't worry," she said under hers. "I'll pay for the chips. Just wait until you taste the *carne asada*." Her main point of contention all along had been that the grilled steak was way better here than at Can-Cun.

Not exactly taking her word for it, I ordered a *carne asada* taco with cheese and a *carne asada* burrito with cheese. I also got a large melon *aguas frescas*, because that was what else she said, that the *melon aguas frescas* were way better here.

She was way wrong. What she must have meant to say was that the *aguas frescas* are nearly twice as expensive and all whipped and foamy and shit, like, you know, at the mall!

As for the food: Yes, the *carne asada* was more succulent than Can-Cun's. However, it was far less enjoyable because the salsa sucked and because I paid so much more for so much less.

The burrito, for example, was about the size of a flour quesadilla at El Toro. It came with beans and meat. No rice. Cheese was extra. Maybe this is a more "authentic" burrito. I wouldn't know because I've never been to Mexico. I *have* been to Southern California, and that's the way the burritos are down there: small. No rice. So we can safely say La Taqueria's burritos are authentically Southern Californian, and possibly authentically Mexican.

One thing they're definitely not is authentically better than Can-Cun's. For crying out loud, the tortillas are steamed instead of grilled. But the main problem with La Taqueria is the salsa, which is bland city. I'm talking about the "fresh" tomato stuff, not the green stuff in the squirt bottle. The green stuff was at least hot. The tomato stuff they put on the tacos and burritos and chips and salsa was nothing. It had absolutely zero zing to it.

The chips were actually good and homemade, but what good are good homemade chips without good salsa? That's the $1 question.

So after all was said and done, I had spent about eight smackers for about the same amount of mealage that I generally get at Can-Cun for about four.

Otherwise: typical taqueria atmosphere, with a nice corn-pickin' mural and general friendliness. I don't think Sushi is the only one who likes the place. They win all sorts of awards, and their business card says: "The Best Tacos and Burritos In The Whole World." I can't speak for the whole world, but they're not the best on Mission Street.

■ TAD'S STEAKHOUSE

Did anyone see Harry Dean Stanton at the Great American Music Hall last week? (Crickets.)

Did anyone see Harry Dean Stanton in *Twister*? (Crickets.)

Wild at Heart? (Clap. Clap. Clap.)

Paris, Texas? (Thunderous applause.)

I don't know, I liked *Paris, Texas,* mostly because of Ry Cooder and Harry Dean, but it did have that one hell of a long, awkward scene toward the end where everything was inexplicably explained. (Hooray for America!)

Tad's Steakhouse
120 Powell Street, San Francisco. (415) 982-1718. Breakfast, lunch, dinner. Cheap.

Wild at Heart . . . no *Blue Velvet,* but, hey, there's Nicolas Cage and the *Eraserhead* guy and Crispin Glover for a split second and—yep—Harry Dean again. Too bad he gets his head blowed off.

Twister—now there's a movie! Plenty of top-shelf Crispin Glover, and Harry Dean gets to keep his head through the whole thing—woohoo!

But why am I talking about movies instead of music? Where was I? Oh yeah: Harry Dean Stanton at the Great American last Monday. I was there. What a show: plenty of fun-loving, meat-eating ballads, some cheeseball rock 'n' roll, Mexicana, Texicana, borderline music . . . he even did "El Paso."

Haywire would've freaked, but he was too busy getting lucky. He also missed out on a hoot of a steak dinner, poor boy, so it was just me and my second-most-meat-eatingest pal, Liked Lee Wayway, down at Tad's Steak Restaurant on Powell.

We had every intention in the world of missing Harry Dean's opening act, a steak dinner being a much more appropriate warmer-upper, you ask us.

And it's cafeteria-style, so you don't have to leave a tip!

Just go in, grab a tray, place your order with the cook (who immediately slaps your meat on the grill), place your drink order and salad-dressing order with the middlemanperson, and then, when all's said and done, give your money to Robocashier.

Now sit down, shut up, and eat.

This place really has character. And characters. What it doesn't have is any sort of mood music, but I'm gonna find out if they have (or can get ahold of) a tape player and make them a few Bob Wills tapes.

In the meantime, like us, you'll just have to listen to some greasy-chinned yahoo whistling the Andy Griffith Show theme song, and Robo-cashier monotoning everyone's dinner debts, like this: "Eight. Point. Two. Four. Eight. Point. Two. Four."

Wayway offered to spill water on the guy to see if he'd short-circuit. But we'd just started eating and didn't want to run the risk of getting kicked out. Anyway, here's what "eight point two four" (seven point five nine plus tax) will get you at Tad's: a pretty thick, good slab of cow (or half a broiled chicken, if you're so inclined), a baked tater slathered with liquid Blue Bonnet margarine, a garlic roll, and an iceberg-lettuce salad with chickpeas. For a buck less, you can get a half-pound hamburger steak, but what would be the point?

I have to say, with or without Bob Wills, our steaks were tastier than all get-out, and every bit as rare as we wanted them to be. In fact, Wayway wasn't certain his was all-the-way dead yet. I think it was.

The baked taters, it goes without saying, would have been better with butter, but they were certainly edible and somewhat enjoyable as were. And the price was right, so who's complaining?

The garlic bread and salad were garlic bread and salad, respectively. Everyone was happy.

How could you not be happy at Tad's? It's a legitimate steakhouse and a real dive at the same time. The ornately red walls, the high ceiling, the hustle and bustle, the satellite weather photos irrelevantly displayed above the cashier . . .

■ KOREA BUFFET

Goddamn it. My Uncle Fatty just died. Not only did he have the best name of all uncles, but, as his great name would seem to indicate, he was at one time a big, big eater. He started out really skinny, which is how he came to be known as Fatty, oddly

Korea Buffet
6314 Geary Boulevard,
San Francisco. (415) 221-0685.
Lunch, dinner. Credit cards
accepted. Splurge cheap.

enough. Then he gradually grew into his nickname. And then he grew back out of it. He became one of those grinning guys in the sports pages, holding their way-too-big pants out from their shrunken waists to prove how much weight they'd lost.

But then he became a good eater again—hooray! But here's the sad part: In the end, according to my dad, he couldn't eat at all. Something was wrong with his esophagus. They offered to run a tube through his nose and down into his stomach, but Uncle Fatty declined. Then he died.

I say a guy with a name like Uncle Fatty deserves to go out the way I want to someday go out: choking on a chicken bone. To die hungry—that's too sad. But I have to agree with him that it would have been even sadder to have a tube in his nose. That's no way to eat.

And now, since I didn't get to say good-bye to him, and since he didn't get to say good-bye to food, I'll dedicate this particularly gluttonous review to the memory of my Uncle Fatty, a good man with a good appetite. Wish you were here.

Me, I'm alive, thank you, but not quite exactly well, in the sense that I've been coughing for about three weeks straight, trying everything I can think of, even medicine, to stop. A few days ago my friend Wayway came up with what sounded like a reasonable plan: Korean food.

I'd never had Korean food before (whereas Wayway is Korean), so I can't say exactly why it sounded reasonable. All I know is he said it—"Korean food"—and I slapped my hand to my forehead, as in, "Of course. Why didn't I think of that?"

Turns out he had exactly the right place in mind: Korea Buffet, a perfect pig-out establishment way the hell out there in the Richmond. The only thing we got wrong was the time of day. We went for dinner ($13.99 per person) as opposed to lunch ($7.99, weekends only).

Either way it's all you can eat, and so either way it's entirely possible to get your money's worth, which we did. We ate from around 8:15 p.m. until closing time, which is 10 p.m. We ate with reckless abandon—a million different things, including seaweed soup, raw garlic, spicy cabbage, and meat meat meat.

I had no trouble falling asleep that night, but I was up like toast at four in the morning, wandering around my apartment in the dark, muttering to myself in tongues. I think it was the garlic. All I know is my stomach was making noises like the radiator makes when the heat comes on at 6 a.m., when I'm still wandering, still muttering.

And still coughing. So, no, Korean food is not the cure for the common cold. However, and all sleeplessness aside, I loved it and would do it again in a hot second—just maybe a little earlier in the day, for financial as well as gastrointestinal reasons.

This was the most fun I've had eating in a long time. I mean, your table has a grill right smack in the middle of it! The hosterperson stokes it up for you, then sends you over to this huge buffet table for you-name-it. There are strips of raw marinated beef, beef ribs, chicken, pork, squid, octopus, and intestines. All that stuff goes on the grill.

Then there are very salty, very crispy, and very delicious already cooked fishes, head to tail. Just dig in. Fried rice, steamed rice, rice noodles, various vegetable things, the soup . . . we just piled our table up with dishes of stuff. And the beauty of it is: no rules! (Just don't forget to cook the meat.)

We were digging in with hands, spoons, chopsticks, pieces of lettuce . . . Wayway said it was OK. "No rules," he said. Yeehaw!

Everything's great, but these are a few of my favorite things: um, girls in white dresses, something-or-other that melts into spring, seaweed soup with gnarled chunks of nameless meat stuff in it, beef and beef ribs, excellently marinated in something garlicky and excellently grilled by Wayway—way better than the chicken, so don't even bother.

These great little cucumber spears, soaked in vinegar or something, were refreshing reminders, now and again, of a nonmeat world. And the raw garlic, dipped in this salty beany thing, had to be the cure for *something*.

I can't wait to go back.

"Danny Boy," says my stomach, "you'll be walking the floor all over again. You'll be growling and groveling, tossing and turning . . ."

And loving every minute of it, Chief.

■ FAMILY RESTAURANT

Paramount Piroshki on Potrero, so you know, is a great place to get a great breakfast or lunch piroshki for only $1.25. Sadly, it's not exactly a restaurant—less and less so every time I go. Two times ago they had one little table in their front room at least. Last time there was only a desk, and it was cluttered with paperwork. But they're still churning out the piroshkis, supplying the city's many middlemenpersons, one of whom just might maybe be your local corner store. Look into it.

Family Restaurant
919 Divisadero Street,
San Francisco. (415) 567-8840.
Breakfast, lunch, dinner.
Cheap cheap.

And while you're doing that, let me tell you about a restaurant that *is* a restaurant. It's called Family Restaurant, and it's right around the corner from my friend Wayway's house on Divisadero.

Do you believe in love before first sight?—because I loved Family Restaurant way, way before I ever went there. I loved it as soon as Wayway told me about it, which was weeks ago. Ever since then I had been tugging on his sleeve like a kid saying, "Tell me again about that place you told me about."

And he'd tell me again, like Grandpa, about how you could get three pieces of fried chicken (actual size) with potatoes or rice, corn bread or bread, hot vegetables and soup or salad for well under five bucks.

"Was it good?" I'd ask him.

He'd shrug. "It was food," he'd say—which is why he has a real job and I'm a restaurant reviewer.

Then, finally, we went there on a rainy Saturday night before going to a party where we didn't realize there would be chicken wings. Family Restaurant. They were out of fried chicken, so we got fried-chicken wings, egg rolls, grilled pork chops, and chicken-fried steak. The pork chops and chicken-fried steak came with all those things the fried chicken comes with, so it was way too much to eat—which didn't stop us from eating it all. Remember: I'm a restaurant reviewer. I needs to know.

The chicken wings were food. Big and good and greasy, with an especially crisp, somewhat two-dimensional breading.

The egg rolls were food, whereas the smashed taters, smothered in a smooth, dark gravy, would best be described as food. "Food" too would aptly portray the soup (chicken noodle) and the corn and the corn bread. The chicken-fried steak, smothered in the same smooth, dark gravy, was slightly dry, slightly tough, and leaning toward thin, but still, nevertheless, truth be told, when all was said and done and chewed and swallowed . . .

The pork chops, in fact, in my opinion, were the one part of the meal that transcended foodhood, but only in the sense that they were interestingly spiced, which is to say, spicy—which isn't to say that I could, under oath, identify any individual spice, in spite of my professed profession. Except rosemary.

I love rosemary. I love Family Restaurant. Unless you eat for two, like me and Wayway do and do, respectively, you'll have a hard time spending more than five bucks. If you don't eat meat, you're looking at grilled cheese or a "Vegetarian Salad" with "avocado, hearts of palm, and assorted cheese." Or, if you get there before noon, you can look at breakfast.

And then there's all the Chinese stuff: various *foo yungs,* fried rices, rice plates, chow meins, and big soups (all of which are reputed to be food). I don't know about you, but I can't argue with an edible meal for under five bucks. Especially when the portions are generous and the service is friendly and there's a flattened cardboard box on the floor to wipe your feet on in lieu of a carpet. The U-shaped counter is conducive to general howdy-strangership and sports-related hobnobbery, and there's also a row of booths or tables (I forget) for the already friended.

■ JOE'S CABLE CAR

Good news. I found a burger that doesn't claim to be the best anything anywhere—but I think it actually is the best burger I've had in San Francisco. The bad news is it'll cost you an arm and two legs (plus tax), assuming you want fries and a medium root beer with it.

When I say an arm and two legs (plus tax), don't forget to take me with a grain of salt. I'm a cheap eater. Sure, I'll spend more than 10 bucks on a meal now and again, but I sure as hell won't like doing it—and I'll probably moan and groan all the way home to my getting-even ground: the typewriter.

> **Joe's Cable Car**
> 4320 Mission Street,
> San Francisco. (415) 334-6699.
> Lunch, dinner. Credit cards
> accepted. Splurge cheap.

In this case we're typing about the best burger I've come across in all my burger-eating years out here, so I don't know what to do. Maybe it was worth it. Let's see: 20-something for two burgers, two fries, and two things to drink between me and my friend Punk, an even cheaper-skate than me, if that's possible.

I don't think Punk had ever been to Joe's Cable Car either before this, but he'd been talking it up for a while, calling it a SF "institution," among other things. Now, when I hear the word *institution,* I hear it with mixed emotions. I mean, some of my favorite restaurants anywhere (Ann's Cafe, Oakland; the Pit, Ohio) are what I would call institutions, but so are hospitals and jails.

And so—for that matter—are some of my least favorite restaurants: House of Nanking, Stars, McDonald's . . .

I could go on and on. In fact, I will:

What, for example, makes an institution an institution? People do, not guns. So one way to tell the difference between my kind of an institution and otherwise is to look at the people who make the place the institution. In other words: Who eats at Joe's Cable Car?

How the hell should I know? Me and Punk a few days ago. In other words: good people.

Good burgers, no doubt about it, but I guess I have to say they're too dang expensive. Punk got a basic four-ouncer with avocado and it was over five bucks. That's for a *quarter*-pounder, mind you. Granted, Joe's quarter-pounders are bigger than, say, Ray Crock-o'-Shit's, being "true serving weight," as Joe's pamphlet so carefully points out.

But a quarter-pound burger, no matter when you weigh it, is still only half of a half-pounder. There's no way around it.

I wanted a half-pounder, but those are two or three hard-earned dollars *extra* extra, so I compromised and got a six-ounce chili burger, figuring the meat from the chili would make up for the missing two ounces. But that came to something like eight bucks, once the cheese was accounted for.

Here's the kicker. Ready? No fries. Fries, if you want 'em (and you know you do), will run you another buck or two, depending on how many you want. And they're not even all that good.

Joe has been doing this to good people for over 30 years now, so you gotta figure he knows what he's doing, and you gotta figure he knows what he can get away with. And you gotta figure he's getting away with it. So I doubt if he gives a hoot what I've got to say on the subject, but here it is anyhow:

Fuck that shit. *Come on, man, throw in the fries!*

OK, let's remember: These are "old-fashioned ground-steak burgers," ground fresh daily. It says so all over the place—even on the napkins, before you get chili all over them. If you still don't believe it, you can actually watch Joe grind.

Ever experience a fresh-ground burger? You really can taste the difference. It's kind of like the difference between freeze-dried Maxwell House and fresh-ground "gourmet shit" coffee. So they really are amazing burgers, made fresh to order and all, with lettuce, tomato, onions, pickles, peperoncini, and even a fresh fruit garnish.

On the other hand, we're looking at a glorified McDoodoo's, atmospherically. Plasticky interior, no table service, styrofoam plates. I don't know. Until they either cheapen up or throw in the fries, or something, I guess I'll eat my great burgers in other parts of the country and stick to burritos out here.

◼ SHALIMAR

Then one afternoon I woke up from a very, *very* good dream, only to find that there weren't no eggs in my larder, nor lard in my egger, nor chickens in my chicken coop, nor nothing nowhere that I could make out—so I checked my underwear, brushed my teeth, hopped on the old bike, and headed for the Tenderloin. Oh yeah, first I called Haywire and said, "Shalimar?"

"Who's this?" he said.

I told him the truth, and I told him what I had in mind. There's this great new Indian/Pakistani restaurant on Jones between Geary and O'Farrell. Shalimar. I gotta thank Home Run Miller, an unanonymous reader, for letting me know about it. I got the impression from H. R.'s letter that she'd never actually been to Shalimar herself. She said she was afraid of it. "It used to be a 24-hour Korean karaoke bar where I only saw people going in and never coming out," she wrote.

Shalimar
532 Jones Street,
San Francisco. (415) 928-0333.
Lunch, dinner. Cheap cheap.

Not to worry, H. R. Not only did me and Haywire go in, but we stayed for over two hours, talking, and then *came out.* I even went back in (to go to the bathroom) and came out *again.* Yeehaw! Not to mention that during the course of our visit several other people were observed coming into and then going out of the restaurant.

So I don't know what was wrong with the old K.K. place, but it's not wrong with Shalimar. In fact, because of its greatness, I predict that lots of people will be in and out of here in the months, years, and hopefully decades to come.

We were both a little leery at first, me and Haywire, I think because the place advertises itself as a fast-food restaurant—which would explain its atmospherelessness. There's no table service, either; you go up to a counter and place your order. But the good news is that they don't just scoop stuff up off of a steam table. They cook it while you stand there and wait and watch.

Well, the tandoori chicken and basmati rice that Haywire ordered was already cooked, technically, but it was also excellent. I tasted both things and can attest to that fact. It was not only excellent but, as you may have guessed, cheap. I ordered spinach and lamb curry and nan tandoori bread, and the bill for the both of us came to eight smackers, total.

While one cook went to work on my curry, the other guy pulled off a hunk of dough, pancaked it, and dropped it into the clay pot. Fast food? Maybe. But it sure ain't McDoodoo's.

I was worried for a minute, when they served up a small-seeming bowl of curry, that it wasn't going to be enough. However, what with the bread and everything, it was deceptively filling. I almost wasn't even ready for a burrito six hours later when Wayway came knockin'—and I'm me!

Now, being me, I haven't eaten a whole lot of Indian food in my life, but I've had it a few times, here and there and in New York. I have to say, this was not only the cheapest (by far), but the best tasting, too.

The spinach and lamb were cooked perfectly: maximum succulence and plenty spicy without being too hot. The nan tandoori—you know, flat flying-saucer bread—was amazing. And the two together . . . well, there are some things that words just can't express—which is why God gave us the yodel.

Yodel-eh-hee-hoo!

▌ PASTAIO

I'll get right to the point: Pastaio. Sixteenth between Guerrero and Valencia in the Mission. Great Italian food for decent prices. I ate there with new pal and excellent spitter Biased Bobo Bolivia, who would rather sleep on broken glass than on a futon in a loft.

Pastaio
3182 16th Street,
San Francisco. (415) 255-2440.
Dinner. Credit cards accepted.
Cheap.

She imparted this important information to me weeks ago or so when me and The Ford were helping her move the softest bed in the world from some Snorth Beach garage into Biased Bobo's swingin' Snob Hill pad. 'Twas then that I knew we would never be more than buddies, because, see, I happily sleep (a) on a futon, (2) in a loft, and, thirdly, in a closet. Furthermore, I'd rather sleep on broken glass than on the softest bed in the world, meaning (at the risk of seeming pre-presumptuous) that any real or imagined potentially possible future "physical" relations between the two of us would have to be conducted standing up somewhere. Or else, I suppose, on broken glass. Which strikes me as problematic.

"Hey—what happened to 'the point'?"

I'll get right back to it: Pastaio. I'd heard it was fairly cheap and good and undiscovered, which adds up to three good reasons to go there.

Number 4 was 'cause I'd just happened to read my Sodini's Green

Valley Restaurant review, in which I'd said that Sodini's raviolis were "the best I'd had in San Francisco," to misquote myself.

Misunderstanding my own misreading of my own misquote, I decided it was high time I take another bath—during which the sobering thought occurred to me that Sodini's were the *only* raviolis I'd ever had in San Francisco. I figured I ought to go try some more.

Biased Bobo, having lived in North Beach, was skeptical about the likelihood of good, real Italian food in the Mission—but she warmed up to the idea as soon as we walked in, smelled the garlic, and looked at the menu. Everything you could possibly want out of an Italian eating experience, including ravioli . . . But guess what? I didn't order it. I was distracted by gnocchi pesto and some side-order sausage. Bobo went with the manicotti.

We also got garlic bread, a generous two-person amount of homemade bread, done exactly the way I like it: next-to-raw garlic, light sprinklings of Parmesan and parsley, and saturated through to the crust with butter.

Rather than browning everything to a dry, crumbly crisp, like many people and places do garlic bread, Pastaio starts with an almost underdone, doughy (i.e., perfect) loaf, and then heats the butter, garlic, etc. into it with a nice, soft touch.

The Italian sausage appetizer was two plump ones in a very good, chunky tomato sauce, with black olives, mushrooms, peppers, and onions. Not only was the sausage itself great, but the puddle o' sauce was perfect stomping grounds for the garlic bread. But on to weightier matters:

Gnocchi, for example, are dangerously dense potato dumplings. They happen to be my own personal specialty, so I've encountered and survived plenty of them in my years, but never before have I eaten restaurant gnocchi that I actually liked almost as much as (if not more than) my own. Pastaio's homemade gnocchi are bigger than mine, but lighter (mine are like black holes; theirs are like, I don't know, quasars). They dished up a heaping big plate of them, with a great nutty pesto sauce that had me spinning in my sleep for the next two nights.

The waitressperson told me she always recommends the gnocchi with pesto. You can also get it with a light red sauce; I almost did, and I'm glad

I didn't. But anyway, I second her recommendation: gnocchi pesto!

As for Bobo's manicottis, they were spinach noodles wrapped around more spinach and ricotta cheese, in a red sauce. Two of them. She seemed perfectly happy, but I tried it and had to yawn—especially after a few of my gnocchis.

Plus, it wasn't enough, manicottically speaking; I can tell because Biased Bobo had to help me clean my plate—and how often does *that* happen?

■ HUNG-YEN RESTAURANT

My mechanically inclined rock-climbing vegetarian brother Jean-Gene the Frenchman was out for a visit, fixing cars, climbing rocks, and not eating meat. I found out he had never eaten Vietnamese food either, so instead of eating burritos one day we biked over to Hung-Yen, that cool-looking place on Harrison at 18th Street. I'd seen it a million times but I'd never been there, but I'd heard it was great. But my brother ordered something other than imperial rolls and pork kebab over rice noodles, so he still hasn't ever eaten Vietnamese food, you ask me.

Hung-Yen Restaurant
3100 18th Street,
San Francisco. (415) 621-8531.
Lunch, dinner. Cheap cheap.

Of course, he's a vegetarian.

I'm not. I ordered imperial rolls and pork kebab over rice noodles, but I also got the spicy beef noodle soup because I saw on the menu that Janet Hazen, famous fancy-pants restaurant reviewer, had listed it among her "10 Dishes to Die For" back in 1992.

Didn't die—but did love the soup, and I was especially happy to see that all these years later, in spite of the good press, the price of the big bowl had not gone up an iota. 'Cause what pisses me off more than almost anything is when I write about how great and cheap a place is, then go back a couple weeks later only to find new menus with all the prices $1.25 more than I said they were in my review, which proudly hangs in the window.

I assume the great J. H. has encountered this phenomenon herself and doesn't like it any more than I do. Not to worry, Janet—Hung-Yen, at least, has not done wrong by you.

This is the first time I know of that my culinary path has crossed with Hazen's. I may as well let her tell you about the soup, because she knows eight to 10 times as much about food (and what all's in it) as I do. See . . . here's what she wrote back in 1992:

"The surface of the lemongrass scented broth was glossed over with a bright red glaze created in part from hot chilies, but beneath the surface lay the real treats—sliced lean beef, noodles, green and yellow onion, red jalapeño peppers, shallots, and plenty of fresh mint. The medley of flavors, textures, and ingredients was at once heartwarming and unusual."

I agree. And since she unfortunately didn't sample the imperial rolls and pork kebab over rice noodles, I'll have to tell you about it in my own words: *mmm. Yummy!*

As for Jean-Gene, the brother, he was just happy to see a vegetarian section on the menu.

"Welcome to San Francisco," I said.

He said he was also happy to see what wasn't on the menu. He rarely even eats Chinese food, back home or anywhere, he said, because it spoils his appetite to see all the duck dishes. Jean-Gene, in addition to being a Frenchman, has several close friends and at least one relation (the dearly departed Spark) who are (or in Spark's case *were*) mallards.

Anyway, he got bean cake with mixed vegetables, and he seemed to think it was very good, but what does he know? Lucky for him, Hung-Yen's portions are huge enough that once I'd sucked all the pork off the top of my food pile there was plenty of rice noodlage left for the both of us—and cucumbers and mint and cilantro and chopped nuts and all that other nice stuff. So at least he got to have a hint of *real* Vietnamese food.

Speaking of cilantro, I don't remember encountering it in this imperial roll/pork dish at other places, and I don't remember Janet Hazen mentioning it in her assessment of the soup, either, but it was there. So they must have added that in the last few years, and also—come to think of it—honkin' heavy-duty pieces of garlic. Plus they give you a plate of add-your-own sprouts, lettuce, and sliced jalapeños in case the soup's not hot enough already. (It is.)

So you see, folks, we're looking at delicious, dynamic, and *cheap* food that stands the test of time.

◼ STEVE'S BARBECUE

I know I've been known to kill a lot of birds with a lot of stones when I write, and I'm sure I've been the death of a good many more when I eat, on account of my addiction to chicken wings. But I think I read

Steve's Barbecue
2521 Durant Avenue,
Berkeley. (510) 848-6166.
Lunch, dinner. Cheap.

somewhere recently that a bird in the belly was worth two in the hand. Now I'm not sure if that means two in *each* hand, two total, or what—and I probably shouldn't mess with math *or* philosophy, let alone both at the same time with my eyes closed . . . but I meditated long and hard over this information, however many chickens it entrails, and I believe that what it means to me is that I will be happier and more prosperous and just generally well fed if I start focusing on one thing at a time.

So first I'll tell you about the food at Candlestick Park, and then I'll tell you about Steve's, this Korean barbecue place over in Berkeley. Deal? Good.

By the way, I'm well aware that Candlestick is no longer technically Candlestick, but like many Candlestick fans I refuse to call it by any other name than Candlestick. Not that I have anything against commercialization, although I do; I just mostly think that if you're going to name your stadium after a business, you should at least choose a business that has a powerful and positive impact on the city. I'm thinking: Taqueria Can-Cun Park.

But that's another restaurant, and this is supposed to be about a Korean barbecue place in Berkeley, which I'll get to in a minute, as soon as I finish telling you about my first personally witnessed 49ers game of the season: Steve Young had 284 yards and three touchdowns passing, . Jerry Rice had six catches for 93 yards and one touchdown, and I had a chili dog, a barbecued beef brisket sandwich, a bowl of tortellini, a bowl of clam chowder, a slice of pizza, and a burrito. All of which was way overpriced, and most of which sucked, but I'm not a sportswriter, so let's talk about something else.

Yeah, like what about that Korean barbecue place?

In Berkeley? Sure, OK. Well, for starters it's called Steve's and it's in the Durant Food Court near the U.C. campus, with all these other kinds of food places: mostly Asian, but also Mexican and American and I think maybe Italian. I didn't try any of that other stuff, so you may as well skip over it too. Go right to Steve's. It's a great little place with just a counter and a few stools. If there's no room inside, don't worry—you can eat out in the middle of everything at one of those picnic tables.

We ate inside because I really liked the decor, which was basically just a nailed-to-the-wall boom box and a handprinted, misspelled sign on the back wall apologizing for having to raise the prices—over a year ago.

I don't know how cheap it used to be, but I had no problem shelling out five-something for a heap of food as heaping and as good as this one was. Steve really piles it on. There was enough rice to feed an entire offensive line, and then about a half of a grilled cow on top of that, and separate compartments of kimchi (spiced-up cabbage) and a tangy sprout salad with cucumbers.

This is the No. 1. There are 10 numbers on the chalkboard to choose from, and I don't remember any of them being geared toward vegetarians. Sorry. I forgot my ruler, but I estimate the No. 1 to have been about 4, 5, maybe 4.5 inches UFS (Up From the Styrofoam). Everything comes with kimchi and sprout salad and rice, and everything I saw was very big.

My lunchmate, Lucky Luciana, the Berkeley person who brought Steve's to my attention, ordered chicken teriyaki, which was the same price and same UFS rating as my steak, only the chicken, unlike the steak, was cut with veggies. I tasted a piece and it was excellent.

Great food, good prices, outrageous portions, and an excellent view of the grill—so you can watch your food sizzle or, in case you get bored, stare at the piles of cabbages in the back room, or ponder the colossal rice steamer, which, as Lucky Luciana pointed out, is big enough to hold a baby. Why anyone would *want* to steam a baby, on the other hand, is beyond the realm of this restaurant review.

■ PUERTO ALEGRE

Believe me, folks, I don't want to write about Puerto Alegre any more than you want to hear about it. It's been my favorite non-taqueria Mexican restaurant since I moved to the Mission. And ever since then

Puerto Alegre
546 Valencia Street, San
Francisco. (415) 255-8201.
Breakfast, lunch, dinner. Credit
cards accepted. Cheap cheap.

I've carefully avoided all but passing references to the neighborhood's coolest hangout.

At first I wanted to keep it a secret (yeah, right!)—well, as much of one as possible. But in the past couple years Puerto has became so out-of-controlledly popular without my help that to give it a good review now would be something like standing up in a crowded bus and saying, "Hey, everybody, sex is *fun!*"

On any night of the week—even Tuesday—the place is packed. Even if you get there at six, you might have to wait for a table or booth or even a seat at the bar. And everyone's always drinking it up and having a real good time, so you might have to wait longer than you want to. The last thing you need, and the last thing Puerto's overworked staff needs, and the last thing I need is a goddamn review.

So why am I doing it?

Three lousy letters: TBN. The Baseball Network. Like everything else that is wrong with the world right now, you can blame it on them. The Baseball Network, some stupid fucked-up system by which this year's play-off games are all being played simultaneously and you can watch only one game, network's choice, based on region.

This system sucks no matter where you live, but in a city like San Francisco, whose Giants aren't even in the play-offs, and whose inhabitants not only unanimously hate the Dodgers but come from all other regions of the country, so that chances are they like the Indians or the Reds or the Red Sox or the Braves, or *someone* far away . . .

Where was I?

Well, if you know a baseball fan, you're probably sick of hearing about it, so I'll complain no further. Suffice it to say that this is the first time in my life the Cleveland Indians have made it into the play-offs, and the only way I can witness any of the action (short of going home) is through the miracle of satellite TV.

As it turns out, most of the sports bars around town were not even able to pick up the Cleveland-Boston series. But Puerto Alegre has Willie, the satellite-dish wiz, and Puerto Alegre is three blocks away.

Ergo: That's where I was at dinnertime all last week, hunched over burritos and enchiladas and tacos and *chile rellenos* and root beer root beer root beer, watching the Indians and Red Sox go at it when I should have been out in the world discovering undiscovered restaurants to write about.

It's true that I could have done something else for breakfast or lunch, but I invariably wound up sitting at home sipping tea and applying sliced white bread to my forehead to combat some wicked root-beer hangovers.

So before I run out of room, let me just tell you in case you haven't been there that Puerto Alegre is a homey, festive, friendly-in-the-face-of-adversity, good-cheap-food, good-cheap-drinks sort of a place that blows the award-winning La Rondalla out of the water in every category except for how late it stays open.

Puerto's main selling point with Mission hipsters is the margaritas. They're apparently cheap and great, but I wouldn't know since a traumatic childhood experience has left me unable to even smell tequila without turning into Vomitman. Plus my aversion to drinking anything out of goofy glasses.

For me, as usual, the point is the food. And lucky for all of us, food is something you can eat any time of day. So go early. The place is seldom crowded before 5:30 or 6 p.m., except maybe on weekends.

Speaking of breakfast, Puerto's *huevos rancheros* are not only great but cheaper than almost anyone's. Same with the burritos. They're restaurant-style, served on a real plate with salsa on top, and every bit as big as any taqueria's. The tacos are decent, although the fresh salsa they use in them is kind of funky—not nearly as good as the spicier unfresh stuff that comes with the chips.

So: (1) the place is comfy even at its bustlingest, (2) the service is slow, so it's real easy to nurse your way through a ballgame, (3) the Indians are on, and (4) sex is fun.

■ SMOKEHOUSE

Here's a poem called "Poem" I wrote many years ago when I used to write poems:

Poem

1. *I never write poems*
   about poetry
   because it is
   like washing the soap
   or eating your stomach
   for lunch, then what will you do with supper?

2. *I never write poems*
   called "Poem"
   it's like calling your dog
   "Dog"
   or your mom
   "Mom"
   when her name's really Alice, or King

3. *I never write poems*
   that don't rhyme
   or flow
   smoothly so that
   or don't make sense

4. *I never go outside without a coat because*
   I'm afraid I might get sick

Smokehouse
3115 Telegraph Avenue,
Berkeley. (510) 845-3640.
Lunch, dinner. Cheap cheap.

Ah, but I'm older and so much wiser now. In addition to never writing poems, period, I have learned to welcome life's little redundancies with an open mind, an open heart, and in many cases, an open mouth.

It was a chili cheeseburger that taught me this valuable lesson. For the longest time, I resisted chili cheeseburgers for the same reason I resisted "poetry" poetry: ground beef on ground beef is redundant, and redundancy is bad. But chili cheeseburgers are good, as I learned at 2:30 in the morning one night at I-forget-which Tenderloin diner when I accidentally ordered one.

That was about a year ago, and since then things have been topsy-turvy for me. Outside of professional sports, there are no absolutes. Life is just one big gray area, especially if you live in the Sunset or Richmond. But even in the sunny Mission, turns out, redundancy can sometimes be fine and dandy and well and good and just what the doctor ordered.

"Washing the soap" or "eating your stomach"—sure, those are mistakes. But what about dreaming you're asleep? What about second helpings? What about having sex with someone while fantasizing about having sex with the same person you're having sex with? What about Doublemint gum, doubleheaders, double plays, and double elimination tournaments?

You see what I'm getting at? According to many commercials and me, you can't have too much of a good thing. Ground-up cows are a good thing, so chili cheeseburgers, even though you have to eat them with a fork, are cause for celebration. And what better place to celebrate the one-year anniversary of my "awakening" than at Berkeley's Smokehouse, where you can double-celebrate redundancy with a *double* chili cheeseburger, a *double* chili cheese dog, chili cheese fries, and a chili cheese milkshake?

I've been there twice now, both times with my Berkeley buddy Satchel Paige the Pitcher. I think I've covered most of the bases, and here's what I can tell you about the food: The burgers are charcoal-broiled and pretty good—better than fast-food ones, anyway, but not in the same league as, say, Joe's Cable Car's fresh-ground expensoburgers. One thing: The Smokehouse is cheap as hell. Two-something for the basic burger (my guess is about a quarter-pound of meat), on up to three or four for the double chili cheeseburger, meaning you can always afford a side of fries for under five bucks, total. That's good.

The buns are "kinda stiff," as Satchel aptly put it. They're supposed to be toasted on the grill, but the grill marks looked shady, like maybe they were drawn on with some sort of a charco-marker.

But the chili is great. It could be a little spicier, but it's got good flavor and big chunks of meat that somehow seem fresher than the burger itself. The serverpeoplepersons really pile it on, too, so there's no need to get chili on your fries.

As for atmosphere, you can eat outside at a picnic table or inside at a picnic table. Even the inside feels like outside. One wall is all windows, the other is white-painted cinder blocks, and because the doors are open, pigeons are entirely possible.

■ JUDY MAY'S M & L MARKET

Things to do in the 10 years I'll add to my life if I stop eating so much meat:
1.
2.
3.
4. . . .

Thank you. Thank you. That's a little poem I wrote a few minutes ago on the can. I thought I'd publish it here since I consider it food-related and relevant, and since I had so much fun self-publishing my last self-published poem, "Poem."

Judy May's M & L Market
691 14th Street, San Francisco.
(415) 431-7044. Lunch.
Cheap cheap.

The thing is that more people than usual have been telling me I should get my cholesterol checked.

I tell you, if I had a cheeseburger for every time I've heard that old line— and a milkshake for every time I've ignored it . . . The thing is, if I were to check out OK, I'd consider it a green light to up my butter intake from one to two sticks a day. Whereas if I were to check out otherwise, I'd run the risk of experiencing pangs of guilt while continuing to eat like I eat.

Recent "You should get your cholesterol checked"–sayers include ex-sidekick Yatee-Yatee-Bing-Eh-Eh-Eh—over a plate of my very own meat sauce, no less. The nerve of her! Yatee-Yatee (whose name I just like to say) is one of the healthiest, wholesomest nonvegetarians I know, and when I reported her *fox paws* to my friend Punk, one of the unhealthiest, unwholesomest nonvegetarians I know, he actually seconded her opinion.

So it would seem to be unanimous: I should get my cholesterol checked.

Instead, I picked up a quart of buttermilk on the way home, emptied the old lard bucket into some frying pans, and fried me and Wayway up some chickens. Then I fried us up some french fries and biscuits in the leftover lard. We were watching the World Series—first game that Cleveland won. So tell me grease ain't healthy! Or at least lucky.

Anyway, the next day I decided to celebrate my lack of medical insurance by discovering hot pastrami sandwiches at Judy May's, a great little three-table sandwich shop at 14th Street and Market. My friend Shellfish had told me about it.

"You know it's good," Shellfish said, "'cause it's where the cops and prostitutes meet."

I liked that idea. I also liked the name of the place. Judy May's. Like a heartbreaker out of some country song. But Judy and May are two different people, and I didn't see any cops or prostitutes there—just late-lunch-breaking nine-to-fivers, poor kids, lining up to the back of the store and getting 'em to go.

Me, I'm not a sandwich guy. I guess I don't see the point in eating something "out" that you could easily slap together at home, in half the time (if you count standing in line) and for half the price.

On the other hand, I have yet to open my refrigerator and find pastrami, let alone hot pastrami. So that's what I got. That and a cup of corn chowder, to be safe.

Now I don't normally mess with chowders that don't have clams or fishes in them, but I'm awful glad I messed with this one. It had a heavily peppered flavor—red, green, and black—plus celery, carrots, two big potato lumps, and all the corn. The amazing thing was that it was chowder, yet none of the vegetables, not even the corn, were mushed. Great and crisp and peppery, and served in a styrofoam cup on an actual plate, with a slice of bread and crackers.

The pastrami sandwich comes in a basket, and it's loaded. Tons of meat. Tomatoes, lettuce, onion, sprouts, American (or Jack or Swiss) cheese, pickles, and scallions if you want, hold the mayo, hold the mustard. And get this: Not only did she actually and unflinchingly hold the mayo and mustard, she also wiped the m-words off the infected knife before cutting my French roll. Now *that's* what I call respect.

She, by the way, is May. She's the one who makes your sandwich. May is a good egg with a great memory, a sense of humor, a big knife, and a mantra: "Next one?" she says over and over. "Next one?"

Judy, who might be May's daughter, is another good egg. She makes the soup. She also rings you up and can talk sports in the process.

The place sells football and basketball cards, other sports-related oddities, a million kinds of chips and sody-pops, candy bars, and all the sandwiches, which range in price from the peanut butter and banana with honey ($1.85) to the Jack special ($4.40). The Jack special is ham, salami, turkey, bologna, and hot pastrami.

Jesus, Jack, you should get your cholesterol checked!

■ GIORGIO'S PIZZERIA

Me and The Ford and Punk and Punker helped our pal Last Straw move into yet another new place yesterday. I was picking my toenails when she called to recruit me.

"What are you doing?" she said.

"Nothing."

"Did you hear about my moving party?"

Last Straw is one of those people who has 10 times as much stuff as everyone else and therefore moves 10 times as often.

"What are you doing? Seriously," she said.

"Nothing," I said. "Seriously."

Me and Punk and Punker love our pal Last Straw, and as long as we live in the same country as she does and don't have arthritis or day jobs or heart conditions, we will drop whatever we aren't doing and help her move from place to place to place. Even if she doesn't take us out to eat afterward, I suppose. But so far she does, so why bother speculating?

Giorgio's Pizzeria
151 Clement Street,
San Francisco. (415) 668-1266.
Lunch, dinner. Credit
cards accepted. Cheap.

Giorgio's was her idea. I swear I didn't plant the seed, although it used to be my favorite pizza restaurant when I lived in the Richmond. Then I sort of forgot about it. But Last Straw remembered. She drove us all there in her charismatic Vehiclemobile.

"You're paying, right?" I said, to avoid any potential awkwardness at the restaurant.

She said she was.

We ordered up an extra-large half-onion, half-sausage pizza with bell peppers and fresh tomatoes. We also shared an order of ravioli with marinara sauce and a large vegetarian salad. Now, as you know, I don't normally necessarily drink when I eat, but since someone else was driving *and* paying, I figured, OK, sure, I can be as suave as the next guy, and ordered half a giraffe of wine. What with wine and tax and tips and all, it came to well over 40 bucks for four people, which ain't exactly cheap by my standards. Luckily, these were Last Straw's standards, so what did I care?

The pizza is still pretty damned good. It's not my favorite San Francisco pizza anymore, but it's up there. The crust was just thick enough and plenty cooked enough to hold its own against the sauce and cheese without sogging under, like so many otherwise edible pizzas do, sadly. There was the perfect amount of cheese—unobtrusive but there—and the toppings were fresh, tasty, and liberally applied. Good, solid pizza.

The raviolis, on the other hand, were problematic on two counts: (1) they didn't taste too great, what with a weak marinara sauce, and (2) there were only 10 of them.

Ten raviolis, $8.88. That's, what, roughly 88 cents apiece? Or another way of looking at it would be like this: Four people pay $2.22 apiece for two and a half raviolis. Fuck that shit. I'm sorry, Giorgio, but no two and a half raviolis in this world are worth $2.22, unless they were made by Bob Casal's mom, Ohio.

So skip the pasta and stick with pizza. That's my advice.

Go ahead and get a salad. The large vegetarian one is plenty good and plenty big enough to be shared four ways. It's a huge plate of lettuce and tomatoes and black olives and peperoncini and mushrooms and a few slices of cheese in a delicious Italian dressing. I like that they don't even give you a choice of dressings, because what else would anyone possibly want? Right?

The house wine was fine by me, but I don't thing Punk liked the coffee too much, 'cause when Last Straw asked how it was, he answered, "Uhhhh . . ."

Of course, Punk may have been a bit punchy, having had his bell rung the night before by Punker, in a bar. Check it out: Punk, drunk, starts throwing Jell-O around and gets Punker in the lip, then some girl in the leg. Drunk, Punker punches Punk in the eye. End of story.

I only tell it because I think it's beautiful.

■ IMPERIAL FAMILY RESTAURANT

My pal Haywire moved to Oakland about a month ago. Then, about a day ago, he moved to Oakland again. This is why he's called Haywire.

The second move puts him four or five blocks closer to Imperial Family Restaurant, but I don't think that's why he did it. I think he did it because of noisy neighbors, rats, and a large man knocking on his window in the middle of the night, wondering what happened to Carol. You know, city stuff.

Imperial Family Restaurant
3219 Lake Shore Boulevard,
Oakland. (510) 893-8947.
Breakfast, lunch, dinner. Cheap.

The Imperial was Haywire's first East Bay food find, but he hadn't actually eaten there yet. He was waiting for me—and then there I was. It was moving day for Haywire, and The Ford was out two to three weeks with a transmission injury, so me and my muscles BARTed under the bay, walked around Lake Merritt for the first time ever, didn't step in dog shit, and managed to wind up at the moving party just about exactly in time for a dinner break.

There was me, Haywire himself, and Jean-Gene the Frenchman.

I got baby beef liver, Jean-Gene got *linguine primavera,* and Haywire got what he always gets, a burger. That's the kind of place this is: American food. Cheapness. Booths, counter, and atmospherelessness, which is one of my favorite kinds of atmosphere.

Off the permanent-lunch-specials menu, baby beef liver with onions or bacon goes for $5.95. The price of indecision: $1. So that's onions *and* bacon, plus french fries (or smashed or spaghetti), plus a mountain of peas, bread and butter, and a bowl of vegetable soup-of-the-day (or salad) for, what, $6.95? I can live with that.

The liver was a touch dry, the onions a tad underfried, and the bacon a wee bit over. The peas were perfect. The veggie soup was great. The french fries were french fries, and the French bread was similarly French. My brother, the Frenchman, once cut his leg open on a broken loaf in France, and I suspect this bread was about as dangerous, although not so much out of authenticity as day-oldedness. I can live with that, too.

Tell you what, though: I'd much rather see linguine in *linguine primavera* than spaghetti, and maybe fresh instead of frozen vegetables. It's spring, for crying out loud! Ah, what the hell, what do you want for five bucks? My brother can live with it.

I liked the Imperial a lot, but it's not nothing to drive out of your way for, really, like say, Ann's Cafe, an exit or two down the road. But if you live in the 'hood, like Haywire does, or if you're just visiting, like me, you may as well check it out.

■ SPAGHETTERIA

I wasn't the same sort of temp as everyone else. I needed the money, but I hated to work even more than I needed the money. If other temps didn't hate me, they should have, 'cause I was making them look bad.

Spaghetteria
318 Kearny Street,
San Francisco. (415) 398-4499.
Lunch, dinner. Cheap.

While they'd try their dilly-dallying damnedest to stretch a two-week assignment into three, I was equally determined to get everything done before lunch so I could go home and listen to records.

Supervisors loved me, and why not? If the average elasti-temp was in fact typing 60 words a minute (like you're supposed to), then I was somewhere up around 945. Jobs were offered.

"No way," I'd say. Then I'd go home and listen to records.

But because I typically finished two-week assignments before noon of the first day, and, if not, worked through my lunch break to make up for it, I was ill equipped, once I became a restaurant reviewer, to answer the oft-asked question:

"Hey, you're a restaurant reviewer? Where's a good, cheap place to eat lunch in the Financial District?"

To which my only answer is: "What the hell are you doing in the Financial District?"

Then they say: "Working, you piece of shit."

Then I say: "Working? In the Financial District? Working? What are you—some feasibility expert for a resource management consulting firm? More shit gets done in one hour at any Mission coffeehouse than in one week in all those fucking sky-risers put together!"

Then they turn to our mutual friend and say, "Who is this idiot?" and the mutual friend shrugs. Punches are thrown, mutual friends are alienated, and nobody is not much wiser for none of it.

Except now, hopefully, this ugly scene will never have to repeat itself, because I finally have something constructive to offer on the subject of Financial District eats: Spaghetteria, the self-proclaimed first gourmet Italian fast-food place.

I was clued in by buddy Earl Butter, country music legend turned para-pseudo-quasi stockbroker, sort of. Him and his Chuck E. Schwab pals do lunch there sometimes, see, and it really is what it says it is: fast and plastic and yellow and red and gourmet. I know 'cause I checked it out yesterday.

It's on Kearny at Pine, smack between Burger King and Taco Bell, and right across the street from a gourmet burrito joint.

The Butter Boy takes his lunch break at 1:15. I was there waiting for him in my ratty K-Mart overalls, and before anyone accuses me of slackerhood, let me tell you what all I'd already done that day:

6:30: woke up, played basketball, ate bagel, took shower.

8–11: office hours, Java Supreme. Read, edited and critiqued a 23-page love story by a fellow fiction writer. Invented a new form of poem, the rhyming three-line nine-syllable progresso-interrogative pastina, which, once perfected, will render the limerick profound, the sonnet simple, and the haiku wordy.

11–12:45: fixed my bike.

In other words, I deserved a lunch break as much as the next guy. What I didn't deserve was Spaghetteria. A guy like me, who basically eats for a living, likes to sit down and stare at a menu for a good long while before ordering.

But fast food is fast food, and to get it fast, you've got to order it fast. I was shuffled through a short, quick line and got what I thought I wanted—*ravioli in rosa* ($6.50) and *insalata mista* ($4)—before I even saw what I *really* wanted: Add $2.25 to any pasta price and get a salad *and* sody-pop. Well, that's why we do this, right? So that you can learn from my mistakes.

I liked my ravioli. It was a handy microwaveable containerful of home-made spinach and ricotta ones, in a deliciously pink tomato-and-cream sauce. Served with three hunks of bread, butter, and a neato plasti-pak: fork, spoon, salt, pepper, and—get this—a toothpick!

The mixed green (and red) salad was nice and big, and the dressing was basic and good (ask for extra, though, 'cause it's not enough).

All else I can say is that Earl seemed to enjoy his *penne con pollo*, and his Chuck E. Schwab pal seemed to enjoy her *fusilli primavera*, but nei-ther one thought to offer me a taste, and I didn't think to ask. We were sitting at an open-windowed counter facing out, and were distracted by the passing downtown throng. At least I was.

Hey, Ray
Lunch today?
Call me, OK?

■ HAHN'S HIBACHI

My good friends Stinky and Pukey are in town from State College, PA, and I've sort of taken it on myself to see that they eat right while they're here. Get this: One of their so-called PA "pals" advised them to eat at Flying Saucer!

Hahn's Hibachi
1710 Polk Street, San Francisco. (415) 776-1095. Also at 3318 Steiner Street, San Francisco. (415) 931-6284, and 1305 Castro Street, San Francisco. (415) 642-8151. Lunch, dinner. Cheap.

So I took them to Can-Cun instead. And the day before that, I sent them to my new all-time favorite cheapo Chinese place, the exact name and location of which I will never, *never* disclose—except under extreme torture, I mean to say, as I have a fairly low tolerance for busted bones and corkscrewed eyeballs and the like.

State College, PA, in case you don't know, is the home of Penn State, the Nittany Lions, the ex-band Yam, and, according to Stinky and Pukey, more bad writers and good Korean restaurants per capita than any other town in America. So they must have been homesick, because they wanted to eat at Hahn's Hibachi, a Korean restaurant—with me!

Whoa, wait a minute . . .

Nevermind.

Hahn's Hibachi on Polk Street is a small, bright place with green tables and a wallful of snapshots of happy customers. What's for dinner is barbecued everything, kabobs and combos, tempura this and that, *udon,* and meat sandwiches. I'm not so sure if it's "Unquestionably the Ultimate in Korean BBQ," as it claims to be, because although I've been to State College, PA, I've never eaten Korean food there. Not to mention Korea!

Anyway, it really is very good, even by San Francisco standards. We went to town, too. Stinky and Pukey are eating for three, so to speak (which explains all the pukin'), and I generally eat for one and a half, as you know—so we ordered about enough food for five, and the whole meal came to only $30.

There was an order of potstickers, a big bowl of shrimp *udon,* BBQ chicken, BBQ pork, and of course I had to order the plate they call Meat Mountain, which is a rib, chicken, and chop combo.

Everything came on huge piles of rice, with kimchi and that sprout salad stuff on the side, and everything came under the same light brown sauce/gravy, with a few bits of carrots and onions. Except for the potstickers and soup, of course.

Pukey wouldn't eat the *udon,* claiming the noodles were too "wormy," but don't take her word for it. That's what *udon* noodles are all about: thickness. And she's more concerned these days with how things are going to look, smell, and taste coming back out rather than going in. Gross, huh?

Which is why she doesn't eat vegetables anymore, she said. Because they take longer to digest. Which brings us to the meat: The chicken was great. The pork was great. I wouldn't waste my time and money on the ribs, if I were you, although they were also great. There just wasn't enough meat on 'em. And, of course, the pork chops were great—probably my favorite inhabitant of Meat Mountain.

An example of the menu's inspired silliness: "Not only do these pork chops taste great, on a cold day it is a festive Korean tradition to fasten them to your ears; it's a great way to ward off frostbite and vegetarians."

Good one. My only complaint is that Meat Mountain didn't have enough meat on it: two ribs, one chop, two strips of chicken, and a thin, fatty, crosscut beef rib section thingie. The Ultimate Meat Platter? The Vegetarian's Nightmare? The Meat Meister? Meatarola? The Meatinator?

Nah. Not even a Meat Mountain, really. I'd rename it Meat Hill.

■ ROSCOE'S CHICKEN AND WAFFLES

Happy New Year everybody. Me, I'm happy just to get rid of the old one. Last year, like the one before it, was my Year of the Bad Decision. And we all know what bad decisions lead to, right?

Bad Luck.

On the bright side, this one promises to be a good-luck year. I don't suppose I need to point out that $1 + 9 + 9 + 6 = 25$, which, divided into 100 (in honor of the almost-ended century) equals 4. What you may not already realize, however, is that this year I'll turn 33 on May 21.

Roscoe's Chicken and Waffles
336 Grand Avenue, Oakland. (510) 444-5705. Breakfast, lunch, dinner. Credit cards accepted. Cheap.

Now if that's not numerically lucky enough, consider that $3 + 3 + 5$ (for the month of May) $+ 21 = 32$, which, divided by 2 (I haven't figured out why yet, but I'm sure there are plenty of good reasons to divide a number by 2) equals 16, the square root of which is 4. Need I say more?

Probably not, but just in case I've been doing everything else right, juju-wise. I spent the last week of last year wandering into and digging myself out of the desert, just generally having visions and staring into the fire. Then, thoroughly smoked, I returned home for New Year's Eve, ate tomatoes, made noise at midnight, threw things, played cards and won, shaved my head, said "Rabbit rabbit," called my mom, ate black-eyed peas, cleaned the kitchen, and showed nothing but respect for the Green Bay Packers.

So all the signs are pointing toward me and my ex-girlfriend getting back together.

If not, then my elaborate good-luck dance will still not have been in vain. It will simply manifest itself some other way, like I'll write that novel or gain 20 pounds or the Indians will *win* the World Series. In other words: general happiness and prosperity, and many many trips to Roscoe's Chicken and Waffles, Oakland.

That's where I ate on the morning of January 2, so it's been a great year for me so far. Of course, I knew from the name of it I was going to love Roscoe's: Chicken and waffles are my two favorite things to eat, and Roscoe is one of my favorite names. No kidding.

Say it: "Roscoe."

Roscoe not only makes the best fried chicken I've eaten in these parts, but he has the presence of mind to serve it with waffles—damn good waffles—for breakfast! And if *that* don't make you happy, then don't bother with antidepressants. Go ahead and jump.

You can get one piece of chicken and one waffle for under five bucks, but who wants one piece of chicken and one waffle? You'd have to have screws loose, which my buddy Haywire has, of course (in addition to stomach problems, poor boy), so that's what he ordered: Denise's Delight, piece and a waffle.

I got the Lord B.J., which is a whole half of a fried chicken and two waffles. Eight bucks. Extravagant, yes, but when you consider that you're basically eating breakfast and lunch in one sitting, you have every right and reason to divide those bucks by two. (Correct answer: four!)

And don't forget that everything was great. The waffles were lightly golden and soft-style, served with enough whipped butter to grease a tank, and enough hot syrup to sweeten an army.

And the chicken! I don't want to die just yet, so let's say the chicken was to yodel for. It was the stuff that dreams are made of. Juicy dreams. Spicy dreams. Good dreams—the ones with full nudity *and* buffet tables.

Yodel-eh-hee-hoo!

I don't think you're supposed to do this (I wouldn't know, being essentially white and from Ohio), but I was cutting up some of my chicken on top of the waffles, like a banana, and eating it all syrupped and buttery. Proper or not, it worked.

Just in case anyone's wondering, there are other things to eat at Roscoe's besides waffles and fried chicken. For example, you can get your Lord B.J. half-chicken smothered with gravy and onions for 50 cents more—but I wouldn't recommend that 'cause it would throw off the math.

Also: grits, eggs, biscuits, corn bread, greens, red beans and rice, smothered taters, chicken sausage patties, chicken burgers, chicken sandwiches . . . come to think of it, all the meat on the menu was chicken meat. Roscoe's got no use for cows or pigs. And if I could do what he does with chickens, I wouldn't either.

■ YAMO THAI KITCHEN

Sure, I love Thai food as much as the next guy—maybe more, if it's *tom ka gai,* the best kind of soup there is, period. Problem is, Thai cooking's always been sort of a rare treat for me because (1) it tends to be

> **Yamo Thai Kitchen**
> 3406 18th Street,
> San Francisco. (415) 553-8911.
> Lunch, dinner. Cheap cheap.

more expensive than other Asian styles of food, and (2) there's never as much of it on your plate. Those are big, big issues with me. Sniff. Sniff. Boo-hoo. Oh help help help . . .

Trumpets, please: *ba-bada-baaaaaaa!*

To the rescue comes Yamo. Yes, Yamo Thai Kitchen, the first-ever Thai dive that I know of—and I use the word *dive* with all due reverence and respect, in case you just joined us.

Thanks to Yamo's essential cheapness and heaping portionality, I've eaten more delicious Thai food in the past three weeks than in the previous 32½ years of weeks put together. It doesn't hurt that Yamo strategically positioned itself just two blocks away, between me and Can-Cun.

Bur*what*o?

All silliness aside, it's true: This great new place recently sprung up where Chris's Hamburger and Lee's Hamburger and Hamburger House used to be—on 18th Street near Mission, between the locksmith and the hardware store, so you know it's going to be a nuts-and-bolts kind of restaurant.

Sure enough, you go in and there's the same small eight- or nine-seater counter, and an entirely different cook/proprietressperson (we'll call her

Yamo). No artsiness. No art. Nothing fancy. Not even music, unless you consider the sizzling of panfried noodles music, which I guess I do.

So, you see, Yamo can afford to deal out more Thai food for less American money than any other Thai place I've been to. And if you don't mind eating like I do—with your head down and your elbows on the counter— you'd better go check it out.

Everything on the lunch menu is $3.95. Let's see, so far I've had the *kao pad khing*, which is sautéed pork (or beef or chicken) with ginger, dried mushrooms, onions, green onions, and chili over rice; the *rad na*, which is panfried rice noodles with broccoli and chicken (or beef or pork) in a bean sauce; and the *guai tiew tom yum*, which is noodles with prawns, pork, fish cake, calamari, and bean sprouts in a hot-and-sour broth.

For dinner I've had the country-style curry, which the menu describes as "choice of beef, chicken, or pork without coconut milk," and which turned out to be a spicy-as-hell big bowl of soup—and, of course, the always insanity inspiring *tom ka gai*, the soup *with* coconut milk, and chicken and mushrooms and *galanga*, lemongrass, and lime juice. Hold me back.

Tonight, to celebrate finding a fiver on the basketball court, I'm gonna splurge on a curry called *kang dang:* "Spicy red curry made from fresh and dried chili and Thai spices. Choice of chicken, beef, or pork cooked with coconut milk, basil, and bamboo shoots." And, as if that don't sound celebratorial enough, you can get it with roasted duck, pineapple, tomatoes, and bell peppers for a buck more. That's what I'm gonna do. Yeehaw!

"Yeah, well, how was everything?"

Everything was great. I can't speak for the *kang dang* (yet), but so far Yamo hasn't let me down. The *tom ka gai* was about as good as any other I've had, only bigger. The country-style curry, which has no "hot and spicy" star next to it, just about set my head on fire. And all three cheapo lunch plates were both hefty and delicious. I'm trying to decide which one I liked best, but—no go. They're *all* my children.

Of course, food always tastes better when it's cheap and there's lots of it. When you get to watch the cook cook it, and when said cook is as cool as our Yamo, well, that's like MSG.

Now, I haven't been everywhere (yet), so I don't know if Yamo's is "the best Thai food in the area," as the menu claims—but as I said in my discussion of Hamburger House, its ill-fated predecessor, I can handle a healthy dose of hyperbole so long as the "best" in question is at least good. Hamburger House's "best burgers in the world" weren't. Yamo's "best Thai food in the area" is certainly good, and it just might be the best. Who knows? I love it, personally, and maybe this goes without saying, but "the area" is a lot smaller than the world. Right?

◼ NATORI RESTAURANT

Funny how a bad decision can lead to a good discovery, how bad luck can lead to good things, and so on. So long as you keep your wits about you, like the French, who turned stale bread into a great breakfast.

In this case, though, it was me and Satchel Paige the Pitcher, trying to have a Breakfast Club together before his biblical 40-week vacation ended. Every day, in other words, we'd eat at one of our favorite restaurants. It was a great club while

Natori Restaurant
327 Balboa Street,
San Francisco. (415) 387-2564.
Lunch, dinner. Credit
cards accepted. Cheap.

it lasted, but he ran out of money after the first day and I got sick of springing for him after the second one. So that was it: two days.

The bad-to-good thing comes into play on Day One. Day Two we ate fried chicken and waffles at Roscoe's. Day One we tried to eat at Roscoe's, but it was closed. We were there around 10-something, hungry as hell, and then disappointed as hell when we saw the "Closed" sign. Of course, if I could read half as well as I write, I'd of knowed they don't open until 11 on Mondays and adjusted my appetite accordingly; instead, we cussed and cursed our lousy luck and headed bridgeward back this way (Ann's Cafe being closed all day Mondays).

I drive like an idiot when I'm hungry, and I don't know how poor Satchel—between pushing his feet through the Ford-boards, screaming his head off, and hiding his eyes—managed to come up with the presence of mind to hit upon what just might maybe turn out to be one of the four or five Best Ideas of the Year:

Natori Restaurant on Balboa near Fifth Avenue in the Richmond, where for $9.75 at lunchtime ($16.50 for dinner, and—get this—"according to height" for the kiddies) you can eat all the sushi you can eat, plus shrimp and fish and soup and crab wings and chicken claws and chow rice and fried mein and all kinds of other great brain-scrambling stuff.

Incredible, huh? But it doesn't get going until 11:30, so we had to kill 45 more stomach-growling minutes with a swiped post-Niners-season *Chronicle* and paper-cupped coffees at the try-not-to-look-at-the-donuts joint next door.

Did I mind the wait? Hell, yeah.

Was it worth it? Hell, yeah—are you kidding me? I left Natori with the stupidest fish-eatin' grin on my face I've probably ever had there. And even though it was mostly sushi, I wasn't the slightest bit hungry again until dinnertime, when eight or nine crackers did me just fine, thank you, and good night. (No lie.)

I'll try to remember what all went down in a moment, but first let me tell you about the place itself. Well, it's big. Big enough for all the everything a lot of people can eat, plus a huge fake fireplace, an indoor tree and goldfish pond, lots of tables, and then—rumor has it—another dining room on top of that. So there's no need to keep it a secret.

Natori!!!!

Take the kids. Grab a friend or three. Go there; just make sure you clean all your plates, 'cause they'll charge you $2 a thing, I think, for whatever you don't finish.

Now I'm not an expert sushi eater. For example: My favorite thing about eating sushi is the way your fingers smell afterward. My second favorite thing is touching the ginger. My third favorite thing is eating the ginger. And my fourth or fifth favorite thing about eating sushi is eating sushi.

That said, here's about all I can say, take it or leave it: Natori's sushi was excellent, mostly of the log-of-rice-with-slab-of-fish-on-top variety, but also a few seaweed-wrapped styles, and of course the selection varies. My favorites were the melt-in-your-mouth mackerel and the less meltable but equally tasty octopus.

Non-sushi favorites: the fish, whatever it was, the eyeball-and-everything shrimps, even though I don't normally go for shrimp, and the curiously sweet fried-chicken wings. Plus crab and—oh yeah—mussels!

And according to Satchel, they also have oysters and lobster parts, but only for dinner.

I also tried the chow mein, fried rice, beef with broccoli, and chicken with something-or-other, and these were all fine tasting, too, but my advice to you (like Satchel's advice to me) is to resist the temptation, like donuts. You can get good cheap those-things anywhere. Stock up on the other stuff, because good cheap sushi and seafood, on the other hand, is a very rare bird.

■ PALACE STEAK HOUSE

Nevermind the gentrification of Valencia Street—has anyone been to Hunt's Donuts on Mission recently? Well, it's no longer technically Hunt's, in the first place. Sniff. It's true: That red neon donut no longer dips into the neon coffee mug over the corner of Mission and 20th Street. It's still open 25 hours, but it's Magic Donuts now, and it's all re-plasticked inside and they've got three types of "gourmet shit" coffee to choose from instead of just regular shit coffee.

> **Palace Steak House**
> 3047 Mission Street,
> San Francisco. (415) 647-
> 2011/6350. Lunch, dinner.
> Credit cards accepted. Cheap.

I went there in the middle of the night one night last week to dunk donuts with that corner's new breed of chichi bike thieves and mentally bankrupt yuppies, and after reading through a two-weeks-old *Guardian*, I leaned back in my chair, smiled donutfully, and thought to myself: Isn't it nice how, no matter what Valencia Street does, Mission's always only one block away, with all its burritos and cheap produce and general realness.

Yep, and McCarthy's bar, where I'd been drowning some sorrows earlier that night, will always be the brightest and best, this city's most heartfelt tunes being kicked out Saturdays by Danny and Nellie and hopefully Dick again soon, if his new heart medicine kicks in.

What with all the dollars they earned off me, and those two donuts counting as breakfast, I wound up with five bucks left to get me through Sunday's lunch *and* dinner.

Mission Street to the rescue!

So . . . moseyed into the oddly named Jelly Bakery Donuts next door to Can-Cun, had a decent buck-fifty cheeseburger, loaded, plus 85-cent fries and dessert: a 40-cent donut (15 cents cheaper than Magic's equivalent) and an honest cup of Farmer Brothers (50 cents). What I'm getting at is that I still had enough cents left to pick up two pounds of tomatoes and a slab of pork for meat sauce for dinner.

But what I *really* want to talk about is Palace Steak House, where you can get a great steak with tater and salad and garlic bread and even something to drink for well under 10 bucks. As with McCarthy's and so many fine Mission Street institutions, you get the sense that potential yuppifiers wouldn't stand a chance here.

The Palace has been around since 1969 and is cluttered with three decades' worth of stuff, mostly flags—big ones, little ones. Many many great nations are represented up on the Palace Steak House ceiling, including the 49ers and the United States, both pre- and post-Alaska and Hawaii . . .

Question?

"Yes, excuse me: Are the 49ers a nation?"

Yes. As I was saying, the Palace also has hanging vines and plants and plastic grapes and strings of garlic and lightbulb candles and hockey on TV. It's a chaotically festive, good-feeling room, with big meat-eater booths, glass-covered red-and-white-checkered plastic-and-duct-tape tablecloths, and a good big guy named Goody (for real), who doesn't mind hollering all the way across the restaurant to me:

"Hey, you want that T-bone bloody rare or just rare?"

Bloody, I told him, and that's how it came. Actually more like "prebloody." It wasn't cooked enough to even get the juices flowing—just sort of flame-licked on either side and raw red meat in the middle. No one has ever meant rare like the Palace means rare, and I love the place for it. It was a hell of a steak.

But as good as the steak was, the highlight of the meal was the tiny taste I got of broiled chicken. See, I was eating with my country-music-star buddies Kid Coyote and Slim Volume, the latter a Palace regular who had decided to try the chicken for a change, and honest engine, I never tasted a broiled chicken better than this one, all crispy-skinned and spiced to heck with I don't know what all.

So go twice: once for the cow and once for the bird, and then I don't care what you do after that.

■ PHU HUONG

Four reviews ago or so I predicted great luck and general prosperity for myself this year, based on the numero-illogical recurrence in my "figgerin's" of the number four. But before that rosy prediction ever even saw the light of day, both me and my Niners had already been dumped, and I owed Bruce a burrito.

Phu Huong
448 Larkin Street,
San Francisco. (415) 885-0965.
Breakfast, lunch, dinner.
Cheap cheap.

Then I get this letter (and some reversal-of-fortune "good-luck money") from a concerned reader informing me that, according to Chinese superstitiology, the number four is about as unlucky as you can get. Basically, as I understand it, it means you're going to die. So unless that good-luck money kicks in, I guess this'll be about it for me. Oh well. But even if I do drop dead—both out of love and, what's worse, with the goddamn Cowsissies on top of the heap—at least my very very worst-ever numero-uno monster fear doesn't stand to be realized: i.e., I won't die on an empty stomach.

Has anyone noticed whatta eatin' streak I'm on? (Knock on wood.) First there was Roscoe's Chicken and Waffles, which I've been back to three happy times already. Then there was Yamo Thai Kitchen, due to which I honestly haven't had a burrito in, count 'em, three (3) weeks. Then there was Natori Restaurant, where I'll be eating myself silly again tomorrow evening, if all goes well. Plus Palace Steak House.

And now this: Phu Huong in the Tenderloin, where I've finally found the bowl of Vietnamese-style hot-and-sour prawn soup I've been searching for ever since my favorite place in Providence, R.I., bit the big one. Technically called *canh chua tom hay ca,* this soup is the only soup I know of that can hold a candle to *tom ka gai,* the Thai-style soup I'm always back-flipping over.

Many Vietnamese restaurants don't even have it, or don't quite exactly have it. Like Tu Lan has *sweet*-and-sour prawn soup and Vietnamese-style "sour fish soup," both of which are good, but for a buck-fifty less at Phu Huong you can get the thing itself, *hot*-and-sour prawn (or fish) soup ($4.50), and it's wally-wally hip-hip yodel-eh-hee-hoo excellent—just like Providence's was, with chunks of pineapple and tomato and celery and mushrooms and mint floating around with the poor dead shrimpies.

The perfect level of spiciness comes from crushed red peppers, and the overall flavor of the soup can only be attributed to what theater people call "ducks in the machinery," or divine intervention. I don't know how else soup can possibly taste this good without chickens in it.

Anyway, Phu Huong is a great place for more reasons than just the best *canh chua tom hay ca* in the known world. For example: It's a great place. It just is. It's a square, wooden-walled little room that could easily have had a big hot tub or sauna in the middle of it, instead of tables and chairs. There's huge protrusion-style art on two walls, and a great little kid, Matthew, age two, who'll sit at your table and play peekaboo with you while you're waiting to order. Other than that, there were Ma and Sis and Granny and Baby, and—let's see—two other guys eating there who were *like* family, so, yeah, it's a pretty homey place.

I was there with pal Yo-Yo, my longtime sushi advisor, who was pissed off over not having been invited to Natori with me—so this was my way of making it up to her. We sat at a big round six-seater because we knew we were going to get a lot of food. And while she scanned the menu (I already knew what I was getting), Matthew, age two, sat across from me and we played peekaboo. Then he fell off his chair.

I ordered the hot-and-sour prawn soup and, of course, *bún cha giò thit nuóng,* or imperial rolls and grilled pork over rice noodles. Yo-Yo added *goi cuon,* or shrimp salad roll, *banh cuon cha,* or "steam meat roll w/ bean sprout," and *ga xao xa ot,* or sautéed chicken with lemongrass.

Everything was great. Nothing was better than the soup, and nothing was weirder than the meat rolls, two of which I took home to my laboratory for further study. But as much as I picked them apart with the tools of my trade—a fork—and as slowly and carefully as I finally finished them, this is about all I can say for sure: ground pork and who-knows-what that curly crunchy brown stuff was in a square, see-through, jellyfish-ish dumpling.

Go there. Get the soup. And one other thing: The kid likes matchbox cars and Doublemint gum, in case you want to get on his good side.

■ MUSEUM KITCHEN

Of course, no one is as sensitive to choosing politically correct word choices as I am—everybody knows that, right?—and yet even I have put my pen in my foot on occasion and by accident, most recently raising the dandruff off of the gay community when I erroneously referred to the Dallas football team as the "Cow-sissies," which, as was pointed out to me by my friends in the gay community, should technically have been "Cowsissypersons." That was a bad mistake, and to atone for it, I resolve to stop referring to the Dallas football team altogether, except in emergencies.

Museum Kitchen
1739 Broadway, Oakland. (510) 832-0280. Lunch, dinner. Credit cards accepted. Cheap.

Well, so my burritoless streak may have ended (thanks to the Green Bay Fairyassmotherfuckerpersons—Hi Bruce!), but my winning streak, I'm happy to say, did not. Thanks to Oakland's Museum Kitchen. I went there with pal Johnny "Jack" Poetry to celebrate the losing of his job. Trust me: When your name is Johnny "Jack" Poetry and you work for Clorox, severance is severe cause for celebration.

After his last day of work we walked down 12th for "a little taste of Africa in America," as the Museum menu says.

It's a quiet, clean bar with a small dining room of a few cloth-covered tables, cloth napkins, general niceness, and this Nigerian guy who does everything from explaining the food to taking your order to cooking it and, presumably, washing your dishes afterward. You know: labor of love, the kind of job you emphatically *don't* want to lose.

So, in the interest of helping him keep it, let me inform you that this Museum Kitchen guy cooks up some delicious and exotic (to me) food. More important, he really piles it on.

I got beans and *dodo*, beans being black-eyed peas and *dodo* being fried plantain, which had to come on a separate dish—that's how many beans there were. Plus your choice of several meats, including goat or fish. Or my choice: some of everything.

Let's see, there were two drumsticks, or one more chicken in a wheelchair, depending on how you choose to look at it, a few find-your-own-meat goat bones, some stew-size chunks of beef, and maybe even a few other animals represented. The mix of meat and beans all stewed up and steaming together in this spicy hot tomato sauce, plus the salty crisp-fried mushy-inside plantain slices . . . well, "comfort food" is what I wanted to get at. But comfortable ain't exactly what I was later that night, tossing and turning and emitting all sorts of noises I didn't know I had in me.

On the other hand, I woke up next morning and, whammo, my killer one-day-old cold was gone—no lie—for which I should rightfully split the credit between Museum's spicy sauce and Yamo's spicy roast duck noodle soup I'd had for lunch.

Speaking of which, you can get all sorts of neato-sounding soups at Museum, like melon soup or jute soup, all served with some sort of neato-sounding "dumpling" material, like *fufu* or pounded yam, for eight or nine bucks. Johnny "Jack" went for the Jollof fried rice, served with the same choices of meats in an even spicier tomato sauce with red and green peppers.

The whole thing, in addition to being good and new and half the cure for a common cold, was dang cheap: 14, 15 bucks total.

On me, Johnny "Jack." Welcome to the wonderful world of Unemployment. It's not quite as prestigious as an NEA grant, but it's easier to get. So here's to all the great work Mr. Poetry'll be kicking out now instead of answering calls from disgruntled bleach bums. Hip hip . . .

■ ELITE

I gotta thank a guy named Will for turning me on to the Elite, on Franklin between Bush and Pine (not to be confused with the Elite Cafe on Fillmore). And then you're gonna have to thank me, I guess, unless Will wrote you a letter, too, in which case this whole review, like life itself, will be pointless.

> Elite
> 1535 Franklin Street,
> San Francisco. (415) 776-8188.
> Breakfast, lunch, dinner.
> Cheap cheap.

Well, Will's point was this: meat loaf. "Spectacular meat loaf," as he put it, cooked and served by "perhaps the most sincere couple that ever ran a restaurant." Right around five bucks, with salad and bread and taters and veggies and "secret cake" and everything.

I was going to write back and say, "Meat loaf?" But it's not like me to write back—just ask my friends—so I simply set out to answer the question on my own. I put on my new Hawaiian shirt, packed a pencil, lowered my head, and pedaled into the mystery.

Meat loaf . . . meat loaf . . . meat loaf . . .

It was one of those beautiful days last week. It was Lover's Day, and I love meat, but . . . *meat loaf?* I couldn't remember my last meat loaf. What *is* meat loaf?

Around about O'Farrell Street, self-hypnotized by the repetition of the words *meat* and *loaf,* I revealed to myself, under hypnosis, that my meatloaf problem stemmed from a traumatic childhood experience: my mother's cooking. My mother's meat loaf—crusty, dry, raisinated, dry. I know I'm gonna fry in hell for saying so, but my otherwise good mom was a bad cook. Then she became one notch worse: a vegetarian. Now, bless her hippie heart, she's rejected refrigeration entirely and can no longer be said to be any kind of cook, on the grounds that she doesn't cook anything. She eats only raw sunflower seeds and organic fruit.

So you see? You see why I yam what I yam?

Well, I solved my personal meat-loaf mystery, anyway, with the help of this here Elite. Truth is, I enjoy a good loaf as much as the next guy (Will), and turns out he's right: Elite's meat loaf is spectacular. Three thick slices of actually juicy, well-seasoned loafed beef next to a mountain of creamy all-the-way-smashed taters, all smothered in gravy. Then a molehill of corn and a bunch of *el blando* mixed vegetables—green and red peppers, carrots, zucchini, onions, and broccoli (if I remember right). Plus two big fat slices of fresh bread with butter.

But before all this there was salad, and before that there was the restaurant itself, and before that there was the word: elite. I don't know why they call it that. *Elite,* to me, implies snobbishness, or at least elitism. It rhymes with *effete* and *mesquite.* At any rate, it doesn't connote dirt-cheap, basic, mostly American food served in an entirely unpretentious atmosphere.

There's nothing fancy about the Elite; it just happens to be a very nice place, low-ceilinged, art-walled, with a couple round tables and then a bunch of really beautiful all-wood two- and four-person high-sided booth nooks, each one individually lamp-lit. You may feel as if you're eating in an old train or something, but I've never eaten in an old train, personally, so I didn't.

They've got a ton of sandwiches, hot and cold; daily special soups; daily specials; hot specials like spaghetti and lasagna and ravioli and *udon* and teriyaki; barbecued ribs and chickens; a few vegetarian items; and all kinds of salads. Almost everything's under five bucks.

Cheap, good, and fast.

Within 10 seconds of ordering my meat loaf I received a fairly large bowl of salad. Real green greens, I mean, with a quarter of a hard-boiled egg, a carrot stick, a celery stick, one tomato slice, one cucumber slice, and one radish slice—exactly. This came with my own personal cruet of Italian dressing. Drench your own—woohoo!

And then, before I finished that, I had the big plate of everything else and bread, and then, before I finished that, I had a little piece of cake for dessert. So that's a heck of a lot of food for a fiver, wouldn't you say? Me and Will think so, and we know what we're talking about.

Well, at least I do. Will made the judgmental mistake of also recommending Bhan Thai, a few blocks away on Polk, over my beloved Yamo, "A+ to C."

One word, Will: wrongola.

■ HON'S WUN TUN HOUSE

I accidentally dissed my own mother's cooking recently—which, all truthfulness aside, is undoubtedly bad juju. So, to make up for it, I'll begin with a list of her qualities:

A fine sense of humor. Weird. Smart. Swears more than me. Antichurch, antigovernment, anti-TV, anti–almost everything. Used to have a goat. Candid about sex. Made an excellent vegetable soup, come to think of it. Less than five feet tall. Italian-Ohioan, and only occasionally gets arrested. Hi Mom!

Hon's Wun Tun House
648 Kearny Street,
San Francisco. (415) 433-3966.
Lunch. Cheap cheap.

And then there's the sad but true case of my artsy ex-sports-talking pal Yo-Yo, upon whom I once relied for off-season insider Niners info . . . the slid-under-my-door bulletin "Dan, K.C. signed Sonny," dated 5-3-94, for example ("Sonny" being our pet name for Steve "My-Goal-As-A-Third-String-Quarterback-Is-To-Be-A-Second-String-Quarterback" Bono), still hangs taped to my wall under a signed (by Yo-Yo) photo of her and Jerry Rice, who, if I remember correctly, smells real good.

See, I rarely if ever even look at a newspaper between football and baseball seasons. So the other day we were having this little downtown power lunch, me and Yo-Yo, and I call it a power lunch only because she was in a hurry to get back to the lab, and I'd just put in a grueling half-hour workweek myself (one of those high-paying consumer research gigs), and you all know what the Financial District does to me, right?

But I happened to remember getting a letter from a downtown temp once almost a year ago, urging me to check out this little soup place on Kearny called Hon's Wun Tun House. So one thing led to another until me and Yo-Yo were sitting there, out of the rain, sipping little plastic glasses of free hot tea and waiting on our soups.

What I'm trying to get at is that I couldn't stop thinking about my favorite cornerback, Eric Davis, so I said something. I said, "What's up with Eric Davis?"

"I don't know," said Yo-Yo.

And that, in a nutshell, is why I call her my *ex*-sports-talking pal. Which isn't at all what I set out to say, either, but ever since that great sentence with both Bono and Rice in it, I've been very deeply lost. Maybe you noticed.

Anyway, Davis, as I write this, is off to pig-pickin' land, which I just found out about between paragraphs, on my way to the post office, and I've had Carolina on my mind, too, so what can I say but, "Hey, thanks, man, for the memories. I mean it." And as for Hon's Wun Tun . . . well, it's not going anywhere. Don't worry.

Hon's is a small, fairly bustling, counter-having soup joint right around the spot where financial yuckiness turns into yeehaw Chinatown. Why is it Wun Tun, by the way, instead of Won Ton? I don't know which is right, but I kind of like Wun Tun because it's said exactly like One Ton, which can't help sounding to me like a lot of food.

Turns out Hon's bowls of soups are not particularly huge. The good news is, they're so cheap you can easily afford two of them: your basic *wun tun* and noodle goes for $3.30, and my basic *wun tun* and noodle with beef brisket goes for $3.84.

More good news is that it's great-tasting soup. The nicely spicy *wun tuns* themselves are packed with explosively flavorful pork, the beef brisket is thick-cut and tear-away tender, and the homemade noodles are plentiful and delicious.

While I was slurping mine down, Yo-Yo explained to me why she wasn't talking the talk. In fact, she wasn't eating the eats, either. In fact, she'd tried to call and cancel our lunch due to a stomach-churning crush on some "good-looking totally unattainable older dude at work." (Dang, coulda been me except for those last two words. And *unattainable*, I guess, which—oops—makes me a "good-looking totally older dude." Dang.)

Yo-Yo also expressed a measure of disappointment in my Phu Huong review because I spent so much time discussing food and luck and barely even mentioned her. I promised to even things out this time around.

No problem: This time there was hardly any food to talk about.

So . . . that's pretty much my pal Yo-Yo for you, in summary—sour on sports, distracted by her own heart, pretty good at tennis and Ping-Pong and poker, taller and less Italian than my mom but way cooler, and *her* parents live in Hawaii! And this is pretty much the point I've been trying to get to all along here: restitution.

■ ANGKOR BOREI

Good news! After midnight last night in the rain, I gave directions to some lost lumberjack from Oregon and he gave me a hug. You don't get that on the East Coast.

Which reminds me of a valuable lesson I learned on Christmas Day at a truck stop down in Barstow, fueling up on fuel, weak coffee, chicken-fried steak, biscuits, and eggs-over-easy with my favorite garnish ever: Bazooka Bubble Gum! Yep sir. Christmas Day, Barstow, Burns Brothers, Mrs. B's Diner, bikers, truckers, Jackie

Angkor Borei
3471 Mission Street, San Francisco. (415) 550-8417.
Lunch, dinner.
Credit cards accepted. Cheap.

the waitressperson, rockin' Yuletide oldies, Bazooka Joe, me . . . and this is what that day your Danny Boy learned: (1) bikers hug, (2) truckers don't.

I was, at the time, on my way to the desert for a week alone with my thoughts and a carton of eggs. And seven days later, on my way back, that was still all I had written in my notebook: (1) bikers hug, (2) truckers don't. So now I can add to that: (3) lumberjacks do. Out here, anyhow. Corner of 18th and Guerrero, California, pouring rain, 12:30, 1 a.m. Sure, sure he was drunk—stumbling, in fact, from the 4, 5, 6, or 700 Club, Bar, or Lounge, as I call it. (Yeah, my memory problem only ever gets worse, curse it.)

Me, I'd been sipping tea that night, if I remember correctly, swapping shop and digesting two tons of great Cambodian food with a ladyperson named Gulliveronica, who speaks languages and has been almost everywhere in the whatchamacallit—world—without ever eating Cambodian food.

Not that I'm any sort of an expert on the subject myself, having only eaten it that one other time at Angkor Wat. Remember? How can you forget? It was me and Ask Isadora—flaming bananas for dessert!

But that was then and this was Angkor Borei, way down on Mission past Army Chavez. Angkor Borei is lower-scale than Angkor Wat—in other words, somewhat fancy-pants for me (i.e., cloth napkins). It's also a bit of a splurge: 30 bucks for the two of us. Holy heck—I forgot to sign the credit-card slip! I noticed just now looking it up, so . . . maybe it was *free,* which changes everything.

Angkor Borei is the cheapest restaurant I ever ate at. Or, assuming they'll have the sense to forge my signature or I'll have the ethical fortitude to square up with them some day, somehow, it's a pricey-for-me but totally-worth-it special-occasion place.

Either way, it's certainly *possible* to eat there for under 10 bucks.

Appetizers run from four-something to five-something, soups and entrées around six, seven, eight, nine. Lunch things go for under five. That's pretty good. And everything we tried was real good, so that's good, too.

Let's see, there were cold Cambodian noodles by way of an appetizer. This was a very refreshing sort of a salad of noodles, cabbage, cucumbers, bean sprouts, carrots, and mint, served with a mild fish curry.

Then there was sour soup, which I insisted on 'cause it sounded so much like my favorite Vietnamese-style hot-and-sour soup: pineapple, tomatoes, celery, scallions, basil, garlic, and tamarind, with shrimp. It didn't taste like my favorite VSH&S soup, but it was mysteriously great in its own right, somehow touching, in fact, aromatically. If I didn't have company, I might have cried.

We got two entrées: shrimp and pineapple curry in a smooth yellow coconut sauce, and *ahmohk,* which they describe as "a mild curry fish moose," if memory serves me, "served in a banana-leaf basket." I think I saw some of them fish mooses on Mutual of Omaha's *Wild Kingdom* once, but I don't remember any of them hanging out in banana-leaf baskets.

Well, the shrimp and pineapple thing was the highlight of the meal; the fish moose, in spite of its exotic presentation, was just too soft and fishy and moosey for me. Which isn't to say I didn't eat it up—especially after I discovered the weirdo zing-zang-zooey salsalike sauce that came along with it.

In summary: nicely presented smallish portions of real good food for some real hard-earned money (maybe), friendly service, and excellent atmosphere. And now, children, in closing, let's review what all else we've learned here today: (1) bikers hug, (2) truckers don't, (3) lumberjacks do; and 4) Gulliveronica? A kiss on the cheek! *Yodel-eh-hee-hoo.*

∎ TROPICANA

You can only be in the restaurant-reviewing business for so long before you get totally fascinated by the people on the other end of things: the waitresspersons and busboypersons and cookerpeople who make your job possible.

Tropicana
2291 Third Street,
San Francisco. (415) 431-1244.
Breakfast, lunch.
Cheap cheap.

I think a lot of food writers come at it from the inside out. They've worked in restaurants; that's how they know what to say about 'em.

Me? Before this I was a temp. Before that I worked in a print shop, at a mental hospital, and on a farm. Sure, I can cook a few things, but the one night in my life I tried waitresspersoning for a living, I was too tired to breathe afterward and almost died. And don't forget that I'm a backyard-tackle-football enthusiast, year-round unprofessional baseball player, and full-court one-on-none basketball star.

Hell, I've held the Ping-Pong table for entire three-day weekends, one-speed-biked the Sierras lengthwise, and danced like a hyena to three ska bands in a row, but I've never felt like I felt back home after that one night of waitresspersoning: like if someone were to set a barbecued chicken six feet away from me, I wouldn't be able to get there.

So this one's for all the restaurant workers. Hip hip . . .

Hooray! Now I'm gonna talk about a place called Tropicana on Third and 20th, crisscross from the Potrero Hill Police Station.

The Tropicana is a great space with an old-timey feel, lots of wood, five tables, and a horseshoe counter center stage. It's American fare for working folks—breakfast and lunch, weekdays only. The price is right—as in five and under—and the food is, you know, *decent*.

But when I go back it'll have nothing to do with any of that. Sure, I'll eat. You almost have to in a restaurant. But really I'll be there to watch two amazing people do some pretty amazing stuff.

Check this out. I went there on a Wednesday, smack in the middle of lunch rush, like 12:30, and they were fairly slammed. I'd say there were 20, 25 eaters at any given time, plus some call-in takeout orders.

I was sitting at the very end of one wing of the counter, back by the kitchen, and I could see the cook in there, cooking, smiling a mile a minute, whistling the "Tennessee Waltz" with the radio, cracking jokes, and hollering good-byes to anyone who got up to go.

Just about as soon as I sat down, the one other worker in the joint, the waitressperson, took my order: beef stew, which she relayed over her shoulder to the cook, and then, whammo, I suddenly had a cup of coffee, a slice of stale sliced bread with butter, and a real-lettuce salad I couldn't eat due to French dressing.

I looked around the counter, took out my notepad, and wrote: "Chicken parm doesn't look too good. Chicken soup looks good."

And then the cook himself came around from the kitchen and slid a big plate of food in front of me. "Stop writing," he said. "Write later. Now you eat. Eat!"

So I ate. The beef stew was just beef, which is OK with me—tender chunks smothered in a barbecuey reddish gravy that was also all over the smashed taters. Then there was a pile of peas and carrots, which tasted better than greasy-spoon pea-and-carrot combos usually taste, meaning they weren't over-un-frozen. Speaking of which: coffee ice cream for dessert!

But I don't want to get too far into the food, 'cause that's not the point. The point is that these *two* took care of *50* or so in the hour I sat and watched. I was impressed from the get-go with their good-natured efficiency in the face of adversity, but I wasn't blown away until I watched a table of five place their orders and realized that I was the only one in the place with a pen. Nobody was writing anything down! Not the waitressperson, not the cook.

Watching them work like that is like watching an NBA highlight film, or Montana to Clark, or, better yet, Steve Young, the consummate do-it-yourselfer. No, here's what it's like: It's like Omar Vizquel glove-handing a wouldn't-be double-play grounder to Baerga, who bare-hands the feed and turns it with time to spare. In other words, poetry in motion *and* under pressure *and* with a great big smile. They even managed to crack each other up once or twice, whispering whatever, so you know it wasn't just showmanpersonship. These two sincerely love their fucking jobs!

I don't know, maybe they're on drugs or something. If so, I'll have what they're having.

◼ EL BALAZITO

He's back! He's my brother, Jean-Gene the Frenchman! *Fratello mio! Lui è ritornato per comprare tutto il frutto putrido nella nostra città, per cucinare le torte.* He's Jean-Gene, the Italian-speaking Frenchman and legendary vegetarian. He's a world-renowned auto mechanic/pastry chef who'd rather be remembered for his flaky crusts than for his transmission work. That's what he told me. I said, "OK."

El Balazito
2560 Marin Street,
San Francisco. (415) 824-6684.
Lunch. Cheap cheap.

You're not gonna believe this, but Jean-Gene brought me a new Ohio-bought Toyota minivan. It's exactly like my old Ohio-bought Toyota minivan, The Ford, in all respects except some: It's clean, it's two years newer (1987), it's got four-wheel drive, it's silver, it's got four-wheel drive, it has 121,387 miles on it instead of 167,509, and it's got four-wheel drive *and* cup holders!

Now, if everyone's done laughing at me, I'll . . . excuse me, is everyone done laughing at me? All right, no problem, I can wait.

[Later] Now? OK, remember how I told you how I got seriously stuck a few times on my last trip away from it all? Well, I've been in a bit of a rut of another kind lately, but instead of picking up and moving to another state, like I've done in the past, I've decided to give four-wheel drive a try. Me and it'll be heading south in a week or two to show some soft sand south of Joshua Tree who's boss. See? It's all very symbolic and poetic and shit.

Speaking of which, I can't tell you how disappointed my brother the Frenchman was to hear that I live on Thai food these days, much as he loves Thai too. It's just that he comes here with Can-Cun on the brain, and who can blame him? But I don't do burritos anymore—just once a month for old times' sake, and we've got two weeks to go until April.

Now, naturally, I've been wanting to spend some quality time with my new nameless car, as well as with my old nameful younger brother, and Jean-Gene has naturally been wanting to spend some quality time with burritos. So we managed to kill at least three birds with one little stone called El Balazito, or the Car Wash Fish-Taco Place. I'd heard a lot about it from a lot of people, but all I knew for sure was it was somewhere off Army Chavez Street near 101 maybe. It took us two days to find it, so I'll try and be a bit more explicit with you.

It's on Marin Street, right off Bayshore Boulevard at the big merge. From Army Chavez you go under the overpass, turn right on Kansas, turn right again, and there it is: a big do-it-yourself car wash with a little taco stand in back, open nine to five every day except Sunday.

I got two fish tacos and Jean-Gene the Frenchman got a super vegetarian burrito and a *taco de nopales* for later. Everything comes with lots of chips, and the lemonade is damn delicious.

There's a place to sit and eat outside—a sort of counter/table with a few stools around it—but I was there to eat in my van. Remember? (Cup holders.) So the atmosphere was great. There was even some weirdo jazz Muzak blaring out over a loudspeaker, so I didn't have to run my battery down for the sake of ambiance.

"What about the food?"

Excellent. Here's a funny thing, though: El Balazito is directly related to El Balazo on Haight Street, which sucks. Goes to show you how smaller can be better than bigger at all things but basketball.

Balazo steams its tortillas and charges about a dollar more for a regular burrito than Balazito, which grills its tortillas. Balazo's *salsa fresca* was *el blando*. Balazito's is almost as good as Can-Cun's. The fish tacos are killer. You know: double-layered grilled corn tortillas loaded with chunks of fresh grilled fishies, a ton of cilantro, onions, and hot salsa.

Jean-Gene seemed to be enjoying his big boy, too. It had some things vegetarian burritos don't normally have: vegetables. Every now and then he'd announce another one: "Carrots." "Zucchini." "Mushrooms."

After lunch we washed my new car.

■ U-LEE

I can't help it. I'm a sucker for thematic unity. I listen to Italian music when I make pasta, calypso when I'm happy, country when I'm sad, punk rock when I'm mad. When I'm driving through the desert, I listen to cowboy songs. When I watch a 49ers game I wear a 49ers hat. Hell, I've got work shirts for working, Hawaiian shirts for ukeing, western shirts for roping steer, and a pair of Cleveland Indians boxer shorts.

> **U-lee**
> 1468 Hyde Street,
> San Francisco. (415) 771-9774.
> Lunch, dinner. Cheap cheap.

Why not? That's the way I figure it. Why not?

So the other day I put on my one and only pair of Lee jeans and called up my one and only pal Wayway, who's first name is Lee.

"You, Lee," I said. "It's me, Dan."

I think he saw what I was getting at, because a little bit later Lee and me were at U-Lee, Hyde and Jackson, Nob Hill, working on the world's biggest potstickers, and some black-bean chicken and pork chow mein, and for the first time in a long time, for a while at least, life seemed to make sense. U-Lee. Him Lee. My jeans. Good food.

Uuurrrp.

Excuse me. I had tried to eat there a few nights earlier with my friend Rob, which wouldn't have made any sense, come to think of it, but they were closed by the time we found a parking space. Sorry, Rob. Maybe we can check out Robert's Corned Meats some time. Or Robert's Hardware. They have a lunch counter, don't they?

Anyhow, Rob and some long-ago letter writer had both told me about U-Lee. Wayway knew about it and had been there once or twice as well. But my dear friend Haywire, who used to live just two short blocks away, on Clay, had somehow or other missed it.

The consensus seems to be this: potstickers. And I'm afraid I'll have to second that. More accurately, I'll have to six-hundred-and-forty-second it, judging from the number of tacked-to-the-wall business cards with scribbled notes and poems of praise.

"Best potstickers in the world!"

"Biggest potstickers in the world!"

"Your potstickers stick to my pot!"

"Potstickers as big as my hand!"

Stuff like that, and for good reason. These were six of the biggest, fattest, meatiest, and bestest potstickers this boy's ever witnessed. 'Bout the size of, well, yeah, realistically, a small fist, I'd say, realistically, and each one packs a ground-pork and ginger and garlic punch that might make your nose bleed.

The black-bean chicken was also great. I love black-bean sauce, and this was a great one, with bell peppers and onions and lots of tender chunks of chickens. If you don't like bones, be sure to ask for "black-bean chicken" exactly, 'cause there's also "boned chicken with black-bean sauce" for 20 cents less, but because of the language barrier, "boned" means it has bones in it.

What else? Well, we got BBQ pork chow mein, because someone had recommended it to Wayway, but I'd have to say it was the low-light of the meal. It had plenty of fine-tastin' pink-edged pig meat, and carrot slivers and celery and stuff, but the noodles were kind of sticky and not quite right. And the noodles, let's face it . . . I mean, chow mein. Right? You see what I'm getting at?

Me neither. Overall, though, U-Lee is a great-food and big-food and cheap-food extravaganza, and I really don't know how Haywire missed it for all those months in the 'hood, unless he was holding out on me, because it's also a great-looking place. It's a very small, attractively unassuming, utterly unpretentious, and homey hole-in-the-wall, with an atmospheric friendliness that pretty much invites you in off the sidewalk, pats you on the back, and says, "Hey, man, enjoy yourself."

Which you will.

■ A TOAST TO MOM: BREAKFAST SPOTS

My own mother, in addition to wearing her clothes inside out and living her life *sans furniture,* does not, as a rule, eat out. For one thing: Like me, she doesn't have any money. For another: Unlike me, she's extremely particular about what goes into her body and generally doesn't trust restaurants any more than she trusts end tables.

Therefore (and also because she lives in Ohio), I won't be taking her out to eat for Mother's Day.

On the assumption, however, that other cheapskates will be taking other mothers out to brave the brunch lines on that impending Sunday, I have assembled a list of practical suggestions based on weeks and weeks of research, cups and cups of coffee, hours and hours of test-eating, and about a minute and a half of serious thought.

In general, the restaurants I'm about to recommend are about to be recommended based on the common decency of their food, relative financial feasibility, atmospherical appropriateness, and the likelihood of actually getting a table before midnight.

I intentionally avoided Haight Street, in light of the last-named condition and in spite of Kate's Kitchen, Spaghetti Western, the Pork Store, and all those other fine places, which are popular enough already, if not too popular.

So these, in no particular order, are some of the alternatives:

The Bearded Lady (485 14th Street, San Francisco; 415/626-2805). I can't think of a better place to take your mom, especially if she's a lesbian. This is just a great place to go, whatever you or your mom is or ain't, and I'll tell you why.

Well, for one thing, it has a peacefully secluded outside eating area featuring five tables, a big blue sky, and a couple of rusty bicycles. I love to eat outside, because that's where food tastes best.

For those folks who, like my own dear ma, are still concerned about the possibility of Skylab falling on them, there is also a comfortable inside eating area.

On the day I went, there was nobody at all inside and just one other guy and then a couple of ladies eating or having coffee out on the patio. I was taking my good old time 'cause it was a beautiful weekday morning; it didn't hurt that I had a heap of delicious food to keep me company. I'm talking about some kind of an open-faced breakfast burrito—a warm flour tortilla topped with scrambled eggs, black beans, melted cheddar, spicy tomato salsa, and sour cream if you want it (I don't). I think it was three-something, maybe four bucks, tops, and I know it was really really good.

I was particularly interested in the dish because it was very similar to something I've been experimenting with at home, unsuccessfully, due to my stubborn insistence upon substituting black olives for black beans and leaving the salsa out entirely.

Anyway, I learned a lot, had a great cup of coffee with one free refill, breathed some relatively fresh air, and went home around five bucks down. (So, if you're bringing Mom, better take, say, 10.)

Sugar Bowl Bakery (3640 Balboa Street, San Francisco; 415/752-7970). Way out in the Richmond, near the Balboa Theater. You can't miss it, cause it's got one of the coolest signs in the city. Also known as "my cousin Drags's favorite place"—but he moved back to Ohio, so I'll have to sing its praises all alonesome:

Sing ho for the Sugar Bowl!/Sing hey, hooray for the Sugar Bowl!/Hey hip mama papa baby wally wally oooh . . . (repeat chorus).

Excuse me, but any mother in his or her right mind would almost have to get giddy here. It's a donut shop/lottery-hangout/bakery, which also serves cheap, mediocre American food and cheap, great Vietnamese food. Due to the multiplicity of culinary amusements, I recommend this place especially for big-eating mothers, like me, who don't do brunch.

I had American food for breakfast, and then Vietnamese for lunch. I mean, for under five bucks I had one pancake, two eggs, four sausage links, toast, muffin, coffee *and* tea. True, the pancake was small and upside-down, the eggs were uneventful, the links were dry, and the blueberry muffin was spongy, but lunch more than made up for it.

After watching all these great-looking Vietnamese dishes passing by while I was working away at breakfast, I had no choice but to order an order of spring rolls and grilled pork with rice noodles—the very mention of which makes me hungry for a return trip.

In sharp contrast to the previously devoured sausage links, this dish's grilled pork was of optimum succulence. The spring rolls were springy and fresh, and the noodles were smooth. I was so won over, I barely even noticed that the dish was utterly mintless. (It usually has mint, right?)

Mama's Royal Cafe (4012 Broadway, Oakland; 510/547-7600). I'm a little nervous about recommending this place in this particular article, but two different people recommended it to me, so—what the hell—we can always blame them.

And, anyway, what with Mama herself being in the title, how could I overlook it?

The food is good. The prices are steep but not too bad, I guess, for special occasions. It's a hip, artsy, and fun place. The service is exceptionally friendly; the waitresspersonpeople seemed to have gone to college or played in bands with everyone in the place except me. The thing that spooked me was a sign-up sheet on the wall in the entrance, which makes me strongly suspect the worst: lines. I was there on a Friday, close to noon, and there wasn't one, but the place was hopping—a bit boisterous for my breakfast money.

There's a small five-seater counter and two cozy rooms with nice wooden booths and a few tables. They have omelettes, *huevos rancheros,* and tofu *rancheros.*

Me, I got a basic two-egg breakfast, with potatoes, toast, fresh fruit, and chicken maple sausage. The toast was good and grainy. The eggs were good and juicy. The taters were good, but there weren't enough. And there was plenty of sausage—three long links—but it wasn't particularly good. Too

---

mild. It was the first time in my life I ever had to add salt to sausage.

A lot of people prefer their breakfast fresh and healthy, and those are the ones who should sign up (if necessary) to eat at Mama's Royal Cafe. It wasn't exactly my kind of place, frankly, but it might be your mom's, so don't rule it out.

Original Mel's (2240 Shattuck Avenue, Berkeley; 510/540-6351). Speaking of lines, I tried to eat at the Homemade Cafe in Berkeley, but it was a Saturday and everyone and their second cousins were waiting for a table. Everyone seemed crabby or distracted. Their second cousins, meanwhile, were drooling on the windows and generally annoying the lucky bacon-munching people inside. The hostessperson was hassled and frantic, understandably.

Nobody was happy, in other words, and being happy is important, so me and my friends whirled around, went back to the car, and wound up at Original Mel's, which was a pretty fine alternative to crabbiness, and I think most mothers would like it better than the Homemade Cafe, anyway. If yours wants a homemade breakfast, stay home and make her one, for crying out loud.

Original Mel's, like all the other Mel'ses, features the old-timey-diner motif, blah blah blah.

What I like is: no waiting, yes cheap, yes decent food.

From the regular menu, I recommend the Pick Four breakfast. You get to choose something from each of Mel's four major food groups: eggs and things like that; toast and pancakes and things like that; potatoes and things like that; and meat.

Don't get the potatoes. They're boring and bad.

Get hash browns, get eggs, get pancakes, get a sausage patty. I got all those things, and they were all well and good.

Tumbleweed Cafe (1245 Van Ness Avenue, San Francisco; 415/474-0200). In many ways, now that I think about it, this would be the ideal place to take your mom, particularly if she's a cowboy. But even Eastern mamas will appreciate the Tumbleweed's '50s deco-style interior, to say nothing of the wide array of fine omelettes, poached-egg dishes, and "scrambles."

My own favorite touch is the genuine cowhide on some of the chairs and all of the booths. These booths, by the way, are as big as Montana. Even if you had five moms, weighing in at 250-plus apiece, you'd all be able to sit together.

It's big, bright, and clean (which many moms like in a restaurant), and we didn't have to wait for a table, not even on a Sunday.

I got the Texas omelette, which was an omelette, yes, but it had little if anything to do with Texas. The "Tumbleweed chili" filling, for example, would have sent my Texan friend Haywire rolling over in his grave— except that he's not dead yet, so he'll have to roll over in his living room instead. This chili was almost entirely meatless and had no kick whatsoever. That ain't Texas! It weren't bad, either, but I think they'd sell more of them if they took out the two little chunks of meat and called it a San Francisco omelette. Beans, tomatoes, cheddar cheese, and onions.

The potatoes are *yeehaw* excellent, and they also have good-looking fresh-fruit pancakes and good coffee.

That said, I've got nothing else to say, except "Hi Mom!"

■ POWELL'S PLACE

Same as I wanted more than anything, when I was a kid, to some day be a major-league baseball player, I now unreasonably aspire to some day fry a major-league chicken. What's wrong with me? I can't bread the perfect bird any more than I could ever hit the ball out of the infield. I set a Little League record for playing the most innings without an official at bat—all walks and sacrifice bunts.

Powell's Place
511 Hayes Street,
San Francisco. (415) 863-1404.
Lunch, dinner. Credit
cards accepted. Cheap.

Team player, right?

Well, if I were really a team player I would do the team a favor and quit. But here I still am, utility infielding my way through my early 30s in San Francisco's Roberto Clemente League, waiting for the big break.

And when that break finally comes—whether it's an ankle or arm or finger—I know I'll never recover quite right *senza insuranza*, as they say. Even if I don't get hurt, I've only got another 12, 15 years of sandlot in me tops, I figure.

So I have to start preparing now for some other futile pursuit to fall back on upon my retirement from unprofessional baseball. That's why, whenever I get the chance, I get together with my upstairs neighbor buddy Wayway, and we break out our old frying pans and practice for fried-chicken stardom—same as I'd go outside and play catch every chance I got as a kid. Now I stay in and mess up the kitchen.

And just as I used to go to Indians games for inspiration, I'll occasionally turn, these days, to the fried-chicken pros. The problem is that, with fried chickens as with professional athletes, good role models are hard to come by. Last night we went to Powell's Place. You know, down there on Hayes Street. It's one of San Francisco's most famous soul food restaurants—you can tell 'cause it's the only one listed under "Soul Food" in the *Yellow Pages.*

I'd had their barbecue once before, but Powell's Place ain't about BBQ; it's about fried chicken. This guy J. C. and some other guys with other initials have been swearing by P.P.'s f.c. for as long as I can r.

Me, I don't swear by it, having discovered Roscoe's earlier this year. But here's what I like about Powell's *pollo*:

Breast . . . $1.65.

Leg . . . $1.

Thigh . . . $1.15.

Wing . . . 75 cents.

See what I'm saying? Hell, I barely even needed a calculator to realize that's half a bird for under five bucks. Four-something, to be exact. And you can get a corn muffin for 45 cents and call it a meal!

Or you can get the corn muffin *and* french fries *and* a large order of yams or potatoes *and* beans and rice *and* chicken livers *and* peach pie, and call it nap time.

We didn't do that, though. We just got the chicken and muffins and smashed taters and took it all down to the Dovre Club to eat it with wine and beer, which is how fried chicken should be ate when sweet tea ain't available.

See, the dining room—which is a great one—wasn't open that time of night, which is just as well 'cause you don't want to order your chicken from the dinner menu anyhow. It's eight bucks that way—although it does include two corn muffins and two side dishes.

Speaking of which, the muffins are moist and delicious and the smashed taters, I can tell you, are piled on and well graviated. And it's a good, greasy meat-eater's gravy.

The chicken itself isn't quite as flavorfully correct as Roscoe's (or Biscuits & Blues's, for that matter), but it's a good, solid, and golden role model.

◼ U.S. RESTAURANT

Now I have a brother *and* a Frenchy sleeping under my Ping-Pong table. The Frenchy, she's my brother Jean-Gene the Frenchman's best friend's sister-in-law, and she's here for two months to learn English and, er, study me for a sociology project.

U.S. Restaurant
431 Columbus Avenue San Francisco. (415) 362-6251. Breakfast, lunch, dinner. Credit cards accepted. Splurge cheap.

So if you think the French have an attitude about Americans now . . .

Well, wait 'til word gets out that we eat with our hands, sleep under Ping-Pong tables, store our shoes on the windowsill, and spend way too much time in the bathroom. Not to mention the egg-carton thing, or Mr. T.

Anyhow, this here Frenchy came over here with a boyfriend, but he could only stay for 10 days, and we only actually played Ping-Pong on one of those days, sadly. He was good—good enough to beat me two out of eight games, which is more than I can say for any of the homegrown competition I've come up against.

On this boyfriend's last night here, to thank him for making me sweat and to send him off with a good taste in his mouth, I took us all out to dinner. They'd already sampled our country's best Mexican and Thai food at Can-Cun and Yamo, respectively. When I tried to find out what else they might be interested in, my worst fear was realized: They seemed kind of curious to try something American . . . you know, while they were here and all.

Fact is, I've been struggling with the issue of American food ever since last summer, when I left the country for real for the first time in my life. Something about the abundance of European Booger Kings and McDoodoo's, on the one hand, and, on the other, the utter lack of chicken-fried steak.

See? Now I'm getting a headache. Let's just skip to the part where we actually eat, OK?—having wound up at the U.S. Restaurant, on Columbus and Stockton, North Beach, but hey, look at the name of the place: U.S. Restaurant. United States Restaurant. Bald eagle and everything on the menu. Now what could be more authentically American than that, short of buffalo burgers and maize on the cob?

Let's see, there was me, Jean-Gene, and the two Frenchies, Muriel and Pascal. Let's see, there was a baked lamb shoulder (Tuesday's special), pasta pesto, a hamburger steak, and a New York steak. Everything was great except for the pesto, which was mediocre, but that's what my brother gets for being a vegetarian. I loved my lamb shoulder—especially because it came on a big huge shoulder bone, so I could pick it up like a chicken leg and go to town, ooga ooga.

"Ha ha, you eat like cowboy," Pascal noted. "We have not zeece in France."

"Urrrp," I said. "No?"

"No. In France we would like to do like zeece, but we are too . . . how you say?"

"Um, weak?" I guessed, wiping my mouth on my shirtsleeve.

Muriel, meanwhile, was taking mental notes. You could tell. But whatever she thought of me, she emphatically approved of her hamburger steak. "Zeece is not MacDonald's," I believe, were her exact words.

All of the meat, including Pascal's steak, was enormous in addition to great. They only give you one side (vegetable or pasta) per order, but they really pile it on. My lamb came with enough lima beans to sink a small ship—and they were meatfully delicious once they'd sat around in the lamb juice a while.

Both Frenchies ordered french fries and kindly let me in on 'em. Fresh-cut and perfectly cooked, these were the best french fries I've had anywhere in this country, probably.

At any rate, everyone was happy.

So check out this here U.S. Restaurant if you haven't yet. It's one of the few things outside of unorganized baseball and maybe Merle Haggard that'll make you proud to be American.

■ HAPPY DONUTS

Speaking of fast food, I tried to muster up the audacity to review McDonald's, but it didn't work. Someone had suggested I go give the McSickeningly promoted Arch Deluxe a fair shake, and to show you just

> **Happy Donuts**
> 761 Third Street,
> San Francisco. (415) 543-1407.
> Breakfast, lunch, dinner.
> Cheap cheap.

how out of it I am, I didn't know what she was talking about. But she fixed me up with a free coupon, and being a good boy, I went ahead and used it.

The rest of what I have to say on the subject goes without saying, so I won't say it, other than to say that this Arch Deluxe is a bona fried piece of shit, just exactly as you'd expect.

Don't forget that I've eaten and enjoyed fast-food burgers, like that Western burger from I think Jack in the Box, or Carl's. But when as dismal a quarter-pound of ground corporate cow as McDoodoo's new "grown-up" burger dares to compete for our Yankee dollars with all the *real* quarter-pounds of *real* American cows out there, with *real* American cheese on *real* American "bakery-style" buns . . .

Well, let's put it this way: When it comes to audacity, McDonald's wins. I lose.

Now let's talk about a real restaurant: Happy Donuts. No, seriously. I mean it. Us Edses have been in the studio with His Lowdown Highness Greg the Great Freebird, recording our next and fourth-ever album, *At the Fish & Game Club*—all of which means, in practical terms, lots of donuts and sandwiches to go, hold the mustard, hold the mayo.

One day I had a Java House chili cheeseburger with onions and jalapeños for breakfast, and another day my brother brought us down some him-made pizzas and a couple pieces of KFC for my vocal chords. (Didn't work.) Other than that it's been all Happy Donuts. I don't know what the connection is, if there is one, between one Happy Donuts and another, but the one I'm talking about is the one on Third and King Streets, China Basin, right across the street from the future stadium. Lucky them.

Greg's studio will be in the left-field bleachers, but I'm still all for the stadium, and so is he. I mean, who *wouldn't* rather watch baseball than record albums? I can see me now, sitting out in the cheap seats, where I like to be, chowing down another two-ton sandwich from 'cross the street, eye-ballin' Barry's butt and remembering how I sat in the same spot once with the same sandwich, trying to decide if the guitar should be louder.

Holy heck, I hope to hell Happy Donuts don't change none, but I suspect they'll be raising their prices to compete with the stadium concessions, and who can blame them? Right now you can get a roast beef, ham, turkey, pastrami, or club sandwich for under four bucks. That comes with potato chips and some sort of salad, and it's enough food to feed a National League umpire. And if you order big or smile the right way, and maybe even if you don't, you're liable to wind up with a bonus donut or muffin or an extra bag of chips.

The woman who made my first few sandwiches was nice enough, but the legendary other one, Alice, takes the cake. In the face of adversity (who wants to work at a 24-hour donut shop?), Alice beams around the place, selling donuts and coffee and slapping together five-inch-high-and-that's-no-lie sandwiches with the world's biggest grin. She jokes with her customers and co-workerpersons and seems to be permanently on the verge of cracking up.

Other than that, it's a donut shop, for crying out loud. Plastic and uncomfortably comfortable and well lit. You've got your NBA Jams, your Ms. Pac Man, a couple of pinball machines over in one corner, your cops, your down-and-outs, your post patterns, me . . . you know the scene.

What you don't know, on the other hand, is the sandwich itself, so let me break it down for you scientifically, and then I'm outta here: eight slices (before I lost count) of meat, or roughly one inch; half an inch of cheese (Swiss, Jack, cheddar, or *real* American); three-quarters of an inch of lettuce; one and three-quarters of an inch of French roll, unless you want some other kind of bread; and then another inch or so of sprouts, red onions, pickles, hot peppers, and tomatoes.

I'm not much of a sandwich guy, but this one's won me over. And best of all, it's there for you 24 hours a day.

■ PAD THAI

It was bound to happen, and then it happened. I've been eating at Yamo Thai Kitchen so much that I accidentally became part of the fambly—meaning free food in exchange for small favors, like adding up stuff and making new menus. This means that from now on you have to take everything I say about Thai food with a grain of MSG.

Pad Thai
3259 Mission Street, San Francisco. (415) 285-4210. Lunch, dinner. Credit cards accepted. Cheap.

Yamo is the best Thai restaurant anywhere, including Thailand, by virtue of being closer to my house. Still, people keep trying to sell me on other ones, just like they try and sell me on a better burrito than Can-Cun's. And it's my duty as a public servant to systematically check all challengers out and shoot 'em down.

Don't worry. It's no big disgrace to lose to the king of a thing. It's like losing to me at Ping-Pong: It goes without saying. Just grin and accept it and go down fighting.

Like Pad Thai, our most recent challenger (i.e., loser), up the road a ways on Mission, near 29th Street. My friend Bearfood tried to tell me once that Yamo's *pad thai* wasn't as good as the *pad thai* at Pad Thai.

Me, I don't particularly understand the popularity of that particular dish, but Bearfood's argument seemed reasonable enough. I mean, a place named Pad Thai had better make good *pad thai*.

They do, but for 30 cents more than Yamo ($6.25), they only put three-sixths as many shrimps into it. And they're 11 blocks farther away. Am I gonna walk an extra 11 blocks to pay 30 cents more for three fewer shrimps? I don't think so.

Wait a minute. What's *pad thai* got to do, got to do with it? Or, as my friend Frank would put it: "*Pad thai*? Fuck *pad thai*! *Tom . . . ka . . . gai!!!*"

He's right, see? *Tom ka gai* is the thing to eat when you're eating Thai food, and Pad Thai's *tom ka gai*, speaking of going down swinging, is actually better than Yamo's (although at $6.25, it's also 30 cents more). They call it *tom khar gai*. If I was them, I'd change the name of the whole restaurant to Tom Khar Gai. It's not only many times better than their *pad thai*, it's also the best TKG I've had anywhere. The extra "h" and "r" means there's extra *heat* and, um, *red* tomatoes in it, in addition to all the regular stuff: the coconut milk and chicken and *galanga* and lemongrass and lime leaves and mushrooms and onions. It's so damn spicy you can just barely eat it without freaking.

That's the good news. The *pad thai* was the no news. And the bad news is the *gaeng daeng,* a red-curry-and-coconut-milk dish I've come to love like one of my own hats.

Now, maybe nothing was going to taste like much of anything after that there *tom khar gai* . . . but then, the *pad thai* tasted like something. The *gaeng daeng* wasn't bad. It just wasn't nearly as good as I'm accustomed to, and there were peas in it. Why? Normally it's just your choice of chicken, beef, or pork with bamboo shoots, peppers and fresh basil. Not that I have anything against peas. I'm just asking, 'cause I've never seen them in Thai food before.

Ah, hell, what do I know?

The place itself is very nice. You know, tablecloths, candles, traditionally garbed and friendly waitresspersonpeople. All of which is especially impressive considering that the prices are at least comparable to Yamo, which Bearfood calls Thai-in-the-Wall.

But they don't have the $3.95 lunch plates, or the general quantitativeness of Thai-in-the-Wall, so if you're going to go to Pad Thai, go for dinner. And bring a date. And for crying out loud, get the *tom khar gai.*

"You like it spicy?" they'll say, like they said to us.

Correct answer: "Yep."

■ KAM'S RESTAURANT

By the time you read this I'll be feeling much better, thank you, but right now it's gloomy tunes and rain rain rain, oh boo-hoo-hoo and fuck you, too. It's muddy-minded madness, romantic frustration, sportslessness, long-gone-lonesome-bluefulness, general confusion, and blisters. Both feet. Too much sleep. Burnt brains breakfast, lunch, and supper, and it's not just me, either. Seems like a lot of my friends, if not all of them, are ailing from some if not all of the above.

Kam's Restaurant
3624 Balboa Street, San Francisco. (415) 752-6355. Lunch, dinner. Cheap.

By the time you read this, though, everyone'll be feeling better—even you. In fact, by the time you read this there will be no chance of rain in the forecast and no sense in patting me on the back either. The sky will be blue, the grass will be green, and we'll all be playing baseball under it and on it again, respectively. In other words, everyone will be so happy and tanned that you'll scratch your head and say: What's this guy talking about?

By the time you read this I'll have a new novel or band in the works, or something, and maybe a new hat or a haircut—for sure a new lease on life. By the time you read this my brother Jean-Gene the Frenchman will have been here to fix everything.

By the time you read this I'll have been back out to Kam's in the Richmond a few more times, probably, 'cause that's one thing that ain't broken or wrong with the world.

A guy with the actual name of Bob turned me on to Kam's in exchange for letting him interview me for a journalism class. If he's able to make anything at all out of the slurps and burps and munches and crunches I laid onto his little tiny tape machine, then give that boy an A+, please. Someone?

How he expected me to speak clearly, let alone intelligently, let alone at all, what with all that food on the table, well, hell, I'll never know.

Sizzling rice soup. Ever had it? Bob says Kam's is the best sizzling rice soup in the city, and I've never eaten it elsewhere, so I'm in no position to argue. I will say this: It's the biggest bowl of soup I've seen this side of dreamland, and it's got more different things in it than Old MacDonald had on his farm. I mean everything up to and including the kitchen sink: cows, pigs, chickens, squids, shrimps, chickens . . . you name it, it was in this soup.

"Deers?"

No.

"Ducks?"

No. No ducks.

"Quail?"

Fuck you.

Anyhow, the main attraction of sizzling rice soup isn't so much the kitten or kaboodle as the sizzling rice, which if all goes well (and at other restaurants it often doesn't, according to Bob), snaps, crackles, and pops all the way from the kitchen to your table.

The bad news is that Kam's soup, for all its sizzle and ingrediation, somehow manages not to taste like anything. BYOMSG. Well, it's worth the five-something and would be, in my opinion, even if it were just boiled white rice in hot water. I mean, the size of the bowl alone will crack you up, and that's a very good thing.

What else we got was chef's gourmet chicken, and beef with ginger and green onions. Both these dishes were totally tasty, totally huge, and totally unnecessary—but we knocked 'em off anyhow, *urrrp*. 'Scuse me.

The chicken was heavily battered, poor bird, and deep-fried with those crispy curly thingamajigs in this sweet-and-sourish red sauce. Trust me, it was much better than it sounds, and I didn't have my ruler with me, unfortunately, but I swear it was stacked five inches up off the plate. The beef was not quite so huge, but it was maybe even tastier, with big strips of munchable ginger in a rich, dark sauce.

And that was everything. And everything was way more than enough. Thanks, Bob. Kam's has the biggest portions of cheap Chinese food I've ever seen, which is saying something. Friendly service. Roomy room. Two rooms, in fact. All else I can think to say about the place is that there's a huge, oddly lit picture of Hong Kong on one wall. And *real* toothpicks, which doesn't go without saying, sadly, in cheap Chinese circles.

Sigh . . .

By the time you read this, who knows, it might even be baseball season. Right now: no. Right now it's raining cats and tractors. Tonight I'm going bowling.

■ HERB'S FINE FOODS

Mrs. Nellie McNalley, senior citizen, wrote me a letter quite some time ago suggesting a review of Panos Restaurant in Noe Valley. I say that she "wrote me a letter"—even though, to be perfectly accurate, it was addressed to someone else entirely—because it somehow ended up in my mailbox. Ergo: However it got there, it must have been intended for me all

Herb's Fine Foods
3991 24th Street,
San Francisco. (415) 826-8937.
Breakfast, lunch, dinner. Cheap.

along, right? Whether Mrs. Nellie McNalley, senior citizen, knew so or not. Whateverwise, I'd like to hereby bounce the suggestion off the back wall and into the wastebasket. I went to Panos, see, but I didn't go in, 'cause it seemed a little fancy-pants for me and my clothing. Dinner things were 12, 13 bucks, and it's true I was out to eat everything but dinner . . . nevertheless, I took it as an omen. And thank you, Mrs. Nellie McNalley, senior citizen, for luring me to lovely Noe Valley of a lovely Monday afternoon. I had a lovely time, in the long run.

Now, Noe Valley ain't exactly the place to be when you're (1) hungry as a horse, and (2) me. Still, there I was, being all of the above, and, what with Panos not panning out, you can add to that: (3) deeply and darkly depressed . . . when what to my hungering eyes should appear but Herb's Fine Foods, serving breakfast and lunch right across the street since 1943, yodel-eh-hee-hoo!

Here's why I yodeled: Because, believe it or not, *it's entirely possible to eat chicken-fried steak in Noe Valley, thanks to Herb!* As far as I know, his is the only really realistic eating place for the empty-pocketed and malfashionably attired in this otherwise upwardly hip neighborhood. Not to Noe Valley bash; it's a great place for children and dogs and Sarnos and coffee. It's got Noe Valley Ministry, Peasant Pies, and a couple of fine record stores, but let's face it: It's no haven for cheap eats.

And that's why I'm so happy about Herb's Fine Foods.

That chicken-fried steak I mentioned, it's just about the most expensive thing on the menu, right around nine bucks. And you can easily have yourself a big enough breakfast or lunch for closer to five. As for me, when I'm in Noe Valley, I can't help thinking about brunch, and when I start thinking about brunch, I always wind up eating both ends of it.

So for breakfast I had a blueberry waffle, and for lunch, of course, I had the chicken-fried steak, which came with smashed taters, veggies, bread, and salad or soup-of-the-day. The day was Monday and the soup was both beef barley and very good. After the soup came the waffle: nice and crispy, four wads o' butter, and enough blueberries for full coverage and then some. Don't get me wrong, Herb's waffle couldn't hold a chicken to Roscoe's, but for this side of the bay . . . hell, I've got no complaints.

As for the meat of the meal(s), the chicken-fried steak: well, no complaints there, either. It was a nice, big, juicy slab of actually rare actual steak—whereas most places'll use cube steak or ground beef under the same noble heading. Chicken-fried steak. Damn, I like those three words, no matter which way you slice 'em.

The gravy was deep and dark and decent. My only complaint—and I can only complain halfheartedly because I ate so dang much other stuff and didn't get to nap—was that the vegetables (broccoli, cauliflower, baby carrots) were oversteamed into a mushy inedibility. The sliced bread wasn't nothing to write home about, neither. In fact, one probably could have written home *on* it.

But these are minor gripes compared to the sheer pleasure, the all-out incongruity of eating chicken-fried steak, the truck-stop classic, in our city's least truckered neighborhood, Noe Valley. At a 50-year-old real-style diner that ain't the least bit trendy or even throwback. It's just still what it always was, I imagine: a friendly, no-nonsense American-food place. Nice big booths against the walls, horseshoe-shaped counter in the middle, and pink-striped Formica everywhere. Even the waitressperson-people seemed to be imported from some other time or neighborhood. I liked them.

So what I'm wondering is, with such a great old-school establishment as this almost directly across the street, what the hell is Mrs. Nellie McNalley doing eating three times a week at Panos, that relatively pricey upstart? Senior citizens these days! . . .

■ EL MAJAHUAL

I had my own problems (a head cold) and Crawdad de la Cooter had hers (severe depression and bilateral physiomotional exhaustion with angstful delusions of work-related worthlessness, corns, and existential

El Majahual
1142 Valencia Street,
San Francisco. (415) 821-7514.
Lunch, dinner. Cheap.

hiccups), and both of them seemed to call for big-ass bowls of animal soup. I was thinking about La Santaneca at Mission and 24th Streets, home of my favorite fish-bone soup, but we fell a little short.

I fell, I'm happy to say, facedown into the biggest and best and only bowl of Colombian-style hen soup I've ever eaten. It had hens in it, and cassava, and potatoes, and green plantains, and the broth . . . the broth was henny, with a little tomato and onion, and a ton of cilantro. We all know what that means, right?

Wally wally.

Why, what with a squeeze of lemon and about a half a bottle of hot sauce, you've got yourself some of the finest-tasting cold medicine ever— but I suppose I should tell you where you're eating, huh?

The name of the restaurant is El Majahual. It's on Valencia between 22nd and 23rd Streets, and I have a feeling it's been there a lot longer than a lot of other restaurants on Valencia have been where they are, but I wouldn't know, because I never noticed it before yesterday. Normally, you see, I walk down Mission, even if it's out of my way, as Valencia scares and depresses me.

Well, there's nothing scary or depressing about El Majahual, unless, I guess, big bowls of soup chase you around in your dreams. It's just a friendly, no-nonsense hole-in-the-wall serving up friendly, no-nonsense Salvadoran and Mexican food, according to the sign outside. But everything I ordered was Colombian. They've got a whole two-sided insert of Colombian dishes stuck in the menu. That's where I found my hen soup, and that's where I found my empanadas. Those are little tiny meat pies with shredded beef and potatoes and a cup of fresh hot salsa on the side for drenching 'em. The salsa had a little bit of tomato in it, and some heat, yes, but it was mostly just cilantro, and we all know what that means, right?

Wally wally.

Speaking of which, hey, have you met Crawdad? She's Crawdad de la Cooter, both borned and breaded in Louisiana, so she says y'all like I say y'ins and you say you, and she puts hot sauce on her cornflakes, speaking of wally wally.

Anyway, Crawdad got the fish soup, and all I can say is that it was a bigger bowl than La Santaneca's, but it didn't taste as good. All the same stuff: fish, bones, eggs, tomato, cilantro, other things . . . well, I can say that Crawdad forgot to squeeze her lemon wedge into it, and maybe that was part of the problem. Or maybe against the greatness of my great hen soup, nothing was going to taste as good as anything else. I don't know.

Let's take a closer look at my great soup: big, huge pieces of mama bird, bone and all; two whole, skinned taters; a couple lumps of cassava; and a lot of green plantains.

Now, I don't know what cassava is exactly, except that it killed Joe Brown in a Jolly Boys song. In fact, cassava makes guest appearances on several of my old calypso records, on which basis alone it's one of my favorite things to eat, just like rum is one of my favorite things to drink, even though I can't stand the taste of it. I asked our waitressperson about cassava, and she said it was yucca or *like* yucca—I'm not sure which. All I know is it was white and mealy and had an inedible spine down the center of it, like a fish. And not like any yucca stuff I've ever eaten.

The plantains, being green, were, well, not exactly rock hard, but *solid,* which is not a bad thing in my book. In my book, a pear, for example, is overripe once it fails to make your gums bleed. So I liked the green plantains more than I generally like other-colored ones.

What all this is adding up to, in case you haven't noticed, is without doubt the heaviest, solidest bowl of soup I've ever experienced, and one of the biggest. Not to mention the topic of our dinner conversation: death.

So we pushed ourselves homeward like wheelbarrows full of Wilmington, Delawarescan cement. Crawdad was so full she thought she was going to puke. All we'd had was soup, for crying out loud, but I felt like I'd eaten a burrito.

You know the feeling.

■ GERMAN COOK

I know you're not supposed to talk about poo-poo in food reviews, but it's hard not to when half of your life is eating and the other half is dealing with the repercussions—minus maybe a few hours a week for writing and car repairs. (See pie chart.)

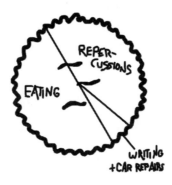

That said, and pie charts seen, let me just add (as ungraphically as possible) that after several days straight of eating nothing but Crawdad de la Cooter's famous and authentic (if somewhat poisonous) seafood gumbo,

> German Cook
> 612 O'Farrell Street,
> San Francisco. (415) 776-9022.
> Dinner. Credit cards accepted.
> Cheap.

I was, well . . . let's put it this way: Keeping my food down wasn't the problem so much as keeping it up.

Nevertheless, I didn't admit to myself that I even had a problem until I reached the point where I couldn't stay off the toilet long enough to get to the kitchen and heat up some more of it. In this way, friends, I starved and dehydrated myself pert-near to death and then, instead of dying, I reluctantly left the last of the great gumbo to green in my fridge and waddled over to Can-Cun for a burrito and about three of those cantaloupe drinks.

That night was difficult. On the plus side, I learned a lot of Italian; not only do I keep my language books next to the can, but my cross-alley neighbors speak it fluently! And their bathroom window, like mine, was wide open.

The next day for lunch I tried Yamo and learned a lot of Italian that afternoon, too.

So for dinner I was determined to do the right thing. I drank a bottle of ginger ale and took a bus to the Tenderloin. I was looking for one of those classic Chinese-American dives where you can get a big bowl of steamed rice and a tall stack of pancakes with a double side of toast for something like $2.50, total, and then, if you're me, write about it.

Good news! I'm not writing this on the toilet. I'm down at Java Supreme, my office away from home, munching bagels and drinking coffee, woohoo! At least part of the credit goes to a wonderful little Tenderloin restaurant called German Cook.

See, I was wandering around looking for just the right Chinese-American dive, when I spotted German Cook, at O'Farrell and Leavenworth, looking a bit upscale for me (not to mention for the 'hood). On the other hand, German food sounded even heavier and solider than rice and pancakes and toast all of a sudden. Meat and potatoes, right? And I don't think I ever reviewed a German restaurant before . . .

So I went on in. There were three booths, a few tables, and a tiny three-person counter with a view of Wednesday-night baseball on TV—so that was where I sat. Nice place. Small. Quaint. Clean. Beers, wines. Bricks, wood, red-and-white-checkered curtains, white-painted chairs with red painted-on roses. Plastic roses in vases on the table.

The place has been there since the '60s, and I imagine lots of people know about it already, but this is for those who don't: Check it out. Don't be afraid of the 10s, 11s, and 12s on the menu. You can always get a dinner special for six or seven bucks. Plus all the sausages, served with bread and potatoes or red cabbage or sauerkraut, go for six or seven or so.

They were out of German meat loaf, so I got the half-baked chicken special—I mean, half of a chicken baked in a tomato and pepper and garlic sauce. It was tear-away tender and flavorful and great, and it came with a boiled potato (or fries, but boiled seemed better for me in this case) and veggies (or red cabbage) and bread and salad (or soup). That's a lot of stuff, and all of it was just what the doctor ordered.

■ KRIVAAR CAFE

I had so much fun putting together that last review's pie chart for you, I thought for this one I'd go ahead and make an actual pie. I went to my secret spot in the city and picked a load of blackberries. It took me two

Krivaar Cafe
475 Pine Street, San Francisco.
(415) 781-0894. Breakfast,
lunch. Cheap cheap.

tries to do the crust right, but it finally came out tasting, well, heavenly, if I may say so myself. And I think I may, being a food critic.

As great as it tasted, though, I gotta tell you it was an ugly son-of-a-bitch (see Figure 1).

FIGURE 1: PIE

Ha ha ha ha ha ha ha ha ha ha ha ha ha. Ha ha ha ha ha ha. Hee hoo ha ha ha ha ha. Whoo! Ha ha ha ha ha ha ha ha ha.

First a pie chart, now a pie. What next?

Hey—I know. Next I'll start illustrating my reviews with the *Chronicle's* little moviegoing guy. Except when he's out like a light, that'll mean it was a great meal at a great restaurant, and when he's up on his seat clapping like an idiot, that'll just mean he had too much coffee or something. OK?

Speaking of out-like-a-light, yesterday I ate me one of the biggest and funnest plates of food this side of Ann's five-pound omelettes. And you'll never guess where . . .

The Financial District! Yeehaw!

I'm talking about the Wowee Plate at Krivaar Cafe on Pine, right around Kearny. This guy with this name—Steve, I think—he wrote and told me about it on pink paper with so many exclamation marks that what could I do? Next time I had any business being downtown, which was yesterday, I went to see for myself.

The place is great. It's 16 years old, but it seems older than that, it's got so much character. And on a block full of yuckiness: Taco Bell. "Old Lady" Fields. Noah's Bagels. McDoodoo's.

Krivaar. Don't be intimidated by the line out the door at lunchtime. It moves very fast and most folks get it to go. But if I were you, I'd stay a while. Food's better when you eat it there. There are four tiny tables in the front of the place, two along the side opposite the ordering counter, and then a few more in back.

The service is very friendly and superefficient. They not only know what they're doing, but they actually seem to enjoy doing it—which is something.

And who wouldn't get a kick out of serving up stuff like the Wowee Plate? It's a dish full of green greens in a great lemon-vinegar dressing, and then all sorts of other-colored stuff on top of that: two falafel thingies, a small wedge of Greek pizza, dolma, pita bread, some tomato-pepper-red onion-cilantro salad, separate piles of hummus, tabbouleh, and Greek potato salad disguised as Greek pasta salad, plus a big scoop of mango salsa.

Now—how good was everything? Well, the tabbouleh was right up there with Jophus Java's. The pasta salad and the dolma and falafel thingies were just fine—nothing special. The pizza was excellent: great dough with some great kind of cheese, a throwaway mushroom, and maybe black pepper, or certainly some sort of spice.

Don't ask me anything else, but I don't mind telling you that the tomato salad and the mango salsa were amazing. And the hummus is probably the best hummus anywhere. I don't even like hummus and I liked Krivaar's hummus, to give you some idea. But someone else who does like hummus said Krivaar's was the best. So . . .

What else you can get there is all sorts of things, mostly Middle Eastern, but also stuff like paella, chicken pesto lasagna, chicken curry over rice, and burritos in a pita. Everying is right around or under $5.

So, you see: cheap. Check it out, and sweep sleetly.

■ HRD COFFEE SHOP

Um . . . I guess I sort of said I'd have a new illustrative rating system for this review, didn't I? And I think I might've even mentioned what it would be: drawings of the Little *Chronicle* Moviegoing Guy either out like

HRD Coffee Shop
521-A Third Street, San Francisco. (415) 543-2355. Breakfast, lunch. Cheap cheap.

a light, meaning he just had a great meal, or jumping around on his seat 'cause he had too much coffee.

Well, I might've been a bit caffeinated myself when I came up with that one. I know I was riding high back then on my newfound graphical success, not realizing that Little *Chronicle* Moviegoing Guys are a lot harder to draw than pie charts. After several 15-hour days in my studio just trying to get the little twit's hat down, I finally decided that, sure, I was most definitely probably talented enough, artistically, to get it right, eventually—but something was holding me back, possibly a deep-rooted subconscious fear of getting sued.

So then I decided to fuck the Little *Chronicle* Moviegoing Guy—what I needed to do was to draw someone entirely original, every bit as lovable, and destined to become as recognizable an icon as he is, only without a hat.

So here it is: Danny Boy's very own and entirely original Mealeating Guy! Hold on a second . . .

There. That's him after a really great meal like the one I had at HRD Coffee Shop (Third and Bryant, downtown) last week. I forget what I dreamed about, exactly, but I know I woke up with a boner.

HRD Coffee Shop is a classic Chinese-American dive. There are a few tables in a small back room, but you counter connoisseurs, like me, will want to be out front where the action is. There's an out-facing one-sided yellow-stooled green-and-brown-chicken-scratched Formica counter with a view of the street, then a similar but two-sided middle-of-the-room counter with a view of the person across from you, and then the ordering counter, with a view of the food, all binned up and ready to go.

Enjoy the view. I know you'll enjoy the prices: cheap cheap cheap cheap cheap. Yep, you'll be hard-pressed to spend more than five bucks at HRD. In fact, I don't remember seeing anything over *four* bucks on the menu.

Now, in honor of that fact, let me just go ahead and draw the too-much-coffee guy, 'cause that's where I'm at now. Java Supreme, writing this. Hold on, here goes . . .

OK, so that's the other one, and if you're good you'll get one more before we're through.

Back to bidness, here's what I ordered. I ordered chicken steak with vegetable. Not chicken-*fried* steak. Chicken steak. It's a mountain of rice with broccoli spears on top, and then four big strips of salty-like-I-like-it, succulently grilled chicken, skin still on.

You want gravy?

No. Skip it. Trust me, I tried it and it sucks. Plus it's pink, and who wants pink gravy on their chicken steak?

Even without the gravy, this is a hell of a pile of food for three-something. In fact, hells of piles of food would seem to be HRD's specialty. I saw one guy get the turkey and they really loaded him up. I mean: carve carve carve carve carve carve carve. Maybe even a few more slices than that, but I got tired of counting.

So on the basis of quantitativeness alone, HRD is a great restaurant, and so are most of the ones I bother to review. Just to be safe, however, and for the sake of reference, I'd better come up with something now for the bad ones.

How about this?

■ ZANTE PIZZA & INDIAN CUISINE

My little sister Car Parts and her boyfriend, Golf Clubs, are out here visiting me. She's a vegetarian and he has bad ankles, so I've been trying to run him ragged—soccer, basketball, Ping-Pong . . . when I'm in Ohio we golf. Maybe we play cards.

Zante Pizza & Indian Cuisine
3489 Mission Street,
San Francisco. (415) 821-3949.
Lunch, dinner. Credit
cards accepted. Cheap.

They live in Ohio.

In other news, Crawdad de la Cooter and I have gone halfers on our very first mutually owned material possession, meaning we're pretty much committed for life, in my book, and everyone else can just back off.

Yep, for just one dollar apiece we picked us up a little sidewalk-sold foldaway crawdad trap, no pun intended. So alls we need now, you gotta figure, is some chicken necks and a river, and we're starin' down the recreational end of happily-ever-after.

As for the business end, well, so, yeah, what's that they say in that book about Man Not Living on Garlic Bread Alone, There Must Also Be Indian Restaurants, or something like that? Or, at any rate, restaurants—and then *someone*'s got to write them up, which is where I come in.

Hi.

The sister and her ankle-impaired man, they came in on Sunday after about a week or so on the road eating nothing but cheese sandwiches and metal shavings.

"What are you hungry for?" I said.

Golf Clubs pointed out that he either likes everything or doesn't like anything—I forget which.

"Italian food," said Car Parts.

So I took them to Can-Cun and Yamo that day, and then the next night for dinner we went to this divey-looking Italian restaurant I'd noticed a while back. It's called the Granada Cafe, and it's all the way out a ways on Mission Street. But Car Parts is a vegetarian, don't forget, and the only meatless dish on the menu was garlic bread. And seeing as how Neither Man Nor Little Sisters Live on so on and so on, as we've seen, well, we dogged 'em and hightailed it down the road to Zante.

Zante is that famous Indian pizza place. Meaning they've got Indian food, they've got pizza, and they've got Indian pizza. Three things. It's highly discovered, I realize, but I've kind of always wanted to eat there someday, and now that I have I can't help saying a few words about it:

The Indian food's great, the pizza sucks, and the Indian pizza's great. I know all this because there were three of us—one for each thing. See? So Car Parts, poor sister, she got her Italian food fix: two plain cheese slices and a salad; and Golf Clubs had himself his first-ever taste of Indian food: lamb *korma;* and I sampled Indian pizza for my first time ever.

Indian pizza has, let's see: lamb, chicken, prawns, spinach, eggplant, cauliflower, ginger, garlic, green onion, cilantro, and later that night Crawdad said she liked my cumin-breath, so I guess cumin. Sound good? Well, fuck you, it *is* good. Weirdo pizza, in my opinion, is the way to go when you're going for pizza in a pizza-dead town like this one.

I took one bite of my sister's regular old slice, and it was every bit as weak as anyone else's. (Interesting, because the Zante guy used to make pizzas in NYC. See? It's the water.)

As for Zante's Indian cuisine, the lamb *korma* was a smooth-ass bright yellow curry with big, tender chunks of lamb and thinly sliced almonds cooked in "a blend of tomatoes and spices." Delicious.

What else? Some basmati rice to go with the *korma,* and—oh yeah—beforehand an order of vegetable *pakora,* or fritters; and even before that, for free, they gave us a sheet of—I don't know—spicy cracker bread or something. All of which was fine and dandy, but especially the spicy cracker bread, which, combined with this super-zingy green salsa stuff, really made my head spin.

So, what with most everything on the menu going for six to nine bucks, this is a fairly dang cheap restaurant, especially considering Zante's award-winning popularity—which, believe me, they won't let you forget. They've got clippings all over the walls, menus, and even on some of the tables. It's deserved. They're great. See?

■ 49 CAFE

Whatever you do, don't go see this movie called *Ed's Next Move.* I'm not saying it's a bad movie (there isn't any food in it, so I'm not qualified to

49 Cafe
2650 Sloat Boulevard,
San Francisco. (415) 664-0476.
Lunch, dinner. Credit cards
accepted. Cheap cheap.

say); it's just that me and my band "occur" three times in the film and we look like complete goofballs.

I just got back from, you know, Hollywood, where we cringingly watched our out-of-context selves on the big silver screen, played a quick set at a postscreening party, hobnobbed with, you know, "industry," and then basically holed up at our paid-for motel, played cards by the pool, and tried our dangdest to per-diem Orion Films back into bankruptcy.

Do you know how hard it is for a guy like me to spend 50 bucks a day on food? Five to 10 bucks a meal—that's, what, 10 or five meals a day? Lucky for everyone, there was a great farmer's market place right across the street with tons of different kinds of cheap and great food: Cajun and California and meat pies and burgers and fries and this and that and the other thing, *urrrp,* "Can I have a receipt please?"

Well, it's good to be back home, back to the grind, so to speak, writing about a great little place called 49 Cafe, way out by the beach, by the zoo. On one block of Sloat, between 45th and 46th Avenues, there's this place, then another old-timey burger joint, Carousel, which makes a kick-ass blackberry milkshake, and then Leon's Barbecue. So it's sort of the Outer Sunset's red meat district. All three are great-looking and in their own way great places, but the 49 Cafe is the cheapest of the bunch. You'd have to eat there 25 times in 24 hours to use up your per diem. Yep, burger and fries for $1.99, but that's only a quarter-pounder, and I was only eating there once, so I ordered the Huge Hamburger Combo, which is a six-ouncer with fries, onion rings, and chicken nuggets.

I ate there on a pre–L.A. beach day with Little Brother Phenomenon, who showers with his clothes on. He ordered the gyros plate, which is basically one-and-a-half-sandwiches' worth of do-it-yourself gyro meat and pita and salad and sauce.

His stuff was better than mine. My burger wasn't bad, but the french fries were weak: small-cut cooked-to-death freezer fries. And I don't generally like onion rings, so I didn't like the onion rings, either. The chicken nuggets, on the other hand, were pretty good. I like chicken.

But sophisticated culinary analysis aside, the real reason to eat at the

49 is for the atmosphere. Or maybe you're a 49er fan. I'm assuming they show the games there, and if not, they should. There's a huge-screen TV that takes up almost all of the tiny dining room (just five wooden booths with red-and-white-checkered tablecloths). Then there's another small-screen TV in the first room, where you place takeout orders or sit at the counter.

By way of art, let's see, there were gyro posters and video games. Racks of *Auto Something-or-Other* magazine by way of reading material. And then, in the oddity department, there's the "Showroom," or rest room, which, according to the sign, you had to be 21 to enter.

Weird place. Oh yeah, when you first walk in, there's a big fish tank to your left, and one of the fishes in it has its brains on the outside of its head. I'm not kidding, it's a sight to see—except that the waitressperson insisted it wasn't an Inside-Out-Headed Goldfish so much as a "Big Hat Fish."

"What?" I said.

"Big Hat Fish," she said.

"If that's a hat," I said, "I'll eat my head."

"What?" she said.

And we left it at that.

■ BERLINER IMBISS

I've been craving sausage like a hole in the head hankers for a hat. My hat has a smiling Indian on it, even though no real Indians are smiling right now. Not only are their buffaloes and land all gone, but they're down two games to none to the fuckin' Baltimoron Oriassholes, even as we speak.

Berliner Imbiss
148 South Van Ness Avenue, San Francisco. (415) 487-0736. Lunch, dinner. Cheap cheap.

But my favorite Indians-hat story is the one where I let Yatee-Yatee-Bing-Eh-Eh-Eh borrow it one time and some Personal Computer person tells her she's offended by it and Yatee-Yatee goes:

"Why? Are you from Cincinnati?"

Which is doubly accidentally funny, see, because people from Cleveland don't even know about Cincinnati, let alone care. They're too busy hating Pittsburgh, which is more of a football thing than anything, a postseason Pirates-Indians matchup in any of our lifetimes being about as likely as the lion and the lamb getting together for coffee and a game of chess—which is why the Browns moving to Baltimore (not to mention the Indians losing to Baltimore) is going to fuck up our continent's climate almost as much as Columbus did. And now the hole in my head is big enough for two sausages.

Enter Berliner Imbiss, *stage left.* The Count *rushes to greet him and women and children holler "wally wally" as* Irving Berlin *breaks into song:*
"Picture this, if you dare . . .
A man with sausages for hair."
[Curtain]
Let's see: sports, theater, American history . . . oh, yeah—food!

I was turned on to Irving Berliner Imbiss by a pet chicken–having friend who was going on and on in a bar one night about sausage and sauerkraut and more sausage and, and . . .

"Wait a minute," I said. "I thought you were a vegetarian."

She smiled slyly and said, "I *was.*"

So I figured any place that could make *one of us* out of *one of them* was my kind of place. I put on my work clothes and went where she told me to go: down to that parking lot between Mission and South Van Ness, where the flea market is on Wednesdays and weekends.

Sure enough, it was my kind of place: just a little tiny orange and orange structure fenced into a corner of the lot with a couple of plastic outside tables, a couple of real ones, a three-stool counter, some nice decorative planter gardens, and a boom box in the window by way of music.

Get the picture? You're eating outside, or you're getting it to go. And what you're eating is not french fries with mayonnaise on them but authentic German-style sausages, maybe some kraut, with a few American concessions: hot dogs, hamburgers, grilled chicken. Stuff like that.

Seeing as how I have a garden now, I got the Farmer's Sausage, which is a fat, juicy, freshly grilled sausage with all the fixin's (tomato, onion, relish, hold the mayo, hold the mustard) in a roll so hard it'll make your lips bleed. Maybe it comes with sauerkraut, too, but they were out that day.

So I had to go back again the next day in order to try The Best

Sauerkraut I've Ever Eaten, No Lie. Due to traumatic childhood experiences, I've always thought of sauerkraut as shredded cabbage and onions boiled for four weeks in vinegar. Berliner Imbiss set me straight. Theirs is a subtle kraut cooked in chicken broth with actual chunks of pigmeat, and it just tastes right for a change.

More good news is I got to sample B.I.'s specialty, the Curry Wurst, which is two grilled farmer's sausages smothered in special-made curry ketchup and sprinkled with more curry powder. The roll's served on the side, for dipping, and it's much better that way 'cause no one gets hurt.

This Curry Wurst, as I understand it, is exclusive even in Germany to Berlin. The Imbiss guy claims no one else in this country or even in that one makes it. He lived in Berlin for six years. That's how he learned to do it.

So happens my baby's in Germany right now, all week, on bidness. But she's in Frankfurt, so I guess she won't be able to bring me home no Berlin Curry Wurst for the sake of comparison. But she did leave a long, boner-inspiring message on my machine yesterday, mostly just describing huge trays of steaming sausages every morning at breakfast. She might've also mentioned missing me. I don't remember.

■ GOLDEN GATE PIZZA

Oof. What a day. Some people are good and gracious losers, but not me. I take it hard, whether it's cards or money or baseball or football or life. Losing makes me want to hit people or cry, and I'm too small and old for either of those activities, so all that was left after the Indians got bonked out of the play-offs was to take a four-hour nap. Which is just what I took.

Golden Gate Pizza
4038 Judah Street, San Francisco. (415) 564-5514. Lunch, dinner. Credit cards accepted. Cheap.

Dreamed the big two, sex and sports, and then woke up all shit-brained and particleboard-tongued right around dinnertime. My little brother Phenomenon and his L.A. pal Pobadaboobidy Luke were talking Yamo Thai Kitchen, which is normally my language, but I needed something new. So I made them come with me instead to Golden Gate Pizza, all the way out in the Sunset, Judah and 46th. And now here I am, up late, writing about it.

The boys are out drinking. Hi, I'm Dan. I eat.

Someone wrote to me about Golden Gate Pizza, or else how else would I have known to go there? Judah and 46th ain't exactly my stomping grounds. Like elephants, though, I'll go where the pickin's is. I don't care. Especially when the pickin's is Indian food and barbecue and, yeah, pizza and pasta and even hamburgers and french fries. It's kind of like Zante plus, in other words—or Zante minus, in the sense that GGP isn't nearly as discovered or award-winning as Zante.

Well, I'm here to tell you that, awards shmawards, Golden Gate Pizza is every bit as good as Zante, far as I can tell.

It's right next door to a Laundromat, for one thing. You have to go down a little ramp to get there, and then the moment you walk in the door it hits you in the face like a soccer ball: the distinctive yet smashed together cornucopiac smells of pizza, barbecue, and curry.

That and the sound of television. They've got a big one blaring there on one of the two tile-top counters you can eat at. Then there're glass-topped tables with paper place mats underneath, and your choice of cloth or paper napkins. In other words: not a particularly focused place. But focus, unlike winning, isn't everything.

Phenomenon ordered lamb curry, which comes with a huge plate of rice, and, yeah, it was good. I tasted it.

I also had a slice-and-a-half taste of Pobadaboobidy's "hot spicy chicken pizza," which is business-meaning pizza. The chicken itself is marinated in something hot and spicy, but the real kick comes from some badass seranno chile peppers. Then there're green onions, cilantro, tomatoes, and a little too much mozzarella.

Cilantro?

Yep. In fact, there was cilantro on everything, and that means everything was great—even the spaghetti and the vegetables that came with my ribs. I couldn't believe it. The spaghetti looked like run-of-the-mill (i.e., bad) side-order pasta, but it was something else entirely. The sauce was only halfway concessional to Italianism, with Indianic spices predominating flavorically. And cilantro.

The vegetables—cauliflower, broccoli, carrot, potato—were surprisingly tasty, too. I believe they were grilled instead of steamed.

The ribs themselves were smothered in a delicious, smoky barbecue sauce and sprinkled with—you guessed it—cilantro. Woohoo! Snapped me right out of my funkiness, in fact, and hopefully we set our waiter-guyperson straight by cleaning our plates—all six or seven of them. He'd tried to tell us we were ordering too much food, and that was before *I* even ordered. I mean, it was only about a two-person pizza, so it's not like we were eating for more than four.

What all we didn't get was burgers or fries or meatball sandwiches, pizza sandwiches, sausage sandwiches, or vegetarian sandwiches. They also have standard pasta dishes ($6 to $8), chicken you-name-it ($8 to $9), seafood stuff, calzones, salads . . .

I know what you're thinking. That's too much. They can't possibly do it all right. Maybe not, but everything we ate was pretty damned good. I think why is 'cause they don't try and make barbecue like Brother-in-Laws', or pasta like mine, or pizza like I-don't-know-whose. Like Frank, they simply do it their way. And their way, like his, simply works.

■ KENTUCKY FRIED CHICKEN

Me and Wayway stopped at KFC on our way to pal Tinzee's house for Monday Night Football. It was five-to-six when we placed our order: two of those eight-piece dark-meat specials with corn and biscuits, one of those chicken potpies, and smashed taters and gravy.

> Kentucky Fried Chicken
> Everywhere.

Tick tick tick . . .

At six o'clock we were deep-grease diving to the tunelessness of Hank Jr., making a mess out of Tinzee's otherwise neat and clean bachelorette pad. And that right there is the singular beauty of fast food: It's fast.

And it's a singular beauty, all right, because the chicken itself was just awful. Soggy-crusted old-ass tastelessness. Not that I didn't scarf down about four or five pieces—but if this is really the Colonel's original recipe, why, he ought to be ashamed of himself, if not executed.

Hey, I've been to Kentucky. I've eaten Ma Kelly's in Richmond, and someone else's in Lexington, for example.

Never mind Kentucky—I've been to Popeye's on Divisadero, for crying out loud, and their chicken's 10 times better than KFC's.

I have to admit, though, I do like the smell of Kentucky Fried. I go by that one on Valencia and Hill, and I don't mind lingering. It's tempting. What can I say?

Plus Wayway said he'd eaten there recently and it was surprisingly good—especially the potpies. As for the chicken itself, he pleaded "inconsistency" and he had a point: the second box was much better than the first. But that doesn't explain the pie, which I'd been led to believe wasn't bad.

Yeah it was. The crust was tough as a linebacker, and it was only on the top. I don't like that. I realize a lot of real restaurants pull the same shit, but that doesn't make it right. Pie is pie. Put a crust all the way around it.

And you may as well make it taste like something inside, too. Sure, there were real chunks of actual chicken in there, but the carrots and taters were mushed to death, and the gravy tasted entirely unseasoned. And where were the peas?

As for the corn, KFC deserves some sort of an award for presentational weirdness. It comes on the cob, cut in half and sucker-sticked, then wrapped in this yellow plastic bag with a twistie-tie around the neck. I expected it to be adhesive—you know how old corn gets with your teeth—but it wasn't. It was just plastic-wrapped cornfulness, choked and suffocated. Mmmm.

The biscuits were all right, and the smashed taters, I'll admit, were actually good, thanks largely to loads of rich, dark gravy—so much more flavorful than the lighter style that . . .

"Whoa, whoa, wait just a cotton-pickin' minute there, Danny Boy. Is this what we think it is: an actual review of Kentucky Fried Chicken?"

No. Of course not. Would I stoop so low?

[Crickets.]

Well, yeah, you're right. I would. But that's not what it is at all. I just wanted to do things a little differently, for the sake of variety, so I figured I'd ramble on a long time about food before finally getting to the point: sports.

The 49ers. Football. My internal sports-clock-calendar hasn't gotten accustomed to this October baseball thing, I don't think, and for two years running now I haven't been able to give my undivided attention to the 49ers until halfway through their schedule. So if we don't go all the way this year, don't blame Steve Young.

Don't blame Wayway. He's spent as much time in the little film room behind his eyes as any coach or player or scout. It's me who's been neglecting my fanly obligations. Hell, I blew whole workweeks working out whether I should wear the blue or the red Indians cap, or no cap at all, not to mention what to eat during the games, where to spit my seeds, and how to act in general. Come Sunday I had one eye on the Niners and both of the other ones on the Tribe.

Now, I don't mean to overdelusionate or anything, because I realize my juju is no more than 35 to 40 percent responsible for whether the 49ers win or lose. Wayway's armchair play-calling also figures big. And then there're miscellaneous variables like player talent, performance, coaching, and biorhythms to be considered. So it's not *all* my fault is what I'm getting at.

But it's largely my fault, and I'm sorry, and I promise, now that baseball is over for me, to make it up to you. For the rest of the football season, starting now, I'm going to pull out all the stops: power juju, reverse juju, double-reverse juju, and even, if necessary, flea-flicker juju. And we'll see if we can't show these goddang Pukers and Cowsissypersons what's what.

■ THAI DISHES

Man oh man, Robert Johnson's singing me some blues right now and Crawdad's in her kitchen cooking up some crawdad étouffée for dinner. Friday night. Weirdo the Cat. Friends. Does it get any better than this?

> **Thai Dishes**
> 1700 Shattuck Avenue, Berkeley.
> (510) 549-0611. Lunch, dinner.
> Credit cards accepted. Cheap.

Yes. Ohio Boy Binko sent me the shirt of a lifetime, for practically no reason! It's an old-time Indians shirt, Bob Feller, No. 19, and it's the most beautiful shirt I've ever owned. I wore it to lunch today with my old-timer pitchin' pal, Satchel Paige the Pitcher. He used to throw for the Indians too, you know, but now he works on the grounds crew at U.C. Berkeley.

In between mowing the infield and raking the warning track (him) and writing restaurant reviews (me), we took a lunch break together and tried to rehash the good old days. The problem is neither one of us was around back then, so the rehashing was shortlived. Plus we had a lot of eating to cram in, 'cause Satch only had an hour and we were at this big-food Thai place over there in Berkeley. It was the first time in my rememberable life I was worried about spilling something on my shirt. Usually I use my shirt as a napkin, but *that's* how great of a shirt this one is.

Thai food. Big food. Great new shirt. Does it get any better than this? Yes. Only $5.95 for a pick-four-things combo lunch special. But you gotta go on weekdays at lunchtime, 'cause otherwise you're going to have to pay regular Thai food prices ($6 to $10) for just one serving of one thing. And I can't vouch for the worthwhilebility of that.

Combo lunch special, on the other hand? Hell, yeah—vouch city.

Let's see, we must've picked eight things between the two of us. There was *pad seeyou*, flat noodles cooked with broccoli and egg in some "black sweet sauce" that wasn't too sweet, thankfully. In fact, this was probably my favorite dish.

My second favorite was either the stir-fried mixed vegetables, which was pretty dang good in spite of its meatlessness, or the *kang ped*—chicken with peas, carrots, and bamboo shoots in a delicious red coconut curry. My only problem with this dish was that it was frighteningly soupy, which wouldn't normally concern me, but what with the shirt…Then there was the yellow curry fried rice with peas and carrots and tomato and green onion. That was all right, but the yellow curry wasn't cutting through quite enough, which leaves you with fried rice—ho hum. The only thing I flat-out didn't like was the barbecued chicken with garlic sauce. It was dry and weird.

What else? There was soup—silver noodle, with lots of cabbage and onions. That was pretty good.

But I'm saving the best for last, and it doesn't have anything to do with food, exactly. It has to do with the no-back bench seats at some of the tables at Thai Dishes. There's one long, comfy cushion that culminates in a built-in triangular back-leaning area, so that you can actually lie down after your meal!

Does it get any better than that? No. Goodnight.

■ ATLAS CAFE

Sunday one of my friends all the way down the bay, Dave, he called me up with a problem. Him and his Mountain Viewing pals were throwing together a little barbecue, see, and instead of some people taking care of this (i.e., chips) and some taking care of that (i.e., chips)—the way these things normally go—everyone this time brought chicken.

Atlas Cafe
3049 20th Street,
San Francisco. (415) 648-1047.
Breakfast, lunch, dinner. Cheap.

"I'm serious," Dave said to me over the phone. "We've got about a hundred pounds of chicken."

"Are you serious?" I said.

"Yeah."

"Well, you called the right person," I said. "Just try and keep everyone calm until I get there." That's what I said, but I was shaking like Katharine Hepburn doing an end-zone dance while I wrote down the directions, and, as a result, I wound up at the wrong barbecue, talking to some old guys in golf shirts and penny loafers.

"I'm a friend of Dave's," I said, shaking hands and showing my credentials. "I understand you have a problem, and I'm here to help."

They said, "Dave?"

So then I found the right barbecue just around the corner of the same house, and sure enough there were about a hundred pounds of chicken. Some of it was South Korean–style fried chicken and some was Mystery Chicken, and while we got to work on those two kinds, the rest went grillward for later. So that's three kinds of chicken. I never ate three kinds of chicken in one sitting before, I don't think. And get this: All of it was dark meat! Legs and thighs—not a breast in the bunch. A hundred pounds. *Yodel-eh-hee-hoo!*

Let's see, a hundred pounds of chicken divided by roughly 10 people comes to roughly 10 to 12 pounds per person, I figure. Which isn't to say that we finished it all. Which isn't to say I didn't carry my weight, maybe even someone else's. I believe I ate about 15, 20 pounds of food that night . . . all of which leads me, at long last, to the point I've been trying to get at:

I ain't been hungry ever since. In fact, Monday, if I remember right, I didn't eat at all so much as I stayed under my Ping-Pong table and twitched. So now would be as good a time as any to review a coffeehouse. See, there's this new one called the Atlas Cafe that some friends have been trying to get me to review.

"I don't review coffeehouses," I said. "I'm a *restaurant* reviewer."

"Three words, Danny Boy: K, F, and C."

"OK, good point," I said, although in retrospect none of those words are exactly words, in my opinion. "I'll be right there."

So there I was, nibbling on a Cuban-style beef sandwich with the Kid—that's Kid Coyote to you. The sandwich is a long, skinny baguette with beef in it, some yellow cheese, tomatoes if they got 'em (which they didn't that day), and pesto and vinaigrette. And a handful of salad (just lettuce and onions).

We chose to sit at one of the couches and we had our food on the coffee table and our reading material under our food and somehow I did something wrong and spilled my whole plate—just turned it right over onto the floor.

I managed to salvage a couple leafs of lettuce off my shoe top. The second half of the sandwich I just picked up, brushed off, and finished. It was pretty good. I can't say it was as great as the Kid had made it out to be, but it was good. And it's a good amount of food, for the price, especially if you don't spill half of it.

The pizza's not bad, either, for coffeehouse pizza. I don't believe they make it there—it didn't taste like premises-made pizza dough—but at least the toppings are fresh. The Kid got a pesto pizza with artichoke hearts. The only other topping choice I remember was salami. I'm sure there were more.

It's a good idea, though, don't you think? Even if you can't make real pizzas, being a coffeehouse, that doesn't mean you can't throw some real ingredients on top of it before it goes in the toaster oven (or wherever it goes). I didn't have my ruler with me, but it seemed like a right-size pizza for one person.

As for the salad, I didn't get to eat enough to know what to say, so I think I just won't say anything.

[Crickets.]

▮ EL POLLO SUPREMO

Speaking of chickens, there's El Pollo Supremo on 24th and Folsom, where you can stand in the window and watch whole piles of them on the grill, doing what chickens do best: sizzlin'.

What a great marketing scheme, to cook your chickens in the window like that. I mean, I've seen about a million of these plasticky-looking chicken-based cafeterias around town—Chicken Coop, Chick 'N' Coop, Chick and Coop, Chick or Coop, Chicken Mart, Wal-Chicken— you know what I'm talking about. You see them all over the place, but you never go in 'cause they look like cheesy fast-food joints. Am I right?

El Pollo Supremo
2801 Folsom Street,
San Francisco. (415) 550-1193.
Lunch, dinner. Cheap cheap.

For example, I've seen El Pollo Supremo many, many times (it's the one with the muscle-chicken logo), but I was always on the burrito side of the street, or else on my bike. It never occurred to me to eat there, and it never would have occurred to me except that I happened to park in front of it one night on my way to check out some other restaurant down the block.

When I went past that window and saw what I saw, man, my knees went weak at the knees. It's a wonder I made it to the other restaurant, but I was with friends, including my girlfriendperson, and a date's a date, in my book, no matter how many chickens are cookin' in a window.

How many?

Oh, I don't know, 67, 68 chickens, give or take about 50.

Which makes you wonder. Between all the millions of KFCs and hundreds of thousands of these kinds of places and Popeye's and Brother-in-Laws and so on . . . and then you multiply all those mind-boggling numbers by the outrageous number of chickens each one of them must be the death of in any given day . . .

Say—whatever happened to Carl Sagan anyway? If he's still around, I wouldn't mind seeing him do a PBS series on chickens, just to hear his turtlenecked self spittin' out something sweet about "zillions and zillions of chickens."

I don't know how everyone else feels about the mass production and general dehumanization of filler-fed no-range birdies, but it makes me proud to be human. I mean, take foxes. They're pretty smart, and they like chicken too, but it would never have occurred to them to make one lousy chain—say, Popeye's—let alone an entire chicken industry.

But enough econobiophilosophizing. Let's get down to the bidness of just how good El Pollo Supremo's pollos really are: Pretty goddamn fuckin' good. I know 'cause I went back to find out two days later.

The sign outside advertises "super delicious charbroiled chicken," and that's exactly what you get, and that's *all* you get. Sure, they've got lots of sides, like salads and beans and french fries and so on, but you can't get a burger or a burrito or a veggie burger. You can't even get a chicken sandwich or fried chicken. One thing: super delicious charbroiled chicken.

They have several daily combination specials wherein, if you play your cards right, you can wind up with half a chicken's worth of chicken plus one or two sides and a drink for under five bucks.

I got a dark-meat quarter-chicken 'cause it was only a late-afternoon snack and I wanted to try a couple different side-order things. I tried *yucca frita,* which was delicious, and Spanish rice, which was nothing special, but fine.

The chicken comes with four foil-wrapped steaming hot corn tortillas and a small plastic thing of excellent salsa, which was great with the chicken but more appropriate with the *yucca frita,* I think. The chicken's got so much flavor already, you almost don't want to mess with it. It's perfectly seasoned, perfectly cooked, with a flame-licked saltiness that'll make your ears twitch.

As always, the skin is the best part, but the remarkable thing about El Pollo Supremo is that the meat itself packs a mean punch all the way down to the bone—so you know they're doing something right marinationally.

Atmospherically, EPS features a plastic, fluorescently lit fast-food interior, as you'd expect. But the chairs, at least, are comfortable, and there's a row of small flags on the counter between the two ordering stations, representing the fact that people and chickens of all nations ought to love one another and try and get along and shit.

■ MISSION VILLA

Mission Villa is the oldest Mexican restaurant in San Francisco. It's 90 years old. That's old. That's older than Grandma Rubino, but it's doing a lot better than her, I think. It has a new menu with interesting new dishes to complement the standard traditional fare, whereas Grandma Rubino falls down a lot.

Mission Villa
2391 Mission Street, San Francisco. (415) 826-0454. Lunch, dinner. Credit cards accepted. Cheap.

I hope Grandma's still kicking by the time I hit Ohio, Thanksgiving Day. She's my favorite and only living grandparent, but she's got some sort of an intestinal tumor, goddamn it, and she's fading fast.

I'm pretty sure Mission Villa, on the other hand, will still be here by the time I get back. It was the first non-taqueria Mexican restaurant I ate at when I came here pert near seven years ago. I ate there just the other night and it was better than ever—although technically, I guess, I can't vouch for the first 83 years.

Me and Crawdad and Wayway and Tinzee were going to check out this Peruvian place on Mission near 20th. Never having been to Peruvia, I was curious to see how they eat there. Well, the food on the menu looked good, but the numbers were all wrong—nines and 10s. Elevens. That ain't cheap eats. So I did my little "this ain't cheap eats" dance and convinced everyone to cross the street with me to Mission Villa, where I wound up spending $8.75.

What's that you say?

Yeah, I know, but here's the difference: $8.75 would've been about the cheapest thing on the menu across the street. At Mission Villa, it was splurge city. I don't mind spending 10 bucks on dinner, so long as I'm spending it at a place where it's at least possible to eat for half that amount.

Mission Villa still has its famous combo plates for three, five, seven bucks, depending on how many items you want with your rice, refrieds, and salad. What you're choosing from, so you know, are enchiladas, tacos, tostadas, *chile rellenos*, burritos, and tamales.

Now you can get a one-item lunch special (with rice, beans, and tortillas, of course) or *pollo frito* with fries and salad for under $5.

But—alas—it wasn't lunchtime, so I went with the *biftec à la mexicana* ($8.75). It sounded like my cup of tea, exactly: sirloin steak simmered in a Mexican-style tomato-onion-green pepper sauce. With rice, refrieds, salad, and tortillas, of course.

First of all, on the subject of small details, points to Mission Villa for coughing up the butter off the bat. (Most Mexican restaurants make you ask.) More points for not putting anything yucky (like sour cream) on the salad—just a dollop of good red salsa, which is all it really needs. Speaking of which: good keep-'em-coming chips and thin, red, very hot salsa.

As for the meal of the meal, the rice and refrieds are so flavorful on their own, you know these aren't no no-lard new-Mission concessionary rice and beans, no sir. And the meat is all that you want meat to be: tender and juicy and every bit as tasty as the next cow.

It was $8.75 well spent, and I was so full afterward I didn't *need* to clean up Crawdad's plate for her. But I did. She'd had red snapper, which came with french fries, oddly, as well as the rice and beans and so on. The fries were fresh-cut and greasefully delicious, and the fish was fine.

Wayway had a pretty cool thing: the "Pancho Villa" plate, which is two beef enchiladas with sunny-side-up eggs on top, not to mention so on and so forth.

'Spherically speaking . . . well, some places are considered "homey"— Mission Villa I'd have to describe as "towney." Main Street runs through the center of the restaurant. Along both sides are rows of real nice wooden booths with bullfighter paintings and coat hooks, further cozified by indoor Spanish-style roofs overhead, slanting down toward the street for better drainage.

In the back, against the kitchen wall, is "town square," a huge round table where the villagers gather on weekend evenings to talk sheep.

■ ECONOMY CAFE

Economy Chop Suey has been on my list of places to check out for three years. It's been on the list for so long that its name isn't Economy Chop Suey anymore. It's Economy Cafe, and it's been remodeled and everything.

The prices have gone up, according to my econoguide E. B. Matt, who

Economy Cafe
399 Eighth Street, Oakland.
(510) 832-9886. Lunch, dinner.
Cheap cheap.

met me for lunch during his lunch break. Temp job, downtown Oakland. That's where this place is, Eighth and Franklin. The prices have gone up, but the name still applies. You'll be hard-pressed to spend more than four bucks at Economy Cafe. The most expensive thing on the menu, I think, is the very first item listed: shrimp and lobster sauce on rice—$4.50.

That's what E. B. got. He's a big spender. I had ginger beef on rice for $3.75. And these are no dinky plates of food, either. I'll tell you what, I showed up 10 minutes early by accident, and I figured I'd go in, sit down, and eat a little something, then eat a little something else after E. B. joined me.

Forget it. There's no such thing as "a little something" at Economy. They don't even have egg rolls. I saw rice dishes, bowls of soup, chow meins, noodle dishes, and fried rices, and they were each and every one of them big enough to feed a small army, or at least a big soldier. Even the soup.

At one o'clock exactly I went ahead and ordered, E. B. being officially late. Plus I'm a slow eater. Plus I was as hungry as a small army. I was sitting at the counter, which is definitely the place to sit. They've got tables too, but they're kind of cramped and boring. The counter seats are comfy, thickly cushioned back-having swivelers (pre-remodeling, I think, because they seemed pretty torn up) with a front-row view of the action: four big woks and one stone-faced wok-man working 'em.

It's a pretty amazing setup, really: the woks, a huge center-stage cauldron of water or oil or broth, two long-neck water faucets. In front there's a four-square container with I figure salt and MSG and soy sauce and something else. And in back there's a little trough for runoff.

The restaurant is bustling and very noisy for such a tiny place, but it's a tight ship at the wok station. Efficient use of space, no wasted motion . . . things move quickly. I thought I was watching, but I didn't even see my food happen until it was suddenly in front of me:

A huge pile of steamed rice with tender slices of beef, onions, and not quite exactly enough ginger in a good, goopy gravy. I compensated for the gingerical deficiency with a few squirts of Red Devil cayenne pepper sauce.

E. B. came along just a couple bites into it and ordered his shrimp-and-lobster-sauce thing, which was, if possible, an even bigger pile of food than mine. I had to help him finish it.

Economy Cafe has some of the biggest and cheapest Chinese food either side of the bay, and at least two of their 70, 80 selections taste pretty darned good, too.

If you've got room for dessert—which you won't—check out Westlake Beef Jerky a few doors down, Franklin near Seventh.

▌ THE BARKING BASSET CAFE

I don't think I ever reviewed a restaurant in Bernal Heights. Did I? I don't think so. I ate at the Liberty Cafe once when my pal Last Straw used to work there, and it was pretty good, sure, but I don't think that I ever wrote about it. I don't know why. Maybe it was a little not-cheap-enough for me.

The Barking Basset Cafe
803 Cortland Avenue,
San Francisco. (415) 648-2146.
Breakfast, lunch, dinner. Cheap.

Last Straw got married and now she and her guy are out there doing what I'll be doing by the time you read this: driving around the country in a car. I don't pretend to know what they're eating right about now, but I can tell you I'll be living on truck-stop chicken-fried steak and smashed taters, iceberg lettuce, and bad coffee. Yeehaw!

Before I go, I think I better review a Bernal Heights restaurant so that I can say I did, before I went. Let's see, how about the Barking Basset Cafe up the hill a ways on Cortland? It's a real five-star head-scratcher, this place, but I'm going to write about it anyway, to prove a point.

Scratch scratch scratch.

Well, I'm sorry, I don't know what to say. Barking Basset is one of the weirdest places I've ever eaten at, and not just because they put cottage cheese in their pancakes. I almost didn't go in, in fact, because from outside it looked sort of fancy. I was looking at the menu on the window and I was seeing a lot of vinaigrettes and Gorgonzola and capers and avocado and goat cheese and steamed apples and crème fraîche, for crying out loud. But then, the prices were decent—$4 to $6 for breakfast, $4 to $7 for lunch. And what appeared to be tablecloths from outside turned out to be white plastic inside. Yay!

I can't say for certain, because I don't have a very good grasp on the true nature of fancy food, but I believe what we might have here is the world's first-ever fancy-food dive. The Barking Basset Cafe. It's got nice-looking splotchy yellow painted walls with cushioned wooden bench seats all along two of them. But then it's also got an ugly-ass worn carpet with lots of crumbs and stuff on it. For art: futuristic dark dreamy world paintings, like potential sci-fi novel covers. Then there's the "permanent collection" doofus dog painting, like a potential month-o-May doggie calendar shot.

Clientele? Let's see, you've got your nerdy Bernal Heights business children, but you've also got the woman across the room from me in a neato astronaut suit, boots included, reading what must have been a fairly sad book, 'cause she'd brought along her own box of Kleenex.

See what I mean?

No? Me neither. Well, let me put it in food terms for you:

You can order a tuna sandwich with capers, peppers, roasted tomatoes, and olive oil along with a goat cheese, apples, and walnuts salad with citrus vinaigrette . . . or you can have a "hot dog sandwich" with french fries.

Me, I got the cottage cheese pancakes, partly because I had to know, and partly because that's the only kind of pancakes they have. You can get 'em with strawberries and crème fraîche, so—what the hell?—I did.

It was lunchtime, but I hadn't had breakfast yet, either. My plan was to have the cakes for breakfast and then try a burger or something for lunch, but the good news for Barking Basset is that I, Dan Leone, was too full to eat anything after my pancakes.

The bad news is that now I can't tell you about the burgers.

The no news is that I don't even know what to say about the freakin' pancakes. Sometimes I liked them and sometimes I didn't. When I did, I was rather enjoying the delicate, surprisingly salty meltedness at the heart of each bite, dancing its cheesy dance with the sweetness of the syrup and strawberries outside. When I didn't, I was thinking: What the fuck is this fuckin' cottage cheese shit doing in here?

For the sake of future generations, I did ask after the burgers. They're five-ouncers—"really good meat," according to my waiterguyperson. Five ounces is pretty small, but I saw the french fries and they were big and fresh-cut and very good looking.

I honestly don't know whether you'd like the Barking Basset or not, but if you're in my ripped-up, worn-out shoes . . . well, let's just say you're a cheap eater, like me, with a taste for fine California-style dining, like someone else, but without the funding to back it, like me. My bet is the Basset'd be worth a try.

■ ALL-NIGHTERS

If I had a nickel for every time I heard someone complain about San Francisco's late-night eating scene, I'd probably have around 35 cents. (As it turns out, I do have 35 cents, but that's not how I got it.)

For my money, the best time of day is the middle of the night. It's quiet, it's all yours, and you can pretty much do whatever you want, like stalking around the apartment in cowboy clothes, shooting fruit flies with a squirt gun.

If you're anything like me, however, you can only take so much peace and quiet and horseplay before you start wanting a hamburger. You never know when the urge is going to strike, and that's why we need 24-hour restaurants in the world.

I complained along with everyone else, to tell the truth, and then I decided to do something about it. I knew they must be out there, so I set out to find them. And I only found one place that I really loved. There were bright spots, sure—a cheap burger here and a cool place there—but the majority of all-nighters were problematic at best. I'm glad I did the research, though, because now at least I know what we're all complaining about. Here are the five best:

Orphan Andy's (3991 17th Street, San Francisco; 415/864-9795). Someone told me I probably wouldn't like this place and they were as wrong as Ponce de León. In fact, Orphan Andy's was easily my favorite all-night establishment and the only one I look forward to revisiting, partly because I forgot to have french fries. The thing that distracted me was a breakfast special: two eggs, two pancakes, two sausages, two bacons.

I'm a sucker for symmetry.

I wish I could say it was 2 a.m. but I can't, 'cause it was 4:30 a.m. I sat at the counter, right in front of the sink where they wash the dishes. At first I was concerned that suds would get in my coffee, which was bad to begin with, and I was thinking of moving down a few stools when the dishwasher said she liked my glasses—so I stayed.

Then the food came and the fun began. My meal and I played a little game of Noah's Ark—only instead of all the water there was coffee.

Later, while the two-of-everythings were settling in and the caffeine was just starting to speak to me, I had even more fun listening to the dishwasher trying to talk some guy into going to sleep.

"I used to think sleeping was a boring thing to do and a waste of time," she said, "but now I can't live without it."

Even without that comment, this would have been a thoroughly enjoyable experience. Orphan Andy's is a fun and friendly little place, and everything was great except for the coffee—and that comes for free with the special, so who's complaining?

Silver Crest (340 Bayshore Boulevard, San Francisco; 415/826-0753). This is an excellent dive that does not quite realize its potential. From the outside, it looks like (and probably is) the most untrendy place in town. Inside, too, it's the closest I've seen to a real "greasy spoon." The atmosphere is totally unaffected.

Bad food, bad coffee, great place.

There are a few booths, but most of the seating is at a long light-blue counter that is U-shaped, so you don't need the mirror trick in order to spy on people. Open windows on one wall present a nice view of the attached bar, where, I would imagine, fights and other interesting things happen. An adjoining wall features a lineup of weird games that are not video games or slot machines or pinball—I don't know what they are. And on the little tiny jukeboxes, every other song is generically called "Greek Record."

I got ham and eggs. The ham was dry, the eggs were weird, the toast was good, and the frozen potatoes were surrealistically greasy. All of this would have been perfect, if only the price was right. But it was $5.95, and everything—even the toast—was small. I could have made the same meal for about 43 cents, and I'm not a restaurant.

Although everything's at least a dollar more than it should be, the place is too great, atmospherically, to pass up. Next time you're feeling sick of trendy restaurants and/or pretentious people, go hang out for a while at the Silver Crest. But don't bother with the food.

Just have a cup of coffee. Maybe a donut.

Pine Crest Diner (401 Geary Boulevard, San Francisco; 415/885-6407). Speaking of expensive . . . here's a downtown diner that is also a great place, but even more overpriced. Get this: Two-egg breakfasts go for over $5, before meat. Omelettes are more like nine! Dinners are over 10. This is not gourmet cuisine, either, folks; it's diner food. I've seen it. I've eaten it.

There is one thing on the menu that is actually a good buy, however, and the trick is to find it and get it. Hint: the half-pound hamburger, for $4.95.

I had a stomachache the night I did the Pine Crest, so instead of the burger I got one of them there gyros (pronounced "gyros") It's a bunch of lamb and cow meat shaved off of some big thing and slapped in pita bread with tomatoes and onions, hold the sauce, thank you.

It was delicious, and just right for a stomachache.

Sparky's (242 Church Street, San Francisco; 415/626-8666). This is the only place I ate at during the day. I tried to go there one night around 4 a.m. but—get this—the kitchen was closed. (That's bad.)

To punish Sparky, I wasn't going to go back, but it's the closest all-night place to my house, and I wound up eating there one day for breakfastlunch.

"Breakfastlunch?"

Yeah. I've always been uncomfortable with the concept of brunch, because it seems wasteful and unhealthy to just toss out "eakfastl." What if that's the part with the sausage links?

So for breakfastlunch I had breakfast (pancakes and eggs) and lunch (pork chops and spicy fries). The cakes were fat and good, but the best part was the spicy fries. The damage: roughly 10 bucks, before coffee.

The place itself is a bit slick for my taste: very clean and black and white, with mirrors on all the walls, so you can watch other people eating from many different angles. There was one guy who was the opposite of me, so I watched him. He ate his sandwich with a fork. (I was eating pork chops with my hands.) And he didn't clean his plate! Also: He was wearing his clothes, and I was wearing mine.

Some people . . .

Lucky Penny Restaurant (2670 Geary Boulevard, San Francisco; 415/921-0836). I don't know if this is called the Lucky Penny or the Copper Penny or both. It says different things in different places. Anyway, its best feature is its counter, which is bright red and embedded with pennies. I don't know if they're supposed to be lucky or copper or both—but there they are, and at 3:30 in the morning I'm easily amused.

I went there the night after a couple friends had expressed concern over my health. I was going to die, they implied, if I kept eating eggs and red meat in the middle of the night, not to mention three times, give or take a time, during the day. I didn't think I was going to die, but I promised I would get a salad as well next time out.

As it happened, I wasn't very hungry anyway, so that's all I got was a salad. I got a chef's salad, which consisted of separate piles of ham and cheese, several stacks of tomatoes, a few carrots, both kinds of pickles, and eggs. Somewhere underneath it all was a big bed of uncut iceberg lettuce, which was impossible to get at until the end.

What can you say about a salad? Well, for one thing, the turkey was conspicuously missing, although the menu had promised it. And one piece of lettuce had some white stuff on the back of it, which I chose to interpret as egg residue, or paint. Other than that, everything tasted like what it was.

The coffee, on the other hand, had the distinct flavor of a roller coaster—one of the old wooden ones that throws you around.

The salad and the coffee came to something like seven bucks. I don't know, but that seems a little steep to me. On the other hand, a guy at the end of the counter was musing philosophically over French toast, and it was worth maybe a buck-fifty to overhear him ask himself: "Why not Chinese toast? Or Italian toast? Why *French?* Why french fries? Why not Hawaiian fries?"

His next question—"How do you know white is actually white?"—was too deep even for me, and I had to leave.

■ ROCCO'S CAFE

Jesus Louise-us, you turn your back for three lousy months on the eat-in'est place this side of News Orleans and York put together, and next thing you know it's the McDonald's Capital of the World. Am I off my

Rocco's Cafe
1131 Folsom Street,
San Francisco. (415) 554-0522.
Breakfast, lunch, dinner.
Credit cards accepted. Cheap.

rocker or are there about 41 brand stinkin' new McDoodoo's around town these days? I personally counted two of them, and I've only been back about a week. And I

haven't been out or about much either.

So my question is this: What the fuck?

And what's this I hear about Ask Isadora implying in print that I was cute? Yes, that would be me running down Valencia, flapping my arms and going, "I'be cude, I'be cude! She said I'be cuuuuude!" Splat.

Now that I've quoted a reindeer, I may as well come right out and tell you that my unscrupulous van, Rocco, is motorically rebuilt and back in action (so watch your step, sidewalkers), and that Rocco's Cafe, on the other hand, is a damn good, friendly, atmospherically fun place to eat, even if it ain't exactly cheap at dinnertime, which only happens on Thursdays and Fridays. Let's put it this way: seven to 12 smackers for entrées, which, for Italian food, ain't bad.

The good news is: gigantic portions of really great grub, and if you want to go for breakfast or lunch, I'll even buy, because everything's a couple bucks cheaper. Wayway, for example, swears by Rocco's breakfasts, and it's true you can come away with a standard two-egger under your belt for under four bucks. Plus they've got Rocco's Favorite Frittata (with sausage, maters, onion, basil, and cheese) for something like six.

The lunch menu is pretty much all the same stuff as dinner, only cheaper. I don't know if the portions are the same or not, but I'll tell you what: I wouldn't mind finding out.

I had a great time at Rocco's one night with a party of four, half of us already drunk and the other half getting there—except for me, I mean, being on duty. Let's see, there was Seattle-bound (sniff) Sorority Girl, who ordered homemade ice, if I remember right. Then there was Tinzee with her great meatball sandwich and weakish "spiced" french fries. And then Crawdad de la Cooter, she got calamari sauté, which she enjoyed very much, although I would have had it over a big pile of linguine if I were her.

Me? I'm saving the best for last: chicken parmigiana. That's a whole big plate full of white-meat chicken just plastered with good tomato sauce and stringfully melted cheese. Very basic and very tasty. And it comes with a side of pasta, but what Rocco calls a side of pasta some places try and pass off as a meal. It's that much. For an extra buck you can get gnocchi or ravioli instead of spaghetti or pesto instead of regular sauce.

Go ahead and cough up the greenback. You can make spaghetti at home. But you probably can't make gnocchi, and these are good ones. I don't know about the ravioli, but I'll tell you what else: I wouldn't mind finding out. You know how filling gnocchi is? Well, you can imagine how happy I was, what with that with a great pesto sauce, plus the parm, plus a lot of bread, what with so many things to sop up, and I haven't even mentioned my soup yet, speaking of sop.

Ever had pastina? Well, I have a cousin named Pastina, but that's neither here nor there. Pastina (the soup, not the cousin) is a thing I haven't eaten since I was a kid sitting at Grandma Leone's kitchen counter. Hurray for Rocco's pastina for bringing me back. (Hi Grandma!) Pastina is a very small, almost microscopic pasta, and when you throw a handful of it into some plain old chicken broth and butter up about a half-loaf of good Italian bread, you're face-to-face with one of life's simplest pleasures, my friend. Enjoy yourself. It's later than you think.

■ CARMEN'S

I won't even try to tell you *Where All I Went* and *What All I Did* during my big cross-country road trip. I'll limit myself to *What All I Ate*.

Let's see, there was Papa Chuy's in the little town of Van Horn, Texas—Papa Chuy's being the self-proclaimed "All-Madden Haul of Fame."

Carmen's
998 Fourth Street,
San Francisco. (415) 495-9265.
Breakfast, lunch, dinner. Cheap.

Seems some years ago or so my man Madden popped into this place and knocked down a few fajitas, liking them enough to then mention Papa

Chuy's in a *Time* magazine interview. Well, technically he didn't exactly mention Papa Chuy by name so much as he said, and I quote: "It's fun going to the Mexican restaurant in Van Horn, Texas. The guy's wife is the cook."

Now, before any wiseguyperson offers to send Mr. Madden to restaurant-reviewing school by way of a dumb-ass crack, let me remind you that he's a football announcer by trade, and the best one we've got, to boot, and that anyone who used to take up as much horizontal space on the Raiders' sideline as Coach Madden used to take up in his prime is entitled to offer an untrained opinion on the subject of eats any old time, in my book.

Anyway, he's right. Papa Chuy's is a fun place, especially since it's become a sort of John Madden shrine, with Madden pictures everywhere, sports shots, and even Madden T-shirts. But the crowning atmospheric touch is a mural on the wall in the back dining room, wherein the entire town of Van Horn is rendered (Papa Chuy's place center stage, of course), and hovering over everything is a huge, haloed head-shot of our Lord and Savior Jesus Christ, arms outstretched like an electric football quarterback over the whole kitten and kaboodle. And in the bottom corner of this picture . . . yes—there it is: the Madden Cruiser, Madden's famous big bus, rolling into town just then presumably for fajitas!

Let me tell you, it's an inspirational sight. In fact, it inspired me and Haywire to go around drawing Madden Cruisers on every religious (or otherwise serious) icon we came across over the next few weeks of our tour. Mostly these were on bathroom walls in bars moreso than church ceilings and such—but, hey, you gotta start somewheres.

Speaking of which, if I don't start spouting local news soon, I'll be in big trouble with the authorities, so let me just gloss over the rest of the country like this: Marfa, Texas has the best chili ever, but I forget the name of the restaurant; I spent enough time in North Carolina to actually get sic [sick] of barbecue; and 3,471 crawfish died for my sins during a memorable week in Louisiana.

One thing I didn't eat out and about out there was Filipino food, so not long after I got back I went to Carmen's, which is a fun, funky Filipino/American restaurant down on Fourth Street, on the water. Where those drawbridges are. Get the picture?

OK, do me a favor and draw a little bus in the bottom corner of it . . . And while you're working on that, let me tell you about Carmen's: There's a wraparound counter with an excellent view of the action. Or you can sit at a table by the window and look out onto the river, or whatever that long, watery thing is. The predominant art pieces on the Peg-Board walls are snapshots of lingerie-wearing women hanging out with fully clothed men. I don't know, so maybe they do lingerie shows or private bachelor parties or something. I know they have karaoke.

As for the food, it's good and cheap. They have pork chops and liver and onions and American stuff, but I ordered *lumpia,* which was seven rolls for something like six bucks. That's less than a buck a roll, if my math serves me, and they threw in a big pile of white rice with what the cook called "gravy" but was actually just a dribbling of thin, orange meat grease.

I had never had *lumpia* before. They're basically egg rolls, only with fresher-looking, more colorful things inside, like peas and green beans and carrots and limas and corn and I think pork—or some kind of meat. I liked that everything still had some crunch to it, except for the mushrooms and carrots, and the overall flavor was flavorful, even without the sweet red dipping sauce.

My friend the Well Baby, who clued me in on Carmen's and ate there with me, says they'll stoke up the karaoke machine for you any time of day. Both the cook and the busboyperson, he says, are gifted karaokers. The Well Baby himself claims to have karaoked on previous visits to Carmen's. Now if only we could get Madden in there.

■ STAR INDIA

I get all excited when I hear about some Polk Street place I gotta get to, 'cause I associate that area with culinary cheapness and an always interesting cast of characters for company. I keep forgetting that the street keeps going until general weirdness turns into yuppie scum somewhere after Steve the Greek and before Alcatraz.

Star India
2127 Polk Street, San Francisco. (415) 292-6699. Also at 3721 Geary Boulevard, San Francisco. (415) 668-4466. Lunch, dinner. Credit cards accepted. Cheap.

Snob Hill? Russian Swill? Little Noe Valley? I don't know what it's called, but if I'd've knowed Star India was going to be in a two-block stretch of street with a Peet's, a Starbucks, *and* a Tully's instead of real coffeehouses (not to mention a Real Foods instead of a real grocery store), I probably wouldn't have gone there in the first place. 'cause not only was I hungry as a hearst, but I hadn't been caffeinated yet either.

Well, it all worked out in the end, because Star India, in spite of its inauspicious location, has one of those $6.95 lunch buffets, and buffet means all-you-can-eat, and all-you-can-eat means happiness and tranquillity, and coffee's not only included but it's the world's weakest and worst-ever cup of joe, as if to say, "Fuck you Peet and Starbuck and Tully." And that's a sentiment that I happen to share.

Don't worry. The food's a lot better than the coffee. And what that says, besides not much, is very little. It's certainly not "The Best Indian Cuisine in Town," as the menu hyperbolates. I know because Shalimar is better, although Shalimar, come to think of it, is not Indian Cuisine so much as Indian Fast Food, by its own admission, so what do I know after all?

I don't stand to learn a lot, either, on the subject of Indian food, because my girlfriendperson and I have an understanding. See, she and her last three guys broke up in Indian restaurants, so us ever going out to eat Indian food together would be a bad idea for a date—something like Kokomo Joe Valentino and Big Six taking a little moonlight stroll down the docks.

So, yeah, I was eating alone. And in more ways than one, because Star India's lunch rush consisted of me and some joggerheaded skinny-ass yup who popped in and ordered an order of plain white rice to go. My point being . . . where was everybody? It's all you can eat! It's Indian food! It's $6.95!

Star India is a colorfully walled, colorfully carpeted, colorfully tabled little joint with authentic Indian music and general friendliness. I can't speak for their dinner menu except to say that everything seems to be about nine bucks. Hey—maybe that's where everyone was. Why would a yupperson in their right mind spend $6.95 for all they could eat when they could stop by later and drop 10 bucks for just one thing?

My favorite buffet item was the chicken *krahi,* tenderfully stir-fried chicken with peppers and onions and garlic and ginger and cilantro and for all I know some other good stuff in a light tomatoey sauce. Be careful not to eat this first, or you may not get around to anything else, what with seconds and thirds and so on.

The tandoori chicken was also pretty good, with a red-rimmed smoky flavor, except I wish they'd leave the skin on. And the *seekh kabab* wins the zing-zang-zooey award. It's kind of like barbecued lamb sausage, all spiced up with cilantro and something hot. It's good and spicy. It's also purple.

The other lamb dishes were good enough, flavorwise, but the meat itself in both of them was dry and tough. Buffet table casualties? I'm talking about lamb *korma,* cooked in a deliciously smooth curry sauce, and lamb *biriyani,* sort of a fried saffron rice with peas and big chunks of meat.

For vegetarians, there was *sag paneer,* a creamy spinach dish, which I tasted and liked. There was also an eggplant something-or-other, which I didn't get around to, and a thing they call mushroom matter, which—what with a name like that—I personally wouldn't touch with a 10-foot fork. Wait. That's not all. They also had soup (lentil, I think), salad stuff (iceberg, cucumber, tomato), that spicy crackerlike material you eat with the great light green sauce, regular flat fried bread, and orange-looking battered onion rings, which didn't sit right with me.

So, given the choicelessness, where did I go for my real cup of coffee after leaving Star India?

That's for me to know and you to wonder.

■ SLIDERS DINER

One night I had to have a hot dog. This would be no sort of a problem for many Americans, such as those living in Chicago or New York or even New Castle, PA, for example. Still, all in all, I'd rather be in San Francisco.

Sliders Diner
449 Castro Street, San Francisco. (415) 431-3288. Also at 1202 Sutter Street, San Francisco. (415) 885-3288. Lunch, dinner. Cheap.

I was walking in San Francisco the night before the other night, and

I said to Crawdad de la Cooter, who was walking with me, I said, out of the blue and for no particular reason, let alone a good one, I said, "You know," I said, "this country's not so bad of a country if you think about it."

Well, that was almost the end of our relationship right then and there, no questions asked, on top of which the whole city seemed to go silent and I had the impression that everyone in the Mission heard me and that I might get kicked to death very shortly by a lot of pretty cool looking boots. I pretended I was joking.

Ha ha ha ha ha ha ha ha ha.

The neighborhood breathed a huge sigh of relief and all the bands playing in all the bars went back to work, and conversations and business transactions resumed and so on, and I still don't know what had gotten into me, but I think it must've had something to do with the impending baseball season.

So I don't know whether or not this was related or not, but the next night I simply had to have a hot dog. Nothing else would do. And I don't often crave hot dogs, mind you, ever since that famous time eight or so years ago when I ate 10 of them in one sitting, to prove a point. Since then my hot dog consumption has been limited to special occasions: baseball games and camping trips.

But I had to have a hot dog so bad that I erroneously imagined there was a little hot dog place on 16th near Valencia, and maybe there was one there for about 15 minutes four years ago, but now it's a little pizza place. You know the one: right down from the Shell Station going toward Dolores.

I kept walking, past the city's greatest art gallery (Creativity Explored), and I just figured I would eventually walk into hot dogs.

Dum de dum de do. Right on Church. Hey, how about sushi dogs! Wouldn't that be something? Wrapped in rice and seaweed paper? Ketchup. There's a veggie restaurant. Tofu pups? Yeah, right. Sparky's? Nope. No hot dogs. Chinese. Left on Market. Boston Market? No.

Stopped to look in the window of the old Scandinavian Deli (R.I.P.), which is now just a pile of boards inside, gone the way of the Sincere Cafe (R.I.P.). Guess there's no room in this town any more for a real-hearted, gimmickless old restaurant. Sigh.

I walked all the way back up to 17th without encountering any hot dogs, not even on the side streets. My stomach was growling like the Angriest Dog, 'cause I hadn't had much breakfast or lunch to speak of.

Orphan Andy's, probably my favorite Castro place, had Polish dogs, but they were five-something and they weren't hot dogs, so I headed up Castro toward 18th. Cove? Nah. Without Reservations? Nope.

My stomach was howling at the moon by the time I crossed the road and noticed Sliders Diner for the first time ever. I mean, I'd noticed it, but I'd never noticed that they had fresh-ground half-pound burgers for under five bucks (although without fries, but that's still cheaper than Joe's Cable Car). Another thing Sliders has is hot dogs. They've got a whole hot dog section on the menu.

I got a chili dog ($3.95), 'cause it was only 70 cents more than a regular dog, and if you're gonna pay over three smackers for a fuckin' hot dog (without fries!), you may as well get chili and cheese all over it. Problem is there wasn't much chili or cheese, but at least the hot dog was a very good, charbroiled, split-down-the-middle, quarter-pound, all-beef dog.

On the way home I went down 18th Street, past the 7-Eleven, and they had quarter-pound dogs for $1.50, so I got one for dessert and kicked myself for not thinking of it earlier. And then I stopped at the 500 Club, just a door or two down from Crawdad's, where I was staying, to wash it all down, and they had hot dogs spinning in their little hot dog thing, and they were free. And I was sad 'cause if there was one thing I didn't have to have anymore, it was a hot dog.

But the next morning Crawdad woke me up craving hamburgers, and I knew just where to take us.

∎ MAI'S RESTAURANT

Someone told me that Burmese food is even better than Thai, so I figured I'd better look into it. "Where?" I said.

"Where what?"

"Where do I go?"

Well, to make a short conversation actual-size, he said I could always

Mai's Restaurant
316 Clement Street,
San Francisco. (415) 221-3046.
Lunch, dinner. Credit cards
accepted. Cheap.

go where he went, which was some unspellable place in the Marina, but, he said, there was a supposedly cheaper place out on Clement that everyone seemed to love, although he'd never been there himself. Burma Super Star.

Never one to make a trip to the Marina when there's a supposedly cheaper place on Clement, I swung through the Richmond last night on my way to the Hotel Utah to see one of my musical heroes, David Thomas (of Pere Ubu, etc.)—playing at the Hotel Utah, of all places!

So where was everybody? I personally invited five different people to go out with me. "David Thomas, man. The Utah. *David Thomas . . .* " No dice. And one of those people even knew who he was.

But first things first. Burma Super Star. Which raises the question, where's Burma? *What's* Burma? All I know is the Joseph Spence song. You know: "Going down Burma Road, going down Burma Road, going down Burma Road, haaarrrrgh, Burma Road."

So there's that, which I was singing to myself all the way there, and there's Burmese food, which I wasn't about to find out about, turns out, because all the fancy-pants restaurant reviewers beat me to it. There were all their reviews in the window, bigger than life, laughing in my face. Ha ha ha ha ha! My pants aren't fancy.

Hit it—going down Clement Street, going down Clement Street, going down Clement Street, haaarrrrgh, Clement Street.

Nah, really I just ducked into the first Vietnamese restaurant I saw, which was Mai's, right across the street. That's how hungry I was. I didn't even check to make sure they had that thing I always get: imperial rolls and pork over rice noodles.

They didn't. But they did have my most favoritest Vietnamese thing of all, which a lot of places don't have: *canh chua tom,* or hot-and-sour shrimp soup, with celery and bean sprouts and tomato and pineapple.

On the basis of this soup alone, Mai's deserves a line out the door. So where was everybody?

Not at the Hotel Utah.

I ate my meal like I ate up Mr. Thomas's postpoetic freak-for-all afterward: utterly alone and alienated and discombobulated and disenfranchised and misanthropicized and uncomfortable and underunderstood and malpracticed and just generally itchy.

And loving every minute of it, Chief!

Besides the soup I had an order of imperial rolls, which were great. I don't know why they're $4.95, but I do know why the soup is $6.25 ($5.50 for lunch): It's bigger and fresher and therefore I guess better than the only other bowl I've found out here, so far: Phu Huong's. And, more important, it doesn't have mushrooms! Which saves me the extra step of having to pick them out.

The celery and sprouts were perfectly crispy, the tomato wedges and pineapple squares were perfectly mushy, the broth made my nose run just exactly as much as I wanted it to, and eight to 10 shrimps may not be perfect, but it's pretty damned good.

Great soup. Now let me tell you about the place itself: It's just a square, carpeted room with sort of pseudo-faux-wood-paneled walls, authentic (I think) Vietnamese artwork, and authentically bad Vietnamese-American pop music, like, "Yesterday", and "I Just Called to Say I Love You"—in two different languages!

The tables have diagonally overlapping mustard-colored and blue tablecloths, then glass, and then paper place mats—so they really expect you to be sloppy, I figure.

License to spill?

■ CORDON BLEU

So happens I've been spending more time at the 'Stick and the 'Seum and various and sun-dried movie theaters these days than at this or that hole-in-the-wall cheap-eats joint. Of course, the obvious Thing To Do

Cordon Bleu
1574 California Street,
San Francisco. (415) 673-5637.
Lunch, dinner. Cheap.

would be to write a little something or other about the culinary fare at some of these stadiums and movie houses, call it a week—I've done worse. But ain't it a sad state of internal American affairs that two of the rock-bottom cheapest and easiest-to-make American meals, hot dogs and popcorn, wouldn't even qualify as "cheap eats," technically?

I'm talking about four-dollar foot-long shlongs and four-dollar buckets of popcorn. Wanna wash that down with something? Tack on two or three bucks, more like four or five if it's a Bud you're after, and already you're up around 10 smackers for a glorified snack.

Now I don't know who's screwing the American public here—whether it's the concessionaires or the theaters/stadiums or the moviemakers/owners or the actors/players or the American public. All I know is that somewhere along the line someone is being mighty mean, and while some people might tell you that greed is the American way, I'm here to say that so is do-it-yourself. A pack of hot dogs goes for a buck-something at the grocery store. So does a big huge bag of popcorn kernels. Boil your own. Pop your own. And let's see if we can't boycott a little common decency into these greedy motherfuckers, whoever they are.

Yesterday, for example, so as not to require popcorn with *Sling Blade*, I stuffed myself silly at the little Vietnamese place next door to the Lumiere, Cordon Bleu. My poetic pal Johnny "Jack" Poetry has been touting this place for years, but I've been ignoring him because "Cordon Bleu" always sounds to me like fancy French food, even if their specialty is five-spice chicken.

That's what I got. It's a half of a roasted chicken, barbecued on the grill. So that makes it five-spice twice-cooked chicken in my book. But for $5.15 for half a bird, I don't care how many times they cook it—especially if it comes on a mountain of meat sauce–smothered rice, with "country" cabbage salad to boot.

Don't ask me what the five spices are. Ask me if I liked it.

"Did you like it?"

Yeah. It was pretty good. But not as good as their imperial rolls. That's what Crawdad, my matinee-mate, ordered: the lunch special with an imperial roll, the same mountain of rice smothered in meat sauce, and country salad. Crawdad maintained afterward that her imperial roll featured an entire "link" of sausage down the middle of it. I had a bite, but I was too busy enjoying myself to notice any such feature, and frankly (no pun intended), I find it hard to believe.

The other lunch special, by the way, is the same thing with a grilled-pork shish kebab instead of the imperial roll. There are only five other meals on the menu, all of which have to do with mountains of meat-sauced rice and country salads and either five-spice chicken, imperial rolls, or shish kebabs—or all of the above.

It's a great little place: just two or three tables and a small counter. The grill's right there. The people are pleasant. Tea's included. Huge portions, tiny prices. Hoppin' location. I was expecting a big crowd, because we showed up right around lunchtime—quarter after 12. But we ate alone, for the most part. I've got no problem with that.

Sling Blade is one heck of a helluva movie.

■ JUST LIKE HOME

Gotta letter from a lawyer yesterday, telling me what to do. I don't always do what lawyers tell me to do, mind you, but when they tell me to go eat a half of a chicken and a *shawarma* sandwich, I'm liable to follow orders.

Just Like Home
1924 Irving Street,
San Francisco. (415) 681-3337.
Lunch, dinner. Credit cards accepted. Cheap cheap.

Especially when they offer to pay for it if I don't like it.

Yep, that's what the man said: "I want you to eat at a little establishment on Irving Street called Just Like Home . . . I want you to try their *shawarma* sandwich . . . I want you to have their roast chicken . . . If you don't like the food, mail me your receipt and I'll refund the price of the meal."

He said some other stuff, too, some of which led me to believe that I probably wouldn't like the food. The guy actually prefers La Cumbre to Can-Cun, for example. And he stopped eating at the Sincere Cafe, he said in his letter, because his girlfriend wouldn't eat there with him, and then after they broke up and he tried to go back, he realized, in his words: "She was right. It really was bad food."

Well, my ex-girlfriend wouldn't eat at the Sincere Cafe with me, either, so what did I do? I ate there without her. Just like before we met. And then after we broke up, I continued to eat there without her. And it continued to be the city's best all-around and cheapest restaurant right up until the very sad day they put the newspaper up in the windows and locked the doors.

All of which . . . well, not *all*, but the stuff about this guy liking La Cumbre and not liking the Sincere Cafe and saying to send my receipt if I didn't agree with him on Just Like Home . . . it was looking like LUNCH ON THE LAWYER to me.

Of course, LUNCH ON ANYONE, anytime, anywhere, is like music to my hairy ears, so one fine day when the sun was bright and the skies weren't gray and the Sunset District seemed not far away—and I had to move my car anyhow, so I made the trip.

Just Like Home. I won't keep you in suspense any longer. You're off the hook, lawyerman. I liked it—although it wasn't anything like my home.

Instead of my mother, for example, there was this serverperson lady I've never even seen before. And instead of 11 kids screaming and scrapping over the last quarter-section of the three donuts my dad brought home from work for dessert, there was me and some business guy, politely placing our orders and paying for them.

Instead of one round table big enough to land a flying saucer, there were four or five square ones, and then a long, narrow room full of blue-seated booths, a cork-boarded wall on one side and mirrors on the other.

Instead of the Jesus who's always looking at you, there was a big painting of some Middle Eastern city. And instead of all our dorky graduation pictures (or baby pictures, depending on how old we were at the time), there was a display case full of for-sale $5 Arabic tapes, all of which featured huge head-shots of the singers—some of whom wore gigantic hairdos and Aunt Ethyl glasses, or otherwise looked every bit as dorky as a graduation picture.

Instead of—

AAAAAHHHHHH! STOP IT! STOP IT! STOP IT!

One more, OK? For the sake of transition . . . instead of cookie trays full of sliced bread with melted cheese on top, what was for lunch was all sorts of Middle Eastern things like falafel and tabbouleh and *baba ghanoush* and so on and so forth. And while none of it was free, it was close enough.

They have half-pound burgers for under four bucks, but I got the baked chicken—chicken *ala kaifak*, they call it—which is half of one with veggies and taters or rice, and the *shawarma* sandwich, which is both parts of a pita pocket stuffed with spike-roasted lamb and lettuce and tomato and tahini sauce.

Lawyerman wanted me to get hummus on there, too, so I did on half of it, but, as I suspected, hummus *and* tahini made for too much goo, so I'm telling you to stick with one or the other.

The chicken was good and flavorful and juicy—miraculously, since it went from the oven to the steam table to a microwave before it ever touched down inside of me. But it was piled with spices and red peppers and onions and tomato and carrots, and we all had us a real good time together.

■ COMBO HOT DOGS

If you thought I was slightly twisted before, you should see me now. This guy Andy Hustle, a personal friend of mine, no less, personally Ray Fosseed me at home plate during a pickup game. The next day I had a league game, but by the fifth inning I couldn't lift the bat up over my shoulder and look at the pitcher at the same time. Nor could I throw the ball as far as the pitcher's mound from second base. But I had to stay in the game because only nine of us showed up.

Combo Hot Dogs
1200-A Polk Street, San Francisco. (415) 474-0979. Lunch, dinner. Cheap cheap.

So now one of my shoulders is lower and less forward than the other and my head will only turn in one and a half different directions and my neck won't even consider doing the Merton Hanks end zone dance, which makes listening to my calypso records next to impossible.

Ergo: general sadness.

On the other hand, my brother Jean-Gene the Frenchman is in town between a meteorologically punishing spring on the Oregonic Coast and a summer in France. Here's the thing: He was living up north with his girlfriendperson, see, and she rudely converted him from vegetarianism to veganism, so now I have three weeks to convert him back before he heads to his homeland. Because no meat is one thing, but in France they kick you out of the country, I think, if you won't eat cheese.

In return for this great favor (which he doesn't yet recognize as a favor, exactly), my brother is converting me back to a more or less normal, upstanding, straight-shooting member of society, which means I should be back out on the ball field spitting seeds and swearing and farting by next weekend, barring any freak writing accidents. It just so happens that, besides veganism, Jean-Gene the Frenchman, being Italian by blood, has recently taken up massagyny—what a guy! He has a book and everything, and a more-than-willing practice back.

So one day after a real good rubdown, I had him pack up me and our pal Tinzee and drive us all down to the 'Loin to check out this Vietnamese place I'd just heard about called, of all the crazy things, Combo Hot Dogs. Now, correct me if I'm wrong, but you've gotta love a Vietnamese restaurant with a name like Combo Hot Dogs.

Right off the bat, I mean, even before you realize that nothing on the menu's more than four bucks, and most of it, in fact, is under $2.50. You believe that? Well, believe it, 'cause it's for real.

Combo Hot Dogs. Polk and Sutter. It's a genuine hole-in-the-wall. The painted sign outside on top of the place is bigger than the restaurant itself, so don't everyone jump at once. But jump. By all means, jump. If all four or five little tiny tables are taken, you can always get it to go. You're going to wind up eating off of plastic either way.

They have a few standard Vietnamese dishes, but the main attraction here is the Combo hot dog for $1.09.

And that's not just a hot dog; it's a hot dog with coleslaw and chili (or in my case just chili) on it. One-oh-nine. Do you realize what that means? You can have five hot dogs with coleslaw and/or chili on them for $5.45, 10 for $10.90!

They're good dogs, too. Thick and real and juicy, on a warm, perfectly toasted bun. The chili, admittedly, looked strange. It was gray, for example. Grayish pink. I don't think it was ground beef. Maybe ground turkey. All I know is there were no beans in it and it tasted great, and *$1.09!*

So I ate about four of them.

Jean-Gene got the only vegetarian thing, the vegetable rice plate, and he said it was great. Tinzee got the pork noodles plate, and she didn't say anything. She'd just got back from Jazz Fest in New Orleans, see, and all she wanted to talk about was how many different ways she ate crawfish there.

Correct answer: nine.

■ GREEN DEW

I was back in the 'Loin again right around eating time, what with the world-famous Breedwads doing the Great American Thing last Tuesday night. Oh, and they did it quite well, I don't mind saying, my lack of music-reviewing credentials notwithstanding.

> **Green Dew**
> 928 Geary Street,
> San Francisco. (415) 928-
> 1906/5269. Lunch, dinner.
> Credit cards accepted. Cheap.

There was me and Jean-Gene the Frenchman and Johnny "Jack" Poetry looking around for a little something to bite on before the big event. Kayla Kupcakes was playing at the Century, but I'm talking about the other big event, the Breedwads. Anyone who was anyone, ourselves included, would wind up at the Great American no matter what was for dinner.

Of course, there's always Lew's, the dive of dives, right there on the corner there, but they've got nothing to offer along the lines of meatless-ness—not to mention veganism.

Did I mention I'm a vegan now?

No? That's 'cause I'm not, you idiot, but the goddamn Frenchy still is, even after a week and a half in my house, *Madonna mia,* so we wandered up Larkin past Lew's—Kayla Kupcakes playing at the Century—left on Geary, and looked into Green Dew, a not-bad-looking Mandarin-style Chinese joint that's called everything else in the world but Green Dew from the outside. (Lunch Special? Something Hunan?) They seemed a little pricey for the 'hood though, so we wandered around some more and looked into more windows and wound up back at Larkin and O'Far-rell. You know how it is when everyone's hungry as a house but nobody has anything in particular in mind.

Well, Kayla Kupcakes was playing at the Century.

I got it in my mind to go to Phu Huong, one of my favorite Viet-namese places, but it's never where I think it is when I need it, so we ducked into some other Vietnamese place right around where Phu Huong wasn't. We were about to be three very happy boys until we suddenly realized . . . nothing meatless on the menu—not to mention vegan.

Did I mention Kayla Kupcakes was playing at the Century?

Well, so then we ran into drummerboy Suave Fuck (S. F.) parking his Suave Fuckmobile (S. F.), and S. F. (the man) turned out to be in need of a little something to bite on before the show too. I remembered to myself that S. F. owed me dinner. In other words, all things considered (including Kayla Kupcakes at the Century), Green Dew was starting to seem more reasonable by the minute.

So that's back up Larkin (everybody sing:) Kayla Kupcakes at the Century, left on Geary, and yodel-eh-hee-hoo, we were finally somewhere, sitting down with amply vegetative menus, fixin' to be four very happy boys.

Everyone ordered what all they all ordered, and I ordered . . . well, I'm too embarrassed to say what I ordered, but I don't mind telling you it was roughly seven bucks. Except for fried rice–type stuff and vegetarian shit and lunch specials, there was nothing on the menu under six—most of it well into the sixes and sevens. Slightly pricey for the 'hood, no? And I also got the appetizer combo, which is some of everything for another seven or so. What can I say? I was hungry as a house, so what's 14 bucks?—especially when it's someone else's bucks.

"Suave Fuck," I said, "remember how you owe me dinner?"

He remembered, all right, but he insisted that this dinner wasn't the dinner; he wanted to take me "somewhere nice." And he mentioned some fancy-sounding Italian-sounding place where everything costs hundreds of dollars. See how fuckin' *suave* he is?

Well, all loyalties to cheapness aside, I'll let someone spend hundreds of dollars on me for dinner any day of the week, so long as I don't have to suck their dicks afterward—but I asked and S. F. said I wouldn't have to. Which put me in such a good mood that I not only paid for my own $14 meal but sprung for everyone else as well!

S. F., naturally, had the best thing, but I don't even know what it was. Some spicy-as-K.K.-at-the-C. prawn dish with broccoli and carrots and celery and so much red pepper that—lucky for me—he burned out on it halfway through, and I easily convinced him to trade me the rest for my soothingly sweet chicken with pineapple in lemon sauce.

Yep, that's what I got.

Now I ask you, who's fault is all of this, philosophically speaking? I mean this review, in general (including what I got). Is it my fault, or the Tenderloin's? Or is it Phu Huong's fault, for never being where I think it is?

Correct answer: Kayla Kupcakes at the Century.

■ PORK STORE CAFE

On one of those hot-as-hell days a weekend or so ago I called up Johnny "Jack" Poetry and you know what he said? He said, and I quote: "Hot enough for you?"

This, mind you, from the mind that has turned such turns of phrase as "yesterday's calzones chock full of Caruso recordings exploding like a pogo stick with a guilty conscience" or "she's swimming the stairs as sexy as any walleyed tropical fish swimming past the wreck in its tank" or "Laura looks great in a bowling shirt."

Pork Store Cafe
1451 Haight Street, San Francisco. (415) 864-6981. Breakfast, Lunch. Cheap.

Mr. Poetry is called Mr. Poetry for some very good reasons—three of which you've just read. Note that I have never nor would I ever refer to Johnny "Jack" as Mr. Customer Service or Mr. Temp or anything like that.

But my next question is this: What can it say of a great, prosperous nation's state of internal and cultural affairs when its very own home-grown poets—purveyors of truth and beauty—are going around saying things like "hot enough for you?"

It must be the greenhouse effect. That's all I can think of. Because the beautiful truth is that it *was* hot enough for me, and I like it hot. I like it very hot.

I also like it rich and thick and oozing with butter and slightly salty—which is why I love the Pork Store, where me and Johnny "Jack" wound up eating on that fine, hot-enough-for-me day. I had strawberry pancakes and a side-order sausage patty. He had the Pork Store Special, which is two pork chops, two eggs, some mighty fine looking hash browns and biscuits or toast.

The Pork Store's pancakes are huge and hot and delicious. They put the strawberries both inside and outside, which is how it should be, you ask me, and they top the whole thing off with an ice cream–size scoop of butter—ooze city!—and a sprinkling of powdered sugar.

As for the sausage patties, they're extra-large—about as big as a quarter-pound hamburger, which would weigh them in right around, oh, say . . . about a quarter of a pound or so. And, almost as important, they're good and juicy. Probably the best overall breakfast sausage I've had around here. Which, you gotta figure . . .

By the way, veggies, don't be scared off by the name of the place. It's Haight Street! There are plenty of concessionary vegetarian dishes on the menu: garden burgers, Nadia's famous vegetarian scramble, even a thing called the "Vegan Delight," a tofu-scramble with, I don't know, some other stuff.

What's for lunch is pork chops, turkey, grilled eggplant, steaks, honey-dipped chickens, and beef liver, plus burgers and salads and you-name-it, for roughly four to seven bucks. We were sitting there talking shop and weather and shit for long enough to get hungry again, almost. But then the guy down the counter started pouring mustard all over his eggs and taters, and that was it for my own personal appetite.

"Holy Mary-mother-of-Jesus, Joseph, and all the apostles except maybe Judas," I mutttered.

"What's that?" Johnny "Jack" said, looking up from his plate with a forkful of pork.

"Nevermind," I said, not wanting to ruin the rest of his breakfast for him. "How 'bout this weather?" I said.

"Boy, you can say that again," he said.

Speaking of which, the Pork Store might be the best-ventilated restaurant in the city. Especially considering its size: small. There's just six tables and an L-shaped counter, and while I'm at it I may as well mention all the Haight Street Fair posters and the Three Happy Pigs paintings and a couple of blowed-up photos of the Pork Store back in the good old days when it was a pork store. All that mentioned, we were sitting at the very top of the L, which is in back of the restaurant, right in front of the grill. Normally this seat is the hot seat, so to speak, but with the back door open and the breeze breezing in and out the front door, or vice versa, well, my pancakes almost even got cold. In fact, the last little bit of extra butter I'd buttered onto them didn't even ever exactly melt.

Hey, butter, hot enough for you?

Answer: no.

■ MEHARRY'S RESTAURANT

Earl Butter's going to kill me for this, but I went to the driving range without him. Yep, less than a week after not going to the driving range with him because my back was outta whack still, *supposedly*, I wound up going there without him. I don't know how it happened. I've lived here for over seven years, and I've always seen the driving range, but I've never gone there. I never even talked about going there. I never even knew how to get there.

Meharry's Restaurant
1200 Sixth Street,
San Francisco. (415) 703-6180.
Breakfast, lunch, dinner.
Credit cards accepted. Cheap.

And then suddenly Earl Butter's sitting at my kitchen table talking about taking up golf, and would I like to go out and hit a bucket with him, maybe show him a thing or two, like how to hold a club and where to put your feet? Not that I'm Jack Nicholson or anything, but I do like to consider myself a jack (so to speak) of all sports except maybe rugby, master of none except maybe Ping-Pong.

Yeah, I used to golf—back when I lived in Ohio, where it was entirely possible to go nine for under five. If I wanted to golf once or twice a year out here, I'd have to get myself a real job, like Earl Butter, and that's a thing that's not likely to happen in my lifetime, not to mention anyone else's.

Speaking of poverty, I was bumming around four days later with my just-back-from-the-Breedwads buddy, Biscuits, who lost her long-term temp job 'cause they got sick of having to get temps for the temp, I guess. Anyway, I say bumming, but really we were moto-bumming. It was Bike to Work day, see, and since we weren't working, we figured we'd drive. So we were poking around for someplace new to eat that didn't have tablecloths or gray carpeting.

Found it! Finally—at the driving range, of all places. You just take Fourth Street from downtown, over the bridge, and turn right right after Carmen's, then go past all the houseboats and housebuses until you get to Sixth. There's Meharry's, and there's the driving range.

A bucket of balls will cost you seven bucks, four more if you want some clubs to hit them with; but I'm not a driving-range reviewer, so let's talk food:

Half a fried chicken, french fries, and coleslaw ($8.25); chili burger with fries ($6.80); other things for other prices ($6.50, $7.75, $5.75, $8.35). It's not a fancy place, either. It's a driving-range restaurant. But if you want to eat for under five bucks, you're eating pancakes or French toast, bub, because everything else—even two-eggers, even a goddamn chili dog—is up and over.

There are certain things in life that you can't put a price tag on, but food isn't one of them. Especially mediocre food, which is Meharry's specialty, far as I can tell.

The burgers are fresh-ground on the premises, and that's worth something. On the other hand, they're smallish—leaning the shy side of a third of a pound, I'm guessing—and overcooked (no guesswork involved), which makes it hard to enjoy their fresh-groundedness. The chili is bean-heavy and run-of-the-mill, and the fries are uninspired freezer fare.

I'll say this much for Biscuits's fried chicken: It was good and juicy. I'll also say that the piece I ate squirted blood down near the bone. I happen to like my chicken erring on the side of salmonella, but I'm less willing to forgive and forget Meharry's ho-hum breading. Hell, for a few cents less you can get Roscoe's half of a real fried chicken with two great waffles, although, true, you'll have to get to Oakland somehow.

We also split a small salad. I wanted matzo ball soup for dessert, but three bucks a cup seemed like too much just to be able to craft some sort of a crack about two-stroke penalties for landing in the chicken broth, or "These are pretty good, but I prefer Maxfli-matzos to Titleist," or something.

I realize Meharry's business is geared toward people who can afford to golf, and those people probably think $6.95 for a chili dog dinner is dirt cheap. But I'm not those people, and neither is Biscuits.

Which isn't to say we didn't enjoy ourselves silly, what with the sheer novelty of eating at a driving range, outside on the porch, to the tune of golf balls being whacked and the smell of cut grass. In the middle of a city! Oh yeah, and jackhammers working on the freeway, and that heavy metallic tamping sound.

Whack, rat-a-tat-tat-tat-tat, whack, wham, wham, whack . . .

If you like pancakes and French toast, check out Meharry's. They serve breakfast all day.

■ CAFE ETHIOPIA

About a month ago I was invited to North Beach by a guy with the same name as mine, Dan Leone, who couldn't believe I had never heard of Gino & Carlo's. Gino & Carlo's, in case you never heard of it, is a North

Beach drinking institution that—

Cafe Ethiopia
878 Valencia Street,
San Francisco. (415) 285-2728.
Lunch, dinner. Credit cards
accepted. Cheap.

since y'gotta eat too (even Bukowski said so)—lays down a kicking multi-course Italian meal every other Thursday.

It's such a novel and popular idea, this eating thing, that they have to sell tickets in advance—from Friday to Wednesday before—and my guess is they almost always sell out. Get this: for 10 bucks you get . . . well, the menu changes every time. But we got Caesar salads, tortellini Alfredos (with seconds and thirds and so ons), bread, free all-you-can-drink house red, and then the main course: half a roasted chicken or prime rib, and potatoes.

It was probably my best and definitely my drunkest and cheapest ever North Beach eating experience—especially since Dan Leone paid for everything.

So, knowing how much a guy named Dan Leone likes to be treated to dinner, I called my namesake recently and said, "Names, now it's my turn." He hung up and came down to my neck of the woods for a late lunch at Valencia Street's latest cafe, Cafe Ethiopia, where the wine wasn't nearly as good or as free as at G. & C., and the food wasn't nearly as Italian, but the end result was exactly the same: I needed a nap.

Cafe Ethiopia is where Cafe Beano used to be, between 19th and 20th. I was never a big fan of Beano, so Ethiopia, even before I ever ate there, was a step in the right direction as far as I was concerned.

Unlike most of the rest of the hyper-hip houses brung in by the restaurantification of Valencia Street these years, Cafe Ethiopia caters to good, honest, hungry people, not yupsters.

Atmospherically, it hasn't changed too much from old Beano. It's still got that back beaded room, for example. In fact, it's still basically a coffeehouse, serving all the same coffees and teas and Toranis as anyone else, plus sandwiches and bagels and all—it's just that now they also have great, cheap Ethiopian grub.

If you're a vegetarian, you can head home happy for five bucks, easy. If you eat meat, more like seven. If you're Dan and Dan Leones, on the other hand, expect to spend about 30, counting wine and food for four. Not that it's an even split. Dan Leone drinks for three and eats for one and a half, while I drink for one and eat for two and a half.

You know how it works: piles of food plopped onto a gigantic, round, flat, spongy bread called *injera*. Then a bunch more *injera* for tearing off and scooping up the goods with. No utensils necessary—yeehaw!—but don't eat with your left hand, whatever you do, because that's the hand toilet-paperless societies wipe their butts with, according to Dan Leone.

Tibsie Dorho, my favorite of the food piles, featured chunks of chicken and diced tomatoes tenderly sautéed with onions and stuff—and the hot peppers go without saying. They were everywhere, and they were hot.

Kitfo was supposed to be "Ethiopian steak tartare," but I guess Ethiopians serve their raw meat cooked, 'cause that's the way we ate it. Which isn't to say that it wasn't great. It was. Maybe they assume no one around here wants to eat raw meat, in which case, well, they're wrong.

We also had the mixed vegetables, which was carrots and taters and cabbage in a yellow curry sauce, with onions and garlic and ginger and, yes, hot peppers.

Then there was the chopped-tomato *fit-fit, fit-fit* meaning "all scrambled up," according to our friendly waitressperson. It was tomatoes and green and red peppers and onions and shards of *injera* flavored with "salad herbs." It tasted fine, but it was kind of redundant served on *injera*, like eating a crouton sandwich. If you want to get this, get it by itself and eat it with a fork, for crying out loud.

And keep an eye out for this namesake of mine. He's every bit as roguish and almost as appetitically endowed as the next Dan Leone, and I understand he's been going around to restaurants I review favorably and dropping our name in order to cop a meal.

Not that I would ever do such a dirty deed, myself, but if I did, for the record, I'd be the one without the mustache.

◼ ORIGINAL JOE'S

Crawdad de la Cooter, who jogs, was going to jog past my apartment any minute and I was supposed to run down and bring her her guitar, which I'd been sleeping with the past couple nights since she left it in my bed.

> Original Joe's
> 144 Taylor Street,
> San Francisco. (415) 775-4877.
> Lunch, dinner. Credit cards
> accepted. Splurge cheap.

She also wanted to know, while she had me on the phone, if I happened to have any "extra hamburgers" lying around or anything, because she was hungry.

"Let me get this straight," I said, already having a fun time imagining her jogging around the neighborhood with a guitar; the thought of a guitar in one hand and a hamburger in the other—or, better yet, the guitar around her neck, bouncing while she ran, and *both* hands on the burger, taking a bite maybe at the light at 19th and Guerrero, jogging in place, ketchup getting all over her Lycra . . .

But, alas, I didn't have any extra hamburgers lying around. I looked in the refrigerator and on the stove, on the table, under the Ping-Pong table, in my bed . . . I looked everywhere, and no extra hamburgers. Not even anything else to eat.

"Sorry," I said. But she wanted the guitar anyway, so I was waiting by the window with it when who should appear on the sidewalk below but Neighborhood Dave, who's always tipping me off to some great steak place or another while I always happen to have an armload of urgent laundry or a couple bags of food or a baseball glove, so that the suggestion goes in one ear and out the other, leaving nothing but a greasy residue.

It occurred to me that, not having any food in the larder (not to mention under the Ping-Pong table, etc.), I hadn't had much more than toothpicks and toothpaste to eat all day, and could go for a little something meaty myself.

So I opened up the window and hollered down to Neighborhood Dave, "Hey Neighborhood," I hollered, "what's that great steak place you're always telling me about?"

"Original Joe's," he said, without skipping a beat, as if the place were so great he walks around with it on the tip of his tongue. "Taylor. Turk and Eddy."

And then he kept walking and eventually Crawdad showed up on the jog and one thing led to another, culminating in me and her and her guitar taking up three counter seats at Original Joe's, an atmospherically excellent old downtown/Tenderloin institution.

Crawdad ordered a sausage sandwich, I got me an 18-ounce top sirloin, and apparently the guitar wasn't as hungry as the rest of us, 'cause it just sat there the whole time, perfectly still, muttering something about pirate ships.

Steak is not exactly cheap eats. Mine was up and over 15 bucks, for example, and it included bread and butter and ravioli (or spaghetti or fries or veggies), but no salad, no baked 'tater, no all-of-the-above.

On the other hand: 18 ounces!

Do you know how big that is? It's bigger than a pound. It's two inches thick, nice and red in the middle, and about as juicy as anything else this side of Freshen Up. Let me put it this way: It was good. Good enough and big enough to command 15 bucks even without the raviolis, which were curiously awful but I ate them anyway.

And I ate all the bread. And I ate some of Crawdad's fresh-cut fries and the second half of her Italian sausage sandwich ($6.25, fries included), which was delicious, especially smothered with this fresh hot salsa one of the cookerpersons was kind enough to whip up for us since the guy down the counter had already knocked off the last of the last batch—and I don't even think it's on the menu!

So the next thing that happened was I was too full to move. I sat there and groaned for a while, which is just what you want to be doing after a not particularly cheap meal, if you're me. And I watched all the bow-tied waiterguypersons and tall-hatted cookers across the counter dishing up gigantic plates of pork chops and meatballs and roast beef and ham and steak and legs of lamb and chickens and so on for all the other soon-to-be-comatose customers in the plush steakhouse-style booths behind us.

Shortly before carting me out of there under one arm like a package of very happy, gurgling cement, the guitar occupying her other hand (and I don't know what *its* excuse was), the great Crawdad de la Cooter was heard to observe:

"Look! We're surrounded on all sides by meat!"

I looked and lost my marbles (but not my cookies). We were surrounded on all sides by meat, which may not be every man's deserted island fantasy, but it sure as hell is mine.

■ DOUG'S BAR-B-Q

I get letters. Three poetic pages, for example, from a guy waxing hysterical over Arthur Bryant's barbecue in Kansas City. The anonymous writer closed his ramblings with an apology for writing in my style,

Doug's Bar-B-Q
3600 San Pablo Avenue,
Emeryville. (510) 655-
9048/9049. Lunch, dinner.
Credit cards accepted. Cheap.

which caused me to scratch my head 'cause I hadn't actually understood most of what he said. Except that he wanted to kill all the people who say bad things about Arthur Bryant's. (So I'll try not to mention that I've been there and consider it overrated, if not downright stinky-poo.)

I also managed to glean from the letter that either Arthur Bryant's has closed or Arthur Bryant has died and his restaurant has fallen into incapable hands—or else why else would this guy be living out here instead of Kansas City?

What is it about great barbecue places? They're always up and disappearing on you. (Take Memphis Minnie's, which I declared my new favorite Bay Area barbecue, I don't know, maybe seven or eight weeks ago.) Already it's gone. Rumor has it they lost their lease and will reopen in a new location, but I wouldn't hold your collective breaths. That same sort of rumor has been circulating for 10 years concerning a Youngstown, Ohio, ex-institution called the Pit, which used to barbecue circles around Arthur Bryant (may he maybe R.I.P.), not to mention Memphis Minnie or anyone else in this wide country.

Despite the rosy rumors, the Pit (sniff) has not reopened, or else why else would I be living here instead of Youngstown?

In fact, I would probably not be living at all if it weren't for occasional doses of what I call "bootleg Pit." See, Mrs. Brown, Pit proprietress-person, bless her heart, can sometimes be persuaded to do up a wingding or two hundred out of her home. For my birthday this year, my friends-for-life out here got my little brother back there to talk Mrs. Brown into whipping up about a gallon of sauce, which was frozen and Fed-Exed, and . . . SURPRISE!

It was my best birthday ever.

That was less than a month ago; the gallon of sauce is already long-gone, and *now-ow-ow I'm lo-o-onesome blu-ue*. But instead of drinking myself to death, like Hank, I keep the empty sauce jug on hand to sniff at when I need a little something extra. (Sniff.)

Speaking of which, this letter writer said in his postscript that he ships 20 pounds of Doug's Bar-B-Q sauce to friends in Kansas City every year. Which intrigued me because Doug's is in Emeryville and Kansas City is in Kansas City. People there take their barbecue sauce very seriously (even if I don't like it). So poor Arthur Bryant must be not only dead but turning on a spit in his grave if Kansas Citians are indeed having their sauce shipped in from Emeryville, CA, these days.

And why shouldn't they? Doug's sauce, although it's too tomatoey and not quite spicy enough for my money, is better than Arthur's. Of course, having recently gulped a gallon of Mrs. Brown's, more or less, it seems ridiculous to me to even discuss anyone else's futile attempt at a sauce.

So let's talk meat.

I went to Doug's right after reading this letter, of course, because I had to know. I'd heard of the place, but I'd never eaten there—maybe because you can't actually eat there. It's takeout only, and I live this side of the bridge, and I'll be damned if I'm gonna drive all the way back with barbecue in the car—so I ate it right there in the parking lot, San Pablo and 36th. An urban picnic, complete with freeways and helicopters, sliced bread, orange pop, and enough napkins to wipe up a small army.

I had a two-meat combo, chicken and beef brisket, for around 10 bucks, beans and more beans by way of sides, because potato salad, coleslaw, and spaghetti were the other options. Lucky for me, the beans were sweet, sticky, meaty, and all-around excellent, as baked beans so often are at barbecue joints (in contrast to spaghetti).

The chicken was delicious, tear-away tender. The beef was good, too. But I also sampled a pork rib and it was way overcooked, tougher than toenails. In fact, it's the next day and I'm still chewing on it.

But my main complaint about Doug's, and my only legitimate one, really, is that it's too expensive. Nothing, not even a chicken sandwich, under five bucks. That and the sad, sad fact that, like every other restaurant I've eaten at in the last too many years (sniff), it ain't the Pit.

▮ TAMPOPO RAMEN HOUSE

Of course, in some necks of the woods, picking berries would be considered a wholesome summertime activity, right up there with sipping lemonade and smearing lightning bugs all over your forehead. This ain't them necks of the woods, though.

Tampopo Ramen House
1740 Buchanan Street,
San Francisco. (415) 346-7132.
Lunch, dinner. Credit
cards accepted. Cheap.

This is San Francisco, big fat urban metropolis, where anyone caught thrashing around in the bushes is liable to be up to something nasty.

Well, there were a lot of kids in the park that hot Monday afternoon, doing whatever city kids do, and there was me, Punk, and Punker doing what us kids do: just trying to pick a pie's worth. Which we did, luckily, between the three of us, so that we had something good and wholesome to show the four arms-crossed cops waiting back at the car—other than all our scratches and bug bites.

See, some particularly parentnoid parent had called us in on the assumption that we were sicko pedophiles, or else what else would we be doing in the bushes in the park, all these children wandering around?

I'd like to know, on the other hand, why these so-called concerned parents weren't sending their kids into the bushes with us. That's what my mom would've done. You seen the price of a handful of blackberries in the store these days?

So, anyway, the jig was up for us bad boys. I had to pop the lid off of my ominous-looking ricotta-cheese container and show these coppers our take.

"Blackberries," I said. "I'm going to make a pie."

It's interesting to note that of the four of them, only the woman one so much as cracked a smile over the relative innocence of blackberry pie as opposed to whatever dirty deed we were suspected of doing. The other three continued to question and insinuate, dead seriously. One even flashlighted through my car windows, looking for weapons or drugs or kiddie porn or something.

"Blackberries," I said again.

The policeladyperson smiled. She understood blackberries. As Punker pointed out later, she'd probably made a blackberry pie or two in her day, whereas the other three pigs had only ever eaten them.

Listen up, coppers, kids, city moms and dads. You might like to know this someday when you grow up: Making a pie is great fun! Not that it's any funner than eating one; actually, it enhances the experience. Pie tastes that much better when you made it yourself. When you picked your own berries, well, words can't describe the feeling, so I'm going to have to yodel: *yodel-eh-hee-hoo.*

All right, then. Made the pie, and in between that and eating it (for dessert), I went out to eat because that's my job. I'm a restaurant reviewer.

Juzo Itami, on the other hand, makes movies. One of them, *Tampopo,* is my all-time favorite food flick, but it's also a restaurant, lucky for me, because Tampopo (the restaurant) is my all-time favorite Japanese restaurant—and now I get to talk about it, being, if I remember correctly, a restaurant reviewer.

Tampopo (the restaurant) specializes in great big bowls of great *ramen* soup for not much money. You can get your basic *ramen* noodles with soy sauce for right around five bucks, for example, or you can get what I got, which was pretty much everything: meat, seafood, roasted pork, and vegetables. I know it was a good amount of soup, and I know I loved every drop of it. The "meat" part is chunks of ground pork, but it's the roasted pork that steals the show: tender, thin slices of great, flavorful pig meat, afloat on a sea of glistening broth—if you'll pardon the poetry, please.

As far as the seafood goes: shrimp. Then there was that possibly fish-related white cloud-shaped thing with the pink swirly in the center. (If you've seen *Tampopo*, the movie, it's what Goro flings onto the mean guy's nose before their first big fight.)

What else? Well, the requisite seaweed, shredded carrots, onions, lettuce or cabbage or something, and some mighty delicious noodles . . .

■ YELLOW SUBMARINE

I know I'm not supposed to write about cats, but what the hell, that's where the money is. And it so happens my girlfriendperson went away for a while and left me her cat, Weirdo the Cat, so . . .

Here are the results of my experiments:

• Cats are very weird.

• They will eat cockroaches and flies, but not boogers (at least not my boogers) or cat food or leftovers or any other kind of food.

> **Yellow Submarine**
> 503 Irving Street,
> San Francisco. (415) 681-5652.
> Lunch, dinner. Cheap cheap.

• Cats will drink bathwater, but not toilet water, tap water, or red wine.

• They don't like any kind of music and in fact can't dance.

• They are easily surprised out of their skin by coffee grinders, door buzzers, joy buzzers, smoke alarms, and banjos, but nothing you can say or do will shock them.

• They absolutely refuse to help out around the house.

• They think they're above it all, and—outside of the publishing world and maybe Broadway—they're dead wrong.

• Duct tape doesn't work.

There. That's roughly one bullet for roughly every day I had to hang with the butt-licking furball in lieu of her sexier and all-around more communicative owner. Now let me tell you what I ate yesterday. I ate my girlfriendperson's cat.

Uuurrrrp, excuse me.

Here's what else: for lunch (for real now), a huge-ass submarine of a submarine sandwich from Yellow Submarine on Irving at Sixth.

Me and my buddy Biscuits were out that way on business, reserving soccer fields and such, when all of a sudden we were hungry. So we called up our pal Jolly Boy, who lives in that neck of the woods, to see what was for lunch. "Sandwiches," he said. And he led us to his favorite sandwich place: Yellow Submarine.

I liked it too. I liked it because I liked the two friendly ladypersons running the joint, and I liked the atmosphere a lot. It's kind of gritty and real, compared to a lot of places around there—not to mention here.

Yellow Submarine has been serving "Boston-style" subs (whatever that means) at least long enough for the price of a large one to have gone from $2.35 to $5.45. See, there's this cool, colorful menu-mural-painting on the back wall of the dining room, in which peppers and eggs and ears of corn and french fries and stuff tell you what they are. It's pretty cool. "Salami," says a salami. And you can still sort of see the old prices through the whiteout: $1.75 for a medium, $2.35 for a large. So how long ago is that?

Anyhow, the main attraction of Yellow's submarines is that they're gigantic. Even at today's prices, 250 cubic inches of sandwichage, roughly speaking, is quite a deal.

I got a large Italian sausage, Jolly Boy got a large meatball, and Biscuits got a medium steak and cheese. Pretty much everything is $5.45/large, $3.95/medium, unless you want something like bologna and cheese, which is slightly cheaper.

Biscuits also got an order of fries. Those are real live taters sliced into slices—almost like thick potato chips—rather than standard french-fry planks.

So those were good, and I can say that the sandwiches were certainly filling. Jolly Boy, a veteran Yellow Submariner, knew to attempt to eat only half of his and take the other half home for dinner. I ate all of mine, being me, and to give you some idea of how happy that made me, being me, my pal Sushi called six hours later to see if I, being me, wanted to get a burrito. My answer: no fuckin' way. And don't forget who I am! (Answer: me.)

The bad news is that it wasn't exactly all that great. At least mine wasn't. The bread was good; they make their own, so that's points for them. And the sausage was just fine, come to think of it, but the tomato sauce that drenched everything was *El Blando* brand. All pasty and no tasty. Come on, ladies, put a little effort into it. Or at least some spices or something.

Maybe it was just a bad-sauce day. That was Biscuits's theory, and Jolly Boy acknowledged having detected qualitative inconsistencies in the past (although he didn't use those words). I don't know, personally, but next time I'm going for bologna and cheese. There's no such thing as a bad-bologna day, is there?

■ ROYAL KITCHEN

Last time I had a favorite Chinese restaurant I didn't say anything because I didn't want it to get House-of-Nankinged. (Yeah, right.) Well, I heard recently that the place was gone. Hopefully it wasn't due to lack of

Royal Kitchen
3253 Mission Street, San Francisco. (415) 824-4219/285-3128. Lunch, dinner. Credit cards accepted. Cheap.

bidness, 'cause that would add up to My Fault, when all was said and done. Not to point any fingers, but just to be safe, I'll shout it out loud and clear this time:

"ROYAL KITCHENNNNNNNNNN!!!!!!!"

But with only one *N*. It's a friendly and fairly unknown and extremely unpretentious (for how good it is) little place way the hell up Mission Street round about 29th. Cloth napkins—but I'm willing to forgive them if they're willing to forgive me and my party for putting them on our heads like hats and necks like ties and mustaches like mustaches, and just generally goofing off.

I was clued to Royal Kitchen by my pal Last Straw and her 5'9" hubby, the Tim Man. You may recall that one year, eight months, and three weeks ago I mentioned in passing that Last Straw moves a lot. Well, she's doing it again. They're going to become Mountain People very shortly, but first we had to have a little dinner together, me and them and Biscuits and Crawdad de la Cooter.

What a feast! We got nine things and six or seven beers (being five fairly heavyweight lightweights) for something like 10 bucks a person— and I'm proud to say that we cleaned the table and closed the place down and cleared out without anyone having been hurt.

Naturally I wasn't taking notes, so you'll have to settle for vague, impressionistic descriptions of everything. My favorite thing, for example, was the house-special squid, which was impressionistically delicious squid rings, vaguely breaded and fried and served in some sort of a sauce. I'm telling you . . .

And the Fresh Ginger Salad. That was maybe my second favorite thing. It had cabbage and maters and red onion and peanuts, hot peppers, cornflakes, crunchy fried peas, and plenty of ginger and cilantro. While mixing it all up for us at the table, our waiterguyperson pointed out that the cornflakes were actually roasted garlic and that the crunchy fried peas were actually crunchy fried peas. The dish itself, he said, was actually Burmese-style, not Chinese.

Four months and a week ago, in case you don't remember, I pointed out that I had never had Burmese food. Well, now I have, by accident, and I'm here to tell you that it's impressionistically delicious.

What else? Hunan spicy chicken. That was yummy. I very much enjoyed the curry prawns with eggplant—at least the curry and prawn part of it. And my least favorite of the bunch was the one I'd called for: chicken with black-bean sauce. Not that it was all that half-bad, either. It just wasn't as great as everything else.

And . . . appetizers. You may or may not recall that 274 words ago I hinted at having eaten nine things. Well, four of them were appetizers, and all four were excellent.

The vegetarian egg rolls were not too greasy and, more important, not too mushroomy. The innards, in fact, were unusually green and fresh. We also got a thing called a *shang-dong* quesadilla from the specials board. It was the approximate size and shape of a quesadilla, and the same basic concept: two round flat things with stuff in the middle. There was pork in there, and there was almost certainly other stuff, but I'll be damned if I can remember what. Cheese? At any rate, I liked it.

But my favorite appetizers were the potstickers and the dumplings. Potstickers are roughly twice as big as dumplings, and they're fried instead of (or in addition to) boiled. I can't say what, other than pork, was inside these guys, either, but I can tell you what I poured all over the outside of them: this great, dark, rich, flavorful sauce with lots of cilantro. You know—one of those sauces (usually involving cilantro) that you want to take home with you and pour all over everything, but especially your pillow.

Sweet dreams. *Zzzzzzzzzzzzzzzzzzzzzzzzzzzzzzzzzzzzzzzzzz* . . .

■ DEER INN

Something about August. I don't know, people coming and going. Vacations. School. Career changes. Plane wrecks. Last Straw last week, and this week I said *hasta lechuga* to an all-around-likable guy named

> **Deer Inn**
> 1900 Folsom Street,
> San Francisco. (415) 621-9413.
> Lunch. Cheap.

Blowtorch, who decided to stop being a bartender and go to work for the vineyards up north. Then after that his plans include moving to Mexico and eating cheap lobsters and just generally writing a book.

But first he had to tell me about an amazing place here in town called Deer Inn, and pretty soon, if you're good, I'll tell you. But first I have to go water the tomatoes. Hold on . . .

OK, I'm back and I don't know how ol' Blowtorch (may he make wine in peace) found out about Deer Inn unless he was in the habit of drinking there. It's a bar first, if not foremost. I mean you walk in and there's a bar. Then there's a great little back room after that. It has six tables with plastic tablecloths on them, and mostly bare walls except for a picture of rows and rows of different flags and a mirror and maybe one or two other things, but certainly not windows or flowers. I think the place has been there for millions of years, and my guess is the back room has seen a lot of poker faces and smelled a lot of cigar smoke and heard a lot of bullshit in its day. Now it hears a lot of bullshit and sees and smells a lot of meat. So long as it's lunchtime on a weekday, at least.

We planned to go there, me and B. T., on a Saturday, the day before he headed out. But we called first to make sure and, sure enough, no one answered. So we decided to go to St. Francis Fountain and research the chili, only we were rudely interrupted by some good-lookingly terrible Mission Street diner.

So that was that and then, a couple days later, Blowtorch having already disappeared into the grapes, I called Deer Inn myself and some old guy's growly voice said, "Hello."

"Is this the Deer Inn?"

"Yeah."

"You open?"

"I picked up the phone, didn't I?" he said. Click.

So I can't say it's exactly a friendly place, but I can say that it rocks the carnivorous world. Deer Inn. Folsom and 15th. Just one or two blocks up from Rainbow, but steer cleer, veggies—there were only two things on the chalkboard menu: beef stew and lamb shank. For six bucks, that'll come with spaghetti, taters, cabbage, and bread. For a buck-fifty more you get soup and salad as well.

Naturally, I coughed up the buck-fifty more, expecting the worst—but it turned out to be well worth it. This was no cup o' Campbell's, no sir; it was a bowl of homemade orange-brothed chicken soup with fresh carrots and celery and parsley, unoverdone pasta, and plenty of actual pieces of actual chickens. It was great.

And the salad was a regulation plateful of real green lettuce with a single piece of tomato on top, in a simple vinegar and oil dressing and a sprinkling of Parmesan. It was great.

And the lamb shank was great: tear-away tender and amply graviated, with plenty of wet stuff left to occupy all my bread and butter. (Real bread and real butter, mind you.) Too bad about the mushrooms, though.

Oh well. The spaghetti was surprisingly good, or at least cooked right, which is rare in restaurants. It was thinly tomato-sauced and sprinkled with more cheese and more fresh parsley.

Other than that, there were two wedges of potato—oven roasted is my guess—and a pile of cooked cabbage and onion seasoned with black pepper and something weird and tangy that I never did identify.

All in all it was a great and huge and meaty meal, and the guy who cooked and served and cleaned up after it was every bit as friendly as the bartender wasn't. Which goes to show you something, but I'm not sure what.

■ STAR LUNCH

Just got off the horn with my dad, Peaches, and he's mildly miffed at me, turns out, 'cause I don't write songs no more, poor boy, mildly miffed at me 'cause I don't write songs no moooore. See, he'll be out here soon—this weekend, in fact—yikes!—hide the *Hustlers* and hooch, honey—I'll go pick me up some disinfectant sprays and cleaning agents, lord

Star Lunch
605 Jackson Street,
San Francisco. (415) 788-6709.
Lunch, dinner. Cheap cheap.

lord, go pick me up some disinfectant sprays and cleaning agents.

All kidding aside, though, Peaches expects to do a little pickin' and grinnin' with me and most of the Bay Area's underground music scene—so get in line and tune up and try and behave yourselves, huh?

How bad am I, compared to some people, what with a four-track-totin', song-spittin' old man and a ma who calls me a sold-out yuppie every time I sell a story for $35 and two copies, oh lonesome, every time I sell a—

"Stop!!!!!!!!"

OK, OK. Jesus, where's your sense of rhythm? I was just trying to illustrate how much I love my mom and dad and they love me, in their own separate ways, even if they can't stand each other. But I wouldn't trade them for anything in the world, short of Mrs. Muckenhoupt and Mr. Beginner and an uncle to be named later. Uh-oh, I think I feel a little something tuneful coming over me . . . Hit it, boys . . .

Off the commode again/I just can't wait to get off the commode again . . .

Ah, nuts, I give up. True as those sentiments may be, I can't write me an honest, god-fearing song any more than Willie Nelson can. So you can see for yourself why I hung up my ukulele. Now if only everyone else would toss in their guitars and drums and paintbrushes and cameras, maybe we could all get us a decent night's sleep. After all, the only real, true way to express yourself honestly is through fiction. Which pays $35 and two contributor copies. Which is why God gave us the restaurant review, so let's see what I can say about Star Lunch.

Star Lunch is a little tiny Shanghai hole-in-the-wall lunch counter on Jackson just off Kearny. You know, right around the corner from Puke of Puke-Puke—or House of Nanking, as some people call it. Unlike Nanking and I, however, Star Lunch is entirely honest and soulful and so on and so forth. The only art on the walls, for example, is an inch-thick layer of grease. Now that's my kind of music!

Speaking of ambience, the recurring theme of my meal there was a pressure cooker letting off a squealing, high-pitched, white-light, nipple-piercing screech that would have split weaker personalities than ours down the middle lengthwise. But we sat it out, me and Dan Leone, calmly conversing about this, that, and Salt Lake City.

What we were eating, since you asked, was braised beef with five spices in noodle soup, preserved vegetable and pork with rice cake in soup, and a couple of appetizers: pork chop and vegetarian beef. *Vegetarian beef?*

I would never order vegetarian beef, personally, so don't ask me. Ask the one with the mustache.

The pork chop was good and fried, I can tell you, but it was also flat-out flat; sprawling, in fact. Not that it wasn't a buck-fifty worth of meat. I just don't think that this pork was "chopped" so much as run over with a steamroller. I loved it.

I also thoroughly enjoyed my soup, the rice-cake one, but Dan Leone's was even better. His was a clear beef broth with glass noodles and cabbage and thin slices of beef and just general deliciousness. Mine had chunks of pork and rice cakes and some sort of greens in a cloudy, whitish broth. The greens were what they meant by "preserved vegetable," I take it, but I don't know why they call them preserved. They were the freshest-seeming and certainly the greenest ingredient in any of the things we ate.

So maybe by "preserved" they mean "kept in the refrigerator." I don't know. The waitressperson tried to explain it to me, but the language barrier was just too great. She was really nice, though, and she didn't seem to mind running around getting things to show me by way of explaining the menu. Rice cakes. Preserved vegetables . . .

So, let's see, we got nice, we got cheap, we got good food, and we got great 'sphere—plus or minus the brain-scrambling pressure cooker, which was a fluke occurrence, according to the waitressperson. All of which equals two bellies up from the Names Brothers, me and Dan Leone.

■ V.A. MEDICAL CENTER CANTEEN

I wanted to make a pie for my dad, Peaches, so I went out and about for blackberries and wound up at the V.A. hospital. Crawdad de la Cooter, who works there, had told me about a mother lode of berries out back behind where she parks. I pictured toxic-waste incinerators and nuclear power plants and thought: cool. Big, juicy ones.

V.A. Medical Center Canteen
4150 Clement Street,
San Francisco. (415) 750-2128.
Breakfast, lunch. Cheap cheap.

But it wasn't like that at all. Well, the blackberries were big and juicy. But instead of smokestacks and puddles of glowing green ooze, all I saw were pretty flowers and trees, some wildlife, and blackberries scrambling down the hill into the open mouth of our lovely bay.

Well, there was one little old dripping pipe coming out of the ground under a bridge between patches of berries. I did see that, but it might very well have been water leaking out of it for all I know, and for all Peaches needs to know.

So anyway, I'm not a cookbook writer or anything, but three cups of berries is how many you need to make a pie. I had four in about 15 minutes, and then when I came back up the hill to the hospital I noticed a wall of glass windows behind which people seemed to be sitting around eating. The V.A. hospital cafeteria! They call it the Canteen, but the important thing is that I remembered something else Crawdad told me after her first day of work. Something about big, fried food and plenty of it.

Seeing as I'm essentially a cartoon character, my eyeballs did that little slot-machine routine and came up chicken and chicken. It was 11 o'clock and I hadn't eaten yet, except for blackberries—so you may as well go ahead and add "hospital cafeterias" to the list of places I would stoop to review.

The V.A. Medical Center Canteen features some of the unhealthiest food you can imagine. Maybe that's why everyone there seemed so happy and full of life. I'm serious. You can get yogurt and salad and fruit, sure, but mostly you can get pizza and burgers and fries and fried chicken and biscuits and chili and yodel-eh-hee-hoo.

I got me a dark-meat-chicken combo with potato wedge and biscuit, plus a big thing of ham and bean soup, plus, what the hell, an order of fries.

Two of my friends were working at the hospital that day, but neither one of them could join me for lunch 'cause they were working, and it wasn't exactly lunchtime, so I had to say what I had to say to four cups of blackberries.

"Hi," I said, settling in to eat.

"You sure do look purty," I said.

"So," I said, "what do you think of this place?"

Personally, I thought the chicken transcended cafetereality. It tasted almost every bit as good as if not flat-out better than most of the fried chickens you get in restaurants around here. Juicy, juicy meat with a well-salted, peppery breading. The potato wedge was boring. The fries were nice and greasy—not bad, but they could've used a shake of vinegar for old time's sake. You know, like at festivals and amusement parks. The biscuit was big and good, but it would've been a lot better with real butter instead of Farm-Fresh Spread. Where do they think we are—down South? I mean, it's not like cholesterol's an issue. Is it?

Oh yeah, and the soup. The soup was really good. Salty as heck with lots of ham chunks and even shreds of pork—at least one piece of meat per spoonful. If you like a lot of crackers in your soup, bring nickels, because they'll only let you have two packages and then it's five cents extra for every two more.

I don't like a lot of crackers in my soup.

By way of atmosphere, well, the Canteen is a two-level, ceiling-fanned, white-walled room with plastic, cushion-backed booths, gray institutional carpeting, and a spectacular view of the bay and the mountains on the other side of it. The glass window wall actually curves up into the ceiling so that the sun comes right in on you—although I don't imagine they get a lot of sun out that way. But this was one of those blue-skied beautiful days right after the rain last week, so maybe that's why everyone was happy.

I know why I was happy. Fried chicken. Four cups of berries. Pie and

Peaches in my immediate future. One wall on out into the big, blackberried world out there, and three more lined with pictures of cartoon characters digging oblivioblissfully into hot dogs and hamburgers and triple-decker Dagwood sandwiches because, like me, they don't have to worry about their cholesterol.

■ EINSTEIN'S CAFE

First I knocked off Rocco the van's driver-side mirror in a parking garage in Reno. Then I solved the problem, like I tend to solve most of my problems, with duct tape. Then, about a month or so ago exactly, more or less, to the day, I finally put a new

Einstein's Cafe
1336 Ninth Avenue,
San Francisco. (415) 665-4840.
Lunch, dinner. Cheap cheap.

mirror on there. I don't know why, but I drove around with the old duct-taped one on the floor in back all this time, and then just this morning, cleaning up a bit, I tossed it into one of those hooded sidewalk trash thingies—freshly emptied, so the decision was irreversible.

Within three minutes, I swear to you, some big bad American two-tone-tanker Mike Tyson van came and bit off Rocco's new driver-side ear, and spit it out in 481 pieces all over Guerrero Street. Right in front of my eyes. So if I sound sad while I'm writing this, now you know why.

Oh sniff sniff sniff. Woe is me—and whoa is me, too, while I'm at it, and what the hell, wow is me and woo and wee are me as well, not to mention who, what, when, where, how, and sometimes why, come to think of it, along with general lamentations, and beating of chests, and pulling of hair, and gnashing of teeth, and renting of garments and then returning them with cheese-corn stains and losing the deposit.

Now, if nobody minds awfully much, I'd like to discuss a colorfully quirky little place on Ninth Avenue between Judah and Irving.

It was a foggy, drizzly, and all-around dreary day in the Mission, so I figured I may as well get my butt over to the Sunset while the gettin' was bad. There was this sandwich place there that I'd been meaning to look into: Einstein's Cafe, which is the bright idea of Youth Industry, the nonprofit group that creates businesses to give on-the-job training to industrious youths. Pedal Revolution (bike shop), Nu2u (thrift store), and now this.

Einstein's Cafe (cafe). They make amazing homemade bread, gigantic real-stuff salads, and soups of the days. Everything is under five bucks as a matter of principle, and that's a principle I like.

I don't particularly like sandwiches, though, so I went with the soup-and-salad combo. I love soup and I love salad. And I loved this salad (great homemade vinaigrette), and I loved the bread that came with it, but the soup had way too many mushrooms in it. I hate mushrooms. It was supposed to be tomato and beef soup, but it had more mushrooms than either, trust me. I counted. (Mushrooms: 9, Beefs: 2, Tomatoes: 5)

Don't worry, I'm not going to let nine little mushrooms get me down. I'm all out of lamentations. And anyway, everything else was great, including the cause, and the place itself. There's the inside coffeehouse-ish room with a chalkboard full of Einsteinic figgerin's, and then there's a funky sort of sunroofed porch, with pictures of old Al and things he said and stuff, and then, best of all, there's an outdoor picnic-tabled garden area, where you can eat with the flowers and trees and bugs, like I like to do.

And guess what? By the time I got there, the dreary, drizzling fog had lifted and the sun was out and the sky was blue and the flowers were real and the trees were whispering haikus about trees and I spilled soup all over my crotch.

■ NEW CENTRAL

At the start of this baseball season I pipe-dreamed about an Indians-Giants World Series. Well, the Indians, sorry as they've sometimes seemed, are going to the play-offs, and the Giants are still in the running, which is more than most people dared to dream—with or without the assistance of pipes.

New Central
301 South Van Ness Avenue, San Francisco. (415) 255-8247/621-9608. Breakfast, lunch, dinner. Cheap.

So I'm heading on out to the 'Stick this afternoon to see if I can't help push the homeboys along, keep that dream a-pipin', so to speak. Big game. Dodgers. Giants beat 'em 2-1 last night, so now they're one game back. That makes today's game the biggest remaining game of the season.

But enough about baseball. How 'bout those 49ers, huh?

But enough about football. It's time to get down to biness.

(New misspelling of the word *business* is courtesy of letter-writer S. Fried, who points out that *real* Clevelanders say biness, not bidness. Um, I meant for the *d* to be silent? Either that or I'm not a real Clevelander but a Youngstowner, and maybe Youngstowners say bidness, but what the hell, I'll switch over to biness if it'll make S. Fried happy, and with a name like S. Fried, how can S. Fried help but be happy—all day every day. Especially if I ever get my ass on over to Mandalay-hee-hoo, the Burmese restaurant S. Fried keeps telling me to get my ass on over to.)

Speaking of letter writers, some other one with some other name sent me a hot tip called something-or-other, an Indian restaurant over on South Van Ness between 14th and 15th Streets. So I went to look into it one afternoon between lunchtime and dinnertime. I was hungrier than a bat out of hell, on account of only having had a bowl of oatmeal for breakfast.

The bad news is the Indian place was closed. The good news is I saw a sign down the block for a cooler-looking place called 307 Cafe, and the bad news is that the 307 was even closeder, as in out of biness. The good news is that just past *that*—and if you feel like a horse being coaxed along by a dangled carrot, imagine how *I* felt (only it wasn't carrots I was after, either)—but just past the 307, same side of the street as everything else, is a Mexican joint called New Central.

Open—*abierto*—open!

And the New Central, it turns out, is the place to be if you ever find yourself malnourished on the east side of South Van Ness between 14th and 15th. For five, six bucks you can pick you up a house special that goes by the noble name of "strips of beef." But first you'll have to sit down and talk to a waiterguyperson.

I recommend the counter, because they have a very good one, but there was no room there for me, so I had to sit at a table. The tables are good, too. They've got these great-shade-of-blue-green-and-white-checkered tablecloths—real ones, but don't worry, they're covered with clear plastic. And then each table has a pink plastic flower centerpiece with false dewdrops.

In fact, New Central is the single most plasticfully flowered restaurant I've ever seen. They're all over the place, all along the walls up high where you can't really tell, but God knows. There's even a huge plastic floor plant, complete with fake dirt, in the corner by the door. Also: beer plaques and TV, by way of atmosphere, and every now and again the jukebox kicks in good and loud for one song, drowning out CNN headline news. Hooray!

Now, about those "strips of beef," well, they're grilled with peppers and onions and 'maters, and that all comes with refried beans, rice, and a small pile of salad with an even smaller pile of guacamole on top. And all that's all well and good, but you also get a big basket of great, thick chips and some great, thin, hot salsa. And, of course, your tortillas, which are three fat homemade flour ones. And (count 'em) five pats of butter, and you don't even have to ask!

My kind of place, in other words, not to mention that that's a lot of food for five, six bucks. They also have standard breakfast stuff and burritos and standard Mexican stuff, including *birria* and *menudo* on weekends—but I've got a ball game to get me out to and a home team to root root root for.

Hey, humor me, OK? I've always wanted to do this, so I'll phone in the final score from the stadium, like a *real* sportswriter. OK? Thanks. Here I go . . .

Final score: Giants 6, Dodgers 5, 12 innings.

∎ RANCHO BURGERS

On one napkin I was writing my picks for Sunday's football games and on another one I was taking notes about the restaurant. I thought I put both napkins into my back pocket before leaving the joint, but all I can find now is you-guessed-which-one—so all good intentions aside, here's who I like on Sunday:

> **Rancho Burgers**
> 5121 Geary Boulevard,
> San Francisco. (415) 386-5678.
> Breakfast, lunch. Cheap cheap.

The Ravens +1½ vs. San Diego in San Diego.

The Eagles +2½ vs. Minnesota in Minnesota.

The Lions +7½ vs. Green Bay in Detroit, because the Silverdome's chili dogs are the best in the NFC, if not the world—which gives the Lions a stronger home-field advantage than most people give them credit for.

I also kind of like the Niners giving 3½ to Carolina, but I personally refuse to ever bet on San Francisco. I get sick enough when they lose without having to cough up any green stuff.

But speaking of chili dogs, what about Mr. Hot Dog Rancho Burgers out there on Geary, 15th Avenue, 16th?

"Good point. What about it?"

Well, you haven't eaten there, have you? I know because *I* hadn't even eaten there until yesterday, and the place has "my kind of place" written all over it. Really it's just called Rancho, but the sign out front says "Mr. Hot Dog" on top of Rancho and "Burgers" below it, so I call it Mr. Hot Dog Rancho Burgers. Hope you don't mind.

Anyway, this million-year-old sign is in the shape of a covered wagon with lit-up wagon wheels and a silhouetted cowpoke up front, but no horse 'cause that would stick out over the street and cause accidents.

I was afraid that Rancho wouldn't live up to its signage, but guess what? It's even cooler inside than out. The floor is painted the color of avocado skins, and the walls are painted funky shades of yellows and reds—at least that's how I remember it. I still can't find the other napkin.

There are real nice, real old wooden booths with flowery, plastic-covered tablecloths; there are antique dairy-can counter stools, a couple of actual wagon wheels behind the counter; there's the "Family Corral," a big huge booth in back with a slat-slanted roof over it.

There's Mr. Hot Dog, wearing a cowboy hat and a gun, plus other antique signs for a smiling slice of "Hot Apple Pie" and "Country Style Flapjacks" and "Mr. Hot Dog goes Cowboy Bar-B-Q." And you know these are for real because they all say "Pennies" with two pegs in front for hanging on the number of cents, scoreboard style.

But my favorite is the "Ham & Eggs with Hash Brown Potatoes" one on the front of the hood over the grill. There's a pig and a chicken running into a frying pan, smiling and laying eggs, respectively. If only life were like that!

It is, kind of, at Mr. Hot Dog Rancho Burgers. Go see for yourself. It's a genuine hole-in-the-wall pre-diner diner, entirely unpretensified. And the food ain't pennies, but it's cheap. I ate breakfast and lunch, for example, for eight-something. Two eggs and pork chop and hash browns and toast (four-something), and a foot-long Rancho bacon cheese dog (three-something). Plus tax. That's eight something, and that's cheap, divided by two.

The taters are hash browned just right, and piled on. The pork chop was done up Chinese-style, and it was good, too. Everything else was just fine, breakfastwise, but the thing to get is lunch.

Hot dogs. They're big, fat, and juicy, and they come with fresh tomatoes, lettuce, onion, relish, and mustard—whatever you want. Bacon, cheese.

I wanted meat meat meat, see, and I didn't trust their homemade chili to have it; that's why I got a bacon cheese dog instead of a chili dog. Because chili round here rarely if ever has meat in it, whereas bacon can't seem to help itself.

I can't make up my mind about the two ladypersons running the joint. They were nice, but they got all suspicious when I ordered lunch right after breakfast. Before the one got my hot dog going, the other slipped me a bill for both meals: eight-something.

"Pay up," she said. "Now."

■ GRAVY'S

Boy oh boy oh boy do I got a good one for you. It's so good that I can't wait to tell you about it. Who cares about postseason baseball or philosophy in general? Who cares that while I'm writing this I'm also knocking off a bowl of Crawdad de la Cooter's catfish gumbo and two meat pies she brought back from Louisiana? Who cares how I found my new favorite soul food restaurant on my way to a baseball game, then went three for four with the game-winning RBI? So you know it's got to be lucky, 'cause I'm not normally much of a hitter.

Gravy's
2511 Geneva Avenue, Daly City.
(415) 337-9122. Lunch, dinner.
Cheap.

The name of the place is Gravy's. It's on Geneva across from Cow Palace, and I know a lot of you don't often always get out that way, but I'm here to tell you that maybe you might oughta start.

It's Daly City, technically, but, hell, it's a lot closer than New Orleans, and if you like gumbo and such, you *need* Gravy's, especially if you're not lucky enough to have a girlfriendperson with a name like Crawdad de la Cooter.

Speaking of great names, the first time I went to New Orleans I stumbled upon a restaurant that was proprietpersoned by a guy named Grease. Now I don't know whether or not Grease and Gravy are brothers, but if so, Gravy must have won the coin toss, 'cause he got Mom. He flew her out from New Orleans a couple years ago, and now it's him and her in the kitchen. Cooking.

In the eating room, eating, it's me and Crawdad and Satchel Paige the Pitcher, who's been having trouble eating and sleeping and everything, poor pitcher, ever since several weeks ago when he made the worst decision of his life: He stopped eating meat. Since which him and his girlfriendperson have broken up and his vanmobile threw a rod clear through the block. In other words, he lost everything, including his meat-eating enzymes, so he was afraid to start eating meat again without them, he said.

"Don't worry," I said, sliding him a chicken wing. "They'll come back." But I don't think it was the enzymes he was so down-and-out about.

At any rate, he had his hands full with a seafood combo dinner, which was four kinds of fishes, all fried, and four sides and corn bread. The red snapper was slightly dry, but the other three kinds (oysters, shrimps, and catfish) were all great, especially the oysters, which were bursting with juiciness. Crawdad said they were the best fried oysters she's ever had, anywhere. Of all the sides we saw, the collard greens and the black-eyed peas (served over rice with chunks of sausage) were my favorites.

Crawdad, being Crawdad, got the gumbo. It goes for $5 or $8, depending on how much you want—a lot, or a whole honkin-duty lot—and it includes shell-and-all crab chunks, bone-and-all chicken parts, and sausage and stuff. Gravy calls himself the "Gumbo Specialist," and he might be right. I loved it. Crawdad said it was the best she'd had around here.

Being me, I got the eight-piece chicken-wing special with fries and bread for $4. Never mind that the fries were perfectly cooked and spicefully seasoned, and never mind that the bread was toasted and buttered, à la breakfast. The point here is the fried chicken.

Powell, Danny Glover, Roscoe, and anyone else whose fried chicken I ever yodeled over—it's time to sit down and start smiling about the good old days. Gravy kicks your collective butts. His breading is spiced right, his chickens have had all their shots, and they're cooked to order, perfectly. Underneath the crisp, golden exterior, these little birdie wings had as much juice to them as some people's whole turkeys. And if you want more than wings, you can get a whole chicken's worth of all dark meat (that's eight pieces), for example, for $6 (that's cheap). That's what I'm gonna do next time.

Atmospherically, Gravy's is right on target: comfy swivel chairs, green-and-white-checkered table plastic, green-and-black-striped curtains that only halfway obstruct your view of Cow Palace, and splattered hot-sauce stains on the linoleum. Plus one free refill on your fountain soda, which isn't technically atmosphere, I know, but they do have RC Cola, which is.

So do your soul a favor and check this place out. If you go on a weekend, take it on down to Crocker and watch me go three for four. I'll be the one spitting out chicken bones instead of tobacco.

■ ELEPHANT BLEU

Everyone's asking me if Gravy's is as good as I said it was. I'll let the facts speak for themselves. I've been back twice already to take away two genetically engineered four-legged, four-thighed all-dark-meat chickens ($6 apiece). In games during which I was eating Gravy's fried chickens, the Indians went 2-0. Without Gravy, they were 1-2.

Elephant Bleu
3232 16th Street,
San Francisco. (415) 553-6062.
Lunch, dinner. Cheap.

But that was the Yankees and this is the Orioles, and luckily it's a seven-gamer, 'cause (speaking of luck) I have a feeling I'm going to have to come up with whole new systems of juju. For one thing, enough is enough (as both Karl Marx and Popeye have pointed out again and again), and I don't think my Chief Wahoo boxers are going to make it another whole week without washing.

But let's talk about the Vietnamese-ification of the Mission. Elephant Bleu. Sixteenth between Guerrero and Dolores. That's good news for me and for anyone else who breaks out in rashes every time they walk past the long line of yuppie hipsters waiting to drop their dollars into the Slanted Door. Of course, I've never eaten at the Slanted Door, so all I can accurately say by way of comparison is that Elephant Bleu is decidedly, definitively better, even if I did find a small green piece of plastic in the bottom of my bowl.

It's better 'cause it's cheaper, see, and it's not overly fancy-pants. It's a converted garage, in fact, which kind of pisses me off because there are plenty of restaurants and not enough parking spots in the neighborhood already. Oh well. At least it's a Vietnamese restaurant and not any other kind, or a coffeehouse.

They didn't have hot-and-sour soup, so I got that other thing I always get, the *bún cha giò thit nuóng*—you know, imperial rolls and barbecued pork over vermicelli with lettuce, mint, bean sprouts, and cucumbers. Punker got vegetarian noodle soup with tofu, tomatoes, mushrooms, and lemongrass. I never did get around to tasting it. Punker seemed to like it a lot, except that he eventually put too much hot sauce in and started to smoke and sputter and cough.

I liked mine fine. There was a lot of it at least, but it was mostly noodles and not enough pork. What pork there was was as tasty as all getout, which only made me sadder about what pork there wasn't. And even the imperial rolls were smaller than at other places. There were two of them, like usual, but they were kind of unimperial: skinny and sickly looking, with a chewy, over-rolled exterior.

Still, I cleaned my plate like a good boy. And then I pulled that little green plastic thing out of my mouth and started wondering what it was.

A "shrinky-dink," Punker guessed. He said I should show it to our waiterboyperson, but I thought it was kind of pretty, so I took it home to keep with the rest of my toys. It looks kind of like an arrowhead, or a fish, or Michigan.

Anyway, I wouldn't let that stop you from checking out Elephant Bleu, and I won't let it stop me from going back. It's an interesting menu. In addition to all the Vietnamese standards (except hot-and-sour shrimp soup), they also have—get this—spaghetti and meat sauce, seafood spaghetti, stuffed calamari, and a couple of rather Italian-sounding omelettes: "Venezia Classico," for example, and "Napoli Fresco."

Question mark?

I'd still rather go to the Tenderloin or the Richmond or Tu Lan, all in all, but it's kind of nice to have cheapish Vietnamese so close to home.

■ RINCÓN PERUANO

While we're on the subject of Mission District holes-in-the-walls, there's a hole-in-a-wall on 26th Street between Capp and Mission I may as well tell you about, while we're on the subject.

Rincón Peruano. Peruvian corner. My pal E. B. Matt told me about it a

Rincón Peruano
3364 26th Street,
San Francisco. (415) 824-2673.
Lunch, dinner. Cheap.

couple Fridays ago, and next thing I knew I was eating lunch there a couple Saturdays ago with him and his girlfriendperson, W. B. Katt. The place consists of the kitchen, which takes up about half of the space, five tables, four orange walls, and a big refrigerator with a little TV on top of it.

The menu's up on one of the walls, and then in the corner right next to it there's a little Peruvian flag and one of those posters that shows you the proper way to choke on a chicken bone. Yeah, there's *art* art, too, but I never know what to say about *art* art. I only know what to say about flags and instructional choking poster art. And food.

That Saturday, for example, I ate *bistek apanada,* or "breaded steak," with rice and salad. By "breaded steak" they pretty much mean "steak," so don't get your hopes up, like I did, for something like chicken-fried.

But go ahead and get your hopes up. It's good food, even if it's not breaded. A pile of rice, some thin-sliced but juicy and well-seasoned meat on top of that, and then a plop of iceberg lettuce with cut-up tomatoes. If I were you, I'd just mix everything together and start spooning the green salsa all over it all—but I'm getting ahead of yourself.

By the time your food comes, you see, you're already going to be addicted to this salsa, I'm telling you. They set you up with it right off the bat—not with chips but with a basket of bread. Never mind the margarine, just spread a spoonful of the green on a slice of white and get ready to yodel. This is the greenest and best green salsa I ever had anywhere, period. It's not like the green salsa you get in taquerias. It's not like guacamole. I think it's just grinded-up cilantro and chile peppers and something magical, because as hot as it is, which is hotter than hell, it's entirely edible. You know how really great music can be really really loud and not hurt you like really loud really bad music does. That's what I'm talking about with this salsa. It's . . . I don't know, it's the Pixies.

We cleaned out a whole little thing of it between the three of us, and the whole time I was thinking and sometimes even saying, "I've gotta get Crawdad here, Crawdad's gonna love this salsa, she's gonna cream her crawpants"—etc.

So, OK, got her there eventually, just last night, in fact, and I don't think she creamed her crawpants, exactly, but we did clean out an even bigger thing of salsa between just the two of us, and we had the cleanest, clearest nasal passages in all of the neighborhood, I believe. I'm still smelling things I never smelled before.

Hold on a second. I smell a cockroach in my kitchen.

Got it. OK, this time—meaning last night, with de la Cooter—I got fried fish (same salad, same rice, same price), and I liked it even better than the steak. Crawdad had fish with oyster sauce and mushrooms, which she liked even better than my fried-fish dish, but the point is that we could have been eating fried flip-flops and sautéed oil rags, respectively, and what with that green salsa all over everything, it would've still been a pretty damn halfway decent meal.

But enough about the salsa. Let's talk about some of the other things you can conceivably put under it at Rincón Peruano, flip-flops and oil rags notwithstanding. They have daily specials, like chicken soup and chicken with rice and a bunch of other stuff beyond my humble ability to translate: *lomo saltado, cau cau o mondonguito a la Italiana, estofado de pollo, y* so on and so forth. The regular, everyday menu is only six things: fried fish (which I recommend), fish with oyster sauce, "breaded" steak, beef fried rice, steak with onions and tomatoes, and seafood soup. All those things are between $6 and $7.

And on Saturdays they have sandwiches for $3.50. We saw some on that Saturday and they were huge and piled with meat and meat and meat. I've been thinking about the implications—all the surfaces a long, fat sandwich like that might afford a certain spreadable green thing. But they only have the sandwiches on Saturdays, so . . . see you Saturday.

■ RICA'S PUPUSAS

There are many, many Jesus Christs. The one I grew up with was the one whose eyes looked right at you no matter where you were, so long as you were in the living room. I think he even had parts of the kitchen covered, come to think of it, which is why I spent most of my formidable years in the cellar or the upstairs bathroom or outside in the maple tree.

> **Rica's Pupusas**
> 3481 18th Street,
> San Francisco. (415) 863-0773.
> Lunch, dinner. Cheap.

Then there's James Tate's "Good-time Jesus," and of course the world-famous "Laughing Jesus." But my second-favorite Jesus of all is the one I call the "Mighty-Concerned Jesus," which hangs on the back wall of the second-closest restaurant to my house, Rica's Pupusas, 18th Street between Valencia and Lexington. Yep, we're still in the Mission, folks, but hang in there please, 'cause I'm calling this Part 3 of a retroactive three-part series on holes-in-the-Mission District-walls, meaning: The end is near.

Someone sent me a list of 10 or 12 Sunset District restaurants that would seem to have my name written all over them, so I guess maybe I'll ride off into the Sunset after this one. Hell, maybe I'll move there for two or three months. But first let me tell you about this "Mighty-Concerned Jesus" I was telling you about. He's sitting at a table or something with his hands sort of interclasped before him—but it's not like he's praying so much as he's wringing these hands of his.

And he's got this look on his face, halo notwithstanding, like he just ordered a hamburger and here it comes only he can't remember if he told the waitressperson not to put mayonnaise on it. Or maybe his team's in the World Series, seventh game, and Jose Mesa just gave up the tying run in the bottom of the ninth, meaning extra innings. On the road.

Jesus, I know the feeling.

"Of course he's concerned!" my friend Haywire said after I described this great painting to him over the telephone. "He has to save the souls of all mankind from eternal damnation, whereas Mesa only had to get three outs."

Well, I had to agree with him there. Except I would've said mankind-persons. (It's not Haywire's fault if he's sexister than me. He comes from Texas!)

Anyway, we talked sports and chicks and chickens and shop for a long time and when I got off the phone I went to Rica's again, 'cause I was hungry.

"Hi Jesus."

"Howdy."

Rica's, for the record, is an oddly shaped, oddly walled sort-of hole-in-the-garage, chaotically decorated with Mighty-Concerned Jesuses, Xmas lights, Last Suppers, Statues of Liberties, posters of Guatemala and El Salvador, mirrors, flags, and a 3-D star-shaped collage of old-timer black-and-white actors and actresses. There's another TV on another refrigerator, just like last week at Rincón Peruano, but this one wasn't on either time I ate there.

The first time I had chicken soup, which was good and tasty with whole pieces of chickens, big chunks of carrots and taters, and a half-ear of corn that was somehow or other cooked perfectly. How often does that happen in a bowl of soup? On the minus side, where were the tortillas?

Maybe you have to ask for them, so when I went back for *huevos rancheros*, I asked for them. Flour ones. Yep—got 'em, and there was no extra charge, so I don't know what to tell you, except that these were the second-best *huevos rancheros* I've had around here. Three eggs with plenty of juice to them and plenty of cheese on top. Tortillas down below. Pile o' rice. Pile o' refried black beans. Yum and yum and yum.

My only complaint on the *rancheros* front is that the dang salsa's got no kick to it. But that's OK, 'cause each table comes with its very own bottle of Tapatío, which is, for the record, my second-favorite kind of hot sauce.

My first-favorite hot sauce is the one I call De La Cooter Juice—but it's not what you think. Don't worry. It's the bottle of stuff Crawdad made out of three kinds of hot peppers from my garden: habanero, jalapeño, and Thai hot peppers. Yodel-*owwww*-hee-hoo!

My first-favorite *huevos rancheros* are at Chava's.

My first-favorite Jesus is the one where he's playing cards with Santa Claus and Rudolph the Red-Nosed Reindeer. What? You don't know that one? That's 'cause it's on a homemade Xmas card to me from the first-most sacrilegious person I know, Haywire. Santa looks like he's bluffing, Rudolph looks suspicious, and Jesus Christ looks wide-eyedly defeated, like he's holding a nine-high hand, nothing wild.

But you never know with Jesus.

■ BASHFUL BULL

I looked up from the sports section into the eyes of Crawdad de la Cooter, whose eyes were looking somewhat waterier than usual, as if she were fixing to bust out crying right then and there in the restaurant. So I looked back down into the sports section.

Bashful Bull
1222 Noriega Street,
San Francisco. (415) 564-1584.
Breakfast, lunch, dinner. Cheap.

"Says here the Indians signed Assenmacher," I said. But that didn't cheer her up none either.

Don't think I'm a knucklehead, or unsensitive or anything, because I'd already been trying to draw her out, so to speak, but she was so unspeakably sad that, well, she couldn't speak. All she could do was shake her head and quiver her lip, and nothing I could say—not even "Drink lots of coffee, quick!"—seemed to help.

There's been a bad blues bug going around ever since the clocks fell back and it started getting dark around lunchtime. Everyone's been feeling it, all over the country. I think it was Haywire, or maybe my cousin Drags, who theorized to me recently that daylight savings time must have been dreamed up by the mental health industry to increase revenues.

In fact, I've been a bit less than chipper myself these past few months, I don't mind admitting, but I'm one of those guys who wraps his emotions up in weeks and weeks of sports sections. It's not that I don't like to cry, it's just that I can't. Not even if a crate of oranges falls on my foot. Not even at the movies.

Not even if I worked at the V.A. hospital, like Crawdad, and it was Veteran's Day, like it was, so I had the day off, along with every intention in the world of spending the best part of it at Ann's Cafe—but unfortunately Ann's Cafe decided to stay home and honor our nation's war veterans too.

So where does that leave us?

How about the Sunset? How about Bashful Bull, Noriega at 19th Avenue, which was the first and best-sounding of the 10 or 12 restaurants on my list of Sunset District restaurants to review? My Sunset informer informed me that their big breakfasts were BIG. All caps.

Well, you can't believe everything you hear, folks, all caps or otherwise, but go right ahead and believe this one 'cause it's true: It's not Ann's Cafe, but the Bashful Bull has the second-biggest breakfast I've had in this here Bay Area. Three pancakes, three eggs, three sausages, three bacons, and biscuits and gravy for $6.25.

Now that would be a pretty good meal deal even if it were two of everything, and even if the pancakes were the diametrical size and approximate thickness of a Kenny G. CD—which is what most restaurants try to pass off as pancakes in their big-eater breakfast specials. But I still don't have a CD player, personally, because records are still bigger and still better, and the Bashful Bull's pancakes, I'm happy to report, are as big as Herb Alpert and the Tijuana Brass on vinyl.

They needed a plate unto themselves, in fact, and then there was another big plate with the eggs and bacons and sausages, and then another smaller plate with a split-open biscuit just smothered in sausage gravy.

There were so many plates, not to mention coffee and water and syrup and stuff, that there was no room left anymore for the sports section, so I had to fold it up and watch Crawdad cry into her Spanish omelette. It came with hash browns and toast, and it was a big omelette by normal standards, but it wasn't five-pounds big and there weren't five kinds of meat in it, and in fact it didn't taste too good.

Not that I tasted it, but I could tell because Crawdad didn't stop crying until I let her eat some of what I was eating. The pancakes were great. The biscuits and gravy were just fine. She didn't try the sausage or bacon or eggs, but those things were good, too, especially since there were three of each of them.

And speaking of three, I returned the favor by eating three-quarters of

Crawdad's two slices of toast for her. Wow, what a meal! The coffee was delightfully terrible, the atmosphere was atmosphereless, and I hear they have good burgers, too, but the important thing is big, big, big. By the time we stumbled on out of there with our respective stomachs, little Ms. de la Cooter and me were giddy and giggly, not unlike we would have been stumbling on out of Ann's Cafe.

But the yeehaw only lasted until about 2:30 that afternoon, when the sun went suddenly down all over again, dang it.

■ JOANN'S CAFE & PANTRY

Here I am about to go getting paradoxical on you, so if you don't think you can handle it, honeybun, hide your eyes. How many eggs are in a three-egg omelette? I'm serious, because last week at Bashful Bull I

> **JoAnn's Cafe & Pantry**
> 1131 El Camino Real, South San
> Francisco. (650) 872-2810.
> Breakfast, lunch. Cheap.

witnessed a three-egg omelette that took up a whole plate almost and probably weighed two pounds. (Not to mention Ann's five-pound three-egg omelette.) Whereas today, on the other hand, I partook of a three-egg omelette that wasn't even half the size or weight of the Bashful Bull's or my name's not Danny Boy *and* I'll eat my hat.

Lard knows I'm still hungry.

I know, I know. I know that eggs, like hats, come in many different sizes, and I know that I was in San Francisco last week and South San Francisco this week and that things are just generally worse in southern California, and I know that "Lard" should technically be "Lord," but some typos turn out to be for the butter.

I know five or six other things too, but what you may be wondering is what I was doing in South San Francisco.

Well, I messed up my foot playing soccer, and now every time I step on it, which is every other step I take, to misquote Sting, I see a different episode of *Love, American Style*. Which was never one of my favorite TV shows, so I'm trying not to walk too much.

So I figured I may as well drive somewhere, so to speak, so long as I wasn't walking nowheres. And so happens there was a restaurant in South

San Francisco that someone had recently e-suggested to me. So you see why I don't read my e-mail very often?

Because the whole bright idea had sprung out of some AOL e-conference on California food dives, during which several e-persons were apparently e-talking up JoAnn's Cafe ("waxing rhapsodic," I believe, were my informant's exact words). "Waxing rhapsodic" sounds good, but technology sucks and so does JoAnn's Cafe. Well, it's not a dive, at any rate—or if it is it's an e-dive for e-people who don't know what they're e-talking about.

Real dives don't charge $7.50 for basic two-egg breakfasts with meat and taters and toast and well, yeah, there was some fresh fruit involved somewhere in there, so that's something. And your choice of meat includes low-fat chicken-basil sausage, and your choice of toast includes bagels and homemade muffins and scones. Standard dive fare.

Yeah, right. About the only things you can get for under five bucks are two eggs and taters and toast without meat, or a bowl of oatmeal—so that was what my down-and-out-of-towner guests got. Carter got the two-egger and Copper got the oatmeal. Me, I scanned the menu very carefully, looking for the silver lining among all those sixes and sevens and eights. The omelette? Six bucks ain't bad for an omelette, I thought, especially if it's as big as that Bashful Bull omelette. Well, it's not. For a buck-fifty more, it's half the size, tops—I'm telling you—and I'll pass on my hat, thanks.

You get two things in your omelette. Want three or four? Buck apiece for extras. So I stuck with Italian sausage and mozzarella cheese, a combination that, you have to admit, makes perfect sense. The sausage was great. It was ground-up style and somewhat spicy, which is how Italian sausage should be. Good meat and good cheese is good, but Italian people like to eat big, and I have a few suggestions for JoAnn:

(1) Go to Ann's Cafe, Oakland. Get the Italian omelette, for roughly six bucks. Note how much meat and cheese and other stuff goes into it.

(2) As for the eggs, either start making six-egg omelettes or stop using robin eggs.

(3) Unrelatedly, make better potatoes. Just 'cause you use those nice, tasteful, redskin ones doesn't mean you don't have to put some spices into them. Sure, I've got salt and pepper on the table, but what about

garlic? What about rosemary and thyme and chile pepper, to misquote Simon and/or Garfunkle.

The muffins are good. I had an apple-walnut one and it was good. Copper liked his oatmeal, which came with thick cream, brown sugar, and some appley goo. Carter liked her real-wheat-bread toast, although she inexplicably ate it with a fork.

Takes all types . . .

JoAnn's isn't for me. If you're a small-eating type who doesn't mind spending more bucks than you have to . . . well, just don't go into JoAnn's expecting a dive. Expect slickness and cleanliness, and wait a minute—what are you doing in South San Francisco anyway?

■ MASSAWA RESTAURANT

The down-and-out-of-towners were still in town, seeing and eating all sorts of things they'd never seen or eaten before and just generally being on vacation. So one day they wanted to wander around the Haight and I said, "Go ahead." I said, "Take the 33 bus." I said, "My foot still hurts."

Massawa Restaurant
1538 Haight Street,
San Francisco. (415) 621-4129.
Lunch, dinner. Credit
cards accepted. Cheap.

Which it did, really, but I'm not saying I wasn't happy about it, for the moment. I was happy.

So I sat around being happy for an hour or three and then I started to be hungry. So I sat around being hungry for about 20 minutes before the phone rang and it was them, wondering what was for dinner.

"Ethiopian?" I said. I was trying to think of something else besides Thai and burritos and Vietnamese and burritos that you can't exactly get in Ohio. And I was right—neither Copper nor Carter had ever had any sort of East African food.

I told them to look around for a place called Massawa and wait there for me. I'd never eaten at Massawa, but a lot of my friends swear by it. In fact, people in general seem to swear by it. They won some sort of a Best Something-or-Other award from the *Guardian*. I saw it hanging on the wall.

Let's see, there was me, there was Copper and Carter, there was Johnny "Jack" Poetry (being one of the swears-by-it friends I was telling you about—so I invited him), and there was Nunzilla, the little windup-monster toy Copper and Carter had boughten for me during their Haight Street wanderings.

You know pretty much what people are like by now in general, so let me just explain Nunzilla to you and then we'll move on to food. She is a three-inch-high fire-breathing ruler-wielding green-eyed nun who waddles when you wind her, shooting sparks out the mouth and looking mean and nasty and just generally instilling the fear of God in long-lapsed Catholics like, for example, all four of us'ns.

The food was great! We got a beef thing, a chicken thing, a lamb thing, and a vegetarian thing, all served family style all over one of those gigantic centerpiece sheets of *injera*. What with recurring decorative piles of lentils, chickpeas, spinach, salad, and something else all the way around the plate, it was easily enough stuff to stuff the bejesus out of four big-eating peoplepersons and a windup plastic nun.

Orange juices, mango juices, Calistoga, and we still weighed in right around $40, so that's, what, 10 bucks a person? (Nunzilla didn't pitch in.) Massawa isn't exactly the cheapest East African food I've had, but it's cheap enough, considering the quantity and quality, and everything's about $1.25 cheaper for lunch (before 4:30).

Well, so here's what all we ate, and I'll tell you up front that everything—even the vegetarian stuff—was great. What it was, the vegetarian stuff, was *alicha,* or mushed-up potatoes, carrots, and bell peppers. We also had *alicha-beggee,* which was pretty much the same thing, only with chunks of lamb in it. These two were the mildest piles of stuff.

The meatiest was the chicken one, the *tsebhi-derho,* which was dark-meat, sadly skinless chicken, still on the bone and smothered in a tomato-based sort of barbecue sauce. My favorite pile, luckily, turned out to be the closest one to me. It was called *kelwa*—that's tender pieces of beef sautéed in "spiced clarified butter," whatever that means, with jalapeños, onions, and tomatoes.

All four of those, like I said, were great. The only thing I didn't like was one of the little side piles, but I'm not sure which one it was. It wasn't chickpeas or lentils or spinach or salad. It was something else.

The place was surprisingly uncrowded for dinnertime on a Thursday night, Haight Street. The service was good and friendly—our waitress-person even brought us "moist towelettes," or whatever you call those things, when all was said and done—as if we needed them! As if we weren't wearing pants!

Atmospherically, there's a lot about Massawa that is the opposite of my closet: It's cavernous, for example. On the other hand, the chairs are on wheels, just like my closet chair, and there are hats and maps on the walls, and the ceiling of the place is painted the same shade of blue as my closet ceiling. So I'm going to go ahead and describe it as homey, even though no one will probably agree with me on that, personally.

■ YOUNG'S CAFE

I was walking down Guerrero Street and a guy asked me if I wanted to join the circus—which is why I live in San Francisco, I guess, because anything can happen. Almost anything. In fact, I'd been trying to explain

Young's Cafe
732 22nd Street, San Francisco. (415) 285-6046. Lunch, dinner. Cheap cheap.

this to my mom on the phone earlier that same day, while she tried to get me to move to Ohio. No dice.

And then there I was, walking, and there was this other guy, who seemed to be struggling with a pile of boxes with a half of a chord organ or a broken accordion on top. He was wearing a large backpack and it had tons of huge pink feathers sticking out of it. Other than that, he looked like any other Mission hipster: young, tall, skinny, amply sideburned, and soul-patched.

"You want to join the circus?" he said.

I did what any normal person in their right mind would've done in my shoes. I said, "Huh?"

"You want to join the circus?" he said.

The thing is—my point is that I thought about it. I actually stood still for half a second on Guerrero Street and considered the prospect of joining the circus. But all I had in all my pockets put together was 14 bucks and a quarter of a stick of butter, and while this guy may have had a few lion tamers and contortionists packed into those boxes for all I knew, my initial half-second image of our circus act consisted of him playing the accordion while I ate a quarter of a stick of butter.

"No thanks," I said, picturing that picture and not seeing much money in it, frankly—not to mention fame or glory or personal satisfaction or babes or nutrition or anything, really. So I reckoned I'd pass on the circus and stick to writing restaurant reviews.

Hey, did I ever tell you about my friend in Ohio named Binko who claims to have eaten an entire stick of butter one night because he was drunk and there was nothing else in the house and that's how hungry he was? No? Well, he did. Or *says* he did. I don't know if I believe him or not. He's a Steelers fan (not that that has anything to do with anything).

Young's Cafe, meanwhile, is a restaurant full of cheap, big, decent Chinese food. It's on 22nd between Third Street and Tennessee. You know: the other side of Potrero Hill.

I ate there with my friend Crack Jack MacWhatever-the-rest-of-his-name-is, who's been talking up the joint for some time between innings. (We play baseball together.) It wasn't until one day Crack Jack out of nowhere turned into Willie Mays, roaming Crocker Amazon's treacherous outfields like anything hit anywhere had his name all over it, that then I started thinking: I'll have what he's having.

If that's one of Young's $2.95 to $3.25 rice plates, no problem. I can live with $2.95 to $3.25. And it's a big plate of food and it's decent, like I said. I don't know if it's worth going out of your way for, but if you work in that neck of the woods, like lots of people do, or if you're already passing through and you're hungry, check this place out.

It's a sort of a cavernous, empty-walled, unpretentious place. It's not big; it's just cavernous, maybe because the ceiling's high. The walls are white and almost entirely pictureless, so that if you take in enough MSG, you can conceivably sit there for a long time filling in the blanks.

The menu consists of 15 rice dishes, most of them right around three bucks, and 64 other standard Chinese things. Only a handful of those are more than five bucks. The potstickers are great. Crack Jack ordered Hunan spicy chicken over rice and I ordered shrimp with black-bean sauce over rice, but what I got was *beef* with black-bean sauce over rice. Both plates contained plenty of meat in flavorful sauces with still-crunchy green peppers and onions and carrots, all sautéed together and then plopped onto this huge pile of white rice. Simple and beautiful, but simple and beautiful Chinese stuff happens like that all over this town, Ma, just like weirdos and one-man circuses and 9,998 other things that you won't find, for example, in Ohio.

I'm not going anywhere.

■ ENCORE HOT POT CITY RESTAURANT

So there we were, on the outside looking in, scratching our heads. There was my head and there was Satchel Paige the Pitcher's. Where we were was Berkeley, CA, home of Satchel Paige the Pitcher's head, as

well as the rest of him, and the heads and the rests of a lot of other smart people. Not to mention Encore Hot Pot City Restaurant and a lot of other smart restaurants.

Encore Hot Pot City Restaurant
2067 University Avenue, Berkeley. (510) 540-8888. Lunch, dinner. Credit cards accepted.Cheap.

The question was: Do we cough up $11.99 apiece for all the hot pot and barbecue we can eat? Dumb question. Of course we do. When it's all you can eat, money is not an object. The only object is getting your money's worth, which is always possible so long as it's really all you can eat and there's no time limit. All-you-can-eat chicken wings, for example, for $1,750? No problem. Just don't expect me to leave my table for six or seven months.

In this case, it took us two hours and 15 minutes to eat all we could eat for $11.99, and then Satchel Paige the Pitcher was too full to go bowling. As for me, well, here's all I ate all day the day after Encore: one waffle, one orange, an ice-cream samwich, some grapes, and a big salad. That's how full I still was.

So, yeah, I'd say we ate our money's worth. I won't say it wasn't a challenge, though, because 12 clams is a lot of potatoes to young bucks like me and Satchel Paige the Pitcher.

Two hours and 15 minutes, on the other hand, is a long time to eat. It's three square meals at 45 minutes apiece is one way of looking at it, and 12 bucks divided by three is $4.80, what with the tip. But enough math, let's get down to philosophy: How full do you have to be to be too full to bowl? (Bear in mind that bowling is not soccer. It's not even baseball.) And while you're working on that, I'll tell you all about Encore . . .

Atmospherically speaking, you're eating at a factory. It's a huge, bright, high-ceilinged place with long tables lined up along three walls and an assembly-line buffet down the middle. Each eating station has a big ventilation hood hanging down from the ceiling, because you cook the food yourself, at your table.

You know how a hot pot works, right? It's a pot of boiling water. You throw raw stuff in, then take cooked stuff out and eat it. Encore's hot pots are encircled by a foil-covered barbecuing surface. In my opinion, gas burners under tinfoil ain't barbecue, but I'll complain about that later.

Right now I want to complain about the lack of help. I mean, they pour water in your hot pot and get the gas going and take your plates away and stuff like that; but what I'd like to see is a little more assistance or advice on what to do with everything. I know people who live and eat in Berkeley are smart, but that doesn't mean they're good cooks. So how about a few pointed pointers and helpful suggestions laminated to each table, or somewhere near the buffet, or something?

Put butter on the tinfoil before grilling. This sauce goes good with this meat, this one with that one. Make sure you cook the chicken all the way. Don't overcook the mussels. Eat your broccoli, save room for dessert—that sort of thing.

I was so excited and hungry and determined to eat eat eat eat eat that I just loaded a plate with raw beef and lamb and pork and chicken and slapped it all down on the tinfoil and went back to see what else there was. There were little plastic things of butter, for example. There was a whole table full of sauces and spices and garlic and stuff. And on the other side of the meat section I'd just pillaged, there were all the same meats, only marinated. I went back to our table and flipped over my burning slices of unanythinged meat. Eat and learn, I always say. Eat and learn.

Well, we learned a lot. I'm happy to report that by the end of the meal we were hot pot hot shots, me and Satch. My own personal specialties were ginger chicken, marinated lamb, and spiced-up fish. Satchel put together a carefully planned and excellently executed chicken soup with spinach and corn and cilantro and lots of other things by way of a closing number, and then for an encore we hit the fresh fruit bar and cleaned them out of watermelon and orange slices.

Lucky for us it wasn't a weekend, 'cause the buffet goes up to $12.99 Friday, Saturday, and Sunday, and I don't think either one of us had another buck of space to fill. The good news is: $8.99 noon to 4 p.m. and after 10 p.m. weekdays ($9.99 on weekends).

■ ABE'S CAFE

Well, it's time to say good-bye, I'm sorry to say, to Johnny "Jack" Poetry. He will be sorely missed at the baseball fields and card tables and coffeehouses and burrito and barbecue joints of San Francisco. The good news is that he's not dead or dying so much as moving to Idaho.

Abe's Cafe
553 Divisadero Street, San Francisco. (415) 885-5932. Lunch, dinner. Credit cards accepted. Cheap.

I know, I know—but it's *not* pretty much the same thing if you have a great girlfriendperson named Taters waiting there for you, and she's got a cozy little mountain home with elk steaks in the freezer.

So when I found out about the elk steaks I just naturally volunteered to haul a minivanful of Johnny "Jack"'s records and poetry and stuff, not to mention Johnny "Jack" himself. Not to mention his cat, Diva "Jack."

Which just naturally necessitated a pre-trip trip to their almost-all-boxed-up apartment, Western Addition, in order to stand around and pull on our beards and stubble and whiskers, reckoning what all would fit in the van and what all would have to be shipped. Not the sort of under-taking one would want to undertake on an empty stomach.

Which just naturally leads us to Abe's Cafe, around the corner on Divis., but not before walking past Brother-in-Laws (count 'em) *four* times, looking for a Carribean restaurant that wasn't either all-vegetarian (Reggae Runnins) or all-overpriced (King Jamaica). Which wasn't easy, mind you—walking past Brother-in-Laws four times, I mean, without stopping in even once just to chew the fat, so to speak—but I needed me something new to write about.

Which . . . well . . . hi, here I am, and here's what I have to say about

Abe's: It (at the risk of writing my first actual sentence in some time) is good.

I got lamb kabob ($5.95) and Johnny "Jack" got the Mediterranean combo plate ($5.50), and those were the two most expensive items on the menu. Abe's is cheap. Cheap and good, but you might not like the atmosphere. Fluorescent lights, nothing fancy, no decor—I think most people get it to go, but not us. We were too hungry for that, and anyway I kind of like decorlessness.

The lamb kabob was great. It was a big burrito-size roll-up of *lavash* with charbroiled chunks of lamb inside, plus broiled tomatoes, peppers, and onions. Lettuce. Parsley. Yum.

My only complaints: not quite enough lamb, too much tahini.

I also ordered a half-pint of tomato salad because I saw it in the display case coming in and it was love at first sight. Tomatoes and cucumbers and red onions and good Greek olives with lots of fresh parsley all over the place and a thick slice of feta cheese on top, as white as death. I loved it, except the feta was so strong and salty it triggered one of my most hideous nightmares ever. (I accidentally went to church and missed most of the 49ers-Packers game.)

As for Johnny "Jack"'s combo plate, I ate one of his three falafels and a forkful of tabbouleh and both were excellent. The rest of the combo plate (which actually took up two plates) consisted of hummus, *baba ghanoush,* tomato salad, one dolma, some feta cheese, some pita bread, onions, and tahini. The combo plate, in other words, is the way to go if you want lots of things and don't mind none of them being meat.

I mind, personally. But I liked my lamb kabob just fine; it was another way to go. Still others are *shawarma,* chicken kabob, all the standard Mediterranean stuff, and even a few American specialties: hamburgers, grilled chicken breasts, and Philly cheesesteaks.

Poor Johnny "Jack." I mean lucky him, and best wishes to him and Taters and Diva "Jack" and happy-ever-after and all that yeehaw. It's just that I don't think he's going to be able to get good Middle Eastern food in Idaho. Not to mention burritos. Not to mention Vietnamese or Thai. Not to mention a million other things.

On the other hand: elk.

■ SZECHUAN TASTE

You probably think I was too depressed to eat after the Packers and the officials and one or two other forces of Evil teamed up to put an end to yet another 49ers football season Sunday, but the fact of the matter is that

Szechuan Taste
917 Taraval Street,
San Francisco. (415) 681-8383.
Lunch, dinner. Credit cards
accepted. Cheap cheap.

I was too nervous to eat before the game, and then afterward I was too hungry to be depressed.

Calls of condolences came rolling in, and I knew truckloads of flowers would follow. But you can't eat flowers, so when Crawdad de la Cooter called and said, "I'm really sorry, I was thinking about you, there's some leftover chickens and carrot soup in my fridge, want me to heat them up or do you want to go out to eat?" I said, "Both."

I figured I'd need the leftovers to tide me over until we could get to a restaurant, see, and lucky thing for that line of figuring, because the restaurant we wound up at was all the way out in the Sunset. Taraval and 19th Avenue, home of J.T.'s Diner (where everything's a buck or three too expensive) and some supposedly good Vietnamese place (but that wasn't where we wound up either).

Where we wound up was Szechuan Taste restaurant, because it was the rock-bottom cheapest (and therefore best) eating place at that intersection. We stood outside in the rain looking at Szechuan Taste's extensive menu: columns and columns of threes, fours, and fives—an occasional six, sure, but who's counting, besides me?

The important thing is that on the other side of the window, happy and dry people were pigging out on huge plates of interesting and good-looking food. And it was my kind of place, placewise: big round tables with those spinny lazy Susan things in the middle, just like I grew up with. Dirty floor, just like I grew up with. Fake-brick walls with red-painted wood trim. Red two-by-fours cross-beaming the ceiling a few feet before the ceiling, and they resisted the temptation to hang grapevines or fishing nets full of toys or flags or laundry or anything else, for that matter.

As soon as you walk in there's a big, murky fish tank with two or three little goldfishes swimming around in lemon-lime Gatorade. There's another tank in back, separating the main dining room from a smaller, three-table back room, where we sat. In fact, this tank was right behind my head, which made me nervous because lobsters instead of goldfish were in it and I had a feeling they were watching me eat, laughing.

I can't do chopsticks, partly because of some football-related cartilage damage in my right hand, and partly because I can't do chopsticks. But I tried, and the lobsters laughed, and then I gave up and asked for a fork, and the lobsters laughed.

What they were laughing at me eating was *kung pao* beef and Mongolian chicken. I also had a barbecued quail, but I ate that with my hands, like chickens, so who's laughing?

Ever have quail? Goddamn they're cute! They're like little mouse-size chickens. Everything's there: cute little drumstick and thigh and breast and wing. Two halves, chopped right down the middle, just like a chicken, but the winner takes the neck and has the option of dangling his or her half by the neck back and forth over the lobster tank, laughing last, ha ha.

Not that I did that.

Anyway, Crawdad didn't like her half of the quail, so I got to eat the whole thing. I liked it. It was cute.

The *kung pao* beef was thin-sliced with crispy carrots, celery, water chestnuts, green peppers, peanuts, and bamboo shoots. Plus slices of fresh garlic and hot peppers. The Mongolian chicken was less stuff—just chicken and onions and green onions and garlic and hot peppers—but the sauce was more flavorful, so I liked it better.

Crawdad wasn't too much impressed with any of it, I think maybe 'cause it wasn't hot enough for her. I'll agree that our stuff, minus maybe the quail, wasn't as good or as interesting as everyone else's stuff looked, but that's 'cause we were first-timers and didn't know what to order, and anyway I liked it fine.

There are about a couple hundred things on the Szechuan Taste menu, some of them involving lobsters dropped live and kicking into large pots of boiling water.

"You'll get yours," I muttered on our way out.

"What?" said Crawdad.

"Nothing."

■ TWO JACKS SEAFOOD

It's all about food, see? That's what it's all about. Pay no mind to all the other hokeypokey, because here we are smack dab between football and baseball and what else is there? Ask Isadora.

All I know is what all I've been eating. Let's see, last week I went to

Two Jacks Seafood
401 Haight Street,
San Francisco. (415) 431-6290.
Lunch, dinner. Cheap.

Idaho and barbecued elk steaks during a snowstorm. And if you think *that* was the highlight of my life, the next night we 'cued up some deer steaks *and* roasted a chicken.

I'd've stayed and stayed, but the state of Idaho was rapidly running out of animals and I figured anyway that Johnny "Jack" and Taters, bless their Idahoic hearts, were wanting to do the hokeypokey, not having seen each other since last year—and there was nowhere for me to go.

So I came home. Hi.

Tonight me and Crawdad are cooking up some crawfish étouffée. Last night we went to Rainbow for nuts and berries and stuff, and walking around looking at all that health food put me in the mood for health food, so instead of eating fried chickens for dinner I ate fried fishes.

Fishes are good for you; I saw it on TV.

Crawdad doesn't care about dinner or health as much as I do. She just wanted to go home and play the piano, so I went on ahead to Two Jacks, my new favorite health food restaurant, without her.

Believe it or not, there are three Two Jacks around town, but the only one I've ever seen is the one on Haight and what? Webster? You know, just a couple doors down from Kate's Kitchen.

The only problem is it's takeout only. No tables. Just three wicker chairs and one plastic lawn chair against one wall, for waiting. And in case you want to look at things, there's a bookshelf with some baskets on it, an empty shopping cart, a floor, a ketchup-mustard-vinegar station against the chain-linked window wall up front, and a foursome of gumball machines center stage. In case you want to chew some gum.

I didn't, but then I did when I saw that one of the machines was called Space Bubble Gum, and instead of "moon sized balls," as advertised, there were those baseball ones that say your baseball fortune: Home Run. Single. Double. Foul Out.

I had to know, so I paid my dime and the one I got didn't say anything. It was just green. What's that supposed to mean?

The only other ambiantic Two Jacks touch was a TV blaring TV shit so loud that I couldn't even hear one of my favorite sounds in the world: the sound of frying.

So when my food finally came up, I got the hell out of there and headed back to Crawdad's, figuring to get down and greasy to the tune of Crawdad's piano-playing, which is one of my other favorite sounds in the world. I'm not a music reviewer or else maybe I could describe it better, but Crawdad playing the piano is a strange and beautiful thing, maybe the most strangely beautiful thing I've witnessed since I was eight or nine or so, when I witnessed my first-ever magazine picture of lesbians doing it like lesbians.

"What'd you get?" Crawdad said, letting me in.

"Fried," I said. "You hungry?" I'd gotten enough for both of us, just in case, but Crawdad said she'd already ate. "What'd you eat?" I said.

"Celery," she said.

Well, I don't imagine I need to tell you anymore than I needed to tell her: Celery ain't dinner, with or without salsa on it. So the dinner music would have to wait until after dinner. Crawdad happily gived in and helped me out with my fried-catfishes samwich and fried-oysters samwich and fried fries and white bread.

By *samwich,* of course, I mean a pile of french fries on the bottom with a pile of fried fishes in the middle and two slices of white bread on top. Hot dang, it was all good and greasy and good-for-you.

The oysters weren't as soft-touched succulent as Gravy's, for example, but they were good enough and a lot closer to home. The catfish, I'm happy to announce, was a catfish, as in bones and fins and everything. Well, everything but the head. It was good, too. And Crawdad liked the fries. And I liked the white bread, although I would've liked it even more if it was maybe toasted and buttered, like Gravy does.

What all else you can get at Two Jacks is red snapper, rock cod, buffalo, prawns, chicken wings, burgers, and sometimes homemade sausage, but not last night, or I'd've got it. I love sausage.

Buffalo?

Don't ask me. Ask Jack.

▌ CLIFF'S BAR-B-Q & SEAFOOD

I turned to the *Chronicle*'s Food section one day, and wouldn't you know it? They did this big spread on Bay Area barbecue joints!

So there I was with suddenly something meaningful to read. Most of the places I'd either been to or didn't ever want to go to, but there was one I'd never seen and liked the looks of. Cliff's. I don't remember what exactly they said about it, I just knew I liked the name: Cliff's.

Cliff's Bar-B-Q & Seafood
2177 Bayshore Boulevard, San Francisco. (415) 330-0736. Lunch, dinner. Credit cards accepted. Cheap.

Cliff's Bar-B-Q & Seafood, technically. It's way the hell out Bayshore, almost all the way to Gravy's, just past this really cool looking 24-hour cafe that pert near sucked me in. Come to think of it . . . the Mission is history. Puke-ification has squeezed out Carl's Pastry Shop, whose red neon has ambiated my living quarters for as long as I've been living in them. And I don't know who this side of Starbuck is going to be able to afford to move in. There goes the neighborhood.

The Sincere Cafe. The Dovre Club, McCarthy's Bar (which I once mal-prophesied couldn't be touched) . . . what's next?

What's left?

Well, I know where I'm moving to, anyway, when Starbuck moves in across the street. I'm moving somewhere between Gravy and Cliff. Bayview? Cow Palace Hollow? What is that neck of the woods there, where Bayshore meets Geneva?

Not that Cliff is in the same league as Gravy, mind you, but he does have something Gravy doesn't: barbecued chickens. And he is open on a day when Gravy isn't: Monday.

Two other things Cliff's got going for him are kickin' fried okra and barbecued you-name-it. Brisket. Rib tips. Hot links. Pork ribs. Beef ribs. Baby backs. And then there're fried chickens and, by way of health food, fried fishes. Gumbo (but that's only on Fridays and Saturdays).

My advice is to go in there looking confused and disoriented, as if you've never eaten barbecue or soul food before in your life. That's what this one young couple did, and the guy behind the counter started heaping samples on them. "Try this. Try this. Try this."

You might maybe wind up with a full meal this way, I don't know, but you'll probably want to buy a little something anyhow, because (1) they're really nice folks, and (2) it's really good food.

Unfortunately for me, I knew what I wanted from the get-go. I'd just had a pretty bad day, and bad days mean barbecued chickens for dinner. Half of one with four slices of sliced bread and one side (mustard greens for me, thanks) goes for $4.50—$2.50 extra if you want all white meat. I was hoping the person before me did, so I could have all dark, but no such luck. And they weren't willing to genetically alter no new chickens for me.

I don't understand. If you can get white meat only, why can't you get dark meat only?

Well, it was good barbecue, both white and dark (but especially dark). The skin was well seasoned and crispy and the insides were tender and smoky and the sauce was dark and deep like Townes Van Zandt, bless his stopped heart.

But maybe my favorite thing of everything was the fried okra. I love fried okras, the explosion of flavors and sensations. There's the fryfulness—the crispy, salty breading and the grease—but then under all that there's this pleasant, juicy vegetableness. And then, as if all that ain't fun enough, you wind up with these little inside-okra balls to play with on your tongue.

I loved Cliff's, and I thank the *Chronicle*, of all papers, for turning me on to it. Great food, great people, and a nice little place. There are three tables in case you want to eat it there, which, of course, I do.

Apparently, some other people love Cliff's, too. It wasn't crowded, but there was a fairly steady stream of takeout customers. I heard one woman say she came all the way over from Western Addition. She lives right across the street from Brother-in-Laws, for crying out loud. And there she was, across town *diagonally*, getting it to go.

Drive safely, ma'am.

∎ TAJ MAHAL RESTAURANT

What the hell does *diurnal* mean? I just finished a book that ended with the line: "'Hey, beautiful!' he asseverated. 'You're pretty damn diurnal yourself.'" And I'm nowhere near a dictionary.

Come to think of it, what the hell does *asseverated* mean? Help me out here, huh? And whoever names that book wins a half-bottle of Walprofen and a perfectly fine AC adapter for a Powerbook 520. Second-place prize is some yeast.

> **Taj Mahal Restaurant**
> 398 Eddy Street,
> San Francisco. (415) 922-9055.
> Lunch, dinner. Credit cards
> accepted. Cheap cheap.

Enjoy the game, and so I can have a little fun too, I hereby announce my intention to learn the meanings of *diurnal* and *asseverated* and use each word correctly at least once before the end of this review.

What do I get if I do it?

I know. How about a round-trip bus ticket to the Tenderloin, one of my favorite eating areas ever and anywhere.

The other day, see, I ran into Luis Yamo, who lives, well, *near* there, anyhow. We were eating lunch at Yamo, where Luis used to work, and where he now eats, like I do, two or three times a week. But I've got a job to do, so when Ana wasn't looking I said to Luis, "Psst, Luis," I said, "you got any good cheap restaurants for me?"

He told me about some Indian place in the 'Loin, but he couldn't remember the name of it. So the next day I was going through my stuff and I accidentally found a menu someone had slipped me some time ago:

Taj Mahal. Eddy Street. "Pakistani and Indian cuisine," and either they use the word *cuisine* loosely or everyone else has been being kind of stingy with it. I don't know, I'm not an entomologist.

Anyway, cuisine to me implies expensiveness, and Taj Mahal is cheap as dirt.

Is this it, Luis? It's real big inside, like it used to be a Denny's or something, and they were too lazy to rip up the awful green carpet and throw out those awful green-cushioned chairs. Green booths . . .

Hey, green is my favorite color! What am I complaining about?

Not the prices: mostly twos and threes, with two or three sixes for the lamb specialties. Like so many Indian restaurants these days, they also have the all-you-can-eat lunch buffet from 11:30 to 2:30. Now it used to be I'd just be getting up around 2:30, it's true, but I'm not nocturnal anymore. I'm more of a daytime kind of guy. I was able to get there by 1:30 or so, no problem.

So I got the buffet, of course.

Jean-Gene the Frenchman, who's even more non-nocturnal than I am these days (so he'd had breakfast), insisted seriously and positively that the regular menu was the way to go. He was sucked in by all those twos and threes, see, but he was done eating his *lahori chikkar chholey* (that's garbanzo beans and stuff) and Taj Mahal Special Rice (that's rice) before I really even got going.

The buffet table had two kinds of chicken: some kind of a pinkish-red barbecued chicken that was all-out smoky and half-out dry, and then this other chicken sort of stewed in all sorts of wet stuff that went great over rice.

There was rice; there was *papadam,* that sort of spicy, crispy cracker stuff with little lentil pieces in it; and there was *naan-e-Taj,* that clay-oven-baked pitalike bread—but I snagged the last piece and then they never restocked.

For vegetarians (and me too): mushed-up spicy lentils, which I loved; mushed-up eggplant, which I didn't; unmushed garbanzo beans with onions and tomatoes and spiciness, same as Jean-Gene was eating only better 'cause I could keep eating and eating them; and some excellent creamy spinach stuff.

The only buffet thing I didn't like was the *mili juli sabzi,* which is mixed vegetables (green beans, taters, carrots, peas, etc.) flavored with "aromatic spices." Well, these spices were a little over-aromatic for my taste. What a great name, though, huh, for a thing? *Mili juli sabzi.*

Some other things they had were four or five sauces, including that light green yogurt-based one that goes so good with the *papadam.* Lettuce, lemons, jalapeños. Free tea. A whole table full of pitchers of ice water, because you'll need a whole pitcher. Almost everything was hot hot hot.

If you like it hot hot hot and cheap and heaping, you'll like Taj Mahal, but I honestly don't know whether or not you'll like being there, atmospherically. We liked it fine, me and Jean-Gene.

What do you want for 10 bucks for two people?

The Frenchman tried to pay, but I asserted myself emphatically, and then we headed homeward on our bikes and got all wet, which has become a daily ritual these days, I'm sorry to say. Dang!

■ EDDIE'S CAFE / TONY'S CABLE CAR

I don't know why, but I can't eat until my car is fixed, provided that my car is broken. In this case, it was broken. I hadn't had breakfast. I hadn't had lunch. I wasn't even hungry. Nevertheless, it was right around noon and I was riding my bike toward the Toyota dealership on Geary. There were four things in my backpack: vice grips, a knife, electrical tape, and a burnt wire with a melted plastic connector at one end of it. No pens, no pencils, no paper, no toothpicks—to give you some idea how "off duty" I was.

Eddie's Cafe
800 Divisadero Street,
San Francisco. (415) 563-9780.
Breakfast, lunch. Cheap cheap.

Tony's Cable Car
2500 Geary Boulevard,
San Francisco. (415) 931-2416.
Breakfast, lunch, dinner.
Cheap cheap.

But there was Eddie's Cafe, at Divisadero and Fulton, and something happened—something supernatural, I don't know how else to explain it—because there I suddenly was, sitting at Eddie's counter, my bike locked up outside. And my car still wasn't fixed.

Great, great place, Eddie's, placewise. Small, boothful, friendly, cheap. It's supposed to be a soul food restaurant, but some of the soul seems to have seeped away. Get this: no gumbo, even though it was on the menu *and* on the specials board.

Smothered chicken was my first choice. "Smothered chicken," I said.

"No chicken," said the waiterguyperson.

"Fried chicken?"

"No chicken," he said. "We don't make chicken anymore. No chicken."

Well, no chicken, in my opinion, is no soul. So first off Eddie's had better stop calling itself a soul food restaurant, even if they do make oxtails and ribs and grits and biscuits and sometimes gumbo.

"I'll have the gumbo," I said.

"No gumbo."

"That's OK," I said. "I'm not eating. The car . . . um." To be polite, I ordered breakfast: eggs and sausage and grits and biscuits.

Not that I actually ate any of it, my car being broken, but I'm here to tell you anyway that the sausage patties were kind of dry, the biscuits were kind of dinner rolls, the butter was margarine, and the grits were good (in spite of margarine), once I busted the egg yolks all over them.

Good thing Eddie's is such a cool place, with such a cool counter, with comfy, cushy, back-having stools and a long mirror across the wall in front of you, so that even if you can't watch the cooks cooking (the kitchen being off to the right somewhere), you can still spy on all the boothbound people behind you, having their little boothbound conversations and eating their little boothbound food as if nothing in the world were wrong with their cars. Because—where was I?—I don't know if I can conscionably recommend Eddie's on the basis of the food I didn't eat.

Not having fixed my car yet, I mean.

How my plate got clean is a matter perhaps best left to theologians and parapsychologists, but there it eventually was—clean—and there I eventually was, back on the old bike, down Divis., left on Geary . . .

Whammo! Tony's Cable Car, right there at the foot of the steepest climb of my trip. What can I say? I'd pedalled 10, 15, maybe 20 blocks since Eddie's. I was famished.

Still, having just not eaten, I rode past and all the way up the hill, in fact, before I turned around and rolled back down. The call of the chili dog was not to be ignored. Maybe it was the one I've been searching for, the chili dog of my dreams . . .

Maybe not. I couldn't tell you, because I didn't eat it. All I know is I ordered it (for something like two bucks) and an order of fries (for something like $1.50). And then, miraculously, it was all gone.

I can tell you that Tony's idea of chili is a lot like a lot of other people's ideas of chili around here: heavy on the beans, that is, with sort of a cameo appearance on the part of meat. I can tell you that his fries are mighty disappointing for such a classic burger joint. I can tell you that, unlike Eddie, Tony at least has chickens on his menu. Fried-chicken sandwiches, to be precise. And deep-fried burritos!

You gotta like that, and you gotta love the atmosphere. It's just a tiny old cable-car-in-the-wall, with two ordering windows, a few plasticky inside tables, and a couple of outdoor ones.

San Francisco Toyota, on the other hand—they wanted 20-some bucks for this little "fusible link," or "linkable fuse," which they couldn't even get until *Friday*.

Well, I can't go on like this, personally—which is where vice grips, a knife, and electrical tape come in.

∎ AL'S CAFE GOOD FOOD

You may have noticed that I've been eating two meals at a time a lot lately these days. Please, don't worry about my cholesterol, whatever you do. You've got enough to worry about. And just 'cause I eat breakfast for breakfast and lunch for dessert, for example, how do you know I don't skip dinner?

> **Al's Cafe Good Food**
> 3286½ Mission Street,
> San Francisco. (415) 641-8445.
> Breakfast, lunch. Cheap.

Well, I don't. But I do eat something light and healthy, like a quarter-pound bacon cheeseburger instead of a half-pounder, or a salad. Yesterday, for example, I had a salad. That was it: dinner.

For breakfastlunch I had eggs and sausage and taters and toast and a chili burger and more taters. Since that's almost exactly some of the same exact things I wrote up a page or so ago, pretty much, I may as well bust right out with a comparison:

Eddie, Tony, you oughta be ashamed of yourselves.

Al, take a bow.

By Al I mean Al's Cafe, or Al's Cafe Good Food, as it is sometimes called. Mission near 29th. Look for Laurel and Hardy wearing chef hats that say Al. Inside, there are life-size cardboard cutouts of Laurel, Hardy, Bogie, my man W. C. Fields, and George Burns, in case you don't have anyone to talk to while you eat.

I had Crawdad de la Cooter. We sat at the counter because we'd rather look at real live cookerpersons and waitresspeople than flat-assed old-timer movie stars, not to mention all the other thematical touches that touch the adjoining dining room: movie posters, a sort of a shrine of old

Broadway musical score books, one of those little tiny Pee-Wee Herman dolls . . .

At the counter, on the other hand, you get to stare at that diner-style silver-tiled wall. Meat slicer. Box o' cornflakes. Burgers a-sizzlin', grease a-glistenin'. There's a great classic-model diner-style waitressperson running the show, re-reiterating orders to a great Oliver Hardy–style cook, who kept smiling long beyond the call of duty.

Yep, I got your BLT, for the 10th time.

I'd've personally bonked her on the head with a skillet or throwed some taters at her at least. But that's why I don't work in a restaurant. I eat there. And I'm here to tell you, folks: Al's Cafe. Good food. Good people.

My pal Biscuits, who pointed me toward it, said Al's was kind of expensive for diner food, but well worth it. Well, she must not've ever been to J.T.'s or Sparky's, or god forbid some of those downtown diners. Compared to them guys, Al's is dirt cheap. I ate for two-thirds of the cycle for just over 10 bucks, and Crawdad, come to think of it, picked up the other third for just over four. But I'm not gonna tell you what she got 'cause I don't want to embarrass her.

I got the eye-opener breakfast special: a small glass of fresh-squeezed O.J., one egg, a sausage patty, home fries, and toast. That was breakfast. Lunch was the chili burger and more home fries. And everything was great, even the home fries, even the egg. The toast had real live butter on it, Eddie, and the chili, Tony, had big chunks of actual meat, real red kidney beans, and honest-to-god tomatoes. It was homemade as heck and it was smothered with chopped green onions and cheddar cheese all over this beautiful, open-faced, very rare burger.

She'd asked me how I wanted it and I'd said rare. Then she'd turned toward the cook, right in front of me, and said, "Chili burger. Medium-rare."

Luckily, he asked me again himself.

"Rare," I said. You see, there's a difference. Cooks know. This baby came out so underdone that Crawdad was scared of it. "Is it cold?" she said. She wanted me to send it in for an overhaul, but I was done with it before she could get the cook's attention—that's how good it was.

And, as good as it was, the sausage was even better. It was a patty, first off, and patties are just naturally better than links, for Freudian reasons alone. And this patty was plump and juicy and flavorful—or, in other words, the exact opposite of the dried-up pigmeat I went down on recently at Eddie's.

Are you guys listening? Is anyone listening? Good, because I'd hate to see Al's get run over by wahoos like "Val 19," for example. On the other hand, Biscuits said she's been there twice already late morning on weekends, and both times old Al was kind of hurting for bidness. So I'll say it, but I'll make it the last thing I say, so that only the very best and patientest and cheapest cheap eaters will know, everyone else having moseyed along to their televisions by now:

Al's is the best dang diner in town.

■ CABLE CAR COFFEE SHOP

I pushed through the heavy glass door of the Cable Car Coffee Shop in downtown South San Francisco, out of the wet and into the smiling stare of an angelic little baby girl in a high chair, right there almost exactly in the entranceway.

> **Cable Car Coffee Shop**
> 423½ Grand Avenue,
> South San Francisco. (650) 952-
> 9533. Breakfast, lunch.
> Cheap cheap.

"Hi," she said.

"Howdy podner," I said, tiny shards of glass dripping off of me like water, tinkling to the linoleum.

"Boggola do carple nonigwiggy," the little girl said, right to my face. "Swanklesmalb nonig do bloobroof a nannygib ba-ba-ba-ba-ba bvweeeef!"

I said, "What?"

She said it again. Her parents laughed. Wasn't she cute?

Well, she was, but I was on duty. "Listen, kid, I'd love to stay and chat," I said, tipping my baseball hat (glass tinkling), "but I've got me some breakfast to eat." And I moseyed along to a booth with a sports section already sitting in it. "Howdy, sports," I said. "Mind if I join you?"

It didn't say anything. I sat down.

Latrell Sprewell was all over the place, the 49ers were getting younger, the Giants had taken a preseason beating and Dusty Baker cared, something about hockey . . .

But I was there for the Pacific Scramble. I'd heard it was good, and it was. And it was a good day for a good thing called a Pacific Scramble—kind of oceanic out, I'd say. Gray and misty. Cold. But I'm not a weatherman, so let's talk food:

Let's see, there were tons o' tiny, angelic baby shrimps in this here Pacific Scramble, plus spinach, scallions, eggs of course, salt, water, and little pieces of people's houses and stuff. There were supposed to be mushrooms, but I'd asked for none, please, because I just don't believe that mushrooms belong in the Pacific.

You might say, Spinach? Scallions?

Well, I see your point, but spinach and scallions could easily be mistook for seaweed, see? And, while mushrooms could also be mistook for certain sea-things, granted (since we're playing like *that*), I don't like mushrooms. I do like spinach and scallions.

So there you have it. And don't even mention eggs, because eggs are everywhere. Take my friend Biscuits. She and the Belle Manor grills have gone in together on a couple of angelic baby backyard chickens. I got to meat the little darlings on my way back from South San Francisco just now, and they sure were purty. Biscuits was blabbing on about futuristic eggs and eggs and eggs, but my own personal free-range imagination was moving in an entirely different direction—you guess which. So even though I'd just eaten breakfast, I started getting kind of hungry for lunch.

Hey, why didn't I eat lunch at the Cable Car for dessert, for crying out loud? I should've kept my streak going. Lard knows they had fried chickens on the menu, along with all other things American (including chicken-fried steak), and all for either under or just-over five bucks. On the other hand, it was a wee bit early for breakfastlunch (9:30).

The beautiful thing about the Pacific Scramble was that unlike most scrambles, which are mostly eggs with a little bit of other stuff mixed in, this one was mostly other stuff—shrimps, spinach, etc.—with a little bit of egg mixed in. In other words: yum.

And it came with toast and home fries or hash browns. Correct answer: hash browns. These were the most perfect hash browns I've ever seen, let alone tasted—a nice, neat rectangle of them, not browned so much as goldened on the outside, and butterfully soft underneath. In other words: googy.

Atmospherically speaking, you're looking at your basic downtown South San Fran old-style joint, but with a fake window on the back wall looking out on the Golden Gate Bridge where no Golden Gate Bridges ever were or will be, with a huge full moon where no huge full moon ever was or could be, astronomically speaking.

There's a skylighted ceiling with a couple of fluorescent boosters, a no-action counter, booths, tables in the window (the real one), planters and plants and general vininess. It's a homey, pleasant place where old S.S.F. ladypersons can have breakfast clubs, little babies can talk to strangers, and soggy seafaring restaurant writers can wash down Pacific Scrambles with 8,000 cups of poetically awful coffee, trying to remember the last line of the Pledge of Allegiance.

■ BILL'S PLACE

Now normally when Rocco and me run the airport shuttle it means that somebody owes us a burrito, but this was different than that. This was Crawdad's mom, and Mawdad and Pawdad sprang for so many crawfeasts last time I was in LA (that's Louisiana, bub), not to mention having sprung into the world my favorite person in the world (sit down, Sandy Alomar), that . . . where was I?

Bill's Place
2315 Clement Street,
San Francisco. (415) 221-5262.
Lunch, dinner. Cheap.

Not Can-Cun. No, I could periodically pick up Crawfolks at the airport well, well into the next millennium, the way I figger, and never ever eat another burrito, as far as that goes. Plus I'm in a bit of a burger-joint rut. Did you notice? Eddie's Cafe, Tony's Cable Car, Al's, that S.S.F. Cable Car, and now this—

Reader, I'd like you to meet Bill. Bill, reader. And speaking of Cable Cars, Joe, you and yours can have a seat next to Sandy's second-place ass, because not only does Bill grind his cows up fresh daily, but he includes the fries *and* they're fresh-cut and 10 or 20 times better than y'all's.

Plus, whereas Joe's Cable Car was plastically a McDoodoo's, pretty much, if I'm remembering right (no table service, styrofoam plates, etc.), Bill's atmosphere is perfect. There's even a patio out back. Inside, there's a counter with a view of the grill, there are real wooden tables, wood walls, incongruous fancy-pants chandeliers incongruously draped with goofy green paper shamrock stuff, and framed presidential china plates by way of art.

Mawdad and me sat right under Abe Lincoln. We'd just been out to the V.A. hospital to say hi there to Crawdad. The V.A. cafeteria was already closed, and I hadn't eaten since breakfast, and Bill's was just down the road on Clement, between 24th and 25th, smack on our way back to the Mission.

The fact that I never knew about it until now is testimony to our big city's amazing greatness, foodwise. I mean, Bill's been there 38 years, churning out fresh-ground burgers for bucks cheaper than Joe's, throwing in the fries—and this was the first I'd heard of him. Which could also be testimony to my amazing dumbness, I know, but I consider myself an optimist, so let's just yodel and move along.

Yodel-eh-hee-hoo.

Let's see, the menu includes a whole page full of "celebrity burgers," but celebrities don't know how to eat burgers. They all want avocados and alfalfa sprouts and fried eggs and Thousand Island dressing and sliced beets and sliced pineapples and coleslaw and stuff on them. As you know, I've got three special words for just such yeehaw, but two of them I can't say in front of Mawdad. So heck on celebrities; order your burgers, like we did, from the basic burger menu.

For roughly 10 bucks total, Mawdad got a plain old hamburger and I got a plain old American cheeseburger with bacon. Hold the mayo, hold the mayo. Rare and rare. Your choice of fries or salad. (Fries and fries, for the record.) Other than which: third-pounders on sesame-seeded buns with lettuce, tomato, and pickles. Howdy, Abe.

Honest, these burgers would've tasted as good as or better than Joe's even if they weren't way cheaper and didn't come with the fries. They weren't as bloody as Al's Cafe's rare ones, mind you, but they were rare enough, and juicy and tasty, and the important thing is that Mawdad was impressed. I don't think they let you get 'em red like that in some parts of the country.

Personally, I was even more impressed with the fries than the burger. They weren't those frozen fresh-cuts some places'll try and sneak past you. These looked fresh and felt fresh and smelt fresh and tasted it and everything. And you can get curly fries, if you want, for 50 cents more.

What else you can get are chicken burgers, veggie burgers, chili, hot dogs, sandwiches, breakfast, pie, ice cream, desserts in general, and "old fashioned" fountain drinks. But we didn't get any of that stuff, so what else can I tell you?

Well, next time I'll see if I can't tell you a little something un-American, for a change. Meanwhile, if you find yourself out there in the Richmond, with or without your grillfriend's (or broilfriend's) mom (or dad), I'd drop in on old Bill's Place and stay a while, I was you. It's the self-proclaimed "Home of the Hamburger," and I can't argue with them on that, 'cause here I am only one day later, closing my eyes and clicking my heels together . . .

■ CURLY'S COFFEE SHOP

Bill, Al, Tony, Eddie . . . meet Curly. Curly—Bill, Al, Tony, and Eddie. I'm Dan. I'm thinking of dropping out of the meat industry and becoming a cab driver. What do you think? It's just that you hardly ever hear anyone complain about how hard it is to flag down a restaurant review in this town, whereas . . . well, how you gonna get there?

Curly's Coffee Shop
1624 Powell Street,
San Francisco. (415) 392-0144.
Breakfast, lunch. Credit cards
accepted. Cheap.

I have a car. Tell you what, I'll pick you up at your door, tell you where you're eating (based on how much money you've got in your pocket, minus fare), and take you there. I'm a good driver.

One night last week, right after running Punker and Punkress to the airport, I reckoned I'd drop in on Crawdad de la Cooter, so to speak. It was a little after 11. She was on the phone with a friend in need, and what this friend was in need of, naturally, was a ride. "Dan's here," I heard her say. "Where are you?" I didn't even take my coat off.

And in between all that and other runnings of other people other places, I was chauffeuring Crawdad's ma, Mawdad, to her cooking classes down near Fishermanperson's Wharf. I generally bummed around North Beach while she was learning how to cook (which she already knows how to do, between the two of us). Anyhow, that was how I met Curly, just a couple doors up from Capp's Corner on Powell. Curly's Coffee Shop. Don't worry—I didn't get a burger.

Because the beauty of Curly's is that, although it's basically a burger and breakfast joint, they also serve Japanese lunches. Teriyaki, *donburi, udon.*

I got *nabeyaki udon.* It's a big bowl of fat noodles in this broth with pickled vegetables (mostly cabbage), chicken, pink-edged processed fishy fish doodads, one large tempurated shrimp, and, above all else, a sunny-side-sort-of-up egg.

Poke the yolk and dig in. It's good.

I especially liked the shrimp. You don't expect to find deep-fried shrimp in soup, but when you do, if you're me, you're yodeling. The batter mushing off of it, like flotsam, floating gently downbowl . . . (not that I know what flotsam is, or anything, exactly, I mean).

So why wasn't there more than one shrimp in the soup? Why weren't there, for example, five shrimps? I personally would have traded all of the little chicken pieces for a few more of those flotsam-flailing fried fishamajigs—which oughta tell you that the chickens part of the soup wasn't the best part. Strange.

The noodles were good. I love *udon* noodles 'cause they're so thick you can pretend they're worms. But luckily I don't have to discuss the soup any further than this, because the next day I wound up back at Curly's, this time for breakfast.

So let me tell you about breakfast. Well, there's a thing on the wall from some North Beach publication whose readers voted Curly's breakfast the best breakfast in North Beach. I don't want to say that these readers are wrong, so let's just leave it like this: If they're right, I'll have my breakfast in some other neighborhood, thanks.

The eggs and toast were fine, but eggs and toast are almost always going to be fine, barring margarine or maybe some egg-related accident. The problem was the hash browns, and the problem with them was that they were dry and crusty and tasteless, especially after the recently-tasted Cable Car Coffee Shop's heavenly hash browns.

The meat I got with this all was corned beef hash, because it was St. Patrick's Day. I don't generally go for corned beef hash, and I sure enough didn't generally go for this one. What is corned beef hash, anyway? Little pieces of leftover potatoes and onions and parsley and, you gotta figure, beef, although it never tastes like beef to me.

I don't mean to complain, because I liked Curly's, overall. It's just a comfortable, clean, coffee-shop-style place with a cute four-stool counter, awful American music, a buzz, and refreshingly bad coffee—the beauty of which is that bad coffee sometimes tastes reminiscent (to me) of good barbecue. Don't ask me why.

But what attracted me to Curly's to begin with was none of the above. It was a couple of out-front outside eating tables, snugfully enclosed by pretty flowers and nature and stuff. It was a beautiful day. It was a big sidewalk cutout of a spatula-wielding chefwomanperson striking what my brother Phenomenon would call a "kung-fu shit" pose.

Eat here or else.

■ NEW AUX DELICES

In case you're planning on getting one of your fingers bent by a football accident in so wrong a way that a ligament pulls a chip of bone away from the bone, necessitating one or two trips to General Hospital, don't worry about lunch. I've got you covered. Suggestion-wise, I mean.

New Aux Delices
1002 Potrero Street,
San Francisco. (415) 285-3196.
Lunch, dinner. Credit cards
accepted. Cheap.

Well, I can't speak for their cafeteria, and it's not that I'm above reviewing such a place, either, as you know. It's just that I haven't had the pleasure of eating there yet, assuming there is such a there to eat at. If not, it oughtn't to be too much trouble (even if you accidentally hurt your foot instead) to walk across the street to one of two little basement-style joints, Potrero between 22nd and 23rd.

There's La Paz, which is Salvadoran and Mexican food, and there's New Aux Delices, which is Vietnamese and French. That's where I went last night, because Jean-Gene the Frenchman was with me. Us—Crawdad de la Cooter was there, too. Jean-Gene the Frenchman is practically

French, and he's all-the-way vegetarian, and the only thing veggie at La Paz is a burrito, which was what he'd had for lunch yesterday, turns out.

New Aux Delices, on the other hand, has a vegetarian section. They also have a French section, but unfortunately for Jean-Gene, who loves ducks in a purely spiritual, "just friends" sort of way, his fellow countrypeoplepersons prefer their ducks *à l'orange,* or in orange sauce. Which implies a certain degree of death, and Jean-Gene doesn't like to see dead ducks, not even on menus. In fact, it ruins his appetite.

So he only ordered one thing: sautéed assorted vegetables in tomato sauce. It was pretty good. I tried it. It was pretty good, but there wasn't any meat in it, so I'm not qualified to elaborate.

What all else we got, me and Crawdad, I mean, was hot-and-sour shrimp soup, ginger chicken, and spicy catfish in a clay pot. Fishes and chickens and fishes. Elaborate away, Danny Boy.

Well, the soup (*canh chua tom* to you) was not one of the better bowls of *canh chua tom* I've ever had, I'm sorry to say. No celery. No tomatoes. Yes bean sprouts and pineapples and shrimps and mushrooms. The broth was plenty hot, in both senses of the word, but not enough sour, for my fiver.

Hey, that's pretty cheap.

It is, you're right, but I'd rather cough up another buck for a bowl of Mai's gloriously superior, celery-laden hot-and-sour . . . hold on a second. I'm gonna have to call Crawdad and ask her to pick me up some on her way home from work tonight. Just talking about it makes me crazy.

I'm back. No go, goddamn it. But where was I? OK, the clay-pot catfish might not have been catfish. It looked like salmon, the way it was cut, but it tasted like catfish: good. Sautéed in a spicy, bubbling hot, dark gravy with onions and stuff. I only wish there had been more of it, because then we might not've cleaned our plates so easily, meaning leftovers in the fridge. (I'm hungry. Can you tell?)

What else isn't in my fridge 'cause we ate it all last night is (was) a fine dish of marinated chicken sautéed with ginger and green onions and still more spiciness. They call it *ga gung,* or "songing chicken with ginger." I asked the waiterguyperson what a "songing chicken" was, and he didn't seem to know, either.

"Ginger chicken," he guessed.

But that would be ginger chicken with ginger, and that wouldn't make sense.

Not that things generally do, but I like to think of there being such an animal as a songing chicken out there somewhere. I haven't worked out the details, such as what such a chicken might sing, but while I'm mulling it over let me just finish telling you about New Aux Delices, placewise.

We'll start with the door. It creaks like a scary movie, and opens into some plants that would best be described as trees. Don't worry, you won't get lost. Just stay to your left and you'll find yourself in a small, square room with wood paneling halfway up the walls, then cool, colorful Asian art.

I don't know about lunchtime, but we were there around 8:30 and the joint was quiet as a graveyard, crowded with empty tables with glass-covered pink tablecloths and paper placemats and upstanding fancy-folded napkins, just standing there all over the place like tombstones or something. Hit it, chickens—

Back to back, belly to belly, drumstick to drumstick, I'm done fried already, oh, back to back, belly to belly, at the Zombie KFC.

■ LA PAZ

La Paz is a lot like New Aux except that it's Mexican and Salvadoran food instead of Vietnamese and French. It's on the same block, right across from General Hospital, and it's got the same church-basement atmosphere—but what am I doing getting right down to bidness when it's baseball season?

La Paz
1028 Potrero Street,
San Francisco. (415) 550-8313.
Lunch, dinner. Credit cards
accepted. Cheap.

Happy season everybody! May the best team lose (seeing as how the best team is liable to be Atlanta or New York) and may the Indians and Giants meet each other in the World Series, this time for sure.

Thinking about baseball makes me think about Gravy's. And thinking about Gravy's makes me think about gravy, which in turn just naturally leads to chicken-fried steak. I tried making it at home for the first time ever last weekend, and I failed miserably. After hours in the film room, analyzing film, I still can't figure out where I went wrong. Unless it was the temperature of the lard. Or, more likely, Jean-Gene the Frenchman adulterated my frying pan with mushrooms and eggplants and vegetable oil and shit while he was here.

I know it wasn't the meat. Instead of using cubed steak, which is what chicken-fried steak usually is, I used thin-cut actual steaks, à la carne asada, and—watch me bring this baby full circle—I got the bright idea from La Paz.

They don't call it chicken-fried steak. They call it deep-fried beef, or something like that, and they serve it with rice and refrieds and shredded lettuce with tomatoes and cukes (which is to say: salad). A wedge of lemon. Homemade tortilla chips. It's $7.50, and if that's two bucks too many for you, you can always get fried chicken (a half of one) with fries, etc., for $5.50.

Not to mention all your standard Mexican and Salvadoran dishes, but I knew I was going to be chicken-frying in a few days, myself, so I went with the chicken-fried, even though they don't call it that. It was two big, skinny, slabs of *carne asada carne*, well breaded and fried to a perfect brownness outside, without toughifying the meat inside. (Now why can't I do that?)

No gravy, mind you, but the refrieds might work, visually, at least. I used a squeeze of lemon and a bunch of salsa, which is probably not as good for you as gravy, I know, but I think it might have tasted even better. And this salsa wasn't even that great. It was thin and red and maybe missing a little something. (Heat? Cilantro?) Hey, can you imagine that great, green Rincón Peruano salsa on chicken-fried? I can. In fact, that's one of the few things I've been imagining, outside of baseball, ever since La Paz.

The place, in case you're interested, is small and bright and friendly. Light green tablecloths under glass. There's this flowery wallpaper halfway up the walls, then, on top of that, on the pink part of the walls, there are paintings of flowers and bouquets of dried flowers. It's just an all-around flowery place, in other words.

Ah spring!

I was there around noon after a little late-morning, early-spring hand-related occupational therapy across the street, and by 12:30 the place was hopping, so that I couldn't get a water refill for the life of me. May I suggest bigger glasses, or maybe more than one waitressperson?

Or maybe order something other than water. There's a precarious shelf full of beer and soda cans and bottles displayed up over the entrance to the kitchen, but I wouldn't worry about earthquakes if I were you. All those other people eating there—they're all nurses and doctors and interns, you gotta figure, and they probably know what to do with cracked heads, if not tweaked hands.

Damn, you hate to start a new season on the D.L.

■ HOT 'N' HUNKY

Me and my grillfriendperson and I have a running argument on the subject of walking-distance burger joints.

Burger Joint, she says. Hot 'n' Hunky, says me. Burger Joint! Hot 'n' Hunky! Burger Joint! Hot 'n' Hunky! (And so on. We never get anything done.)

Hot 'N' Hunky
4039 18th Street,
San Francisco. (415) 621-6365.
Lunch, dinner. Cheap cheap.

OK, I concede that B.J.'s burgers are better and fresher, meatwise—which, what otherwise is there to a burger? Granted. But Hot 'n' Hunky has better fries, better atmosphere, and that all-you-can-eat peperoncini-and-pickle station. Hot 'n' Hunky has the Italian Stallian burger with black olives and mozzarella. Hot 'n' Hunky has the Ms. Piggy (bacon and cheddar) and the Swisher (bacon and Swiss).

But most important, Hot 'n' Hunky has the Macho Man, which is *three*-quarters of a pound of cow, with good ol' American cheese, for $4.70. In other words, that's one and a half half-pounders for under five bucks. You have to pay $1.25 extra for your fries, but who's complaining? Not me. That's a lot of meat and taters for $5.95. And, in case you don't go for Macho Men, you can easily do some other, lesser burger-and-fry two-step for under five. Don't worry.

So one day recently I tried to go a whole day without eating meat, not so much for the sport of it as to give my cholesterol level a little breather, just in case what everyone was saying was right. I had four eggs without bacon for breakfast, and two grilled-cheese sandwiches without bacon for lunch, so naturally I was feeling somewhat malnourished come dinnertime.

I found an old can of tuna fish and an even older can of peas in one of my cupboards. I knew I had a half of an onion somewhere in the fridge, but no pasta, so I went across the street to the corner store and bought a bag of baby shells. I don't know what I was thinking. Pasta à la cans of peas and tuna fish, I suppose, with onions. In light of which, who can blame me if I threw cholesterol to the wind, took the scenic route back across 18th Street, and wound up four or five big blocks away at Hot 'n' Hunky, going down on a Macho Man and fries and a side of all-you-can-eat peperoncini and a medium root beer, a one-pound bag of baby shells for company?

On the way there, come to think of it, two different people had hit me up for cigarettes.

"I don't smoke," I had to say, showing them the bag of baby shells, "I eat." I had to say this twice, to two different people. "I don't smoke. I eat." And neither one of them hit me.

The miracle of the Macho Man is that, although it's three quarter-pound patties instead of one three-quarter pound wad of ground beef, it's still got quite a bit of blood to it. That's 'cause they ask how you want it, and when you say rare, they believe you.

I also like that they don't give you a fork or knife or anything. And if you think you're going to lift this big boy with your hands, let alone get your mouth around it, think again. Come to think of it, I don't know *how* you're going to eat the damn thing. I know how I ate it, but unlike most people, I have very little pride and absolutely no table manners. Just ask that bag of pasta.

Don't listen to Crawdad, Hot 'n' Hunky's fries are delicious. They're not the best in the city (see Bill's), but they're better than B.J.'s. They're fresh-cut and skinful and crispy, and they've got a bottle of vinegar at the peperoncini-pickle buffet. Drench away.

Say hi to Marilyn. Give your quarters to the jukebox. Spy on other people in the mirrored walls. Spy on yourself. Wipe your mouth. Wrap your hands around the imaginary microphone and sing a little something.

Speaking of crazy people, I was walking home afterward, just minding my own bidness, chatting with my bag of pasta, when this loony-tunes dude with three big suitcases and one tiny-wheeled bike pirouettes out of some shadow onto the sidewalk in front of me, and—get this—he *doesn't* ask for a cigarette.

He asks for a wrench.

What can I say? I shake my head no and hold up the only thing I have, other than a bellyache, to show him. "Pasta," I say.

■ SUGAR BOWL BAKERY & RESTAURANT

Of all my friends who I tend to eat with, none have had as many different names as my friend Biscuits, which makes sense 'cause she's my oldest friend. And now I'd like to officially change her name to Bikkets,

> **Sugar Bowl Bakery & Restaurant**
> 480 Toland Street,
> San Francisco. (415) 824-4800.
> Breakfast, lunch. Credit cards
> accepted. Cheap.

because why would anyone want to say *Biscuits* when they can just as easily say *Bikkets?*

While you're working on the answer to that, let me tell you about the Sugar Bowl. Not the one out on Balboa Street in the Richmond, the one I think I might've mentioned already. No, this Sugar Bowl is out there on Toland where all the junkyards and warehouses are. The produce district? Bayview?

Whatever it's called, me and Bikkets were looking to eat us a little breakfast in that neck of the woods. Believe it or not, there are some pretty cool looking places around there, like the Bonanza, a long, skinny, almost doorless, dungeonesque dive where Evans forks into Whatever and Whatever, a sandwich shop with a big truck on its sign a couple doors down from that, a fancy-painted Mediterranean place, and this really meat intensive cafeteria hiding out behind enemy lines at the produce market.

All those places are kind of lunch-oriented, though, and we were looking for breakfast, so we wound up at the Sugar Bowl Bakery & Restaurant, which is kind of everything-oriented. They have American, Vietnamese, and Chinese food. They have donuts. They have an eating counter *and* a drinking counter. They have beer-babe posters all over the cinder-block walls, lingerie shows after work on Fridays, a gigantic taxidermed swordfish, satellite TV, and an entire display rack dedicated to birthday candles: soccer ball candles, football candles, "forty and sporty" candles . . .

In other words: woohoo!

Too bad they can't cook. Well, they can't cook breakfast, at any rate, but if they're anything like that other Sugar Bowl, they make some mighty fine Vietnamese stuff and donuts. Unfortunately, it was 9 a.m. in the morning: breakfast time.

I shoulda got *bún cha giò thit nuóng* for breakfast is what I shoulda done, but I went with steak and eggs instead. That's three eggs, mind you, hash browns (or home fries), and toast.

"How do you want your eggs?" the waitressperson said.

"Sunny-side-up."

What she didn't say, and what I didn't realize she didn't say until too late, was "How do you want your steak?" Still, you would think a cook would know that anyone who wants their eggs sunny-side-up would also want a little juice left to their steak.

Damn, it *looked* good. It was a big-ass slab of crisscross-charbroiled meat, and it gave me an even bigger boner than the beer-babes did—even the one with the pool cue. And it tasted halfway decent once Bikkets pointed out that I could always pour Tabasco sauce all over it. Which I did. Before that it only tasted maybe an eighth of the way decent.

There were a ton of hash browns sprawling across the plate and even snuggling in under the steak. Unfortunately, they tasted like they were cooked in engine oil instead of butter, and nothing, not even Tabasco, was going to fix that.

Bikkets got Eggs in the Nest, two eggs grilled into buttered toast with four bacons and home fries and a side of tomato slices. The bacon was good and crispy and good. The home fries were better than the hash browns. The eggs in the nests were cooked a little too hard, but the tomato slices helped. So she won.

On the other hand, she's gotta lotta problems in her life right now, and she chewed my ears off over them, and I'd rather eat an overcooked steak and engine-oil taters than my hairy old wax-filled ears. Ha ha ha ha ha ha ha ha ha. Ha ha ha ha ha ha ha ha ha ha ha ha ha ha ha ha ha ha ha. Ha ha ha . . .

Shit. Still here? OK, I'll go ahead and tell you about her problems, then, but this is off the record, OK?

1) Tax time, and she got nailed.

2) Made a $3,000 mistake at work.

3) Her man's too damn cynical. "I'm tired of cynicism, Dan," she said. "I'm tired of that kind of line: 'People are so stupid. Everything's all wrong. I hate everything.'"

I nodded.

"I mean, where do you go after that?" she said.

I shrugged.

"I mean, after that, you can't even play miniature golf!" she said, and she was right. The steak wasn't all that half-bad after all.

◼ KAMAL'S

Remember Haywire? Remember how haywire he used to be? Well, he still is and is, respectively, only now he does what he does on the East Coast. He moved from here to rural Maine because he couldn't deal with high rents and crazy neighbors, and then, when he could no longer deal with birdies and blueberries, he moved to Brooklyn, NY.

> **Kamal's**
> 2246 Jerrold Avenue,
> San Francisco. (415) 695-9481.
> Breakfast, lunch, dinner.
> Cheap cheap.

Next stop: here again, is my guess, because that's the way Haywire operates. He operates in circles, like atoms and planets and Swedish meatballs. It's perfectly natural.

I call him Haywire for other reasons.

Speaking of Pepto-Bismol, we've been eating a lot of burritos and drinking a lot of coffee together, me and Haywire, just like in the good old days. He's out visiting for two weeks, see, trying to cram in two years' worth of *carne asada*, and teaching me a thing or two about philosophy along the way.

Yesterday, for example, I learned that you can't doubt you are doubting while you are doubting, according to Descartes. And I wonder what his copy editors were up to on the morning he came up with that one.

Anyway, since another thing you can't do, according to my mom, is eat burritos five days in a row, we thought we'd try a little something Middle Eastern yesterday. I was thinking about that place out near the produce market, the one with the colorfully painted painting on the outside of it. Bikkets had already eaten there, and she said they had great falafel.

So there we were, me and Haywire, for lunch. Ironically, neither of us ordered falafel, nor anything else from the Middle Eastern section of the menu. I was personally distracted by a tin bin of baked chickens, and Haywire, for his money, couldn't resist the piroshki. In addition to all the classic Middle Eastern stuff, Kamal's also makes American breakfasts, American sandwiches, burgers, and, apparently, piroshki. Which is Russian.

And then, as if all that weren't sufficiently cornucopious, while we're eating, the woman behind the counter comes out from around the counter and starts ladling Indonesian peanut sauce onto our plates! It was peanuty and nice and spicy, sure—but mainly it was the thought that counted.

This woman, bless her heart and soul and stomach lining, is out of the same mold that created Franny the Great, of Ann's Cafe fame. Which is to say that she won't let you get away hungry. And she's got a certain streak of showmanpersonship in her, as well—not to mention a philosophy or two of her own.

Overheard: "Time is unlimited until you die."

Yeah, well, here's what I thought about the food: The chicken was delicious. Dark meat. Dark gravy. In fact, there was a ton of juice to it, and it oozed nicely into the bed of rice upon which it was served. There was also a pile of tabbouleh that might not have been tabbouleh. It had tomatoes and cucumbers and parsley and an eye-watering amount of lemon—but no bulgar wheat, nor any other discernible grain.

No problem. Who needs grain in their tabbouleh when you can have Indonesian peanut sauce, apropos of nothing? Plus she gave me two kinds of salad, which was one kind beyond the call of duty. (The other was tomatoes and stuff with tahini, and it was just fine.)

Haywire got two kinds of salad with his piroshki too. He got two, in other words *three* kinds of piroshki, because before we even ordered, she chopped up a potato and cauliflower one and let us taste it. Then she gave him a beef one and a spinach one. But he didn't exactly want the beef one, so I ate most of it and she threw in the rest of the potato and cauli-flower one for Haywire for free. Follow?

Me neither. The important thing is that all this and more (i.e., a couple of bananas for dessert) set us back only about five bucks apiece. And the piroshki, like everything else we did and didn't order, including falafel, according to Bikkets, were excellent. Haywire especially liked the potato-cauliflower one. I especially liked the other two. Which worked out nicely.

As for the "place" of the place, I think you're going to like it. Like so many other buildings around there, it's basically a warehouse, with high blue walls and ceilings, and a permanently open garage door, windowed in for the sake of natural light. The restaurant itself is pretty small, but adjoining it is a big dance floor (in case you like to dance to Middle East-ern food), and more tables and a stage (in case live music is more what moves you). They have bands on weekends, apparently, but that has nothing to do with Kamal's.

■ MILLBRAE PANCAKE HOUSE

Or another thing you can do is hop on the freeway and find yourself in Millbrae, although I wouldn't necessarily recommend this activity, unless you happen to know the Brioschi Kid and Caterin' Caroline. They live in Millbrae. They're good people. They have a dog, a table, a budding pepper empire, and a favorite pan-cake house: the Millbrae Pancake House. Me and Haywire, liking pan-cakes, went there with them.

Millbrae Pancake House
1300 El Camino Real, Millbrae.
(650) 589-2080. Breakfast,
lunch, dinner.
Credit cards accepted. Cheap.

More sentences are as follows:

It was a fine and sunny Tuesday morning. An afternoon Giants game loomed in Haywire's and the Kid's and C. C.'s immediate futures, but not mine. No, me and the Rock were about to run an important airport shut-tle, seeing the world's greatest remaining rock band, 100-Watt Smile, off toward Germany. Knowing them, there would be little if any margarine for error, timewise, so it wouldn't hurt, I reckoned, to run a little test-run—get Rocco's juices flowing, make sure I remembered the way, scout

out the traffic situation, eat pancakes . . . I mean, the last thing in the world you want to be doing if you're me—and, trust me, you're not—is waiting around for a whole band to get their shit together on an empty stomach. Yours, that is, which is to say: mine. Stomach, I mean.

Now that that's settled, let's talk about the Millbrae Pancake House. Or better yet, let's talk about what we all were talking about over our pancakes: "senses of urgency" and, I'm sorry to say, "anal leakage"—two of the many strikes, according to early published warnings, according to the Kid, against this new kind of anti-oil, olestra, or oleanstra, or oleoleo, or whatever. Beware! Even if they've ironed out the "sense of urgency" and "anal leakage" issues, you don't want to be messing with anything that deprives your body of lubrication. Bodies are like cars, with butter being Valvoline, vitamins being gas, gas being exhaust, valves being valves, and I don't know what to do with cup holders, but I do know that in any and all possible cases, "anal leakage" is a bad idea.

You know this, don't you? You do, I know, so I'll crusade no further. Millbrae Pancake House pancakes come with about a pound and a half of whipped butter on top of them, and that right there is my fondest memory of the meal. The 'cakes were good, sure—especially the Kid's 'cakes, 'cause he got corn 'cakes, and there were six of them, rising up into the Millbrae Pancake House atmosphere like something out of Dr. Seuss. And there were real kernels of corn in them, and they were just like the menu described them: "tasty!" (I tasted them.)

Me and Haywire both went for the special: two blueberry pancakes, two eggs, and two sausages or bacons for under five bucks. I can't speak for his'n's, but mines'n's were just fine, except that I accidentally poured boysenberry syrup on part of the pile, and I hate boysenberry syrup. It tastes like medicine. I tried to drown it out with good old maple, but it didn't exactly work. Haywire, on the other hand, forewent maple in favor of boysenberry. Being a hypochondriac, he loves boysenberry syrup. He eats medicine like candy. Sometimes he eats it for dinner.

Caterin' Caroline got an egg-related breakfast, and lucky for me she let me in on her toast, a side order of which would've set me back $2.05. Even our waitressperson, who was a damn good old-fashioned pancake-house sweetie, agreed that $2.05 was way too much for a side of toast. Two bucks, or in other words a buck apiece for two slices of bread, is ridiculous in and of itself. It's the extra .05 that kills me. After all those dollars, do they really need the nickels? They must just not like making toast.

And my only other complaint has to do with an utter lack of sausage patties. I'll take links over bacon 10 times out of 10; what I'd really rather choose between is links and patties, especially at a pancake house, which should have both. Don't you think?

Although they did have special chicken-apple sausage, link-style, which is what C. C. got with her eggs, and it was pretty good, she said, yeah yeah yeah. So there's that. And there's the general friendliness of the waitresspersonpeople. And that atmosphere that the Kid's Seussian corn stack was poking up into was some mighty fine atmosphere.

Big, comfy, cushy pancake-house booths. Deliciously bad pancake-house coffee. Unintrusively classical pancake-house music. A sky-blue pancake-house ceiling (for that outdoorsy effect pancake eaters so love). Hanging pancake-house copper pans, by way of art. And pancakes.

■ JUST FOR YOU

You know me. I'll write about anything, which is why, if you really do know me, you have to be careful what you say and do in my presence, especially over lunch, 'cause it's libel to wind up in print. Off the record, of course.

Just For You
1453 18th Street,
San Francisco. (415) 647-3033.
Breakfast, lunch. Cheap.

I don't make records anymore.

I'm a writer.

So there I was, a writer, in my favorite Potrero Hill hole-in-the-hill, Just for You, having a very serious lunch meating with my favorite Potrero Hill publisher, Russian Hill Press. Hey, don't look at me. You know where I stand on the issue of life's little anomalies. I stand right behind them. Russian Hill Press in Potrero Hill! What fun!

Well, actually, RHP was relating to me a very seriously sad sob story, so that both of us, both writer and publisher, were just oozing tears and tears into our crab cakes and Filipino sausages, which were good and salty and juicy enough to begin with, in my opinion. The Filipinos, in particular, were bursting with sweet, wholesome succulence.

Ever eaten at Just for You? Well, why the hell not? What are you, a vegetarian?

There used to be a Just for You up there on Church Street, just for Noe Valleysters, but that one's closed. But the Potrero Hill one is still open. It's just two tables and a counter. Me and RHP were sitting at the end of the counter, crying, like I said, and toward the end of the meal, our waitressperson/proprietressperson overheard RHP sob something about the *Bay Guardian,* which got her getting a little emotional herself. Only she was too tough to cry.

"I gotta problem with the *Guardian,*" she said. "I tell you, if I ever meet that Dan Leone," she said, "I'm gonna put my foot right up his ass."

I couldn't see, from my side of the counter, what size or type of shoe she was wearing, but my guess is there was some sort of an expression on my face, because she stopped herself mid-rant and said, "You guys aren't him, are you?"

"No. No. Not me," I said, shaking my head.

RHP was quick to point out that he wasn't Dan Leone either.

"Good. I don't understand why he doesn't review this place," she continued. "It's his kind of place. I mean, it's not super-cheap, but it's cheap enough. And it's good."

And all the meat, and the atmosphere . . . yep, she was absolutely right. It was my kind of place exactly. And I'd eaten there before, and I'd loved it, and I'd even thought about writing about it, but for some reason . . .

"Maybe he doesn't know about it," I said. "You should write him a letter."

"I should," she said. And then she let it slip that she was leaving town for a week, and I made a mental note to go back and take actual notes while the cat was away, so as to avoid any possibility of recognitions, associations, puttings of two and two together, and subsequent foots up my ass.

Folks, friends, neighbors, editors, apartment managers, I'm about as kinky as the next guy, so you know, and maybe even open-mindeder, but foots up my ass are one thing I don't even like to think about.

Sausages, on the other hand, and lots of butter . . . and homemade toast and just generally excellent, meaty meals with a spicy, Louisianic tint to them! All that oh-my-goodness is right up my alley.

So to speak. So I happily went back for more of it the following week, this time with a writer friend of mine. And if there's one thing weepier than a writer and a publisher having lunch together, it's a writer and a writer. If I'd've taken any actual notes, they'd've been too tear-streaked to read right now anyway.

Suffice it to say that everything was great. I had scrambled eggs with chili and cheese and onions all smothered all over two slices of toasted homemade bread (for five-something, if memory serves me). A side of Louisiana hot sausage. A taste of my comrade's eggs and chorizo scramble . . . everything, I'm telling you, was delicious.

Even the potatoes. They're salty, spicy, red-coated home fries with absolutely no subtlety to them. Which, if there are two things in this world that don't belong together even more than foots and asses don't, that's what two things they are: potatoes and subtlety.

Even the things we didn't get looked great, like the Hangtown Scramble, I think they called it, which had oysters and bacon in it, for seven-something. Burgers, eggs, crab cakes, sausage, sausage, sausage . . .

I'll definitely be back, and I hope to see you there. I'll be the tall, muscular, clean-shaven gentleman with a briefcase, curly red hair, a three-piece suit, and a tie with lots of little ducks on it.

■ CHILE LINDO

My cousin Choo Choo Train, who used to be called Drags, has recently re-relocated here, and he's making Haywire look like a burritoteetotaller, averaging better than a burrito a day through his first week back. That's

> **Chile Lindo**
> 2944 16th Street,
> San Francisco. (415) 621-6108.
> Lunch, dinner. Cheap.

pretty good. Haywire, the mama's boy, only had one a day, and only for five days running. I'll admit, I thought that was pretty impressive at the time. But these are different times; from now on anyone who thinks they eat a lot of burritos is going to have to reckon with the Choo Choo Train.

I don't eat a lot of burritos. I reckoned I'd go eat some Chilean food instead, because a hot tip I got said that Chile Lindo, 16th and Capp, was an excellent alternative to Mission District burritos and donuts. I don't eat a lot of donuts, either.

I called Choo Choo and said, "Are you sick of burritos and donuts yet?"

"Donuts?" he said.

He wasn't sick of burritos, either, but he said he'd meet me for lunch as soon as his laundry was done.

"Laundry?" I said. I was too hungry to even think about laundry, let alone wait for it. So I persuaded the Train to leave laundry out of it and hop the hell onto his bike, and next thing I knew there we were: Chile Lindo, 16th and Capp. Capacity: five.

Number of things on the menu: very few. Just sandwiches and salad and the Health Nut Special, which is what Choo Choo got, being not so much a health nut or even a nut as another goddang vegetarian. (Actually, to me he's the original vegetarian, dating back to the early '70s, Ohio, which was the first I'd ever heard of the abnormality.)

The sandwiches all have meat in them. Steak, to be exact. I got the one called Chacarero, because in addition to steak and tomato and *pebre,* which is "Chilean mild hot sauce," which I'll grapple with in a minute, the Chacarero also has string beans. String beans! Homemade round bread. Mayonnaise.

"No mayonnaise," I said and said and said. I said it three times.

"We put very little mayonnaise on them, anyway," the proprietress-person said, smiling.

"*No* mayonnaise," I said. Four.

The Train laughed at me.

"You don't understand, Chooch," I said, dead serious. "It takes three or four times, at least. Sometimes it takes more than that."

And a few minutes later, as if to prove my point, here came my sandwich with mayonnaise on it. Albeit very little mayonnaise. But to a mayophobe of my caliber, even a very little is way too much.

Choo Choo tried to tell me those little white spots were butter, and I guess I wanted to believe him, 'cause I loaded the sandwich down, just in case, with extra *pebre* (which is Chilean mild hot sauce, which I'll get to in a moment) and I took a bite. Mayonnaise.

You can't hide it from me, proprietpeople, sandwich makers of the world, scofflaws and poo-paws and mayonnaise meanies . . . if it's there, it's there, and I can taste it and I'm going to puke. All over your restaurant, one of these times, which is bad for business.

In this case I just gulped a bunch of soda, gave the infected bottom half of the sandwich, meat juice and all, to Choo Choo, who happily ate it, meat juice and all—so he's not as big of a baby as I am. Thanks to gravity, the top part and most of the middle were clean, so I was able to eat it, but it was too late for any real enjoyment, string beans notwithstanding. And steak and great homemade bread.

And *pebre.* Which, lest we forget, is Chilean mild hot sauce, yet another in a long line of life's little knuckleballs warranting yet another rousing chorus of "Oh Susanna, Don't You Cry for Me"—mayomemories notwithstanding.

That sung, let me take care of a little more business: Chile Lindo is a hell of a hole-in-the-wall, maybe the tiniest restaurant I've ever eaten in. And, mayomemories notwithstanding, it's a pleasant place, operated and presumably owned by friendly if short-memoried folks. The five counter seats face out the window onto 16th Street, beautiful day, like a painting, and behind you the other three inside walls are also painted sky blue, with wisps of clouds, winds out of the west at 15 mph, and a slight chance of early evening showers.

Steak sandwiches go for just over five bucks. You can get them with avocado or cheese if you don't like string beans, or if you don't believe they belong on sandwiches. Health Nut Specials go for just under five and consist of brown rice, soy sauce, *azuki* beans, and salad, all mixed up. Choo Choo Train was perfectly satisfied with his meal, but don't forget he also had half of my sandwich's bread.

I personally needed a burrito for dessert.

■ MR. PITTMAN'S PIT

So there we were, sitting around the edge of the pool, dabbling our toes into the barbecue sauce and talking about this, that, the other thing, and how we all knew each other. It was Crawdad de la Cooter, me, his

Mr. Pittman's Pit
1117 Fillmore, San Francisco.
(415) 885-2357. Lunch, dinner.
Credit cards accepted. Cheap.

royal newness J. F. Bird Nouveau, J. F. Bird's grillfriendperson Mama Bird Biker Bird, and this other bird called Circus Boy. It was Friday evening, Memorial Day weekend.

Ah summer!

For the record, Crawdad and myself met on the dance floor, El Rio, Spring '96, slosh-dancing through my spilt red wine to Red Meat's rendition of George Jones's "He Stopped Loving Her Today." I knew his newness 'cause our x-bands used to play together, and him and Mama B-3 go way, way back. I don't know where Circus Boy came from, but I was happy to have him aboard, even before he lit a book of matches on fire and ate it.

"How's it taste?" I said.

"Bad."

"Have some sauce," I said, and he dipped on into the pool and had some. "How's it taste?" I said.

"Good."

Him eating the book of burning matches was not entirely out of the blue, for the record. How it happened to happen was like this: I was minding my own business, fishing for chickens and ribs and briskets with a plastic fork, pretty much popping them down like Popeye pops a can of spinach—only instead of getting strong and walloping Bluto I was sweating like a pig and wiping my nose a lot. The sauce was hitting me pretty hard, but I was taking it like a man. I had sliced bread and grape pop on my side. I was going to be fine.

And then Circus Boy, who had stopped eating for a few minutes, said, "This sauce kind of hits you a few minutes after the fact."

Uh-oh, I thought. I looked over at Crawdad, who can handle heat as well as anyone I know (except now Circus Boy). Her nose was running. "Uh-oh," I said. "It's hitting me immediately." And I continued to scarf stuff down, hating to think what would happen if I stopped. Luckily, there was a lot of stuff, a swimming pool full of chickens and ribs and briskets afloat in this hot hot hot sauce, plus beans and spaghetti on the side.

"I should mention," mentioned Circus Boy, "that I eat fire for a living."

"Glad you mentioned it," I said, slowing down and breathing easierly. Of course, I'd seen Crawdad eat the equivalent of fire, but I'd never seen anyone eat fire fire, so we got to talking about how fire fire is properly eaten, and that was what led to the matchbook demonstration. Which was only a demonstration, mind you.

Normally Circus Boy eats kerosene torches.

Sounds yummy, but I reckon I'll stick with chickens and ribs and briskets—for now at least. Truth is, that was all we could think of, me and Crawdad, all through that three-day weekend last weekend, was chickens and ribs and briskets drowned to death in that terrifyingly delicious sauce. Crawdad kept saying it was the best barbecue she's ever had out here. Then she kept saying that, of course, she hasn't had an awful lot of barbecue out here.

Well, I have, and I think I can say, without fear of overhyperbolating, that it was up there. Not quite as cheap as Brother-in-Laws. Possibly better, though. And definitely better, by about a hundred million times, than Flintroy's, which used to mark the spot. For the record.

I won't get into the East Bay. It's been so long since I've been to Everett & Jones . . . it might as well be in Ohio, I'm sorry to say. And my onetime SF favorite, Memphis Minnie's, which is now a part of Johnny Love's, might as well be in Arabia, with Lawrence, I'm even sorrier to say.

So, yeah, why not? Mama Bird Biker Bird, who lives upstairs from Mr. P's and eats his 'cues all the time, she'll back me up on this. Sure, 18 hard-earned bucks is a lot to pay for a three-way, but this is easily a three-feeder three-way, four or five if you eat like birds, and two if you eat like me and Crawdad. Which is still nine bucks apiece, which isn't bad for such a magnitudinous feast.

I mean, this wasn't a plate—it was a swimming pool, or a sandbox, or a table, or at least a lasagna tray filled with meat and meat and meat. We had a tiny bit of help from our friends, sure, but they all had their own stuff to worry about.

"Look," Ms. B. B. B. said to our waiterguyperson, "they ate the whole thing!"

We were proud and sweaty pigs, me and Crawdad. And happy.

"I'd rather clothe them than feed them," the guy said, heading back into the kitchen.

I watched the door swing closed behind him and thought: oink?

■ BAYSIDE CAFE

Sitting at the counter, staring into a five-gallon, two-ton pile of whipped butter, trying to collect my thoughts . . . the butter is not my breakfast. My breakfast is a chili omelette and hash browns and toast. The butter is on the counter behind the counter, between the machine that spins milk shakes and the other machine—the one that isn't exactly a toaster but still manages to make toast out of slices of sliced bread. Like the meaning of life or a one-bedroom apartment with hardwood floors and a bathtub and a big closet for under four-arms-and-four-legs . . . you know it's out there somewhere, you can see it, you can almost even taste it, and yet it remains just out of reach.

> **Bayside Cafe**
> 2011 Bayshore Boulevard,
> San Francisco. (415) 467-2023.
> Breakfast, lunch, dinner. Credit
> cards accepted. Cheap.

Think, Danny Boy. *Think!*

Um . . . the name of the restaurant is Bayside Cafe. It's a 24-hour diner known, according to the menu, for its "fabulous food" and "spectacular views." There's a drawing of the Golden Gate Bridge and five of the Seven Sisters on the menu, but I don't think you can see either of those spectacular views from the Bayside Cafe. I think you can see the big hill between Candlestick Park and the freeway, some houses, a tiny bite out of the downtown SF skyline, and the spectacular traffic patterns of the intersections of Bayshore and Third with Highway 101, just before it splits into 280. There's a lot going on right there.

There's a lot going on inside the restaurant, too. Two waitresspeople are running around like chickens with their heads still on, somehow managing to move things along quite nicely in the teeth of a wicked late-morning, prelunch rush. A party of 17 is taking up all the booths in the smaller part of the L-shaped restaurant. The big bad-ass cook is cooking his big bad ass off, keeping up. I'm staring on into the butter.

Trying to think here. You know, I asked for grits with this omelette, and you know what I got? Hash browns. If I had grits, grits'd have a big ball of butter on them, I know because I've watched other orders of grits go by with big balls of butter on them. If those were my grits, I'd watch that ball slowly turn into a puddle of yellow and I'd push my fork through it, mixing yellow into white, maybe come up with something. Some other color, or a clue.

My toast has butter on it, but not enough. If I ask for more, I know they will slide me a scoop of butter on a small white dish with light blue trim, and I will be able to see butter up close, maybe feel butter with my finger, eat it with a spoon, who knows? Maybe think a legitimate thought like that one I thought back in 1991, after which everything fell into place.

But there's a party of 17 and a lot else going on, and I can't get anyone's attention for the life of me. Another glass of water would be nice. Coffee . . . the chili omelette is good and big and good, with cheddar cheese and chili but not lettuce or salsa, like the menu said. Onions would be nice. But I don't think the menu said onions. For five, six bucks, it's a helluva lot of food. "Generous portions," the menu says. Yep.

The burgers look good. But the best-looking thing I've seen passing by between me and butter was a sliced-beef quesadilla with grilled onions on two huge, burrito-size tortillas. Don't remember seeing that on the menu, so maybe it's a special order. In any case, they did it, didn't they?

Waterlessness notwithstanding, I have to smile. The outside walls of this L-shaped diner are all windows, and the inside walls are all mirrors, so that even us'n's sitting at the counter, looking in, could conceivably look out—if it weren't for, in my case, butter. And outside of here there's a Thrift Lodge and another, taller, restaurant called Russia House, which is round and bigger-windowed, with, one would imagine, still more spectacular views of traffic patterns and houses and hills.

I'm stuffed. I can't move. I've got a lot to do, but I'm not going anywhere until I get another glass of water. "Excuse me. Help. I've got a lot to do." I'm thirsty. At home, on my kitchen table, there is an almost empty bottle of wine, two purple-bottomed wineglass jars, a pencil, and a junk-mail envelope numbered one two three.

Marriage? Children? Shirts? (Money? A story? This review?) . . .

breakfast, lunch, and dinner, and here I sit at this here counter, open 24 hours, staring into a five-gallon, two-ton pile of butter, thinking: butter.

■ CAFFE COZZOLINO

Found a place. Yep. Having thought about it, me and the great Crawdad de la Cooter are moving on in together, lack of closet space notwithstanding, meaning, among other things, I have to get used to furniture and plants and art and drinking out of glasses that don't necessarily say 49ers on them.

> **Caffe Cozzolino**
> 300 Precita Avenue,
> San Francisco. (415) 285-
> 6005/6006. Lunch, dinner.
> Credit cards accepted. Cheap.

There were a few moments of panic during the big search, most notably while checking out one place that was actually more than three blocks away from Can-Cun. It hit me in the kitchen. I opened the refrigerator door and there was nothing at all inside of it, not even a ripped-open box of baking soda. I don't remember if I'd eaten yet or not, but it didn't matter. A series of synapses synapted inside my brain, connecting the sight of an empty refrigerator to a *carne asada burrito, con queso,* right around the corner. Then I reckoned where in the world we were, did the math, and folded to the linoleum. Crawdad had to help me up and away from the place, and even if we'd wanted it, the apartment manager surely would have rejected our application on grounds of "insufficient balance" or "lack of character."

In such a rental market as ours, sadly, there is little if any margin for error, let alone fainting spells and nervous breakdowns. You might as well write down "shopping cart" where they ask for your vehicle make and model and so on.

Well, luckily, in the end, although we did have to leave our neck of the Mission, our new apartment is—get this—three blocks away from the new Can-Cun, Mission and Valencia! Some other businesses that stand to benefit from our relocation are Royal Kitchen, my favorite Chinese place; Al's Cafe, the great breakfastlunch joint; Rincón Peruano, the green salsa champions of the world; and El Rio, whose rancid red wine is offset by an excellent card-playing patio.

As for Caffe Cozzolino, the cozy little Italian restaurant just across Dog Shit Park from our pad-to-be, Precita and Folsom . . . yeah, well I suppose maybe they'll benefit, sure, but mostly, I imagine, we'll get it to go. Get this: Everything's about two bucks more if you eat it there, and that's for lunch. For dinner, it's more like four bucks more. What's up with *that?* as our Southern CA neighbors say. (And I suppose that in a week or so I'll be one of them, Army-Chavez Street being the dividing line, right?)

Crawdad braved the famous dog shit of Dog Shit Park to cross over and grab a takeout menu one day while we were waiting to meet our new landlordladyperson. I liked what I saw: pasta dishes for five or six, meat and seafood for seven or eight, pizza, free delivery after five—which could conceivably come in handy if, say, I ever break both of my legs at the same time.

Anyway, that was last week. This week, on account of missing my new neighborhood-to-be (which is possible, trust me), I went ahead and went to Cozzolino with my new neighbor-to-be, Bikkets. We almost left when we saw the numbers on the eat-in menu, which were eights and nines for lunch, tens and elevens for dinner. But then we stayed, because what the hell? It was nice in there, and we had to know.

The spaghetti with clam sauce was pretty goddamn weak, in spite of some really cute baby clams. The vermicelli with tomatoes and basil and garlic, on the other hand, was pretty goddamn delicious, and it was one of those magic bowls of pasta that starts out looking kind of small but never seems to get any smaller. I was slurping away at it for an hour, it seemed, sopping up the soupy sauce with bread and bread and bread (and butter and butter and butter)—and it wouldn't go away! I almost even got sick of it.

We also sampled some soups, speaking of soupy. Bikkets had minestrone, which was great, and I had soup-of-the-day, which was pastina. Which wasn't great. The broth was kind of gloppy. Either don't cook the pastinas in the broth, or don't cook them as long, is my advice. To them.

To you, dear reader, my advice is to get it to go. Avoid the temptation of those comfy, cushy chairs and that cheesy classic Italian music and the general coziness of Cozzolino. If you don't live across the street, there are benches and tables right there in Dog Shit Park.

And if you happen to see anyone not cleaning up after their dog, do me a favor and harrass the hell out of them.

FOR SALE: Ping-Pong table. (Sniff.)

■ CHER'S GRILL HOUSE

I wish I could say I went downtown to check out Bonnie O'Bounty at the Market Street Cinema, but why I was down there was way more embarrassing than that. In fact, I'm not going to tell you why. It's too embarrassing.

> **Cher's Grill House**
> 138 Sixth Street, San Francisco.
> (415) 522-1183. Breakfast,
> lunch, dinner. Cheap cheap.

Well, OK, I'll tell you, but this is just between me and you, OK?

OK. I had to pick up a pair of alterationed pants at Banana Republic, and exchange a shirt at—get this—Brooks Brothers! Yep, me, wearer of same-thing-every-day hand-me-down castoffs, conducting business with the Big Boys. It's hard to believe, I know—especially if you know me. On the other hand, if you know me, you'll know that last month was my birthday, and next month I'm going to Florida for a sorta pseudo de la Cooter family reunion. And apparently Crawdad would prefer for some of her Crawfamily to think of me as a "restaurant reviewer" rather than "the cheap eats pig."

Ergo: birthday presents.

Now, if you don't know me except through these reviews, you may well picture me as a somewhat huge person—understandably, on account of how much I eat and how much of how much I eat tends to be fried in lard. What's interesting is that even my closest friends consider me more girth-ful than I actually am. Crawdad, for crying out loud, hugs me on a regular basis, and often without clothes on, I'm happy to report. She of all people should realize I'm a Medium, not Large, and a size 32 Waist, not 42.

In her defense, maybe she has an uncanny ability to see into the future. Plus it must be hard for girls to think in boy-sizes, particularly when the boy in question generally wears T-shirts and tagless thrift-store "action slacks," and wouldn't even know his own waist size (32) if it weren't for having to break down and pick up a new pair of undies every 10 to 12 years or so.

New clothes make me nervous, in part because I tend to spill things on them, but for other reasons too. After only five minutes in Banana R. and 15 in Brooks B., I was beyond nervous. I was fuckin' freaked. By way of re-grounding myself in reality (mine), I reckoned I'd swing past the bus station on my way home for some cheap cheap cheap Chinese food.

Unfortunately, the great Chinese joint that used to be in the bus station is gone gone gone, and crying, according to Lefty, won't bring it back. So then I started thinking about the Tenderloin, but on the way there I had to pedal past Sixth and Mission, where there happens to be a Filipino dive I'd been meaning to get to—not to mention a lot of important-looking gentlemen hanging around on the sidewalk.

Hi boys! Keep an eye on my bike for me, will you?

Man, I love Filipino food. Filipino food is basically meat. Which is beautiful, but the most beautiful thing about this particular Filipino hole-in-the-wall is the name of it, which they miraculously manage to spell three different ways in about as many square feet of restaurantage: Cher's Grill House, Cher's Grille House, and Cher's Grilhouse.

What's for lunch, for me, is Chicken Adobo, which is basically chicken and gravy over rice, and two *lumpia*, which are basically egg rolls, sometimes known to have things like peas and carrots and vegetables in them, but these ones were solid rolls of pork. Nothing else. Beautiful.

For breakfast, well, I didn't eat breakfast, but I saw pictures of it: beautiful shots of fried eggs and meat over big piles of rice. Then a sign over the ordering area: "Breakfast—Garlichicken—$2.50." Beautiful.

The food was fine, and certainly cheap, but once again I'm going to have to encourage you to get it to go. Not 'cause of the neighborhood; because of the loud, staticky radio, which inflicted me with my worst nightmare, Whitney Houston, and because of a gone-awry door chime that chimed every time anyone walked by on the sidewalk outside, either side of the street.

I don't know which was more annoying. Probably Brooks Brothers.

■ GASPARE'S

I'm rich, I'm rich! No kidding, yesterday at this time I had a grand total of one dollar in my wallet (none in my checking account), and today at this

Gaspare's
5546 Geary Boulevard, San Francisco. (415) 387-5025/5039. Dinner. Credit cards accepted. Splurge cheap.

time, 11:31 in the morning—I just counted—I have $103. Here's how I did it, and how you too can get rich quick, in five easy steps:

1) Have friends.

2) Go out to dinner with them, the more the merrier.

3) Lots of food, lots of wine, dessert, coffee . . .

4) When the check comes, say, "I'll put it on my credit card."

5) Put it on your credit card, and your friends will all slide you cold, hard cash, happily. Your friends are your friends! In some cases, depending on how much they've had to drink, they may even thank you. Often they will overpay. And even if you don't wind up with more money than the check and tax and tip added up to, it's still a cash advance, you gotta figure, minus the finance charge.

Plus all the food and wine and so on and so forth.

Some get-rich-quickers like to order big, 'cause that jacks up the overall price of the meal, and most groups of friends, friends being friends, divide the grand total by the number of friends present, so that some poor sucker who only had a salad and a glass of water winds up handing you a crisp twenty just like everyone else, saying, "Thank you."

"No. Thank *you*."

I would never pull such a stunt, myself. Last night at Gaspare's out in the Richmond, for example, I ate *gnocchi alla Bolognese*, meatballs, sausage, calamari steak, and pizza—but I only ordered three of those things. The others I bartered for or just grabbed. And I did drink a lot of wine, but it wasn't me who kept asking for another bottle please.

The pizza was pretty good. It's almost $20 for a giant *margherita*, which has a tetch too much garlic, a tetch too much olive oiliness, and about the right amounts of basil, oregano, and cheese. It's a thin-crust pizza, and by thin I mean *thin*—as thin as my wallet was yesterday at this time.

What else I didn't order was the *calamari steak doré*, whatever *doré* is; but I enjoyed it immensely. It was a tender slab of squid sautéed with garlic and a lot of lemon, almost eye-wateringly tangy. And it comes with a side-pile of spaghetti with meat sauce, which was decent.

I'd traded a bunch of my gnocchi for a bunch of this calamari (and a little spaghetti), and I traded well. Which isn't to say that the gnocchi was all that half bad. It leaned toward the chewy end of the spectrum, but the Bolognese sauce was good and meaty and good.

Speaking of meaty, Gaspare's meatballs are pretty good, but the sausage takes the cake. It was broiled like I like it—to a crisp on the outside, without sacrificing any essential inner juices—and then smothered in more meat sauce. Next time I go I'm getting the sausage entrée.

Either that or Danny's Pizza, which is salami, which I like, and mozzarella and sauce—because that's who I am—Danny Boy—and what better reason is there to order a thing?

Well, it almost doesn't even matter at Gaspare's, because the point, in my opinion, isn't the food. It's the atmosphere. It's the grapevine ceiling with hanging, half-basketed bottles of winelessness. It's the beautiful green booths with individual jukeboxes. It's "Funiculi Funicula" on the jukebox, and then "Funiculi Funicula" again on the jukebox, and then again, with maybe "Arrivederci Roma" or some old American song in between—say, "My Ding-a-Ling." And it's those long, long paintings of San Francisco or Venice or what?

My cousin Choo Choo Train loves Gaspare's. He loved it when he lived here before, and now that he lives here again he still loves it, and the only thing he's ever ordered is a *margherita* pizza. He says it's his favorite pizza in San Francisco, but he hasn't eaten at Tommaso's yet. That's where me and Crawdad are taking everyone who helped us move—on us, and no credit-card get-rich-quick schemes, either.

There are still two or three things at my old place, by the way, if anyone's hungry. A Ping-Pong table, some ketchup . . .

■ HUNGARIAN SAUSAGE FACTORY

Some guy accused me yesterday on public radio of never leaving the Mission, but I don't even live in the Mission anymore, so my accusers are going to have to start accusing me of never leaving Bernal Heights or else run the risk of being wrong. To help them along, I hiked over the Heights yesterday to Cortland Street to look into the Hungarian Sausage Factory,

Hungarian Sausage Factory
419 Cortland Street,
San Francisco. (415) 648-2847.
Lunch, dinner. Credit
cards accepted. Cheap.

which I'd learned about on public radio yesterday.

Nice view up there on those Heights, huh? Well, hell, those are some pretty high Heights. I realized going over them, in fact, that I don't live in Bernal Heights, really. I live in the Bernal Foothills. And I realized coming down onto Cortland Street that I don't live on the happening side of the Heights, either.

Which is fine by me. I've had it up to here with happening neighborhoods. Most of what happens in them is shit. Which I guess tends to happen in Dog Shit Park, too, but it's different when it's dogs. I'll tell you what, I'd rather step in dog shit, for example, than into the new, yuppified "original" McCarthy's, my old ex-favorite Mission District bar. Seen it lately?

Well, the deal with the Hungarian Sausage Factory is sausage. They make it, and you can either take it home and cook it yourself or have a seat in the adjoining dining room, let them do the work. In which case, there are all sorts of other Hungarian things you might choose to eat, like herdsman's beef stew, stuffed cabbage leaves, or *palacsinta,* which is a crepe. At lunchtime, the price range ranges between about $3.50 and seven bucks, and after 5:30 you can expect to pay a few dollars more, like seven to 14—but you also get live music.

I showed up at the best possible time: 5:15. I got to get it from the lunch menu, and I was the only one there, *and* I got live music. I got to listen to an amazing duet between cello and cricket. The cellist was warming up for the evening's performance, trying to decide between two new bows, the cheapest of which, I overheard, would run him around $800 (so I hope cellists make more money than ukulele players).

What the cricket was up to, I couldn't tell you. Probably hanging out in the wall wondering what the hell crickets are supposed to eat in a Hungarian Sausage Factory. But if you've never heard a cello and a cricket make music together, I suggest you check this place out. The sausage was good, but the live music was out of this world.

The cello, as you know, begets such sounds as are only otherwise heard after midnight near the core of the earth, when molten lava lulls solid rock to sleep with gazillion-year-old traditional folk tunes about the origin of matter. And this is with any old bow. Imagine such densely flowing sonic awesomosity invoked by a pair of alternating $800+ new ones, and then imagine the resultant magnificently majestic heaviness accompanied by a little cricket going, "chirp chirp, chirp chirp," and there you have it. Now you know why I was glassy-eyed like I was glassy-eyed at the Hungarian Sausage Factory yesterday between 5:15 and 5:45 p.m.

It wasn't the sausage. The sausage was great, but no food this side of a five-pound omelette can compete with Duet for Cello and Cricket in B Minor when it comes to inducing euphoria.

I got the sausage—*kolbász,* by name—because no matter how good herdsman's beef stew sounds, which is pretty damn good, you have to get sausage. It's a sausage factory. You can get a sandwich for cheaper, but I got the platter. It had one long sausage, a pile of deliciously simple sauerkraut, a pile of deliciously simple cucumber salad (which was supposed to be potato salad, but I hate mayonnaise—in case you just joined us), three pickles, two slices of red onion, two slices of white one, one slice of tomato, and a basket of thick-cut, darkishly great bread. Lots of butter.

All of which, including the music, added up to Naptime, but I fought off the big snooze and went to play soccer instead. Get this: two goals and two assists for Danny Boy, so you know the meal was magic, 'cause I'm usually lucky to get my foot on the ball without falling down.

Atmospherically, the Hungarian Sausage Factory is highly atmospheric, for a factory. The floor is concrete, sure, but the walls are appropriately arted and the tables are tableclothed and flowered and there's a piano and a low ceiling and just general coziness. Good food, good service, good music . . .

Crickets.

■ TOMMY'S JOYNT

They'll charge you four dollars for a wineglass of wine at the Great American Music Hall. Otherwise, it's a beautiful place. I was there the other night for some Great American Music, but you're probably more

Tommy's Joynt
1101 Geary Boulevard,
San Francisco. (415) 775-4216.
Lunch, dinner. Cheap.

interested in what I ate before-hand, right?

Burgundy beef over rice, a tomato salad, and a roll.

All right, let's talk sports. I don't see any honest-to-goodness, God-fearing pennant races shaping up on any of the six horizons, except maybe the American League West. And we're already this side of the All-Star Break, which can only mean one thing: Football season's just around the corner! Other certified facts are as follows: (1) I'm writing this at the airport, waiting to pick up Johnny "Jack" Poetry and Taters, in from Idaho to play pitch with me all weekend, give or take a few meals and/or naps; (2) plane's late; (3) I was up most of the night last night listening to my stomach make noises I didn't know my stomach had in it (such as "Ping!"); and (4) it wasn't Tommy's fault. Just 'cause he doesn't know how to spell, that doesn't mean he can't cook.

He can cook. More important, he can ladle. And even if he couldn't and couldn't, respectively, I'd still have to recommend Tommy's Joynt, the famous Geary and Van Ness corner sports bar/hofbräu, with all my heart and valves and arteries, because you can drink a *pint* of wine there for the same price, give or take a buck, as a *glass* of wine around the corner at the Great American.

Scout's honor. It's two bucks for a "small" glass of wine, $2.50 for a large—and by large they mean a half-pint. Two kinds to choose from. I forget the other one, but I got burgundy to go with my burgundy beef, and it was damn fine wine, considering it came from a tap. Shit, for $2.50 a half-pint, it can come out of a rusty can for all I care.

The beef burgundy was great: big, huge chunks of tender beef and per-fectly taut, skinned potato balls, all smothered with plenty of orangishly greaseful juiciness, which oozed quite nicely into the rice, thanks. Did I mention that they really pile it on at Tommy's? Yep. Whether it's wine or meat or salad . . . but you probably know all this already. Tommy's Joynt is not exactly undiscovered. Even all the tourists seem to know about it. It's colorful and cool, just like San Francisco in general—only it's also cheap. And meaty.

In fact, the whole reason I was eating (and drinking) at the world-famous joynt, besides for being in the Great American neighborhood, was 'cause Wayway thought it would be a fine idea to pack some meat into our marathon-running pals Tinzee and One-Cents before the big event (SF Marathon, Sunday).

One-Cents didn't show, so I wouldn't put any pennies on her winning any marathons last weekend if I were you. Wayway, for the record, ate a big bunch of turkey sloppy joes. (I wouldn't put any money on him running any marathons ever, but that's another story.) For the record, he seemed disappointed in Tommy's sloppy joes 'cause they were made out of actual—rather than ground—turkey. I liked them fine.

Tinzee, for the record, had the special of the day, which was a gigantic sandwich of steak—ground, on the other hand, when it probably shouldn't have been. It tasted kind of overdone for my money, but it wasn't my money, so . . . and anyway, its dryness was covered by a fine brown gravy, and there must have been about a half-pound of meat or more, plus salad I think and maybe even something else for I-forget-how-much. (And if that ain't a fine example of journalism . . .)

Well, good luck everybody who's running (ran) in the SF Marathon. Time will have already told, by the time you read this, and I don't believe it's possible to jinx someone retroactively, so I don't mind predicting that Tinzee's going to win.

■ CHEUNG HING CHINESE RESTAURANT

Of course, a lot of amateur eaters seem to believe that a Chinese restaurant full of Chinese people is automatically a good restaurant. My personal, professional opinion is this: maybe. Maybe it's not so much good as authentic, which isn't always necessarily good. Or maybe all those Chinese people aren't Chinese, or maybe they're good friends

> Cheung Hing Chinese Restaurant
> 2339 Noriega Street,
> San Francisco. (415) 665-3271.
> Lunch, dinner. Cheap cheap.

with the cook, who may be a great guy, for all we know, with lots of funny jokes and friendly advice and nickels for the kiddies, but it so happens he can't stir-fry his way out of a paper bag.

So don't take anything for granted, OK? In food as in life, you can't judge a book by how many people are reading it—even if all the people reading it are writers, or book reviewers, or Chinese. Personally, I've been reading Chekhov's short stories, and I don't care how few people showed up at his funeral, the cat could tell a fuckin' story!

That said, let me just say that Cheung Hing Chinese Restaurant in the center of the Sunset is a great goddang restaurant, but not because of the line of getting-it-to-go Chinese people lined up all the way out to the sidewalk. No, it's a great restaurant because I ate there and it was great.

Hi, I'm Dan Leone, white guy. Never been to Hong Kong, not to mention China in general or several other places. But I know meat when I see it, and Cheung Hing is meat city. Rows of whole, hooked, hanging ducks and chickens, roasted, barbecued, five-spiced, soy-sauced, cold-boiled . . . other animals, other parts: heads, organs, feets and ears, feets and ears. Yes, I know meat when I see it.

I saw pork. I was standing in line, waiting to order what I thought I wanted—"Marinated Assortment"—when a guy comes moseying out of the back of the place with a whole roasted pig, on a hook, and he hooks it onto this whole-roasted-pig hanger right there pretty much in the middle of the restaurant. I thought: cool. I watched him hack a few parts off with a big butcher knife, and then I looked away for maybe a minute, thinking about other things (ducks, chickens), and next time I looked it was half of a whole pig, lengthwise, just hanging there, looking good. I hoped and prayed that some of it would find its way into my "assortment."

But when I got up to the counter, finally, and said what I wanted to say—"Marinated assortment," I said—the butchermanperson behind the counter didn't seem to know what I was talking about.

"Huh?" he said.

I pointed to the BBQ section of the takeout menu. "Number 69. Marinated assortment," I said.

"You want 'Two Items'?" he said—Two Items Together being Number 70.

I didn't feel like arguing, so I said, sure, chicken and pork, and an order of roast duck noodle soup. For here.

"For here? Sit down," he said, and he sent someone over to take my order, so I'd waited in the getting-it-to-go line for nothing.

No problem. It moves pretty fast. And there was no wait whatsoever for one of the seven or so glass-topped tables. And if there would've been a wait, it would've been worth the wait. I'm telling you, if you love meat like I do, check this place out. It's right across from the Safeway on Noriega, between 30th and 31st Avenues.

Except for Two Items Together, there's nothing on the menu over $5, and the portions are huge, and the meat is freshly hooked catch-of-the-day material.

The roast duck noodle soup was a huge bowl of great dark broth, great tender ducks, and great skinny noodles, with a little bit of green onion for color. No spoon, just chopsticks and a fork, and an empty plate for duck bones, and a plastic glass of hot tea. Don't be afraid to pick up the soup bowl and drink from it. I wasn't.

And the Two Items Together (TIT) was a huge mound of rice, a little bit of steamed cabbage, and I think three kinds of meat. I'd asked for roasted pork and chicken, but I swear there was some duck in there too. At least I think it was duck. I know meat when I see it, as I think I might've mentioned, but that doesn't mean I know what's what. All I know is all of the what's-what in this TIT was just as succulent as, well, you-name-it.

There was at least two meals' worth of mealage involved in the meal, all said. Excuse me now while I go eat the other one.

■ CHAVITA'S RESTAURANT

Wow, when I read in the *Bay Guardian* that Chevy's—*Chevy's!*—was the Bay Area's best Mexican restaurant, according to readers of the *Bay Guardian,* my first impulse was to stop reading the *Bay Guardian.* My

> **Chavita's Restaurant**
> 3006 Mission Street,
> San Francisco. (415) 285-6927.
> Breakfast, lunch, dinner. Cheap.

second impulse was to move to some other city. My third impulse was to lie down for a while. It wasn't until my fourth or fifth impulse that it even occurred to me to go eat at Chevy's.

After all, I mean, readers' polls don't lie, do they? How can they? Readers, like me, simply have their opinions. Sometimes they're wrong. Sometimes they're right. Can-Cun, for example, won *two* awards—presumably from the same readers. So my next impulse was to stop eating at Can-Cun. In short, I was very very very very very confused. I'd never been to Chevy's, because I always imagined it to be a sort of yucky suburban mallville wahoo mainstream-Americanization of Mexican food for people who had just enough sense not to eat at Taco Bell, but not quite enough sense to go to Chava's. Plus it's a chain, and chains are inherently mean and nasty, right?

Well, maybe not. Maybe all my preconceived notions were malpreconceived. This much was certain: There could be only one way to find out, definitively and responsibly, and that way would almost have to entail a trip to Chevy's. By me, Danny Boy.

So I put on my goofy-glasses-false-nose-and-fake-mustache disguise and headed off toward BART. Problem is, if you live where I do, the walk to BART'll take you right past Chavita's on Mission and 26th, across from the Tip-Top Inn. And if you're as hungry as I tend to be—in you go, Chevy's be damned.

Hey, and there was my friend the Liver Lady, sitting at an otherwise empty table with a drink and a menu!

"Hi, Liver Lady!" I said.

She said, "Who are you?"

So I took off my goofy-glasses-false-nose-and-fake-mustache disguise and she said, "Oh, hey," and we wound up having a great meal together. She got Steak Ranchero, which was juicy little pieces of steak with crunchy little pieces of peppers and onions and stuff, smothered in a delicious *ranchero* sauce. I got the grilled-chicken plate, which was grilled chicken. Both meals came with rice and refrieds, of course, and shredded-iceberg salad with a single slice of tomato on top, like a hat. And my dish had a small pile of great fresh tomato salsa, so hooray for me.

What we talked about while eating all this, and—oh yeah—chips and salsa and homemade tortillas, too, was this, that, the other thing, and our favorite kinds of liver. A typical conversation between me and the Liver Lady, so you know, goes something like this:

ME: Chicken liver.

HER: Calf liver.

ME: Deer liver.

HER: Sushi liver.

And so on, until we both break down crying, because that's how much we both love liver—but especially her because her name's the Liver Lady. Some other things you should know about her are (1) don't sit next to her on an airplane; and (2) if, on the other hand, you should wish to seek out her company—which I strongly recommend for liver-related conversation—follow the trail of crumpled napkins she tends to leave on the floor behind her. At the end of the trail, that's the Liver Lady.

Whoa, wait a minute, Danny Boy. Is this another one of your imaginary friends?

Nope, not at all, and my proof is that there's no way I could've eaten all that food myself, good as it all was—and there were nothing but empty plates on our table at Chavita's last night. Nothing but crumpled napkins on the carpet under her chair when we left.

Besides for which, the atmosphere at Chavita's is nitty-gritty bare-boned basics: tables, chairs, walls, jukebox, TV with Mexican soap operas, then baseball, and a sort of a shrine to Budweiser, the King of Beers. The service is exceedingly cute. ("Would you like something to drink, more?" our timid waitressperson timidly sputtered at one point.) The prices are cheap: burritos for $3.50, meat plates for $4 and $7, seafood stuff for $7.50 or so, and breakfast things for $4 to $6. *Birria* and *menudo* on weekends.

Did I mention that the grilled chicken was great? Yep. Skin-still-on, superseasoned, tenderfully juicy meat, and with a bunch of that cilantroful salsa on top, chased by a bite of those wonderful homemade tortillas and a swig of Corona . . . Folks, if it's any better than this at Chevy's, I'm there.

■ TOMMY'S RESTAURANT

Went out to the V.A. hospital to get blackberries, it being that time of year again, and I took with me my friend Wayway and I took with me my friend Tinzee. Note: I did not take with me my friends "Wayway and Tinzee," so to speak, because they are no longer, sad to say, a couple, having broken up several months ago, which I still haven't gotten over.

Tommy's Restaurant
5929 Geary Boulevard,
San Francisco. (415) 387-4747.
Lunch, dinner. Credit cards
accepted. Splurge cheap.

But they have, and that's what matters, I guess. So I don't mind taking them both with me places—especially when two more people means three times as many black-berries. (It works out mathematically, don't worry.)

Well, it was so foggy out there on the corner of the world that you couldn't hardly see five feet in front of you, as the saying goes. But the black-berries were shining through like golf balls, and we were pickin' 'em. And out on the ocean the foghorns were singing mournfully deep ditties to each other, so that the ships all knew where all the ships were at. And Wayway, in his own way, was answering their call—so that we all knew where he was at, too. And Tinzee was going "ouch . . . ouch . . . ouch," and I was laughing at both of them, so no one got lost or shipwrecked or hurt or anything.

And then seven o'clock rolled around and the voice of Crawdad de la Cooter, who works at the V.A. hospital, was heard by us up the hill somewhere saying, "Are you guys done yet? I'm hungry. Let's go. Are you done yet?"

It being pretty much dinnertime, we were pretty damn hungry too, Wayway's sonic soundings notwithstanding (not to mention all those blackberries), so we swam up out of the fog toward my sports utility vehicle, Rocco, and we all piled in and headed for Chevy's, San Francisco's Best Mexican Restaurant (according to readers of the *Bay Guardian*).

To get there from that part of the world you go over to Geary and turn left, then head downtown. You'll pass a store and a gas station and a the-ater and another store and so many restaurants that if you aren't hungry you will be, and if you already are, you'll be way too hungry to make it all the way to the Embarcadero.

Which is where Tommy's Restaurant comes in. Right there on your right, Geary between 24th and 23rd Avenues. It's where the fog-dwellers eat their Mexican food and drink their margaritas and tequila and stuff instead of Mission Villa and Puerto Alegre and, I suppose, Chevy's.

Crawdad said the V.A. people are always talking Tommy up, and Wayway said some friends of his swear by it, too, and Rocco said, "Look! A parking space!"—so we reckoned old Chevy could wait another week and in we went.

"Hey there, Tommy."

"Yo."

Tommy and his wife established this place in 1965, two years after I was established, but it's already exceeded me in at least two major categories: popularity and menu items. Yep, it was pretty crowded—downright hopping, in fact—but we got us a nice corner table in the back room, no wait, and before too awfully long we were chowing down on chips and salsa and salads and chimichangas and *carne asada* and pork chops and barbecued chickens, beans and rice. Tortillas.

Sounds good, don't it?

Was. But it was kind of expensive, for my money. As in 10 bones for half a chicken. (That's what I got.)

The *carne asada* was probably the best *carne asada* I ever had, which is saying something. The menu said it was marinated in lemon juice and garlic, then panfried with onions. But I think the menu might've been wrong, because with all due respect to panfrying, this meat was too flavorful not to have been grilled. It was a little thicker than most *carne asada,* and therefore juicier, and it was well salted and peppered and smoky, I swear, and actually red some in the middle.

The chimichangas were similarly out of this world. But chimichangas are deep-fried burritos, so you expect them to be out of this world. One was beef and one was chicken, and the chicken one was far further out of this world than the beef one. It had guacamole on top instead of sour cream, for one thing, and I don't know—biting into it just made me feel like I was a kid again, at an amusement park. And chicken chimichanga was my favorite ride.

If I go back, I'll ride that ride—over and over again. But I don't honestly know if I'll be back. The barbecued chicken and the pork chops were dry. The place was over-bustling. The atmosphere was over-atmospheric. I don't like tequila. Ten bucks a meal . . .

The carne and chicken chimis were worth it, yes, but why go all the way out to the Richmond for Mexican food? Unless you're already there, I mean, like us. I mean, Chevy's is right downtown.

■ LOS JARRITOS

South Van Ness is not a good way to get to Chevy's. Mission Street's only a block away, and it calls out to you, like Sirens. And even over everything—the traffic, the other sirens, the bass-bouncing speaker-tearing convertible rap riffs, gunshots in the post office—Mission Street manages to be heard. *Ssshhhhh* . . . listen: the gentle bubbling of vats of lard, chips a-crispin', on-the-block

> **Los Jarritos**
> 901 South Van Ness Avenue, San Francisco. (415) 648-8383. Breakfast, lunch, dinner. Credit cards accepted. Cheap.

carne asada, chop chop, *mmmmm,* beans a-simmerin', beers being opened . . . and, hey, is that the Can-Cun jukebox I hear?

Yeah, if you stand any chance at all of making it all the way downtown on an empty stomach on South Van Ness, better take the sports utility vehicle, and better crank your Dolly Parton as loud as she'll go. Keep the windows up, so as not to accidentally smell anything other than the damp T-shirt and dirty soccer socks someone left on the passenger-side floor two or three pickup games ago. Tie yourself to the mast, in other words and so to speak, and whatever you do, *don't* turn your head in either direction at any intersection, or you're liable to catch a passing glimpse of Chava's or Panchita's or some other entirely enticing ma-and-pa joint, and—just like that—so much for Chevy's, the best Mexican restaurant in San Francisco (according to readers of the *Bay Guardian*).

Speaking for myself, and for Tinzee and new guy Wally-Wally, we were knocked off track this time by Los Jarritos, which must mean millions and millions of little tiny cups, because that's what's hanging all over the walls of the place, like string-strung garlic or hot peppers. Little tiny cups. They're everywhere. Other atmospheric touches include hanging dolls, sombreros, clothes, and a back room with shelves of fuzzy eagles, bulls, and dogs and stuff. Sort of like at a carnival. Throw a baseball at a bowling pin, or shoot the cute little ducky, or guess how much the weight-guesser weighs, or whatever, and pick out a stuffed animal—only these animals aren't stuffed so much as fuzzed, and I don't think you win them so much as buy them. Theoretically.

But my favorite feature, placewise, is the color of everything: great shades of blue and red and green and pink chairs and tables and walls and ceilings and counter and counter stools. Nice hardwood floors. It's a pretty and pretty interesting looking little restaurant.

Foodwise . . . well, I still haven't ever eaten at San Francisco's best Mexican restaurant, Chevy's, so I can't say exactly how Jarritos rates, but it's gotta be up there.

I had Huevos Divorciados, for example, and they were *muy deliciados.* You get two fried eggs topped with both *chili verde* (which is chunks of pork stewed in this green sort of tomatillo sauce) and *chili Colorado* (which is chunks of pork in red sauce). The porks were oozefully tender and both colors of chili were great and juicy, and the Colorado River and the Green River converged and flowed together into the yellow reservoired runoff from the sunny-side-ups and that, my friends, was poetry in motion—especially when a rolled-up corn tortilla got involved.

What with all that free-for-all, and some particularly moist beans and rice, salsad silly with the hot, thin, red stuff from the table . . . hold on a second, I'm crying.

Which isn't to say, by the way, that I didn't get in on Tinzee's and Wally-Boy's meals, which were fried steak and Deanna's Mole. Guess which one I liked and which one I didn't.

Right. The fried steak was thickish and nicely battered and well seasoned and, above all else, *fried steak,* which I'm pretty much always gonna like, even if it's truck-stop freezer fried.

On the other hand, Deanna's Mole (be sure to pronounce it right or else you might not like it either) was two enchiladas—one chicken and one beef—smothered in mole sauce, which is sort of a chocolate sauce, or "chocolate gravy," as the menu called it.

I call it "blech," but then I don't exactly like chocolate. I don't like chocolate in cake or ice cream or chocolate kisses. Put it on something as pure and beautiful as a chicken or beef enchilada, and I don't even want to talk about it.

So ask Deanna, or ask Wally-Wally.

All else I want to say is that I once ate a bowl of *birria* one Sunday at Los Jarritos between playing baseball and soccer and that, if you'll forgive me please for veering once again into the wide world of sports, it was a damn good bowl of *birria.*

■ BOTANA

Some people live in the Haight. My cousin Choo Choo Train, for example, isn't one of them. But he doesn't live in the Mission, either, and yet he routinely eats as many as two burritos a day.

I've been known to bite into a burrito on occasion myself. Lately, however, it's tamales I'm interested in. My favoritest of all tamales—with due respect to Roosevelt's Tamale Parlor, not to mention the one that Satchel Paige the Pitcher gave me once two and a half years ago, but I remember it like it was one and a half years ago—my favorite tamales of all tamales are the Tamale Lady tamales. The Tamale Lady being a local superhero who materializes out of nowhere in Mission District bars with coolers full of hot ones, right around the time Mission District bargoers are getting thirsty for something to eat for a change.

> **Botana**
> 422 Haight Street,
> San Francisco. (415) 863-9113.
> Dinner. Cheap.

Sadie's. Sunday night. Satchel Paige the Pitcher is pitching a few tunes toward a small audience of $1 Pabst drinkers. I've had one or two myself, in fact, and it's starting to feel like dinnertime, even though I already had dinner. It's getting late. Satch ran out of songs five songs ago, but such is the nature of Satch's tune-pitching genius, he's still going, making them up off the top of his head. Until . . .

"Thank you. Goodnight."

"One more. One more. Sing an invocation to the Tamale Lady."

Which he sings—*"Please, Tamale Lady, please, Tamale Lady, please"*—and there's almost immediately a smell of cornhusks in our noses, the taste of hot sauce on our tongues. Then, there she is: the Tamale Lady, and everyone's going nuts, getting in line for the best tamales they've ever eaten. One dollar.

Am I dreaming? Maybe, maybe not. All you need to know is that a few days later I started thinking about tamales all over again, wondering, naturally, if they have them down at Chevy's, San Francisco's Best Mexican Restaurant (according to readers of the *Bay Guardian*). If so, I reasoned, they might well be the best tamales in San Francisco, maybe even better than the Tamale Lady's.

So I went and picked up my cousin Choo Choo Train in Ashbury Heights, or whatever it's called up there, and we headed for the Embarcadero via Haight Street, which seemed safe, 'cause I've always hated Haight-Mex cuisine, expecially compared to Mish-Mex.

We'd've made it, too—I swear—if it weren't for Botana, this cool new joint in the Upper Haight, or Lower Haight, or whichever Haight it is that has Kate's Kitchen and Spaghetti Western and, more important, Two Jack's. In fact, Two Jack's is the last Haight Street place on the right, Botana is the last one on the left. That's how close we came to making it to Chevy's. So you know.

I'd heard good things about Botana from separate sources, including an e-mail from the Wise One, who e-praised Botana's *carnitas,* mole, and *rellenos,* so I didn't get any of that stuff. I got tamales. Choo Choo, of course, got a burrito.

So you see, between the three of us, we've got a lot of bases covered. Plus I heard someone say they liked the enchiladas. Choo Choo seemed to enjoy his burrito, even though it contained roasted vegetables and tofu and mole instead of *carne asada* and cheese and all. I will say this: They grill their tortillas. They don't steam them. And they fry their chips in-house, thick and good.

Other than which, I can vouch for the tamales. You get two of them, plus rice and beans and salsa, for roughly $5, more like $6 if you want a bunch of meat on top, and you know you do. I got *carne asada.* You can get that, or grilled chickens or shrimps, *chili verde, carnitas,* or chicken mole. The *carne asada* was decent. The refrieds and rice were great, mostly because the fresh tomato salsa I mixed up with them was great.

The tamales themselves consisted of black beans and a few tiny bits of carrots and zucchini, tightly packed in tamale matter. You can also get them with cheese and peppers inside, but I forgot to specify and they picked for me. They also take the cornhusks off for you—which I wish they wouldn't do. Well, the tamales weren't nearly as good as the Tamale Lady's, but that's like saying Choo Choo's burrito wasn't as good as the Can-Cun one he'd had for lunch. It isn't fair.

No table service, but really nice folks behind the counter. Nice place, too. There are red and green and blue lights, and a big old 3-D lizard and moon on the wall, in case you forget to remember you're still on Haight Street.

Which may or may not beat being at Chevy's.

▌CHEVY'S

It's a colorful trick of nature that Concord grapes, my favorite kind of grapes, come into season right at the height of the inner-city blackberry scene. So if you saw someone walking around town last weekend with the

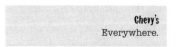

Chevy's
Everywhere.

purplest tongue you've ever seen, that was me. Why I was walking around town instead of going camping, like everyone else, was because Concord grapes were in season.

It's a short season. You hate to miss it.

Another thing about Concord grapes is that, as good as they taste at the kitchen table with a sports section and a spittoon, they taste even better outside. All food does—that's why picnics and barbecues are so popular, and why hot dogs taste better at the ballpark than in restaurants. Trust me. I spent hundreds of thousands of your tax dollars studying this phenomenon for the U.S. Government's recently dismantled Bureau of Picnics and Barbecues and Ballpark Hot Dogs. And nowhere in the culinary kingdom is the superiority of outdoor eating more evident than in the case of the Concord grape, which explodes (outside) with zingy, zangy purplicious flavor, stimulating not only the taste buds but nasal membranes, spinal nerve endings, and the region of the brain that regulates patriotism.

Plus you get to spit the seeds wherever you like and stick your tongue out at little children, to freak them.

So that's how I spent my Labor Day weekend. Crawdad left town. She flew to Tennessee and flew back Monday morning with a horrible head cold. I showed her my purple tongue. I even kissed her with it, fearlessly; hell, I had enough vitamin C in me by then to French-kiss Typhoid Mary herself.

"Hi, Hudey, I'b Hugry," Crawdad said.

I took her straight from the airport to Chava's for a big bowl of chicken soup with chicken legs and lots of other stuff floating around in it. *Birria* for me.

This is not a review of Chava's. Chava's is too good to review. Anyway, you've already probably heard me waxing goo-goo over their *huevos rancheros*, which, what with three eggs, about a pound of melted cheese, *ranchero* sauce, and spoons and spoons of that great red table salsa ... well, let's put it this way: You won't have to wonder what to do with your pile of steaming hot homemade tortillas. The *birria*'s great, too. And the lemonade. And the atmosphere, and the counter, and the long community tables, and the small ones, and the sidewalk umbrellad ones, and the jukebox, and the beers and beers and food food food flying by.

Man oh man oh man, it's hard to imagine a better Mexican restaurant in the world, let alone San Francisco ...

So, anyway, before I stray too far from the digression at hand, after lunch we went back home and did the hokeypokey, and you know how it is when you haven't had any hokeypokey in a little while, and it's hot as hell out and your skin's all sticky, and hers, and her nose is plugged, and your tongue's still purple, and her throat hurts, and your arm does, and the Chava's is sloshing around in both of your bellies, and the windows are open and Weirdo the Cat is sitting on Crawdad's dresser, where she tends to sit, doing what she tends to do: staring down an old black-and-white photo of Crawdad's ancestors ...

Yodel-eh-hee-hoo!

In other words, it was some of the best hokeypokey that two people ever hokeypoked, and I firmly believe that at least part of the credit should rightfully go to Chava's, but this is not a review of Chava's, so let's fast-forward through the next couple of days to yesterday, dinnertime, when our pal Tanya Trucker trucked in from Pennsylvania, via Vegas. She'd been living on animal crackers and radiator water for at least a day, as I understand it.

"What do you want for dinner?" I said. "Chinese?"

"Sure," she said, shrugging.

"Mexican?" I said, and she said sure again, but this time with feeling.

Damn. I was kind of in the mood for Chinese, myself. I've been eating a lot of Mexican lately, you might've noticed. But what can you do? You know how it is with guests, especially ones from Pennsylvania who've been living on animal crackers and radiator water—not that Pennsylvania cuisine's any better than that, in general. And they're only here for a couple of days, so you have to show them the best of everything. If T. T. wants Mexican, in other words, she gets to get the Best Mexican Restaurant in San Francisco (according to readers of the *Bay Guardian*). Do you see where this is heading?

Sorry Chava's. Sorry Mission Villa. Sorry Roosevelt. Sorry Puerto.

I took her to Chevy's. She liked it. Me? I'm so sick of Mexican food, it was all I could do to look at the menu, let alone the restaurant, let alone T. T.'s plate o' cheesy "fresh Mex."

I had a hamburger (kiddie's menu, four bucks). It was OK.

■ BIG JOE'S 2

Wellsir, it looks, sounds, smells, feels, and tastes like if I juju'd myself into a nasty head cold with that crack about French-kissing Typhoid Mary, not to mention the great and infectious Crawdad de la Cooter. Bud

> **Big Joe's 2**
> 717 Monterey Boulevard,
> San Francisco. (415) 333-2878.
> Breakfast, lunch. Cheap.

de good dews is that conventional wisdom tells us to "feed a cold, starve a fever," if I remember correctly. (I tend to remember it the other way around when I have a fever.)

Now, I don't know if conventional wisdom was thinking of hamburgers and french fries and root beer, or chicken soup and hot tea and orange juice, or what and what and what. All I know is I believe in the power of dreams. Not the ones where all hell breaks loose and people turn into other people and die or do something impossible, like coming back to life or going for a kite ride. I believe in sex dreams and food dreams, inasmuch as your body, I believe, is trying to tell you something, like "eat more vegetables," or else "get more nookie," or *else*.

Here's the dream: I was standing there, fully clothed, eating handfuls and handfuls of raw ground beef. The End. Mmmm. God bless NyQuil.

So, OK, woke up, changed my underwear, and went to work, which is to say that I ruffled through my latest batch of suggestionary letters. *Eat here, eat there,* everyone was saying, and the beautiful thing was: I could! I could go anywhere in the world, I realized, now that I'd finally made it to Chevy's. I still can't firsthandedly verify whether it is the Best Mexican Restaurant in San Francisco, as readers of the *Bay Guardian* seem to believe, but I can tell you this, for sure: It ain't the best burger joint.

No, that honor's going to have to go to Big Joe's 2, Monterey and Gennessee, recommended to me by this guy Gary. Thanks, Gary. Congrats, Big Joe. Sit down and shut up, Hot 'n' Hunky—I still love ya, but Big Joe's got a burger that'll make your three-quarter-pound Macho Man question his manhood. Joe's burger is 5⅜ inches tall (actual size, I measured). It's one whole pound of meat.

I know, I know, size isn't everything; but it is a hell of a lot of things, if you're talking about food, and especially if you're talking to me. Because there's no way around it, mathematically: A one-pound burger is four quarter-pounders, two half-pounders, and for six, seven bucks, *with fries,* not to mention cheese and bacon and grilled onions and, and . . . well, not even a good, strong yodel will accurately express my stupisatisnackasnoozifaction. All else I can say is, *oof.*

What a breakfast! Poor Tanya Trucker, she had to get a vegetarian omelette, being a vegetarian. For all I know, she had woke up dreaming about vegetarian omelettes. This one had mushrooms and avocados and cheese and stuff, sure, and it was big enough for Tanya, and she seemed perfectly happy, but—no matter how you look at it—it wasn't a one-pound bacon cheeseburger with grilled onions, so I couldn't help feeling sorry for her.

And for vegetarians in general, because they'll never know the ethereoserendipmystic joy of Big Joe's big boy.

It's *one pound of meat,* for crying out loud! Do you know how big a burger that is? Too big to get your mouth around, for example, without making at least two incisions. Too big to finish without serious gastrosomniferous repercussions.

But I finished it, and I napped, and I'm here to tell you that, in spite of its bigness and cheapness and medium-rare-when-I-asked-for-it rareness, this was one fine, fresh, and juicy burger. Charbroiled on a grill, not grilled on a griddle.

The fries were decent. Other than which: salads, sandwiches, soups (the Fridays-only New England Clam Chowder, according to Gary, is "positively addictive"), eggs, pancakes, waffles—you get the picture.

There are a couple other Big Joe'ses around the Bay Area. One in Belmont, one in San Leandro (and one somewhere in Maryland, but nevermind that). And don't forget Joe's Cable Car, and Original Joe's. I don't know what, if anything, they all have to do with each other, but I'm beginning to think that Joe runs the San Francisco red-meat racket the way Ray makes all the pizza in New York.

∎ EM'S PLACE

Me and the Trucker were legging it toward Can-Cun the other day in a somewhat speedy manner, since it was way past lunchtime and we didn't want to run the risk of becoming malnourished, having the both of us skipped breakfast. Anyway, we were approached by an oncoming winoperson who looked like he'd missed a few meals in a row, so I put my hands in my pockets to feel out the spare-change situation, but it turned out all he wanted was information.

> **Em's Place**
> 154 McAllister Street,
> San Francisco. (415) 552-8379.
> Breakfast, lunch, dinner.
> Cheap cheap.

"Who's up—McGwire or Sosa?" he said. He had me pegged, I guess, for a sports fan, by the big Chief Wahoo on my shirt.

"McGwire," I said, "by two," because that was how it sadly stood at the time.

"Thank you," he said, and then he was gone and so were we, Ms. Trucker wondering aloud who McGwire and Sosa were and what two things the former was up by, myself musing warmly to myself on the nature of streetpeoplepersons these days. They care. They care which millionaire has more home runs than the other, and that, to me, is beautiful—especially if Sosa winds up with more than McGwire. Right now they're tied at 65.

Yeah, yeah, I know now that someone licked our president's burrito and he went and lied about it, I'm embarrassed to admit—embarrassed to admit to actually *knowing* about it, I mean, but what can you do? The sports section comes wrapped up in all these other goddamn sections, and sometimes the print's so goddamn big you can't help seeing it on your way by. And anyway they're even talking about it in the sports section these days. That's the bad news.

The good news is that Sosa caught McGwire at 65 (as of yesterday), streetpeoplepersons care, the Indians are in the play-offs, the play-offs are now, and I'll be eating a lot of Gravy's fried chicken, as of now, because last year it got us as far as Game 7 of the World Series, where we had no right being, and this year we've got no right being anywhere either (I say for the sake of juju). By "we" I mean me and the Indians.

But why am I talking about sports?

Today doth the great Crawdad de la Cooter turneth 30, right now while I'm writing this, and when she comes home from work we're going out to take in a couple of big fat juicy fancy-pants steaks, which is what Crawdad wants to take in for her birthday, so . . . *happy birthday to her, happy birthday to her, happy birthday to Crawdad de la Cooter, happy birthday to her.*

Yesterday, in honor of steak in general, I moseyed around the Tenderloin and wound up eating at Em's, this great Chinese-American dive on McAllister between Hyde and Leavenworth. You can get a steak-and-eggs breakfast at Em's for under five bucks. You can get chicken-fried steak for under five bucks. You can get fish 'n' chips. They have steak dinners, burgers, sandwiches, all-day breakfasts, Chinese rice plates, wonton soups, fried rices, and chow meins. They even have a cute little vegetarian section. But the important thing to remember is that nothing is over six bucks, not even steaks. Most of it is under four.

So . . . cheap. You might not like the place, placewise, but I loved it. They have Norman Rockwell all over the walls, for example, ugly gray tables, ugly gray institutional carpeting, butt-beaten but very comfortably cushioned chairs, fake flowers, and Muzak. But my favorite touch of all is the green wood lattice-style ceiling, which features unobstructed views of heating ducts, water pipes, and electrical shit where grapevines and strings of garlic and nets full of swimming-pool toys would be in more pretentious restaurants. Let's hear it for Em's for showing us the plumbing! Hip hip . . .

No, no, I mean it, I loved this place even before the food came. Well, it didn't technically come so much as I went and got it. It's cafeteria style, only the food isn't sitting around in bins—at least what I got wasn't.

I got combination chow mein. It was a heaping, heaping plate of noodles with shrimp, beef, pork, and chickens. The noodles were soft and sticky and good, and the carrots and green onions and white ones were also very tasty. The shrimp and beef were fine, but the barbecued pork tasted slightly off in that Chinese-American Tenderloin dive kind of way that barbecued pork sometimes tastes. And as for the chickens, well, the chickens were less than succulent, but that's 'cause Em's only uses chicken-breast chickens, which they seem to think is an advantage.

So I'd recommend getting the chow mein with just beef or just shrimp, or even just—gasp—vegetables. Maybe. Maybe.

■ CAFFERATA PICCOLA CUCINA

Well, here I am smack in the heart of visitor season. Of course, if you come from Ohio, like me, and you have 10 brothers and sisters like mine, who drive around the country like some people drive around the

> **Cafferata Piccola Cucina**
> 659 Columbus Avenue,
> San Francisco. (415) 392-7544.
> Lunch, dinner. Credit
> cards accepted. Cheap.

block—not to mention cousins and extended cousins and friends of the fambly—well, visitor season tends to run roughly from the third week of March to the first week of March,

following year. With just that one two-week spell where no one's sleeping on your floor—at least that's the way it seems.

No lie, I recently received a letter from Cugino Stefano in Rome, who depicted himself stick-figuratively parachuting out of an airplane and into my house, in case I didn't understand his English. I didn't. I wrote back in Italian, saying, in effect, "Now is the time when something is seen to be many small difficulties almost out of my control very much, it displeases me to say."

And then, in case he didn't understand my Italian, I drew a little picture of his parachute only partways opening, off-coursing him into St. Mary's Hospital with a severely sprained ankle and possible ligament damage to both knees. I tried to depict the resultant falling nightmares, psychological scars, and just general urinary tract difficulties—but I'm not that good of an artist.

I can cook. When you have houseguests, however, you want to take them out and about, right? It's San Francisco! Phenomenon, my significant other brother, likes Italian food like I like fried. So I figured I'd take him and his girlfriendperson, Phrannie, to North Beach. By the time we left we had attracted a crowd: One-Cents, Bikkets, Choo Choo Train, and the new neighborhood superhero, Otherman. That makes seven, counting me, so let's hear it for minivans.

On the other hand, we couldn't quite fit into Golden Boy Pizza, which is where I wanted to eat when the Gold Spike turned out to be closed (on *Wednesdays,* for crying out loud). So that left us with Tony Bennett's favorite place, Cafferata Piccola Cucina, across from Washington Square Park, on Columbus. Sure, sure, there were one or two other restaurants in that neck of the woods, but they were all either too crowded or too expensive, or else they hadn't been recommended by Tony Bennett.

I'm not saying I'm *not* a personal friend of T. B.'s, but his recommendation wasn't exactly a personal, private one. It's right there in lights, Columbus and Whatever: "Tony Bennett says the Cafferata has the best Italian homemade food." You can't miss it. And then the neon sign marking the spot: Cafferata Piccola Cucina. Hot Food. Since 1886. Open.

That's a long time, a hundred and some years, so you gotta figure they've done better business than they did last night, when it was pretty much just the seven of us and a lot of light and a wallful of pictures of barely recognizable stars—Captain Kirk, Captain and Tennille, Sammy, Fr. Guido Sarducci, and a lot of people who might maybe have been Tony Bennett or else related to him.

What else? Well, a couple carafes of wine, cheese ravioli with meat sauce for me, spinach gnocchi, fettucini Putanesca, gnocchi pesto, linguine alla something-or-other . . . Everything was under 10 bucks, salads included. That's cheap, for North Beach. And, incredibly, all of the pastas were fresh-made, or at least seemed to be.

Unincredibly, they were all overcooked. The gnocchi were of a strange consistency, even for gnocchi. They were soft and chewy, not melty, like you want gnocchi to be. The linguine that came under Phenomenon's tomato-and-basil sauce were homemadefully tasty, in spite of their over-doneness. Same with Bikkets's fettucine. And her Puttanesca sauce was one of the better ones. The pesto was weak but workable.

I tasted everything, even my own raviolis, which were great big ones with a nice ricotta filling . . . (meat sauce, meaning a pasty tomato sauce with ground beef all over in it). I tasted everything, and everything was kind of good. Not great. But who needs greatness for eight, nine bucks in North Beach?

The place is under new management as of last week, according to the menu, according to my brother, so maybe they'll get it all-the-way together yet. In the meantime, I personally will settle for slightly over-cooked fresh pastas and slightly off-kilter sauces, so long as the Cafferata promises to do something about the music, because Top 40 crap radio isn't going to cut it.

What would Tony think?

■ IL POLLAIO

Last week, on our merry way to Tony Bennett's favorite restaurant, I couldn't help noticing another promising North Beach place called Il Pollaio, or "The Chickaien."

I laiove chickaiens. I'd've duckaied in and eaten some, myself, but I was with, among other things, a vegetarian and a brother whose idea of Italian food, like most people's, is pretty much pasta and/or pizza. Well, there ain't no pasta at Il Pollaio. There ain't no pizzas, either.

Il Pollaio
555 Columbus Avenue,
San Francisco. (415) 362-7727.
Lunch, dinner. Credit
cards accepted. Cheap.

There are chickens, rib-eyed steaks, pork chops, rabbits, and lamb chops. Yum and yum and yum and yum and yum. And, oh yeah, sausages. Yum.

So this week, when I got a call from the Duke o' Luke, wanting to meet for dinner maybe, I knew just what to say.

"You eat meat?" I said.

He did, so I led him to Il Pollaio. Columbus Avenue, between Gold Spike and Michaelangelaio, same side of the street. Like so many Columbus Avenue establishments, Il Pollaio is triangular. It's a small triangle with not a lot of tables, but the turnover's pretty quick, so if you have to wait for a table, it won't be long.

Will it be worth it?

Hmmm . . .

I got the lamb chops, for example, which go for $9, including salad or fries. Salad for me, thanks. And salad for you too, I'll assume, because when you see the salad plates setting on the counter there, getting ready to go, with piles of beans and greens and tomatoes, mayoless coleslaw buried somewhere underneath—that's called the combination salad, and it's irresistible. You can get just bean salad, or just coleslaw, or just a green one—or just french fries—but I'm assuming you've got your wits about you.

So there was that, the salads, and bread and butter, and we split a side order of Italian sausages—one mild and one hot, theoretically, but in my opinion they were both pretty damn mild. One was just redder than the other. But they were juicy and good, hotlessness notwithstanding.

And then the lamb chops, I thought, were excellent. Two of them. I'd asked for them rare, and guess what? They were! How often does that happen? And they were sprinkled with fresh parsley and accompanied by two or three little potater balls. And there was plenty of juice to keep my bread and butter occupied, and myself, therefore, happy.

As for the Duke o' Luke, poor guy, he got the half chicken ($6.75 with salad, $4.50 without), and I don't imagine he was as happy as I was, 'cause I borrowed his drumstick, poor drumstick, and it was dry city. Some people like it that way, I know. I might not have minded it so much myself, chickens being chickens, but I'd had Gravy's for lunch, as luck would have it (Indians 4, Yankees 1), and my taste buds were still on their feet, cheering.

But wait a minute. Is it fair to compare fried to grilled chickens? Probably not, but just like everything is fried at Gravy's, everything is grilled at Il Pollaio. They do mostly chickens, I take it, because there were a bunch of halfs of 'em hanging around on the grill in various states of doneness, waiting to get ordered. Whereas I didn't see any lambs or steaks or bunnies, and when I initially asked for rabbit, which I initially asked for, the waitressperson warned me it would take a half hour—which is a good sign, freshness-wise, but I was too hungry to wait.

Where was I? Yeah, so the chicken was dry. Who cares? The Duke was drinking imported Italian beer, which I never knew existed, and I was partaking of the house burgundy, and everyone was happy, but especially me because he picked up the check. Let's hear it for expense accounts!

And in sports:

Let's hear it for the damn Yankees! In fact, let's more than hear it for them—let's take off our hats and close our eyes and kneel on one knee and make the sign of the cross, or curtsy or bow or sacrifice pepperoni pizzas or other animals in honor of their almighty almightiness. The Yankees are great! The Yankees won 114 games! Hooray Yankees! Go Yankees! Babe Ruth was a Yankee! Lou Gehrig. Mr. Coffee. Roger Maris. Graig Nettles. The Yankees are the best team ever, the best *anything* ever! The Yankees are the Mark McGwire of baseball teams! Nobody can beat the Yankees! Nobody! Everybody loves the Yankees! Everybody—the media, God, Bob Costas, Yankee fans, Yankee haters, lesbians, all of us, oh 1998 New York Yankees, we every single one of us close our eyes and plug our noses and lick your heroic, historic, immortally pinstriped asses. Bend over.

∎ GOLDEN BOY PIZZA

While we're on the subject of North Beach, we may as well stick around for one more restaurant and call it a three-part series. Remember them? Well, here we go again, only I neglected to announce Parts 1 and 2.

> **Golden Boy Pizza**
> 542 Green Street,
> San Francisco. (415) 982-9738.
> Lunch, dinner. Cheap.

This, though, is without a doubt Part 3 of a three-part series on North Beach restaurants.

Did you know I was editor of my college newspaper? Yeah, well, I'm not saying where I went to college. All I'm trying to establish is that having been a college newspaper editor, I have a keener-than-common understanding of the ins and outs, the insides and outsides, the intricacies and outricacies of the three-part series, not to mention the most useful of college newspaper editorial phrases, *Something must be done.* (As in, "The quality of education is rapidly deteriorating. Something must be done," or, "The chemistry building is on fire. Something must be done.")

All of which more than adequately credentiates me to write about what I'm about to write about: pizza. Because if there's one thing around here about which something must most definitely be done, it's the pizza. Let's review the facts: East Bay has Zachary's—enormously popular and deservedly so, since their Chicago-style deep-dish pizzas are actually better than Chicago's. But on this side of the water, well, the only operative words I can think of are "blech" and "yucky." Yeah, I get a lot of mail from a lot of SF pizza places whose pizzas really are really great because they use, you know, cornmeal and tofu and nothing but the finest homegrown organic artichoke hearts.

That ain't pizza! Pizza is sauce and cheese and crust, with maybe pepperoni on it, or sausage—and not chicken-apple sausage, either; *sausage* sausage.

That said, my favorite SF *pizza* pizza so far is Tommaso's. My favorite by-the-slice place, as of last night, is Golden Boy Pizza, which used to be Crawdad de la Cooter's favorite pizza place when she used to live in North Beach. It's basically a boxcar pizza bar. You can get microbrews on tap or little, plastic, practically Dixie cups of wine for $3. Johnny Cash on the stereo . . . The walls and the ceiling are corrugated tin or aluminum or sheet metal or *something* that goes "clink" when you throw a quarter against it. There's a counter facing the kitchen, and there's another two-tiered wall-facing counter in back. That was where me and Crawdad sat and ate and talked and threw quarters at the wall.

I forget what we were talking about. I remember what we were eating: square-style pizza, like I like it, like I grew up on. You don't have a lot of choices at Golden Boy. You can get a plain square slice, pepperoni, sausage, pesto veggie, or clam and garlic, and I think they have a combination slice with everything, even mushrooms. Blech. Yucky.

So Crawdad had a plain cheese slice, and I had a sausage one, and then a pepperoni one, and then another sausage one. But you don't need three to fill up; I just didn't like the pepperoni slice as good as the sausage one, and I like to end a meal on a positive note.

The only problem with the pepperoni one was that the crust was so soggy you couldn't even pick it up. And the plastic fork and knife they gave me weren't much help. So I had to sort of lap it up, like a dog. Which is a fun way to eat, don't get me wrong. It's just that the sausage and plain ones were pretty damn perfect—maybe 'cause they'd been sitting around in the window for a while, whereas the pepperoni was hot out of the oven. I don't know.

The sauce was great, and it wasn't overwhelmed by too much cheese, and the crust was thickish yet light, with pockets of air, and valleys and hills, little lakes of cheese, sausage boulders—that's how square pizza's supposed to be. You don't talk about it in terms of texture so much as *terrain*.

Great terrain.

Great place. And for $9.50 for four thick slices—that's not too bad, pricewise. Of course, for $9.50 you can feed a whole Sicilian family in Ohio. And even in New York City, street slices are, say, 50 cents cheaper.

And, speaking of N.Y., the Yankees are in the World Series. Again. Something must be done.

■ YUM YUM FISH

I'm not a Laundromat reviewer, but I was doing my laundry yesterday—mine and Crawdad's, technically—and it was time to take everything out of the dryers and stuff it all into pillowcases and carry it all home. I fold at home.

Yum Yum Fish
2181 Irving Street, San Francisco. (415) 566-6433. Lunch, dinner. Cheap.

Hi. I live across the street.

So I'm working on the one dryer, and out of the corner of my eye I notice someone else seems to be working on the other one. It's an old geezer guy with whiskers whiter than mine, and blue jeans dirtier than mine, and a more general air of disorderliness than mine, and he's tugging on one of Crawdad's crawbras. The bra, so happens, is hooked into one of those tumbler holes, so it's not exactly going anywhere. So I've got a moment to think.

All right, I think, either this geezer is me 40 years from now, just lending a helpful if somewhat paranormal hand is all . . . or else it's not, and then I don't know what to think.

"Those clothes are mine," I say, to test him.

If he's me, you see, he'll say, "Mine too," or, "Well, technically, they're Crawdad's." Instead, he just lets go of the bra, backs away from the dryer, and doesn't say anything.

But it's clear from the way he looks around the place—like if he just woke up, almost—that he doesn't have clothes in any of the other dryers, either. He's trespassing. Loitering. Confused. I can't be mad.

"What are you looking for?" I ask him.

His eyes dart and he takes another step back. He looks at me and looks away, puts his hands in his pockets. "Something," he says.

I believe him, and for the rest of the day I'm sad.

Do I tell Crawdad about it? No.

So what *she* was so sad about I can only guess, and my guess is it was the mayonnaise. She doesn't fear mayonnaise like I do, but I don't think she wants it in her sushi—who would?—and there it was. Mayonnaise.

Where we were was Yum Yum Fish, a Sunset District fish store/sushi place that Crawdad had heard about at work. Yum Yum, she'd heard, sold fish to other sushi restaurants and sushi to people in general for way cheaper than other sushi restaurants. The catch is you have to get it to go or else be atmospherically open-minded.

No problem. Most sushi places kind of annoy me with their foofiness. Yum Yum is a fish store: three or four little tables with fish-print table-cloths under glass, fish-chart art along the wall, and fish-price signs all over the place. BYOB. There's a tiny black-and-white TV across the counter, World Series blaring, which would normally veer me off into sports, but I'm trying to ignore this one, thank you. Can't bear to see the bad guys win.

As for the good guys, well, we ordered conch, yellowtail, and grilled eel *nigiri*-style, the white tuna with green onion hand-roll special, an eel and cucumber roll, a yellowtail roll, and a spicy tuna roll. Wait, that last one was a bad guy; it was the one with unannounced mayonnaise all over it. It was also, sadly, the biggest of the bunch. Crawdad ate half of one piece and became despondent.

Everything else was great!—and I should know because I ate

everything else myself. The conch was good and chewy, the yellowtail was good and melty, the eel was eely. The white tuna hand roll went down smooth as ice cream, and I couldn't interest Crawdad in a lick of it.

I'll bet the fish soup would've been good for her, but the guys at the next table got the last of it.

"How is it?" I asked them.

"Mmmph," they said. They looked happy.

Finally I talked Crawdad into a flying fish roe roll—which, if that don't at least tickle your curiosity, you might be dead. Crawdad, being a crustacean, kind of likes fish eggs. I tried a piece and liked it OK, I guess, but I'd've liked it a lot better if the flying fish roes would've acted like pop rocks when they hit your tongue.

So we got out of there, when all was said and done, for something like 15 bucks total—which is damn cheap for sushi.

Crawdad cried all the way home, I still don't know why, 'cause I still hadn't told her my little Laundromat story. Anyway, I slept through my own personal sadness pretty good, what with all those little fishies swimming around in my stomach.

I had every intention of waking up on the right side of the bed, having a cheerful and productive day today. But it was all I could do to sit and stare out the window all morning. The fog, the Laundromat, the dogs shitting all over Dog Shit Park . . . and I didn't even know yet that the Yankees had won.

■ CANTON RESTAURANT

I got a bunch of lunch buffets for you, starting with Canton Restaurant in the Castro, but first I'd like to say something mean and nasty about PG&E.

Um . . . let's see, how can I put this without stepping on any toes, I mean, or anything . . . well, PG&E bites. Whatever all else they've done wrong, my own biggest beef with the Poopy Goons & Eelbutts has to do with the racket and ruckus

Canton Restaurant
524 Castro Street,
San Francisco. (415) 626-3604.
Lunch, dinner. Credit cards
accepted. Cheap cheap.

they're raising around Dog Shit Park these days, 7 a.m. to sometimes 5:30 p.m. Tearing up sidewalks and streets and sidewalks—two weeks running and no end in sight.

I can't even hear myself tinkle, let alone sleep or type or read or listen to Harry Belafonte records; and Weirdo the Cat, poor cat, thinks she's back in 'Nam, what with all the rat-a-tat-tat. She's running around like a chicken with its head blown off, shitting her fur, and just generally not having any fun. And for what?

We got gas. We got electric. Leave us the fuck alone.

While we're on the subject of biggest beefs, remember Big Joe's 2, the home of the one-pound burger? Well, the same guy who sent me there sent me to Canton Restaurant in the Castro. Gary. And anyone who steers me toward a one-pound burger is on my list of reliable sources for life. So there I was at Canton Restaurant yesterday, lunchtime, eating all I could eat with my friend Jolly Boy, who lives where I used to live, lucky guy.

The Canton is on Castro near 18th. There's a bunch of preprepared takeout stuff on display up front, or you can sit down in the dining room in back and order something fresh from the menu for four, five, six bucks.

But you want the buffet. For $4.15, between 11:30 and 2:30, you can have your way with eight bins of stuff, plus Chinese chicken salad, plus pork buns, plus complementary starter bowls of soup, and—oh yeah— fried onion rings if you get there early enough, but we didn't, but I don't like onion rings anyway, but Gary says they're killer.

The soup, a hot-and-sour eggdroppy glop, was good enough, working around the mushrooms and tofu. The chicken salad, with cilantro and peanuts and green onions and those little fried noodlelike thingies and let us not forget lettuce, yuk yuk. I mean, yuck. There was a strange, unpleasant flavor to this salad. I never did figure out where it was coming from, so I don't know what to blame. PG&E?

Just skip the salad. The pork buns were good, so long as you realize they're pork buns. If not, they might scare the hell out of you, 'cause they're sticky sweet on the outside, and then—*surprise*—salty, piggy, saucy sweet in the middle.

But I liked that pork better than the pork in the pork-fried rice or the, um, what is it with wide noodles? Pork chow something-or-other, or pork whatsit mein? Fun? Lo? Chow?

Lo, and the chow was fun, in general—ha ha yucca yucca *ding!*—'cause it was all-you-can-eat. If you don't like something, fuck it. Go get something else.

I recommend the chicken wings. They had fried ones and they had graviated ones, and both were good, but you know what I'm gonna tell you to do, don't you? Get the fried ones and scoop gravy onto them, 'cause that there equals smothered chicken wings, for crying out loud, and that's double-good.

Also: half-decent potstickers, damn decent sweet-and-sour chicken, a ho-hum vegetable pile with broccoli and carrots and cabbage and water chestnuts, and an untried tofu dish.

Atmospherically: nice tile floor, vertical Chinese art, plastic flowers, weirdo jig-jagged heavy metal chandeliers, early bird Christmassy garland shit hanging over the buffet table, and no background music save for my favorite kind of background music: the low, lonesome gurgle of fried stuff frying from the kitchen.

Which beats the hell out of jackhammers, Jack, so you and Jolly Boy can just walk on home without me, huh?

I think I'll hang out here for a while.

■ SCHNITZELHAUS

There's a guy name of Wetfoot who I play football and soccer and basketball and baseball and pitch with, and now I guess I eat all-you-can-eat German food with him too. Ooof. All-you-can-eat German food

Schnitzelhaus
294 Ninth Street,
San Francisco. (415) 864-4038.
Lunch, dinner. Credit
cards accepted. Cheap.

is a lot different than all-you-can-eat Chinese food.

It's a few bucks more, for example, and you have to go to an entirely different restaurant.

Schnitzelhaus. Ninth and Folsom. And after German all-you-can-eat it's all you can do, if you're me, to stay awake, let alone write about it.

In fact, I think I might just maybe close my eyes for a minute or five, call it a nap. If nobody minds . . . and in place of the three or four paragraphs

of insightful culinary commentary I might well have written in those minutes, for all anyone knows—hey, it could happen—what the hell, here's a
poem by our country's greatest living poet, Haywire Winterwire.

The Fool in Shakespeare
by Haywire Winterwire

Amongst Shakespeare's works, many works
contains The Fool. The Fool
appears on over 18 works
by Shakespeare. Shakespeare
utilizes The Fool to underscore
human frailty. He reiterates
this in several of his works
in which The Fool re-appears.
Similarly, one of the things
we see in Shakespeare
is a thing
called "foolishness." "Foolishness"
occurs in several passages
involving "The Fool." "The Fool"
enters into the scenes
where The Fool is called for.
Therefore, Shakespeare
uses The Fool
throughout his countless works.
These novels ensconce the need
for many things, including
The Fool, "foolishness,"
characters who are not The Fool,
and Hamblet.
In conclusion,
"foolishness" is a thing
created by The Fool
in Shakespeare.

Snort. Wha—oh, hi, hey, hello, it's me again, Danny Boy, and I'm here to tell you all about all-you-can-eat German food at Schnitzelhaus—ha ha, as if the above-taken nap and replacement poem don't tell you all you need to know about all-you-can-eat German food at Schnitzelhaus!

What, are you kidding me? It's great! It's meat and taters and cabbage and meat and goulash and gravy and meat and rice and meat. Soup. Salad. $6.95. No buffetwursts or sausages of any kind, but you can get a sausage-centered lunch special for $3.75. Which we did, by way of dessert—the bratwurst one—and it came with more taters, a slice of sliced bread, and some meaty-ass sauerkraut I think I might've liked even better than Berliner Imbiss's.

The brat was all right, but the buffet stuff was better: great goulash with chunks of beef and general sweetness, some pleasantly battered fried pigmeat, these salty hamburger-like thingies (which were surprisingly good considering how cooked they were), chicken drenched in a smooth-fully rich paprika sauce, decent red cabbage, plain white rice, and deli-cious roasted potatoes. And last as well as most, this great stewful of I think pig knuckles and chicken fat and maybe even other parts of other animals for all I care, the way it greased up a pile of rice, googy-googy. It was, for me, the highlight of the buffet.

But everything was great. And considering everything had been sitting around in buffet bins, it was defiantly hot and fresh and juicy.

Well, the soup was so-so—sort of a shredded cabbage and onion deal, yawn—but it comes free with the buffet, so who's complaining? Not me, I'm saving up all my cantankerousness for the service, which, frankly, sucked.

I don't believe the waiterguyperson hated us, exactly; and if he did, I can't imagine why, unless he sensed ahead of time that we were going to eat him out of a job or something. At any rate, we didn't get our Coke and waters until after our second trip to the buffet, and our soups until after that, and I think he would have forgotten our dessertwurst entirely if Wetfoot hadn't've jumped up and done his famous Where's Our Dessertwurst? dance. (He's a famous dancer, you know.)

Well, yeah, they were a little lunch-rushed, yes. And there was only the one waiterguyperson. But that doesn't explain how parties of four who came in 10, 15 minutes after we did and sat at a table connected to ours, so that the waiterguyperson had to go around us to get to them . . . where was I? Oh, how can it be that these four were washing down their complementary soups with waters and Cokes and great big beers before we had any of the above. And then we had to tug on his sleeve to get them.

"It's like we're invisible," Wetfoot said.

And he was right. That was exactly what it was like.

■ JAVA 'N' MORE

This review-slash-sports page-slash-literary magazine's all-you-can-eat pick comes courtesy of the known world's most prodigious all-you-can-eater (after maybe me, *maybe*), Jimmy Buffet (pronounced Buf*fay*), and his grillfriendperson, Buffy. It's not technically a restaurant, technically, but I haven't let that stop me in the past, and now is no time to start letting shit stop me.

> **Java 'N' More**
> 1351 Church Street,
> San Francisco. (415) 824-6601.
> Breakfast, lunch, dinner. Cheap.

So . . .

Java 'N' More, Noe Valley. Church and Clipper. Coffeehouse. It's yet another of the millions and millions of Java Fill-in-the-Blanks around town. Only this one has all-you-can-eat Middle Eastern food on Saturdays and Sundays, 11 a.m. to 4 p.m. $5.95. So if you stay the whole time, that's what?—a little over a dollar an hour to eat and eat and eat, etc.

We only stayed for an hour or so, because I had to go play football and J. B. had to go take a nap and I forget what Buffy Buffet had to do. Probably write a poem or story or something. She's a writer.

Hey—me too, so let's get down to bidness:

It was a muddy, blustery afternoon at the Mission football field, and in spite of heroic performances on both sides of the ball by Wayway and Andy Hustle, the guys with the white shirts fell by one touchdown to the guys with the dark shirts, because Georgie Boy's back hurt and Danny Boy kept cutting his pass routes short in order to burp up tabbouleh and hummus and stuff.

There was some controversy over the winning touchdown, as the empty Coke bottle marking one side of the Dark's end zone had blown over and rolled to what would have been the one- or two-yard line, you ask me. There were also, however, complaints from the Darks that the Whites were slurring their one-Mississippi, two-Mississippi, and so-on-Mississippis, saying, in effect, "Missippi." Replays were inconclusive. Nevertheless, this week the rules committee will meet to consider changing the rush to six-Mississippi and/or requiring the rusher to spell out rather than simply say (or sort of say) the word.

I have an idea! How about "Vegetable Magloubeh" instead of Mississippi? It's harder to slur—not to mention digest. That's another one of the things I was burping up instead of getting open and catching footballs and scoring and so on.

The beauty of vegetable *magloubeh* is that it has chickens in it. The beauty of chickens is that, even if they're dry and tough, like these ones were, they still beat the pants off of vegetables. Without chickens, for example, vegetable *magloubeh* would just be rice and peas and carrots—not even fried!

Not only that, but the chickens in the vegetable *magloubeh* were the only animals of any kind anywhere in Java 'N' More's buffet. There was an empty bin marked "Baked Chicken," but it was empty. Sniff. Ah, I can't complain, really, because everything was really good. The tabbouleh was nice and zingy, the hummus was good and garlicky, and the dolmas were sweet even without meat. I liked the falafels a lot, and I don't always like falafel, because it seldom has any succulence to it.

I also liked the pasta salad with tomatoes and red peppers. My favorite thing of all, however, was the salad salad with this mysteriously great purple-specked dressing. There was a bowl of undressed greens next to the tahini, and almost anything else you might want to toss into it, like tomatoes and black olives and red onions and stuff. But the already tossed salad had all that *plus* pita-bread croutons and mint—not to mention the better-than-tahini purple-specked dressing, which I think I might've mentioned.

So I had about three plates full of that, plus a falafel sandwich in a pita pocket, plus a plain falafel with some dipping hummus, plus two or three servings of the *magloubeh*, plenty of tabbouleh, and a couple of dolmas, *uuurrrp*.

You know the scene, atmospherically. It's just like any other Java Fill-in-the-Blank coffeehouse. If you accidentally wind up there on a weekday, or before 11:00 or after 4:00 on a weekend, you can still eat Middle Eastern stuff, or bagels, calzones, soups, salads, sandwiches. You know the scene. And I didn't have any coffee, but both Buffet and Buffy said it's great coffee. Music and poetry and performance open mics happen on Thursday, and comedy night is Saturday night, in case anyone's interested. I'm not. I eat.

■ NEW ERITREA RESTAURANT AND BAR

Satchel Paige the Pitcher loaned me a book to read by Satchel Paige (the pitcher) called *Maybe I'll Pitch Forever*, by Satchel Paige (the pitcher), as told to David Lipman. If I ever get to tell a book about me to Mr. Lipman, I think I'll call it, *Maybe I'll Eat Forever*, by Dan Leone (the eater), as told to David Lipman. Hey, who knows? Maybe I *will* eat forever, or at least until the buffet runs dry.

New Eritrea Restaurant and Bar
907 Irving Street,
San Francisco. (415) 681-1288.
Lunch, dinner. Credit cards
accepted. Cheap.

Which could very well be the premise of a very good blues song, don't you think? The buffet running dry, I mean. Unfortunately, I'm not a songster anymore, so I'll pass along the idea to any one of the four songsters I ate and ate and ate and ate and ate lunch with yesterday. Where we were was New Eritrea Restaurant at Irving and 10th Avenue in the Sunset. Who we were was me, Satchel Paige the Pitcher, Punk, Punker, and Finnegan King—who had his viol-axe with him, come to think of it, so where was the dinner music?

It was there, actually, but it was coming through the speakers. It was Eritrean music. Now, I'd never heard Eritrean music or even heard of Eritrea the country, let alone eaten Eritrean food, before yesterday; but you don't have to be a rocket geologist to know Eritrea has something to do with Ethiopia (or vice versa), because the food's pretty much exactly the same. According to Satchel Paige the Pitcher, Eritrea was once part of Ethiopia, and now it's its own country. Well, I'm not a rocket political scientist or anything, but my guess is the big split had little if anything to do with what was for lunch:

Injera, the flat, spongy bread that you eat stuff with, and then the stuff, which was mushy and spicy and colorful and just generally delicious. Let's see, there was the yellow lentil mush; the slightly spicier orange lentil mush; the brown mush, which I don't know what it was other than still spicier and creamier than anything; the spinach with onion and tomato; the unmushed potato and carrot mixture; rice with peas and carrots and onion; iceberg salad with cukes and tomatoes; *fit-fit* (at least that's what Cafe Ethiopia calls it), which is chopped up *injera* sort of saladified with more 'maters and carrots and hot pepper pieces.

Meat. Chicken drumsticks either stewed with carrots and taters or drenched in a sort-of barbecue sauce. Beef in the same stuff.

Everything was great! That's a lot of everything, too, for $5.95. All you can eat, 11:30 a.m. to 3 p.m. weekdays and I think Saturday, too. They're open for dinner, but everything's more expensive and it's not all-you-can-eat. So go for lunch. But go, if you know what's good for you.

It's a pretty cool restaurant, with a full bar and an entirely enclosed patio, if such a thing is possible, with a glass roof and diagonally mirrored walls for maximum natural lightfulness. But we didn't eat out (in) there. We wanted to be as close as possible to the buffet table. What else I can say, atmospherically, is that I liked the hangy stringy beady things, and I didn't one-bit mind the painted animal pelts that decorate New Eritrea's tables between the tablecloths and the glass. I liked them, in fact, but you vegeterrestrials might not.

Of all the above-mentioned foodage, my favorite stuff, predictably, was the pert-near-barbecued chickens and beefs. The red sauce starts out subtle and then kicks in big-time after a second or two.

Satchel Paige the Pitcher liked the potatoes and carrots best, and I liked them too, but I liked them even better in the stewed chicken, because it was basically the same stuff only soaked in chicken juice, which is how taters and carrots, to my way of tasting, taste their best.

Even the meatless buffet items were damn tasty, and damn fun to eat, as Eritrean/Ethiopian food always is. You eat with your hands!

Although, come to think of it, there were forks. Hey, maybe that's what the big split was over. Eritreans wanted to start using forks? Or maybe they wanted to be free to have all-you-can-eat lunch buffets, because I don't remember ever eating all-you-can-eat Ethiopian.

Or maybe, maybe—I mean, I'm not a rocket philosopher or anything, but maybe there's more to life and politics and countryhood than *what's-for-lunch* and *how-we-gonna-eat-it* . . .

Yeah, maybe, but I wouldn't put money on it.

■ BRENNAN'S

Nnnyes. It makes perfect sense, in a perfectly nonsensical way, that the poet who would advance the literary genre of the two-word poem to the lofty heights to which, to wit, Sir Shakey could be said to have advanced the sonnet, for example, or Sir Rodgers the yodel—indeed, as I was saying, it makes perfect sense, I say, that the so-called according-to-me maestro of the two-word poem should have four names in his name. Christian Jon Bevins Chambers.

Brennan's
720 University Avenue,
Berkeley (510)
841-0960. Lunch, dinner. Credit
cards accepted. Cheap.

I say!

Nnnyes, and the poem (which I'll publish in a moment, hold your horsies) has been the subject of heated debate amongst literary-circle squares, with my side saying basically what I just said (vis-à-vis this treatise's opening paragraph) and the Empiricist Tweedheads arguing, in effect, "What the fuck are you talking about? The poem can't possibly be the quintessential two-word poem, since—all quintessentiality aside—neither of the words is even technically a word, or, if they are, then they are two words apiece."

Ah, but guess what, Empiricist Tweedheads—this is *my* restaurant review-slash-sports page-slash-literary magazine, and I personally am willing to grant anyone with four names in their name Poetic License for Life, simply on the grounds of how many names they have in their name, to say nothing of the greatness of the work in question, which I hereby publish not because I need a nap but because I maintain this poem to be *the* predominant two-word poem in the English language this century, vis-à-vis, that is, the apropos squid-pro-quota persona-non-gratuity de-facto clause, so to speak, with lots of frosting on top.

Here then, the poem:

> Untitled
> by Christian Jon Bevins Chambers
>
> *Overcaked bakeman*

Which poem was related to me in the absence of the author himself by a four-named two-word-poem writer in his own right, Satchel Paige the Pitcher, over meat and smashed potatoes last night at Brennan's.

Brennan's is a restaurant. Hey—and I'm a restaurant reviewer! Here then, the review:

Meat meat meat meat meat meat meat meat meat.

Other than which, Brennan's is just this sports bar, see, over in Berke-ley, see, by the water. Big-screen TVs, little-screen TVs, trophies, *hof brau*–style grub, long tables, lots of wood, lots of guys, meat (as I might've mentioned), drinking, and just general ooga-ooga.

Only we weren't drinking, me and Satch. We weren't even watching TV, against all odds, except for a little while when one of the televised participants in a bowling contest (see basketball strike) appeared to have a perfect game going through seven innings. But then he blew it in the eighth, and we returned to our meals and loftier thoughts: "poetry," and "our meals."

His was the roast-beef plate, mine the turkey leg, and both were damn delicious, only mine was funner because you can pick up a turkey leg by the bone and gesture with it between bites, speaking of ooga-ooga.

But the roast beef had plenty of redness (and therefore juice) to it, and that's fun, too. And the smashed potatoes were very real, and the gravy was great. And the steamed vegetables were good-for-us. And I got stuff-ing as well, which is why I went with the turkey, because you get stuffing too, gravy all over everything . . . and it's all only $4.75.

And—get this—you can get turkey necks for $2, tails for 75 cents, and an entire turkey carcass for $3.25. Of course, what you want to do with

those items is none of my business, but they sound like soup to me. ·-.
Speaking of which, we also partook of a couple of salads on the side.
Satch had a green one with shrimps and stuff in it, which looked great,
although I didn't get to taste it because I accidentally glanced down at my
napkin, and when I looked back up it was gone. I, on the other hand, let
Satch in on plenty of my three-bean salad—not 'cause it wasn't good, 'cause
it was, but that's how hungry the big boy was, and how fast he eats, and
anyway there were a lot more than three beans in it, ba dum dum, pssshhh.

*Contributor Notes: Christian Jon Bevins Chambers is a person. In
addition to existing, he is credited (by Satchel Paige the Pitcher, who similarly exists) with authoring several works of two-word poetry, including
"Untitled" (or "Overcaked Bakeman"). More recently, his credentials
include disappearing.*

■ SAIGON SANDWICHES

I'm getting married. It's official. Me, the Cheap Eats guy, and who else but
Crawdad de la Cooter? We haven't decided who's taking whose name
yet—she's the girl, technically, but I have every intention of being the
mom. Not in the sense of bearing
children so much as staying home
and cooking and cleaning and just
generally writing books. Shoot me,
I'm a traditionalist. On the other hand, it's the '90s. On the other hand,
it's the USA. On the other hand, it's San Francisco. And we both have
pretty good names already. The Cheap Eats guy and Crawdad de la
Cooter. Hmmm . . .

> **Saigon Sandwiches**
> 560 Larkin Street,
> San Francisco. (415) 474-5698.
> Breakfast, lunch. Cheap cheap.

Well, there's only one way to settle the matter, in my mind, and that's
to put everything in a blender and see what happens, as in: Crawdad Eats
Cheap Cooter.

All kidding aside, though, don't be offended if you aren't invited to
our wedding, 'cause we're not having one. We're simply marching down
to the police station, or wherever you have to go (I haven't researched it
yet), saying we do, or whatever you have to say, and then kicking off our
happily-ever-after in the honeymoon suite at Gravy's—that's the table

with the swivel chairs.

And before anyone accuses either one of us of being a cheapskate, let me assure you that we're going to order fried chickens *and* gumbo *and* the seafood combo platter—in honor, respectively, of me and her and all the other fishes in the sea, as they say, who are going to have to go home crying now that me and Crawdad are out of the pool. Officially.

What? Oh—January. We'd do it sooner, but Crawdad reckoned it'd be better juju to get married in 1999 than 1998, and I have to agree—and so would Prince, the artist not currently known as anything. But he was a fine, fine artist in his day. Don't you think? I mean, having anticipated the Year 2K glitch and all before anyone else, even Todd—and him not even a computer guy, to my knowledge. Prince, that is.

What? Oh—you know, "Two-thousand zero zero party over oops outta time," and so on, the very typing of which makes me want to jump up and dance, but I can't 'cause I've got too many Vietnamese sandwiches inside of me.

What? Oh—Saigon Sandwiches in the Tenderloin. I forget who told me to go there, but I'll go back in a hot second, because you can't beat $1.60 for a roast-pork sandwich, for example, $2.10 for a BBQ-chicken one. That's tax and everything, folks, and under four bucks (tax and everything) for two sandwiches, if you'll excuse the expression, is yodel-eh-hee-hoo in any language, even French.

One thing, though: It's very important to remember to ask for no mayonnaise—unless, of course, you like mayonnaise, in which case, don't even think about kissing me, OK? Anyway, my crawmama-to-be'll whap you one, and we don't want anybody getting hurt.

So, yeah, they use mayo. Exercise caution. Other than that, it's the meat of your choice—chicken, pork, meatball pork, fancy pork, or liver-wurst—plus carrots, onions, and cilantro on a crispy French roll. It's kind of smallish, as sandwiches go, but don't forget: two of them for under four, three for six—and three would be a big-time feast, even for me.

Now, I know what you're thinking—you're thinking, "meatball pork?"—and all I can say, is, hey, I'm right there thinking it with you.

I can speak for the roast pork and BBQ chicken: These babies are loaded with succulence (that's sans mayo, don't forget), and full of flavor—especially once you get into the cilantro.

What else you can eat, besides sandwiches, are prewrapped to-go spring rolls, imperial rolls, and stuff like that. Plus there are tons of colorfully sweet-looking things. Green. Yellow. Pink. (In case you needed a few examples of colors.)

Atmospherically, we're looking at two invisible paintings, a clock, a no-smoking sign, and a stack o' sody-pop boxes. We're listening to Vietnamese soft rock. Yep, Saigon Sandwiches is a hole of a hole-in-the-wall. There's one small table and a four-chair counter (total capacity: six). The rest of you are getting it to go, which most people seem to want to do anyway.

Me, I liked it in there. I can't wait to go back with my sweet pea. We'll be the ones with the googly grins and probably by that time wedding rings, living happily ever after.

∎ LA LIMENITA

Earl Butter will back me up on this. He was there six, seven years ago at Community Thrift, helping me find a good, big drinking glass. Those were Earl Butter's drinking days. These are mine.

Back then I was into water. I didn't want just any old glass, you understand. "I'm looking for something special," I remember saying to old Earl, "something that will give me a new lease on life"—and I remember him understanding entirely. New lease on life. A good glass. Sure!

La Limenita
3161 24th Street,
San Francisco. (415) 824-2833.
Breakfast, lunch, dinner. Credit
cards accepted. Cheap.

And then we turned a corner and there it was, standing out among all those millions of mix-matched thrift-store glasses like Sister Darla Jean at a monster-truck show. It was one of those moments, rare and perfect and beautiful, because it was one of those glasses. Rare. Perfect. Beautiful. A tall, heavy, stein-style glass with a handle and, best of all, a proud and simple 49ers helmet. No words or extraneous logos like Shell or the NFL or Super Bowl XXV or anything like that. Just the helmet. Buck-fifty.

So . . . there I was with my new lease on life, the love of my lips, drinking water. On top of the worl*urrp*. Excuse me. Years passed. The 49ers went to and won the Super Bowl again, more years passed, and then just the other day, a couple days before New Year's Day, I was washing dishes, thinking about the 49ers, as always, about how they're finally falling off the top of the world and into a puddle, according to everyone.

Thinking these thoughts, I happened to see my 49ers glass down the counter with some water in it (as usual), and I got to thinking how I hardly ever wash that glass, on account of only ever drinking water out of it. So then I got to thinking (as usual) that maybe it was all my fault. Maybe it had nothing to do with salary caps, free agency, the aging process, or the lack of a front office. Maybe all the bad juju had been building up in the crusty bottom ridge of my glass all these years, and alls I had to do was wash the dang thing for a change and we'd go back to being on top of the world all over again.

Well, in the process of washing the alleged bad juju out of my beloved glass, I'm sorry to report, I knocked it over in the sink and shattered it into 4,900 pieces. And then, adding injury to insult, I managed to drive a half-inch sliver of it into my thumb, cleaning up.

The point being that I've been too sad to drink anything but wine, let alone water—what? outta some water glass that *doesn't* have a proud and stately 49ers helmet on it?—ever since. I've been drinking wine out of wineglasses, so you know. I personally imported the wine (a whole vanful of my brothers' home-hatched hooch) from Ohio (and it's already half-gone).

I got the wineglasses from my cupboard.

And don't worry about me dehydrating, OK, because I know how to take care of myself: soup. That's all I've been eating, starting with about 10 gallons of matzo-ball wedding soup (did I tell you I was getting married?), and then, let's see, Mai's hot-and-sour, Wayway's Korean noodle, and—oh yeah—last night I drowneded my sorrows in a bowl of Caldo de Gallina from La Limenita, this great Peruvian place on 24th Street.

I felt right at home in spite of the eights, nines, and 10s on the menu, because they had some Spanish-speaking soap opera on TV and everyone was crying, but then some little kid sang this cute little song, and then everyone cried again and somebody died, and everyone cried some more, and then the kid sang another song. So maybe it was a musical soap opera. The thing to remember is that Peruvian food rocks. Not that it's any better than any other kind of food, in and of itself, but you get that googy-googy green salsa, like at Rincón Peruano, and I'm telling you, even on plain old bread, it's enough to cheer a feller up.

It's also hot hot hot, so what you gonna drink?

Soup. Small bowl, but there was a whole big piece of overboiled *gallina* sticking up out of it, plus spaghetti, green onions, and cilantro in a clear, simple chicken broth. To eat: a tamale with chicken, hard-boiled egg, and black olives in it, a pile of red onions on the side, but, most important, it was yet another flat surface to paint green.

▮ BOBBY'S BACK DOOR CAJUN BBQ

I have taken up smoking. Ribs, chickens, fishes, turkeys, short ribs, spareribs, ribs, sausages. All of these things have I smoked in the past three months. I don't have it down yet, but if I don't die of lung cancer first, I figure I will (have it down) by summer. And then all of the Bay Area's many fine barbecue joints will have no choice but to go out of business, because I won't be their customer anymore.

> Bobby's Back Door Cajun BBQ
> 12891 San Pablo Avenue,
> Richmond. (510) 232-9299.
> Lunch, dinner. Credit cards
> accepted. Cheap.

Which isn't to say that I'm the only person in the Bay Area who eats barbecue on a more or less daily basis. I know because I got a letter recently from a Complete Stranger waxing all-out poetic over a place in Richmond, CA, called Bobby's Back Door Barbecue. She'd eaten barbecue everywhere around here—including Flint's, including Brother-in-Law's, Memphis Minnie, etc., etc.—and Bobby's was her favorite. It was the best *and* cheapest, she said. So poetic did she wax, in fact, that I actually wrote her back, which is saying something because I don't normally even write back to my friends. Ask 'em.

Well, and plus "Bobby's Back Door Barbecue" has a certain ring to it, which, with all due respect to "Cliff's" and "Mr. Pittman's Pit" and "Big Nate's," resonates more beautifully than any name of any place since Fat

Ed's Hickory Pit went down for the count. So I'd've eventually wound up at Bobby's even if it were in Richmond, VA—and that was before I learned that its full, god-given name was actually Bobby's Back Door *Cajun* Barbecue, and that they have free live Cajun music on Thursdays and Sundays, blues Friday and Saturday.

So next thing anyone knew me and Crawdad and Tinzee and Wally-Wally (who are finally back in town, hoorah) were over the bridge picking up Satchel Paige the Pitcher (who never left, hoorah) in Berkeley, and then meeting this Complete Stranger, Queen BBQ, at my new favorite place, Bobby's. Richmond. San Pablo Avenue. Sunday night.

There's a bar, Abalone Gardens, or something like that, and then there's a stage and a dance floor, and then a little eating area, and then, in the very back of the place, a barbecue dispensary. Around back, outside, is a gigantic barrel-style smoker and a couple of picnic tables. So I suppose you can eat out there when the weather's nice. But you might not want to, either, what with the great Cajun music inside, and generally excellent atmospheric touches, like the hottest beer-babe poster in beer-babe-poster history, colorfully festive wall trimmings, and—get this—a Ping-Pong table, which was folded up in the corner, out of service, or else I'd probably still be there.

There being six of us, we ordered two three-ways for something like 16, 17 each. One three-way was ribs and chickens and beef links, and the other was ribs, sliced beef, and smoked pork sausage. Both come with bread, potato salad, and baked beans, but we traded one of the orders of bakeds for red beans and rice, which was good and meaty and good. The baked beans were all right. The potato salad, of course, I didn't touch, although everyone else seemed fairly happy with it.

But enough about things that aren't meat. Let's talk about me.

I liked the ribs best. You could tell because they were gone the fastest (except for the chickens, but that was 'cause there was half as much chickens, and their part of the styrofoam was closest to me). You could also tell because Satchel Paige the Pitcher was eating the bones. Rib bones. I don't remember him eating any chicken bones.

But the chickens were great, too, you ask me. And I loved the sliced beef, although I did hear a few fat-related complaints from our party, I'm embarrassed to admit. As for the sausages, they were the last to go, and even then only after a couple of dancing breaks and beer runs.

Anyway, I wasn't too thrilled with the beef links, and the Cajun-style pork sausages, good as they were, are not part of the regular menu. If you're only getting one three-way, I'd recommend ribs, chickens, and beef. Get the sauce hot. You can handle it. I can't say it was the best sauce I've had around here, because Cliff's is better, but Bobby's is the best everything else. And at under $40 for six big-eating people, it's probably also the cheapest.

Too bad it's in Richmond. I mean, good thing it's in Richmond. Something tells me a place so real and unpretentious and uninhibitedly fun as this couldn't happen in the city.

■ ANA'S RESTAURANT

By the time you read this I will be Mr. Crawdad Eats Cheap Cooter, so congratulations to me, and a little more respect, please. Thank you.

Tomorrow is the big day. Tonight I am quietly enjoying my last night as the Cheap Eats guy. No bachelor party. No cards or dice or booze or stripperchickpersons popping out of cakes. No friends even. Just me and my congestion and a big bowl

> **Ana's Restaurant**
> 4499 Mission Street,
> San Francisco. (415) 334-6100.
> Lunch, dinner. Credit cards
> accepted. Cheap.

of Seven Seas Soup at Ana's Restaurant, Nicaraguan and Salvadoran food, way the hell out Mission.

Crawdad and her grillfriends, on the other hand, are at Osento, or "Girl Soup," as they call it, having a *mikvah*. That's a Jewish tradition whereby the bride-to-be goes out and gets naked and wet with all her naked and wet grillfriends, not only as a sort of a symbolic spiritual cleansing, but also to make sure once and for all that she's not a lesbian.

Me? Not only do I know for a certified fact that I'm not a lesbian (at least not a textbook example of one), I'm also not much of a partaker in traditions, not even the ones that call for stripperchickpersons to pop out of cakes. Not that I have anything against tradition. I think there's something to be said for doing things the way your parents did them. I'm just not going to be the one to say it, let alone do it. I'm more for making up your own, individual, original "traditions," such as having the stripper-chickperson pop out of a tray of lasagna.

Marriage, for better or for worse—and I can speak now from experience, if not intelligence—is all about tradition. Even if you do it in court, with a couple of witnesses, only one ring, and Gravy's looming, you're still liable to make at least one of your parents happy. Therefore, I can't conscionably recommend it to all you cheap eaters out there who may be scratching your heads over bowls of soup right now, for all I know, wondering whether you should or shouldn't.

Don't! There's only one person in this world worth all the yeehaw—and I beat you to her. Your best bet is to stay single.

Tell you the truth, I was going to eat *menudo* tonight. Because I never had *menudo* before. Because I believe in that old philosophy about Ping and Pong—you know, where there's good and evil and dark and light and meat and tofu, or, in simpler terms, elk and non-elk, and then shall the lion and the lamb lie down together and give birth to the modern computer, wherein the one needs the zero to mean one and the zero needs the one to mean zero, and God needs to both exist and not exist for anything at all to get done, right? Well, so I was thinking that if Crawdad was going to take the pure-and-cleansed approach, then I had better eat me some *menudo*. You know, to balance out the juju. *Menudo* being basically animal-scrap soup.

Unfortunately, it smells entirely too awful to eat, no matter what all you pour into it. So I left the barely dented bowl on the *taqueria* table and moseyed on down Mission to Ana's, this cute hole-in-the-wall with light blue wood trim along the walls and—would you believe it?—little-red-heart-patterned tablecloths!

Take that, *menudo*. Take that, cynicism and philosophy. Take that, Danny Boy.

What can I say? If I still wrote songs, I'd write a love song. If I were a painter, I'd paint Crawdad's portrait, nude, for the sake of posteriority. But, alas, I'm the Cheap Eats guy. So . . .

The broth was rich and buttery, like the skin at the base of Crawdad's neck, no, like the skin at the back of her knees, where she won't let me go on account of ticklishness. Hell, like all her skin! Why not? And the fish itself, still on the bone, like I like it, in part tenderly delicious and in part downright dangerous—that would be her brain. And the calamari, with its jiggling tentacles, that's easy: the hair, which I wish she'd cut shorter, as much as I love calamari, on account of my own ticklishness and because it somewhat diminishes my view of her beautiful scallops, which is to say, face, with its smooth, tender, smile-a-minute expanso-expressiveness. Ah, and the shrimp, split-curled and still in its shell, that's the laugh, the raucous, rollicking guffaw that grabbed me by the ear and fell me in love with her at first listen, no lie. If I can keep being funny—just think—I get to hear it for the rest of my life! The crab, that one big claw, so tough to break into and so worth it, that's her heart, and her dirty sense of humor, and all the other inside stuff, like the stomach and liver and shit. And the clams and mussels, well, I don't need to tell you what those represent, but I would like to point out that the soup came with two small, round, thick-style homemade tortillas!

So you see? You see why I'm getting married tomorrow?

■ JOHN'S OCEAN BEACH CAFE

The wife and I, being married people, are trying to get more mature and adultlike than we used to be, so as not to arouse any suspicions or anything. To start the ball rolling, we had a contest to see who could go the longest without being immature. If I didn't immediately lose by virtue of suggesting the contest in the first place, I lost two and a half seconds later when I proposed that picking one's nose should not count, so long as any results were disposed of in a proper, discreet manner and not wiped on the other person's arm.

John's Ocean Beach Cafe
2898 Sloat Boulevard,
San Francisco. (415) 665-8292.
Breakfast, lunch. Cheap.

Then we decided to make the contest ongoing and to keep score, and I'm proud to announce that since my initial goof(s), Crawdad has easily overtaken me. She currently leads the family in immaturity by a score of 5 to 1. A few of her less shocking offenses, as documented on the official scorecard, include "lewd hand gestures of a masturbational nature" and "making chicken noises."

I, on the other hand, have been on my best behavior, especially while Crawdad's looking. It wasn't me, for example, who stole the World's Hottest Beer-Babe Poster off the back wall of Bobby's Back Door Barbecue to hang up in the garage and look at whenever I change my oil. Even if she *was* already falling down at one corner anyway, and probably would've wound up in the recycling bin, or worse.

Well, so there we were Sunday night, in Richmond, my new favorite city, digesting Old MacDonald's whole farm, practically, on Bobby's dance floor. The whole gang was there except for Wayway, who's still on crutches ever since his Achilles tendon unzipped on the basketball court, goddamn it, and for no good reason.

(Moral: stretch.)

Anyway, everyone else was dancing with everyone else, myself included, and all of a sudden I started feeling a little funny around the ankle, and I remembered the look on Wayway's face when it happened, and I remembered his description of the post-op staples coming out, and I didn't remember stretching before dancing, because nobody stretches before dancing, because nothing could be more uncool than warming up to dance. Nevertheless, I thought it would be best to sit the next number out, so I was standing at the bar, dropping quarters and keys and things by my feet and bending down to get them, *one two one two*, when up comes my pal One-Cents and says to me, she says, "You're not stretching, are you?"

"No no," I said. "I just dropped something is all."

"Oh, OK, cool," she said, and then she started talking about a breakfast place out by the beach she likes to talk about, and did I like cinnamon toast? Sure, I said, thinking she musta not've got enough barbecue to be thinking about breakfast already. But for all I knew I'd be hungry again too after a good night's sleep, so we made a plan to go get some cinnamon toast first thing in the morning.

First thing in the morning rolled around at roughly 12:30 in the afternoon, and luckily John's Ocean Beach Cafe was open, because they're not usually open on Mondays. But this was not only Monday; it was President's Day. So they were open, I guess.

So we ate. We ate cinnamon toast, and One-Cents got an Italian sausage scramble, and I got a chili burger.

John's has 45 kinds of omelettes, so you know. Some of them have things like crabs and asparagus and stuff in them, so you know. But I wouldn't know, because I had to have a chili burger. Dumb choice, even if you don't mind taking long, oniony naps all afternoon.

The burger wasn't that good. It came with fries, which is good, but the chili was mostly beans, just three big chunks of meat, and the burger itself was one notch overdone, and the gigantic bottle of Tabasco sauce was entirely necessary.

One-Cents's scramble, on the other hand, tasted like something. I tasted it. I love Italian sausage. It came with toast and taters for around seven bucks, which might be a buck too much, unless they start letting you pick cinnamon toast for your kind of toast. Because we had to pay $2.95 extra for our cinnamon toast, and it was good, sure—thicker cut than normal, with sprinkled cinnamon and powdered sugar and granulated butter granules. Delicious, but . . . $2.95?

The best thing about John's is the atmosphere. Chicken-scratched yellow Formica booths, a nice counter, great waitresspeoplepersons, and posters of Elvis, James Dean, Marilyn, Mr. Wayne, Clint, and Rudy V. None of which I stole, for the record.

And now if you'll excuse me . . . I drove to Ocean Beach and back this week. Time to change the oil!

▌DELI 42

Bad posture is bad for your back, sure, but good posture has its own special problems. Since I started walking around town with my chin up, for example, I've stepped in dog shit on average six to eight times a day.

Also, I don't make nearly as much money as I used to make. Those nickels and pennies add up!

> **Deli 42**
> 42 29th Street,
> San Francisco. (415) 282-4200.
> Lunch, dinner. Cheap cheap.

Still, bad posture is bad and backaches ache, and I want to play baseball again someday soon, so my slouchful days are all-the way over. Clean up after your dogs, please, you dumbass shit-for-brains asswipes, or I might just start to become cross.

Oh, yeah, which reminds me: babies too. Why, just yesterday morning I was riding around the neighborhood with my neighbor, Bikkets, feeling pretty good about the fact that I wasn't walking around the neighborhood, stepping in dog shit. So we got where we were going, which was the little grocery store on Cortland, and as Bikkets parked in the little parking place across the street, I was distracted by what looked like a ridge of icy slush or snow on the ground. All I could think was it was a lot colder than I thought out there, or else this had just fallen off of an airplane or a very fast car coming from the Sierras. Thinking these thoughts, entranced by the shimmering snow ridge yonder, I stepped out of Bikkets's car into a very used baby diaper.

"Shit," I said, and I went to clean my shoes in the miraculous slushy icy snow ridge, but—*aaaaaaahhhhhhh!!!*—it wasn't a slushy icy snow ridge; it was some gelatinous artificial jellylike goo.

"Run for it!" I screamed. And we dashed across the street into the store and calmed down and shopped. Coffee, bread, tangerine juice, peas. And afterward I got back into her car on the driver's side, backseat, thanks.

The moral of the story is that six hours later I still didn't have much of an appetite. Which was lucky for me because I wound up eating lunch at Deli 42, and they only put three thin layers of salami and one little layer of cheese on their salami sandwiches. And the cheese is extra. Sheesh.

So that's $3.50 plus 40 cents, or right around $3.90, for which you could get a four-times-as-much-meat-and-cheese sandwich *plus* chips *plus* salad at Happy Donut, for example—but sometimes you can't make it all the way to China Basin. Sometimes you have to walk to the Bernal Heights Post Office on 29th Street to mail a thing, and you're kind of grossed out already anyway, or on a diet, but you gotta eat *something*, and for just such occasions I heartily recommend Deli 42.

It's right there. It's a friendly, straightforward little place with hot dogs and salads and soups-of-the-day, too. Minestrone. Buck-fifty for a small one, and it was OK. Pastas, carrots, kidney beans, green beans, peas, celery, taters—that's a lot of things, but there was only about two or three of each of them floating around in a lot of glossy orange broth. Good thing I wasn't hungry!

And another thing 42's got going for it is the special garlic spread, which is a delicious garlic and oil and parsley mixture. Mayophobes of my mayophobic proportions love to see alternative sandwich spreads in action, and this one didn't disappoint. All the other condiments: lettuce, tomatoes, pickles, red onions, jalapeños . . . they were plenty present, and the sweet roll was nice and fresh.

And I don't think the sandwichladyperson was being a meany by holding back on the meat and cheese; she seemed very nice, in fact. I just think she doesn't know how to make a sandwich. No crime there. Not everyone knows how to make a sandwich, or a bowl of soup—I mean a great one, or a great one. I don't, which is just one of the reasons I don't run a deli.

So here's what I'm going to do: I'm going to mosey back down to Deli 42 some day real soon and buy a bag of chips or something, and sneak three five-dollar bills into her tip jar. One for a trip to Happy Donut down by the new stadium, one for a trip to Judy May's on 14th and Market, and one for a trip to Soups, in the Tenderloin. Those are three hot hot hot tips for anyone who wants to make sandwiches or soup and, in the process (and more important), make people happy happy happy to eat them.

That's what I'm going to do.

What she's going to do, as I imagine it, is watch me leave her place with my bag of chips, not knowing about the tip yet, and wrinkle her nose and make a funny face and say, "What's that *smell?*"

∎ HUNGRY JOE'S

Life is loaded with minor mysteries. Take the Case of the Missing Thermos, for example. And why does the red neon–lighted sign in the 3300 Club's window say "Nancy" instead of "Budweiser" or "Coors" or "Open" or "3300 Club"? What ever happened to Danny and Dick and Nellie, the old-timers who used to play at McCarthy's before McCarthy's got gentrified? (Happy St. Patrick's Day, sniff.) Where are the Hardy Boys when you need them? And how in the world can people look

Hungry Joe's
1748 Church Street,
San Francisco. (415) 282-7333.
Breakfast, lunch. Cheap.

at an 800-pound drool-jowled mastiff such as Juicy the Dog, and say, "*Cute*"???? Which they invariably say, I know, because I hung out with Juicy on Sunday morning on the sidewalk in front of Hungry Joe's, Church and Day.

Juicy was chained to a parking meter. I was chained to a Super Sausage Scramble and home fries and toast, and a side stack of banana-walnut pancakes. The Choo Choo Train was there, helping me with the side stack, and Crawdad, and Juicy the Dog's proud and happy owner, Ally McEats— not to be confused with the popular TV personality, Ally McDoesn'tEat. Ally McEats eats, or else I wouldn't have been eating with her.

Hungry Joe's. Sidewalk table, so the atmosphere was a sunny Sunday morning, Noe Valley. Cars. People walking by, goochy-gooing Juicy the Dog, saying, "Cute." Juicy the Dog isn't cute! She's big and beautiful and strong and good and goofy and lots of other things, but not cute.

Ally McDoesn'tEat isn't cute either, by the way, in spite of her diminu- tiveness. I walked in on her program a couple weeks ago while someone whose name I won't name was watching it.

"Why?" I asked.

"Because she's pretty," she said.

Well, she's about three burritos a day away from being pretty, in my book, so maybe the show's good or funny or something. I couldn't bear to watch long enough to find out. And anyway, I'm not a TV show reviewer, so what the hell am I doing reviewing one?—speaking of great big mysteries.

Let's get back to Juicy the Dog. Now, if I were an 800-pound mastiff, which I'm not, but if I were and if every gene in my body were program- ming me to be big and powerful and fiercely loyal and seriously somber and gently protective of Ally McEats, queen of the corner of Church and Day, the last thing in the world I'd want to be called would be cute. But Juicy the Dog, to her credit, didn't bite anyone's head off or anything. She took it like a good doggie, drooling and barking and begging for table scraps.

My point being this: Go figure.

What all she scored, for the record, was a piece of bacon from Ms. McEats and a few forkfuls of banana-walnut pancakes from Crawdad. She said to tell you that the bacon was "snarf" and the pancakes were, in her opinion, "slobber slobber slobber."

And now that I've completed my application for the position of Bazooka Joe's joke writer, let me just tell you what I personally thought of Hungry Joe's food, by way of not quitting my day job. Well, I didn't have any bacon, so you'll have to take Juicy's word for it. (Snarf, in case you forgot.) As for the pancakes, yeah, I liked them too. In fact, I loved them dearly. They were big and airy and crispy-edged with mushy middle banana pockets and big chunks of walnuts. In other words: slobber.

The sausage scramble was great. Chopped-up sausage links, tomatoes, onions, and probably some other stuff, like eggs or something. And it came with a pretty big pile of home-fried potaters, which were pretty good, in spite of mushiness. They were interestingly spiced, at any rate. Lemon pepper, or something lemony. When was the last time you had lemony home fries?

They're pretty good.

Hungry Joe's, according to me and Juicy and lots of other people and dogs, is a great place for breakfast. And probably lunch. I had lunch there once a long time ago, but I can't remember if I liked it or not. Anyway, it's not as popular—or at least it wasn't as crowded as most of those other Noe Valley weekend breakfast hangouts, but it was fairly hopping. I'd go on a weekday, I was you. And I'd sit inside. It's nice in there. They have a long counter and general diner-style atmosphere, only without any pretentiousness—kind of like Herb's Fine Foods, my other favorite Noe breakfast nook.

But the best thing about eating inside is you won't feel any pressure to share your food with dogs or restaurant reviewers, or at least dogs. I guess I'm still allowed to go into places, personally, for now. Hey, man, you gonna finish that toast?

▮ CHILI UP!

Crawdad de la Cooter and I Roccoed down the coast all the way almost to Carmel, to the Inn at Spanish Bay, or something like that, where our favorite Ruskie was celebrating her 50th birthday at a very long banquet table. You wouldn't believe what all I ate, but you probably will believe

Chili Up!
The Irving Street Chili Up! has closed, but the restaurant's still kicking at 5 Embarcadero Center, San Francisco; (415) 576-0811. Also at 50 Post Street, Third Floor, San Francisco; (415) 693-0467, and 101 Spear Street, San Francisco; (415) 243-8096. Lunch, dinner. Cheap.

that I was the only one eating it with my hands.

Not that there was a shortage of forks—I think I counted four of them at my place alone. But I'll be damned if I'm using a fork on a piece of lamb, for example, that's still got a bone sticking out of it.

Anyway, I was sitting in the bathtub the next afternoon, trying to recover from a fancy-food hangover, and the telephone was sitting on the Coleman cooler I keep next to the tub. It started to ring.

"Hello?"

It was Crawdad, calling from the UCSF library to see if she should pick up something edible on her way home.

"I've got one word for you, Chugga, and I'm only going to say it once," I said. And then I said that word: "chili."

Chugga being my pet name for Crawdad, you see, and chili being, everybody knows, the only tried-and-true cure for a hangover. Another thing everybody knows—and no one knows better than I do—is that this isn't a chili town any more than Wichita, Kansas, is the fresh-seafood capital of the world.

But what Crawdad didn't know, and what you still don't know, unless you skipped ahead, you cheater, is that I had something up my sleeve. It's called Chili Up! (the exlamation mark is theirs), and it occurs three times downtown, once at Candlestick, and once on Irving Street between Eighth and Ninth Avenues—or not far from the UCSF library—so I asked Crawdad to meat me there and I washed behind my ears and hopped out of the tub and onto my bike.

It was a beautiful late afternoon, early evening, even in the Sunset. At the corner of Eighth and Irving, I spotted Crawdad sitting out front of Chili Up! at a sidewalk table, waving. I waved and hopped off my bike and started walking it across the street and an N-Judah train came along and cut me in half at the waist. Not only that, but I'd left the house naked!

So there I was, exposed to the world in every way imaginable, and a long line of half-chickens started filing out of my two hollow legs and heading toward the park. I could hear Crawdad calling out to me, and I was trying to decide between "Don't take your guns to town, Bill," "Cross the Brazos at Waco," and "One little kiss and Felina, good-bye."

In fact, I still can't decide, so I'll just go ahead and tell you that Chili Up!'s deal is all chili, only chili, and "gourmet" chili. And the chili's pretty good. I can speak for the "Lean Mean No Bean" version. They describe it as "traditional 'Texas-style' chili," but that's only in the sense that it's beanless. Texas chili is ground beef, not actual chunks of beef, and it's not served over basmati rice, no.

All the Chili Up! chilis come over rice and under onions, cheese, and cilantro. Besides the lean mean one, there's "Pork 'n' Tomatillo," the hottest of the bunch, with black beans and lime juice. There's chicken and black-bean chili, and there's chicken and corn chili with white beans in a cumin-infused broth, for crying out loud. There's also one called "Ancho-Turkey," and two vegetarian chilis: one with mushrooms and black beans and stuff, and one with tomatillos, white beans, and stuff.

They all come with corn bread or a tortilla. Go with the corn bread. I'm telling you. It's good and sweet and moist, whereas the tortillas suck. My only complaint about the chili itself—and I tasted almost all of them, 'cause you can—is that the large bowl isn't as large as it should be. I don't like to go home hungry.

Placewise, Chili Up! is pretty much what you'd expect from Irving Street these days: small, hip, happening. Not exactly my cup of tea, atmospherically, but, hey, that's life.

Life is not a bad dream or a great cowboy song. It's a journey, and at the end of it, you had better have something mighty profound and meaningful to say, podner, like Kit Carson, whose last words were, according to the writing on the wall out back at Chili Up!'s patio (and I have no reason not to believe it): "Wish I had time for just one more bowl of chili."

FOOD TYPE INDEX

BARBECUE

BREAKFAST SPECIALISTS

BURGER JOINTS

CAJUN

LOCATION INDEX

SF Neighborhoods

RESTAURANT INDEX